# Good Housekeeping Recipe-a-Day Collection

First published in 1997

1 3 5 7 9 10 8 6 4 2

First published in the United Kingdom in 1997 by Ebury Press
Random House, 20 Vauxhall Bridge Road, London SW1V 2SA

Random House Australia (Pty) Limited
20 Alfred Street, Milsons Point, Sydney, New South Wales 2061, Australia

Random House New Zealand Limited
18 Poland Road, Glenfield, Auckland 10, New Zealand

Random House South Africa (Pty) Limited
Endulini, 5a Jubilee Road,
Parktown 2193, South Africa

Random House UK Limited Reg. No. 954009

A catalogue record for this book is available from the British Library.

ISBN 0 09 185283 8

Edited by Maureen Callis
Designed by Jerry Goldie Graphic Design

Printed and bound in China by L Rex Ltd.

# Good Housekeeping

## Recipe-a-Day Collection

365 inspiring recipes for every day of the year

EBURY PRESS
LONDON

# CONTENTS

# INTRODUCTION

*Good Housekeeping Recipe-a-Day Collection* is a superb cookbook which will give you inspiration throughout the year. The easy-to-use, wiro-bound design allows you to flip through the cards to select a new recipe for each day, so you will have an endless source of delicious ideas at your fingertips. The 365 recipes in this collection range from hearty soups and light salads, vegetarian and pasta dishes, to more sophisticated recipes for special occasions, glorious puddings and mouthwatering cakes and biscuits.

Each recipe is accompanied by a full-colour photograph, showing you exactly how the finished dish should look and all have clear step-by-step instructions, making preparation and cooking as simple as possible. And, in the knowledge that each recipe has been double-tested in the Good Housekeeping Institute kitchens, you can be assured of successful results. In addition, the book includes all the features which make Good Housekeeping recipes so reliable and easy to use, including preparation and cooking times and calorie counts, as well as suggested variations and handy Cook's Tips.

Packed full of recipes for every day of the year, *Good Housekeeping Recipe-a-Day Collection* will be the ideal companion for every cook.

## COOKERY NOTES

◆ Both metric and imperial measures are given for the recipes. Follow either metric or imperial throughout as they are not interchangeable.

◆ All spoon measures are level unless otherwise stated.

◆ Ovens should be preheated to the specified temperatures given in the recipes.

◆ Use freshly ground black pepper unless otherwise stated.

◆ Freezing notes indicate the suitability of the dish for freezing. Where a stage is specified in brackets, the dish should be frozen at the end of that stage.

◆ Calorie counts are given per serving or appropriate portion of the dish. Where the calorie count ranges from a higher to a lower figure, this reflects the fact that the dish may serve a large number of people, in which case the portion size and calorie count are reduced.

◆ Use fresh rather than dried herbs unless dried herbs are suggested in the recipe.

◆ Large eggs should be used unless otherwise stated.

◆ The young, the elderly, pregnant women and those suffering from immune-deficiency diseases should not eat raw or lightly cooked eggs.

---

### HOW TO USE THIS BOOK

This book has been designed with a folding base so that you can stand it up while you cook. Simply turn the pages over as you work your way through the recipes in one direction and then, when you reach the end, turn the book around and go back the other way. Each chapter is colour-coded, making it easy to find the recipe you need.

# BOUILLABAISSE

PREPARATION TIME: **15** MINUTES ◆ COOKING TIME: **45** MINUTES ◆ FREEZING: SUITABLE (STEP **3**) ◆ **285** CALS PER SERVING ◆ SERVES **4**

900 g (2 lb) mixed fish fillets and shellfish, eg whiting, John Dory, red mullet, cooked peeled prawns and mussels
400 g can chopped tomatoes or 225 g (8 oz) fresh tomatoes
pinch of saffron
45 ml (3 tbsp) olive oil
1 onion, sliced
1 leek, sliced
2 celery sticks, sliced
2 garlic cloves, crushed
1 strip of pared orange rind
15 ml (1 tbsp) sun-dried tomato paste
2.5 ml (½ tsp) fennel seeds
1.1 litres (2 pints) fish stock
45 ml (3 tbsp) chopped fresh mixed parsley and thyme

**1** Cut the fish into bite-size pieces.
**2** If using fresh tomatoes, immerse in boiling water for 15–30 seconds then peel away the skin. Cut in half, remove the seeds and roughly chop the flesh. Place the saffron in a bowl and pour over 150 ml (¼ pint) boiling water.
**3** Heat the oil in a large pan, add the onion, leek, celery and garlic and cook for about 5 minutes or until beginning to soften. Add the tomatoes, orange rind, tomato paste and fennel seeds and cook for 1–2 minutes. Add the stock with the saffron and its soaking liquid, then season to taste with salt and freshly ground black pepper. Bring to the boil, then simmer for about 30 minutes.

Adjust the seasoning.
**4** Add the fish and mussels and cook for 5–6 minutes, until the fish is just cooked and the mussels have opened (discard any that remain closed). Stir in the herbs and prawns. Serve with French bread.

# SUMMER VEGETABLE SOUP

PREPARATION TIME: **15** MINUTES + CHILLING ◆ COOKING TIME: **22** MINUTES ◆ FREEZING: NOT SUITABLE ◆ **425** CALS PER SERVING ◆ SERVES **6**

50 ml (2 fl oz) olive oil
1 small loaf ciabatta bread, cut into strips
sea salt and freshly ground black pepper
15 ml (1 tbsp) chopped fresh thyme or 5 ml (1 tsp) dried
2 garlic cloves, crushed
125 g (4 oz) red pepper, cored, seeded and finely chopped
125 g (4 oz) cucumber, finely chopped
1 large ripe avocado, finely chopped
3 spring onions, finely chopped
30 ml (2 tbsp) lemon juice
30 ml (2 tbsp) chopped fresh basil
two 450 g (1 lb) cartons fresh tomato soup, chilled
basil leaves, to garnish

**1** Preheat the oven to 200°C (400°F) Mark 6. Put the oil in a roasting pan, add the bread and toss well. Sprinkle with sea salt. Cook for 15–20 minutes or until crisp. Add the thyme and garlic and return to the oven for 1–2 minutes.
**2** Place the prepared vegetables, lemon juice, chopped basil and tomato soup in a bowl and season well. Chill for at least 30 minutes. Garnish with basil leaves and serve with the ciabatta.

# INDEX

# CREAMED CELERIAC AND FRESH PARMESAN SOUP

PREPARATION TIME: **25** MINUTES ◆ COOKING TIME: **35** MINUTES ◆ FREEZING: **SUITABLE (STEP 3)** ◆ **370** CALS PER SERVING ◆ SERVES **8**

30 ml (2 tbsp) oil
175 g (6 oz) onion, chopped
1 garlic clove, crushed
450 g (1 lb) each celeriac and potato, roughly chopped
1.1 litre (2 pints) vegetable stock
bouquet garni
568 ml (1 pint) milk
284 ml carton double cream
15 ml (1 tbsp) lemon juice
salt and freshly ground black pepper
120 ml (8 tbsp) freshly grated Parmesan cheese
toasted Parmesan cheese, to garnish (see Cook's Tip)

**1** Heat the oil in a large saucepan, add the onion and garlic and cook gently for 4–5 minutes or until golden brown.
**2** Add the celeriac, potato, stock and bouquet garni, bring to the boil, then simmer for 20–25 minutes or until the celeriac and potato are tender. Remove the pan from the heat, cool slightly and discard the bouquet garni. Purée the soup in batches in a food processor or blender until smooth. Return to the saucepan.
**3** Add the milk, cream, lemon juice and seasoning and simmer for 10 minutes.
**4** To serve, put 15 ml (1 tbsp) grated Parmesan cheese in the bottom of each serving bowl. Ladle in the soup, grind over some black pepper and garnish with toasted Parmesan cheese.

### COOK'S TIP

To toast Parmesan, sprinkle 25 g (1 oz) finely grated Parmesan cheese on to a baking sheet. Place under a hot grill until melted and golden. Cool, then crumble. Store in an airtight container for up to one week.

# SPINACH AND BLUE CHEESE SOUP

PREPARATION TIME: **25** MINUTES ◆ COOKING TIME: **40** MINUTES ◆ FREEZING: **SUITABLE** ◆ **560** CALS PER SERVING ◆ SERVES **6**

450 g (1 lb) fresh spinach
50 g (2 oz) butter
225 g (8 oz) onion, roughly chopped
350 g (12 oz) leeks, roughly chopped
600 ml (1 pint) vegetable stock
284 ml carton double cream
350 g (12 oz) blue cheese, eg Stilton, Roquefort or Dolcelatte, crumbled
freshly ground black pepper
crumbled blue cheese, to garnish
2 extra leeks, to garnish (see Cook's Tip)

**1** Remove the stalks from the spinach and rinse the leaves well under cold running water.
**2** Melt the butter in a large, heavy-based saucepan, add the onion and leeks and cook for 20 minutes or until golden and very soft, stirring occasionally. Add the stock, cream and cheese and bring to the boil, then simmer, uncovered, for 10 minutes. Add the spinach, bring back to the boil, then simmer for 5 minutes.
**3** Cool the soup slightly, then purée in batches in a food processor or blender until smooth. Push the purée through a fine sieve.
**4** Return the purée to the rinsed pan and bring to the boil; adjust the seasoning. Serve in warm soup bowls, garnished with crumbled blue cheese and crispy leeks (see below).

### COOK'S TIP

Thinly slice 2 leeks, soak in salted water for 15 minutes, drain thoroughly and pat dry. Heat 150 ml (1/4 pint) oil in a large pan and cook the leeks in batches until golden and crisp. Drain on kitchen paper.

# LUXURY CHRISTMAS CAKE

PREPARATION TIME: **1** HOUR + MACERATING ◆ COOKING TIME: **3-4** HOURS ◆ FREEZING: SUITABLE (STEP **5**) ◆ **315–235** CALS PER SLICE ◆ MAKES **30–40** SLICES

225 g (8 oz) dried apricots, chopped
175 g (6 oz) stoned prunes, chopped
grated rind and juice of 1 lemon and 1
   orange
225 g (8 oz) each currants and raisins
125 g (4 oz) sultanas
150 ml (¼ pint) brandy, rum, porter or
   sweet stout
175 g (6 oz) glacé cherries, halved
175 g (6 oz) unblanched almonds,
   roughly chopped
125 g (4 oz) chopped candied peel
350 g (12 oz) self-raising white flour
10 ml (2 tsp) mixed spice
300 g (10 oz) unsalted butter, softened
300 g (10 oz) soft dark brown sugar
6 (size 3) eggs, beaten
60 ml (4 tbsp) treacle

**1** Put the apricots, prunes, citrus rinds and juices, currants, raisins and sultanas in a large bowl. Add the brandy (or other liquor), cover and leave to macerate overnight, stirring occasionally.
**2** Preheat the oven to 160°C (325°F) Mark 3. Line a 25 cm (10 inch) round or 23 cm (9 inch) square cake tin with a double or triple layer of greaseproof paper. Grease with butter.
**3** Add the cherries, nuts and peel to the macerated fruit mixture and stir well. Sift the flour, spice and 2.5 ml (½ tsp) salt together. In a large bowl, cream together the butter and sugar until fluffy. Gradually beat in the eggs, beating well between each addition to prevent curdling. Stir in the treacle, then fold in the flour and fruit.
**4** Spoon the mixture into the cake tin, level the surface, then make a slight hollow in the middle. Bake in the oven for 1 hour, then lower the temperature to 140°C (275°F) Mark 1 and bake for 2–3 hours. Cover the cake with buttered paper if browning too much. Test by inserting a skewer into the cake - if it comes out clean, the cake is cooked.
**5** Leave in the tin until cool, then turn out onto a wire rack to cool completely in the paper. When cold, keep one layer of greaseproof paper on the cake, then wrap in foil. Store in a cool dry place. Ice and decorate as wished.

# TOMATO, CELERY AND APPLE SOUP

PREPARATION TIME: **15** MINUTES ◆ COOKING TIME: **50** MINUTES ◆ FREEZING: **SUITABLE** ◆ **160** CALS PER SERVING ◆ SERVES **6**

50 g (2 oz) butter
300 g (10 oz) onion, roughly chopped
1 head of green celery, about 400 g (14 oz), roughly chopped
400 g (14 oz) cooking apples, peeled, cored and roughly chopped
2 garlic cloves, crushed
two 400 g cans plum tomatoes
300 ml (½ pint) apple juice (see Cook's Tip)
450 ml (¾ pint) vegetable stock
pinch of sugar
salt and freshly ground black pepper
basil leaves, to garnish

**1** Melt the butter in a large, heavy-based saucepan. Add the onion and celery and cook for 10 minutes, stirring occasionally, until the onion is soft and golden. Add the apple and garlic and cook for 5 minutes, then stir in the tomatoes, apple juice and stock. Bring to the boil then simmer, uncovered, for 30 minutes.
**2** Cool the soup slightly, then purée in batches in a food processor or blender until smooth. Push the purée through a fine sieve.
**3** Return the purée to the rinsed pan and bring back to the boil. Add a pinch of sugar and adjust the seasoning. Serve in warm soup bowls, garnished with basil leaves.

### COOK'S TIP
For a richer-tasting soup, replace the apple juice with the same quantity of medium cider.

# CARROT, PARSNIP AND LENTIL SOUP

PREPARATION TIME: **20** MINUTES + SOAKING ◆ COOKING TIME: **55** MINUTES ◆ FREEZING: **SUITABLE** (STEP 3) ◆ **280** CALS PER SERVING ◆ SERVES **6**

75 g (3 oz) green lentils
30 ml (2 tbsp) oil
200 g (7 oz) chorizo sausage or peppered salami, cut into cubes
350 g (12 oz) onion, roughly chopped
225 g (8 oz) each carrot and parsnip, roughly chopped
5 ml (1 tsp) ground cumin
1.7 litres (3 pints) vegetable stock
2 bay leaves
a few thyme sprigs
salt and freshly ground black pepper
croûtons, to garnish

**1** Soak the lentils in double their volume of cold water for 6 hours or overnight.
**2** Heat the oil in a large pan, add the chorizo or salami and cook, stirring, for 5 minutes or until golden. Remove with a slotted spoon and set aside. Add the onion to the pan and cook for 10 minutes or until soft and golden. Add the carrot, parsnip, cumin and drained lentils and cook, stirring, for 5 minutes. Stir in the stock, bay leaves and thyme. Bring to the boil, then simmer for 30 minutes or until the vegetables are tender.
**3** Cool slightly, remove the herbs, then purée the soup in batches in a food processor or blender until smooth.

**4** Return the purée to the rinsed pan, bring back to the boil and adjust the seasoning. Transfer to warm soup bowls, add the fried chorizo and garnish with croûtons.

# SAFFRON SCONES

PREPARATION TIME: **15** MINUTES + INFUSING ◆ COOKING TIME: **10–12** MINUTES ◆ FREEZING: SUITABLE ◆ **110** CALS PER SCONE ◆ MAKES ABOUT **12**

1/2–1 sachet or 2.5–5 ml (1/2–1 tsp) saffron
   strands (see Cook's Tips)
about 150 ml (1/4 pint) milk
225 g (8 oz) self-raising flour
pinch of salt
5 ml (1 tsp) baking powder
40 g (1 1/2 oz) firm unsalted butter or
   margarine, diced
30 ml (2 tbsp) caster sugar
beaten egg, to glaze

**1** Preheat the oven to 220°C (425°F) Mark 7. Lightly grease a baking sheet. Roughly break up the saffron strands and place in a saucepan with half of the milk. Bring just to the boil, then remove from the heat and leave to infuse for 20 minutes.
**2** Sift the flour, salt and baking powder into a bowl. Add the butter and rub in using the fingertips until the mixture resembles fine breadcrumbs. Stir in the sugar.
**3** Stir in the saffron milk and half of the remaining milk. Mix with a round-bladed knife to a soft dough, adding the rest of the milk if the mixture is too dry; it should be soft and slightly sticky.

**4** Knead lightly and roll out to a 2 cm (3/4 inch) thickness. Cut out rounds using a 5 cm (2 inch) cutter. Place on the baking sheet and brush the tops with beaten egg. Bake in the oven for 10-12 minutes, until well risen and golden brown. Transfer to a wire rack to cool. Serve split, with butter or clotted cream and fruits.

## COOK'S TIPS

Use either 1/2 or 1 sachet saffron strands, depending on the strength of flavour required.
Bake the scones immediately as the baking powder is activated as soon as it comes into contact with liquids.

# WAFER BREAD

PREPARATION TIME: **30** MINUTES + RISING ◆ COOKING TIME: **12** MINUTES EACH BATCH ◆ FREEZING: NOT SUITABLE ◆ **240** CALS PER SERVING ◆ MAKES **16**

450 g (1 lb) strong plain white flour
7.5 ml (1 1/2 tsp) salt
7.5 ml (1 1/2 tsp) easy-blend yeast
olive oil
45 ml (3 tbsp) finely chopped mixed
   fresh herbs, eg flat-leaf parsley, chives,
   thyme, marjoram
freshly ground black pepper

**1** Sift the flour and salt into a bowl, stir in the yeast with 300 ml (1/2 pint) warm water and 30 ml (2 tbsp) olive oil and mix to a stiff, sticky dough.
**2** Turn out on to a lightly floured surface and knead for 10 minutes or until smooth and no longer sticky. Alternatively, put the dough in a food processor with the dough hook or flat beater attached and leave on a low speed for 5–10 minutes.
**3** Place the dough in a lightly greased bowl, cover and leave in a warm place until doubled in size.
**4** Preheat the oven to 200°C (400°F) Mark 6. Divide the dough into golf ball-size pieces, dip each ball in the chopped

herbs, then roll out to a wafer-thin round on a floured surface.
**5** Place on a baking sheet and lightly brush with oil and sprinkle with pepper. Cook in batches in the oven for 10–12 minutes or until golden brown and crisp. Transfer to a wire rack to cool.

## VARIATION

This bread dough can be made into 20 rolls. Add the chopped herbs at step 3 and divide into 20 pieces. Shape into rolls and place on 2 baking sheets. Leave to prove for 15 minutes, then brush with beaten egg. Bake in the oven for 10–15 minutes or until golden.

# BEETROOT AND ORANGE SOUP

**PREPARATION TIME: 15 MINUTES ◆ COOKING TIME: 2 HOURS 25 MINUTES ◆ FREEZING: SUITABLE ◆ 230 CALS PER SERVING ◆ SERVES 6**

700 g (1½ lb) medium raw beetroot
50 g (2 oz) butter
225 g (8 oz) each onion and potato, roughly chopped
1.3 litres (2¼ pints) vegetable stock
300 ml (½ pint) each medium-dry sherry and orange juice
salt and freshly ground black pepper
orange strips and finely grated rind, to garnish

**1** Preheat the oven to 200°C (400°F) Mark 6. Trim the beetroot, wrap in foil and place in a large roasting pan. Cook in the oven for 1½ hours. Leave to cool, then peel and roughly chop.
**2** Melt the butter in a large, heavy-based saucepan, add the onion and cook for 10 minutes or until golden and soft. Stir in the beetroot and potato and coat with the buttery juices. Add the stock, sherry and orange juice, bring to the boil, then cover and simmer for 40 minutes or until the potato is tender. Cool slightly.
**3** Purée the soup in batches in a food processor or blender until smooth. Return to the rinsed pan, adjust the seasoning and bring back to the boil.

**4** Serve in warm soup bowls, garnished with orange strips and finely grated rind.

# ROASTED BUTTERNUT SOUP WITH CARAMELISED APPLE

**PREPARATION TIME: 20 MINUTES ◆ COOKING TIME: ABOUT 1 HOUR ◆ FREEZING: SUITABLE ◆ 345 CALS PER SERVING ◆ SERVES 6**

2 butternut squash, about 1.6 kg (3½ lb) total weight
125 g (4 oz) butter
salt and freshly ground black pepper
5 ml (1 tsp) ground cinnamon
freshly grated nutmeg
225 g (8 oz) each onion and carrot, roughly chopped
75 g (3 oz) celery, roughly chopped
2 rosemary sprigs or 10 ml (2 tsp) dried rosemary
3–4 parsley stalks
300 ml (½ pint) white wine
750 ml (1¼ pints) vegetable stock
30 ml (2 tbsp) maple syrup
3 Granny Smith apples, peeled, cored and thickly sliced

**1** Preheat the oven to 200°C (400°F) Mark 6. Cut the squash in half lengthways and scrape out the seeds. Place cut side up in a roasting pan just large enough to hold them.
**2** Melt 25 g (1 oz) of the butter and lightly brush the squash. Season generously with salt and pepper. Sprinkle with the cinnamon and nutmeg. Pour 150 ml (¼ pint) water around the squash. Cook, basting occasionally, for about 1 hour, until very soft; cool.
**3** Meanwhile, melt 25 g (1 oz) of the butter in a large pan, add the onion, carrot and celery and fry for about 5 minutes. Add the rosemary, parsley stalks, wine and stock, bring to the boil,

then cover and simmer for about 35 minutes until tender.
**4** When the squash is cool enough to handle, scoop out the flesh. Place the flesh, any roasting juices and the vegetable mixture in batches in a food processor or blender and purée until smooth. Push through a fine sieve.
**5** Melt the remaining butter with the maple syrup in a large non-stick frying pan. Add the apple slices and fry over a high heat, turning occasionally, for 5–6 minutes or until they turn a caramel brown colour. Keep warm.
**6** Gently warm the soup, adjust the seasoning and ladle into warm bowls. Garnish with the apple slices.

# CITRUS ECCLES CAKES

PREPARATION TIME: 35 MINUTES + CHILLING ◆ COOKING TIME: 12–15 MINUTES ◆ FREEZING: SUITABLE ◆ 160 CALS PER CAKE ◆ MAKES 20

**PASTRY**
225 g (8 oz) plain white flour
pinch of salt
175 g (6 oz) firm unsalted butter, diced
5 ml (1 tsp) lemon juice

**FILLING**
175 g (6 oz) currants
50 g (2 oz) chopped mixed peel
50 g (2 oz) soft light brown (muscovado)
    sugar
finely grated rind of 2 lemons

**TO FINISH**
beaten egg, to glaze
caster sugar, to dust
50 g (2 oz) unsalted butter, melted

1  Sift the flour and salt into a bowl, add the butter, lemon juice and 100 ml (3½ fl oz) iced water. Mix to a soft dough, adding extra water if it is too dry.
2  Knead lightly, then roll out on a floured surface to 30 x 10 cm (12 x 4 inches). Fold the bottom third up and the upper third down, keeping the edges straight, then give the pastry a quarter turn. Repeat the rolling, folding and turning 4 more times. Wrap in greaseproof paper and chill for 30 minutes.
3  Mix the filling ingredients together.
4  Preheat the oven to 220°C (425°F) Mark 7. Grease 2 baking sheets. Roll out half of the pastry to 50 x 20 cm (20 x 8

inches). Cut in half lengthways, then cut each strip into 5 equal pieces.
5  Make three 2 cm (3/4 inch) cuts, 5 mm (1/4 inch) apart down the centre of one piece of pastry. Make 3 more rows of cuts either side of the first so that when the pastry is pulled apart it creates a lattice. Repeat with remaining pastry. Brush the edges with egg.
6  Divide half of the filling between the latticed pastries, placing it in the centres. Bring the edges up over the filling, pinching together.
7  Repeat with the remaining pastry and filling. Brush with egg and sprinkle with sugar. Bake for 12–15 minutes. Pour a little butter on to each cake, to serve.

# ORANGE FLOWER BISCUITS

PREPARATION TIME: 10 MINUTES + CHILLING ◆ COOKING TIME: 8 MINUTES ◆ FREEZING: NOT SUITABLE ◆ 65 CALS PER BISCUIT ◆ MAKES 20-24

125 g (4 oz) plain white flour
15 g (½ oz) cornflour
100 g (3½ oz) firm lightly salted butter,
    diced
50 g (2 oz) icing sugar, sifted
20 ml (4 tsp) orange flower water
icing sugar, to dust

1  Lightly grease a baking sheet. Preheat the oven to 200°C (400°F) Mark 6. Sift the flour and cornflour and place in a food processor. Add the butter and blend until combined. Alternatively, sift the flours into a bowl and rub in the butter.
2  Add the icing sugar and orange flower water and blend until the mixture binds together. Knead lightly and chill for 30 minutes.
3  Roll out the pastry thinly on a lightly floured surface and cut out rounds using a 6 cm (2½ inch) cutter, re-rolling the trimmings to make more biscuits.
4  Place on the baking sheet and bake in the oven for about 8 minutes, until beginning to colour around the edges.

5  Transfer to a wire rack to cool. Dust generously with icing sugar to serve.

### VARIATION
Use rosewater instead of orange flower water, or add the finely grated rind of 1 orange or lemon.

# BEAN AND TOMATO SOUP

PREPARATION TIME: **10** MINUTES ◆ COOKING TIME: **30** MINUTES ◆ FREEZING: SUITABLE ◆ **300** CALS PER SERVING ◆ SERVES **4**

15 ml (1 tbsp) olive oil
1 large onion, chopped
2 garlic cloves, chopped
1 red pepper, cored, seeded and thinly
   sliced
3 celery sticks, thinly sliced
150 g (5 oz) spicy chorizo sausage, thinly
   sliced
15 ml (1 tbsp) sun-dried tomato paste
two 400 g cans chopped tomatoes
300 ml (1/2 pint) chicken or vegetable
   stock
salt and freshly ground black pepper
400 g (14 oz) can flageolet beans,
   drained and rinsed
flat-leaf parsley, to garnish

**1** Heat the oil in a large saucepan, add the onion and garlic and cook over a low heat for 5–7 minutes or until the onion begins to soften.
**2** Add the red pepper and celery and cook for 5 minutes.
**3** Stir in the chorizo, tomato paste, tomatoes, stock and seasoning and cook over a low heat for 15 minutes.
**4** Add the beans to the pan and simmer for 5 minutes. Adjust the seasoning. Serve in warm bowls, garnished with parsley.

# MUSSELS IN SAFFRON CIDER BROTH

PREPARATION TIME: **15** MINUTES ◆ COOKING TIME: **15** MINUTES ◆ FREEZING: NOT SUITABLE ◆ **630** CALS PER SERVING ◆ SERVES **4**

3 kg (6 1/2 lb) mussels
50 g (2 oz) butter
225 g (8 oz) onion, chopped
2 garlic cloves, crushed
300 ml (1/2 pint) cider
large pinch of saffron strands
284 ml carton double cream
30 ml (2 tbsp) chopped fresh herbs, eg
   parsley, dill or chives, to garnish

**1** Rinse the mussels very carefully under cold running water (see Cook's Tip).
**2** Melt the butter in a large saucepan, add the onion and garlic and cook, stirring, for 10 minutes, until soft. Add the mussels, cider and saffron strands, bring to the boil, then cover and bubble vigorously for 1 minute or until the mussel shells have opened.
**3** Drain the mussels in a colander, reserving the liquid. Return the liquid to the saucepan and add the cream. Bubble for 10 minutes or until reduced and syrupy. Meanwhile, discard any mussels that have not opened and add the remaining ones to the sauce. Simmer for 30 seconds to reheat and serve

immediately, garnished with chopped fresh herbs.

### COOK'S TIP
Most mussels from supermarkets have been cleaned but do check for open or damaged shells, which should be discarded.

# WHITE CHOCOLATE BROWNIES

PREPARATION TIME: **20** MINUTES ◆ COOKING TIME: **30–35** MINUTES ◆ FREEZING: SUITABLE ◆ **490** CALS PER BROWNIE ◆ MAKES **12**

500 g (1 lb 2 oz) white chocolate
75 g (3 oz) butter
3 eggs
175 g (6 oz) caster sugar
175 g (6 oz) self-raising white flour
pinch of salt
175 g (6 oz) shelled hazelnuts, roughly
 chopped
5 ml (1 tsp) vanilla essence

**1** Preheat the oven to 190°C (375°F) Mark 5. Grease and line a baking tin measuring 21 x 29 cm (8½ x 11½ inches) across the top and 19 x 26 cm (7½ x 10½ inches) across the base. (Or use a tin with similar dimensions.)
**2** Roughly chop 400 g (14 oz) of the chocolate and set aside. Break up the remaining chocolate and put in a heatproof bowl with the butter. Place over a pan of simmering water until melted. Leave to cool slightly.
**3** Whisk the eggs and sugar together in a bowl until smooth, then gradually beat in the melted chocolate. Sift the flour and salt in, then fold in with the hazelnuts, chopped chocolate and vanilla essence.

**4** Turn the mixture into the prepared tin and level the surface. Bake in the oven for 30–35 minutes, until risen and golden and the centre is just firm to the touch (see Cook's Tip). Leave to cool in the tin. Turn out and cut into 12 squares. Store in an airtight container for up to 1 week.

## COOK'S TIP

When cooked, the mixture will still be very soft under the crust; it firms up during cooling.

## VARIATION

Use any nuts you like - almonds, walnuts, pecans and brazil nuts are all suitable.

# COCONUT SQUARES

PREPARATION TIME: **10** MINUTES + COOLING ◆ COOKING TIME: **35** MINUTES ◆ FREEZING: NOT SUITABLE ◆ **500** CALS PER SQUARE ◆ MAKES **10** SQUARES

75 g (3 oz) butter,
200 g (7 oz) demerara sugar
175 g (6 oz) ground rice
2 eggs, beaten
pinch of salt
1–2 drops of vanilla essence
75 g (3 oz) desiccated coconut
75 g (3 oz) hazelnuts, chopped
45 ml (3 tbsp) apricot or raspberry jam,
 plus extra for brushing

**1** Grease a 28 x 18 cm (11 x 7 inch) shallow cake tin. Preheat the oven to 180°C (350°F) Mark 4
**2** Cream together the butter and 75 g (3 oz) of the sugar until light and fluffy. Stir in 150 g (5 oz) of the ground rice. Spread the mixture into the prepared tin and bake in the oven for 15 minutes. Leave in the tin to cool for a few minutes.
**3** Mix together the eggs, remaining sugar and rice, salt, vanilla essence, coconut and hazelnuts.
**4** Cover the baked cake with the jam, then spoon over the egg mixture. Return to the oven for 20 minutes.
**5** Leave to cool, then brush with a little

warmed jam. Cut into squares. Leave in the tin to cool completely before serving (see Cook's Tip).

## COOK'S TIP

The squares can be wrapped in greaseproof paper and stored in an airtight container for 3–5 days.

# JERUSALEM ARTICHOKE SOUP

**PREPARATION TIME: 30 MINUTES ◆ COOKING TIME: 1¹/₂ HOURS ◆ FREEZING: SUITABLE ◆ 370 CALS PER SERVING ◆ SERVES 6**

125 g (4 oz) butter
175 g (6 oz) onion, chopped
1 garlic clove, crushed
50 g (2 oz) celery, chopped
900 g (2 lb) Jerusalem artichokes, chopped
125 g (4 oz) carrot, chopped
300 ml (¹/₂ pint) dry white wine
1 bouquet garni
salt and freshly ground black pepper
142 ml carton double cream
Goat's Cheese Crostini, to serve (see right)

**1** Melt the butter in a large saucepan, add the onion and garlic and cook for 2 minutes. Add the remaining vegetables and cook for 5 minutes.
**2** Add the wine, bring to the boil, then simmer until reduced by half. Add 1.1 litres (2 pints) water and the bouquet garni. Bring back to the boil, then simmer until the vegetables are tender, about 1¹/₄ hours.
**3** Cool slightly, remove the bouquet garni, then purée in a food processor or blender until smooth.
**4** To serve, gently reheat the soup, season to taste and add half of the cream. Ladle into warm bowls and drizzle with the remaining cream.

Serve with the crostini.

## GOAT'S CHEESE CROSTINI

**150 CALS PER SERVING**

Toast 6 thin slices of French bread on both sides until golden brown. Spread 125 g (4 oz) goat's cheese on each piece of bread. Sprinkle with cayenne pepper. Grill until brown, about 1 minute. Garnish with herbs, such as thyme, and serve.

# BACON AND CELERIAC SOUP

**PREPARATION TIME: 10 MINUTES ◆ COOKING TIME: 35 MINUTES ◆ FREEZING: SUITABLE (END STEP 5) ◆ 190 CALS PER SERVING ◆ SERVES 4**

350 g (12 oz) lean smoked bacon
15 ml (1 tbsp) vegetable oil
1 large onion, finley chopped
1 garlic clove, finely chopped
350 g (12 oz) celeriac, sliced
900 ml (1¹/₂ pints) vegetable or chicken stock
salt and freshly ground black pepper
thyme sprigs, to garnish

**1** Trim any rind and fat off the bacon. Reserve 4 rashers and finely chop the rest.
**2** Heat the oil in a large saucepan, add the onion and garlic and cook for 5–7 minutes or until the onion is beginning to soften (see Cook's Tip).
**3** Add the chopped bacon and cook for 5 minutes. Stir in the celeriac and cook for 5 minutes.
**4** Add the stock and seasoning and bring to the boil, then simmer gently for 15 minutes or until the celeriac is very tender. Cool slightly.
**5** Purée the soup in batches in a food processor or blender until smooth.
**6** Grill the reserved bacon until crisp.

Reheat the soup and adjust the seasoning. Serve in warm bowls, garnished with bacon and thyme.

## COOK'S TIP

Cover the saucepan with a tight-fitting lid when cooking onion with oil to soften. The steam will help to prevent it from colouring.

# APPLE AND BLACKBERRY SCONE

**PREPARATION TIME: 15 MINUTES ◆ COOKING TIME: 50 MINUTES ◆ FREEZING: SUITABLE ◆ 300 CALS PER SLICE ◆ MAKES 6 SLICES**

1 cooking apple, about 175 g (6 oz)
25 g (1 oz) caster sugar
8 cloves
75 g (3 oz) blackberries
10 ml (2 tsp) cornflour
200 g (7 oz) self-raising white flour
pinch of salt
2.5 ml (½ tsp) ground cinnamon
5 ml (1 tsp) baking powder
75 g (3 oz) unsalted butter, diced
25 g (1 oz) medium oatmeal
50 g (2 oz) soft light brown sugar
90 ml (3 fl oz) milk

**TO FINISH**
milk, to glaze
demerara sugar and medium oatmeal, to
    sprinkle
75 g (3 oz) blackberries

1  Preheat the oven to 200°C (400°F) Mark 6. Lightly grease a 19–20 cm (7½–8 inch) spring-release cake tin. Peel, core and thinly slice the apple. Place in a bowl with the sugar, cloves, blackberries and cornflour; toss gently to mix.
2  Sift the flour, salt, cinnamon and baking powder together in a food processor. Add the butter and work until the mixture resembles breadcrumbs. Add the oatmeal and sugar. Add most of the milk and process to a soft dough; add the remaining milk if the mixture is too dry.
3  Roll out two-thirds of the dough on a floured surface, to a 23 cm (9 inch) round and use to line the tin, so that the dough comes about 2.5 cm (1 inch) up the side. Pile the apple and blackberry mixture into the centre and brush the edge of the dough with a little milk.
4  Roll out the remaining dough to a 20 cm (8 inch) round and lay over the filling, pressing the edges together.
5  Brush with milk, sprinkle with demerara sugar and oatmeal and bake for 30 minutes, until risen. Lower the temperature to 160°C (325°F) Mark 3.
6  Scatter the scone with the remaining blackberries and sprinkle with more sugar and oatmeal. Return to the oven for 20 minutes, covering with foil if the scone appears to be over-browning. Leave in the tin for 5 minutes, then transfer to a wire rack to cool.

# CHERRY STREUSEL SLICE

**PREPARATION TIME: 20 MINUTES + COOLING ◆ COOKING TIME: 40–45 MINUTES ◆ FREEZING: SUITABLE ◆ 480 CALS PER SLICE ◆ MAKES 8 SLICES**

**Serve sliced - preferably with spoonsful of lightly whipped cream - as a teatime treat, or dessert if you prefer.**

two 425 g cans pitted black or red
    cherries
10 ml (2 tsp) cornflour
5 ml (1 tsp) vanilla essence
250 g (9 oz) self-raising flour
5 ml (1 tsp) ground cinnamon
grated rind of ½ lemon
175 g (6 oz) unsalted butter, diced
165 g (5½ oz) caster sugar
50 g (2 oz) ground almonds
1 egg
icing sugar, to dust

1  Drain the cherries, reserving 90 ml (3 fl oz) of the juice. Blend a little of the juice with the cornflour in a small pan. Add the remaining juice and vanilla essence and bring to the boil, stirring. Add the cherries and cook, stirring, for 1 minute, until thickly coated in the syrup; cool.
2  Grease a 1.5-litre (2½-pint) loaf tin. Line the base and long sides with a double thickness of greaseproof paper, allowing it to overhang the sides. Preheat the oven to 180°C (350°F) Mark 4.
3  Place the flour, cinnamon and lemon rind in a food processor. Add the butter and work until the mixture starts to cling together. Add the sugar and ground almonds and process until the mixture resembles a coarse crumble. Weigh 150 g (5 oz) of the crumble and set aside for the topping. Add the egg to the remaining mixture and mix to a fairly soft paste.
4  Use half of the paste to line the base of the tin. Roll out the remainder and cut strips about 2.5 cm (1 inch) wide. Use these to line the sides of the tin, pressing them to fit around the corners and base, eliminating the joins.
5  Spoon the cherry filling into the centre and sprinkle with the crumble. Bake in the oven for 40–45 minutes, until golden. Leave in the tin to cool.
6  Loosen the edges at the ends of the tin, then lift out the cake, using the greaseproof paper. Dust with icing sugar.

# CAULIFLOWER AND TOASTED CHEESE SOUP

PREPARATION TIME: **20** MINUTES ◆ COOKING TIME: **1** HOUR ◆ FREEZING: **NOT** SUITABLE ◆ **715** CALS PER SERVING ◆ SERVES **4**

**Try this soup as a warming starter next time you're entertaining, or serve it with plenty of hot garlic bread for a light lunch.**

1 cauliflower, about 700 g (1½ lb)
50 g (2 oz) butter
350 g (12 oz) onion, finely chopped
25 g (1 oz) plain flour
900 ml (1½ pints) milk or milk and cream mixed
salt and freshly ground black pepper
350 g (12 oz) strong cheese, eg mature Cheddar or Gruyère, coarsely grated

**1** Finely chop the cauliflower, reserving any small outer green leaves for garnish. Melt the butter in a large saucepan and stir in the cauliflower and onion. Cook, stirring, for at least 10 minutes or until the onion is very soft and a golden colour.
**2** Stir in the flour and milk. Season to taste and bring to the boil, then cover and simmer gently for about 45 minutes or until the cauliflower is very soft. Meanwhile, drop the reserved cauliflower leaves into boiling water for 1–2 minutes. Cool in cold water and set aside.
**3** Cool the soup a little, then purée in a food processor or blender until smooth. Sieve, if wished, for a finer texture.

**4** Preheat the oven to 200°C (400°F) Mark 6. Return the purée to the rinsed pan and reheat gently. Dilute, if necessary, with a little extra milk and adjust the seasoning. Stir in all but 50 g (2 oz) of the cheese. Ladle the soup into individual heatproof bowls and sprinkle with the reserved cheese. Place in a roasting pan, surround with hot water and cook in the oven for 10 minutes or until golden and bubbling. Garnish with the cauliflower leaves and serve immediately.

# CRAB AND TOMATO SOUP

PREPARATION TIME: **40** MINUTES ◆ COOKING TIME: **45** MINUTES ◆ FREEZING: **NOT** SUITABLE ◆ **270** CALS PER SERVING ◆ SERVES **6**

one dressed crab, about 200 g (7 oz)
60 ml (4 tbsp) olive oil
125 g (4 oz) onion, chopped
1 celery stick, chopped
60 ml (4 tbsp) port
1.1 litres (2 pints) light stock
550 g bottle or carton passata or creamed tomatoes
45 ml (3 tbsp) mayonnaise
5 ml (1 tsp) tomato ketchup
1 garlic clove, crushed
few drops of Tabasco and Worcestershire sauce
salt and freshly ground black pepper

**TO SERVE**
1 small French stick, thinly sliced
50 g (2 oz) Emmenthal cheese, grated
single cream

**1** Separate the white and brown crab meat and set aside. Roughly crush the shell.
**2** Heat 30 ml (2 tbsp) of the oil in a large saucepan, add the crab shell, onion and celery and cook for 5 minutes, stirring. Add the port, bring to the boil and bubble until all the liquid has evaporated. Pour in the stock and passata or creamed tomatoes and bring back to the boil. Add the brown crab meat, then cover and simmer for 30 minutes.
**3** Strain the crab stock through a sieve, pressing to extract the juices. Discard the shell and vegetables.
**4** Return the soup to the rinsed pan and bring to the boil. Whisk in the

mayonnaise, tomato ketchup, garlic, Tabasco, Worcestershire sauce and seasoning.
**5** Toast the French bread on one side under a preheated grill. Drizzle the remaining oil over the untoasted side and sprinkle with the cheese. Cook under the grill until bubbling.
**6** To serve, stir the flaked white crab meat into the soup and heat through for 1–2 minutes. Ladle the soup into warm bowls, garnish with a swirl of cream, float the warm croûtes on top and serve immediately.

# ALMOND AND APRICOT ROULADE

PREPARATION TIME: **20** MINUTES + STANDING ◆ COOKING TIME: **20** MINUTES ◆ FREEZING: NOT SUITABLE ◆ **380** CALS PER SLICE ◆ MAKES **8** SLICES

**The roulade is best made a day in advance and filled shortly before serving, preferably with strong dark coffee.**

**ROULADE**
25 g (1 oz) flaked almonds
5 eggs, separated
150 g (5 oz) caster sugar
5 ml (1 tsp) vanilla essence
125 g (4 oz) white almond paste, grated
45 ml (3 tbsp) plain flour
45 ml (3 tbsp) amaretto de Saronno
   liqueur

**FILLING**
6 ripe apricots
300 g (10 oz) crème fraîche
caster or icing sugar, to dust

1  Preheat the oven to 180°C (350°F) Mark 4. Grease a 33 x 23 cm (13 x 9 inch) Swiss roll tin and line with greased non-stick baking parchment. Scatter the flaked almonds evenly over the paper.
2  Whisk the egg yolks with 125 g (4 oz) of the sugar until pale and fluffy. Stir in the vanilla essence and grated almond paste. Sift the flour over the mixture, then lightly fold in.
3  Whisk the egg whites in another bowl, until stiff but not dry. Gradually whisk in the remaining sugar. Using a metal tablespoon, carefully fold a quarter of the egg white into the almond mixture to loosen, then fold in the remainder.
4  Turn into the prepared tin and gently ease the mixture into the corners. Bake in the oven for about 20 minutes or until well risen and just firm to the touch. Cover with a sheet of non-stick baking parchment and a damp tea-towel and leave until cool, or overnight if possible.
5  Remove the tea-towel and invert the roulade (and paper) onto a baking sheet. Peel off the lining paper. Sprinkle another piece of baking parchment with caster sugar and flip the roulade onto it. Drizzle with the liqueur.
6  Cut the apricots into small pieces. Spread the roulade with the crème fraîche and scatter over the apricots. Roll up the roulade, transfer to a plate and dust with sugar to serve.

# RASPBERRY MOUSSE GÂTEAU

PREPARATION TIME: **1½** HOURS ◆ COOKING TIME: **30–35** MINUTES ◆ FREEZING: SUITABLE ◆ **845–630** CALS PER SERVING ◆ SERVES **6–8**

**HAZELNUT CAKE**
175 g (6 oz) shelled hazelnuts, toasted
4 eggs
125 g (4 oz) soft light brown
   (muscovado) sugar
125 g (4 oz) plain flour, sifted
2.5 ml (½ tsp) baking powder
25 g (1 oz) butter, melted and cooled

**FILLING AND TOPPING**
450 g (1 lb) raspberries
1 egg, separated
25 g (1 oz) caster sugar
7.5 ml (1½ tsp) powdered gelatine
450 ml (¾ pint) double cream
150 ml (¼ pint) Greek-style yogurt

1  Preheat the oven to 180°C (350°F) Mark 4. Grease and line a 20 cm (8 inch) round cake tin. Chop 25 g (1 oz) of the hazelnuts and grind the rest in a processor.
2  Whisk the eggs and sugar in a bowl over a pan of simmering water until thick. Remove from the heat and whisk for 3 minutes. Fold in the flour and baking powder alternately with the ground hazelnuts and butter.
3  Spread in the tin and bake for 30–35 minutes, until firm. Cool on a wire rack.
4  Rub half of the raspberries through a sieve. Whisk the egg yolk, sugar and raspberry purée in a bowl over a pan of simmering water until thick. Remove from the heat and whisk until cold.
5  Sprinkle the gelatine on 30 ml (2 tbsp) water in a heatproof bowl, then stand in hot water until dissolved. Whip 50 ml (2 fl oz) of the cream and fold into the raspberry mixture; stir in the gelatine. Whisk the egg white until peaks form.
6  Line a 20 cm (8 inch) spring-release tin with cling film. Cut the cake into 3 rounds; place one in the tin. Whip 150 ml (¼ pint) of the cream, fold in the yogurt, then spread over the cake. Scatter over a third of the raspberries, then a cake, then the mousse and another third of raspberries. Add the remaining cake, then chill for 2 hours.
7  Whip the cream and spoon over the cake. Scatter with raspberries and nuts.

# MUSHROOM PÂTÉ

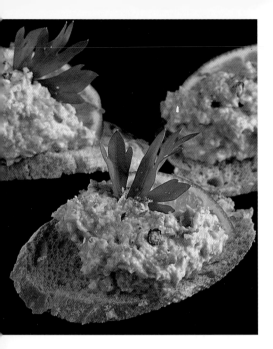

PREPARATION TIME: **15** MINUTES ◆ COOKING TIME: **15** MINUTES ◆ FREEZING: NOT SUITABLE ◆ **60** CALS PER SERVING ◆ SERVES **4**

**Try serving this pâté with baked *ficelle* (narrow French bread) instead of toast for a change.**

30 ml (2 tbsp) olive oil
350 g (12 oz) brown-cap mushrooms, finely chopped
2 celery sticks, finely chopped
1 garlic clove, crushed
15 ml (1 tbsp) lemon juice
200 g carton reduced-fat soft cheese
2 anchovies or 5 ml (1 tsp) anchovy paste
salt and freshly ground black pepper

**TO SERVE**
toast
slivers of lime and flat-leaf parsley

1  Heat the oil in a frying pan, add the mushrooms, celery and garlic and fry gently for about 10 minutes or until soft and all the liquid has evaporated. Stir in the lemon juice.
2  Leave the mushroom mixture to cool slightly, then place in a food processor or blender with the remaining ingredients and blend until smooth. Adjust the seasoning.
3  Serve the pâté on small squares of toast and garnish with lime and parsley.

COOK'S TIP
If you use a food processor to chop the mushrooms, cut them roughly and put through the tube with the machine running. Be careful not to over-process them or they will liquefy.

# TARAMASALATA

PREPARATION TIME: **15** MINUTES + SOAKING ◆ FREEZING: NOT SUITABLE ◆ **195** CALS PER SERVING ◆ SERVES **8**

**This traditional Greek appetiser usually served with others as part of a *meze*. Make up your own with olives, crispbread or biscuits.**

50 g (2 oz) smoked cod's roe
150 g (5 oz) white olive oil bread, eg ciabatta or pugliese, crusts removed
45 ml (3 tbsp) lemon juice
3.75 ml (3/4 tsp) anchovy paste or 1 anchovy fillet
50 ml (2 fl oz) sunflower oil
75 ml (3 fl oz) olive oil
freshly ground black pepper
olive oil for drizzling
black olives and thyme sprigs, to garnish

1  Soak the cod's roe in cold water for 1 hour. Cut the bread into chunks and soak in a bowl of cold water for 2 minutes; squeeze out excess liquid.
2  Drain the cod's roe and remove the thin skin. Place in a food processor with the bread, lemon juice and anchovy paste or fillet and blend for 4–5 seconds. With the machine still running, gradually add the oils in a thin stream until the mixture is smooth and light in texture and colour. Season with pepper.
3  Place in a serving dish, drizzle with olive oil and garnish with black olives and thyme.

COOK'S TIP
If the mixture it too thick, add 30–45 ml (2–3 tbsp) hot water.

# APPLE STRUDEL WITH MAPLE FUDGE SAUCE

PREPARATION TIME: 30 MINUTES ◆ COOKING TIME: 40 MINUTES ◆ FREEZING: NOT SUITABLE ◆ 230-170 CALS PER SERVING ◆ SERVES 6-8

grated rind and juice of 1 lemon
25 g (1 oz) fresh white breadcrumbs
30 ml (2 tbsp) caster sugar
700 g (1½ lb) cooking apples
6 sheets filo pastry, about 50 g (2 oz)
25 g (1 oz) low-fat spread, melted
icing sugar, to dust

**MAPLE FUDGE SAUCE**
75 g (3 oz) butter
150 g (5 oz) soft light brown
   (muscovado) sugar
30 ml (2 tbsp) maple syrup
75 ml (3 fl oz) half-fat double cream

1  Preheat the oven to 190°C (375°F) Mark 5. Mix the lemon rind with the breadcrumbs and 15 ml (1 tbsp) of the sugar. Peel, quarter and thickly slice the apples. Drizzle with a little lemon juice to prevent discolouration. Mix the apple with the breadcrumb mixture.
2  Lay 3 pieces of filo pastry side by side on a clean tea-towel, overlapping the longest edges by 5 cm (2 inches). Brush with low-fat spread. Place the remaining filo on top and brush again.
3  Place the apple mixture on the filo pastry. Using the tea-towel to help, roll the filo from the longest edge to form a thick roll. Roll it on to a non-stick baking sheet, seam-side down, curling it slightly

if necessary to fit the sheet. Brush with the remaining low-fat spread and sprinkle with the remaining sugar.
4  Bake in the oven for 40 minutes or until the pastry is golden brown and the apples are soft. If necessary, cover the pastry loosely with foil to prevent it becoming too brown.
5  Meanwhile, make the Maple Fudge Sauce. Melt the butter in a heavy-based pan, add the sugar and maple syrup and cook gently until the sugar has dissolved completely. Stir in the cream and bring to the boil; cool slightly.
6  Dust the strudel with icing sugar, cut into slices and serve warm with the sauce.

# WALNUT TORTE

PREPARATION TIME: 25 MINUTES + COOLING ◆ COOKING TIME: 30 MINUTES ◆ FREEZING: NOT SUITABLE ◆ 530–425 CALS PER SLICE ◆ MAKES 8–10 SLICES

**Folding whisked egg whites into a creamed mixture gives a soufflé-like quality to this airy sponge, so expect it to deflate slightly after baking.**

150 g (5 oz) unsalted butter
150 g (5 oz) caster sugar
5 eggs, separated
grated rind of 1 orange
150 g (5 oz) ricotta cheese
40 g (1½ oz) plain white flour, sifted
165 g (5½ oz) walnuts, lightly toasted
   and chopped

**TO FINISH**
90 ml (6 tbsp) apricot jam
10 ml (2 tsp) orange juice
25 g (1 oz) plain chocolate, in one piece
   (at room temperature)

1  Preheat the oven to 190°C (375°F) Mark 5. Grease and base-line a 23 cm (9 inch) spring-release cake tin.
2  Cream the butter and 125 g (4 oz) of the sugar together in a bowl until pale and fluffy. Add the egg yolks, orange rind, cheese, flour and 125 g (4 oz) of the walnuts and mix gently until evenly combined.
3  Put the egg whites into another large bowl and whisk until stiff but not dry. Gradually whisk in the remaining sugar. Using a metal tablespoon, fold a quarter of the egg white into the cheese mixture to loosen it slightly, then carefully fold in the remainder.
4  Turn the mixture into the prepared tin

and gently level the surface. Bake in the oven for about 30 minutes, until risen and just firm. Leave to cool in the tin.
5  Heat the apricot jam in a pan until melted, then press through a sieve into a bowl and stir in the orange juice to make a glaze.
6  Brush half of the glaze around the side of the cake. Using a palette knife, coat the side of the cake with the reserved walnuts.
7  Brush the remaining apricot glaze over the top of the cake. Using a swivel vegetable peeler, shave curls from the chocolate and scatter over the top of the cake to serve.

# WARM SPLIT PEA DIP

**PREPARATION TIME: 5 MINUTES ◆ COOKING TIME: 55 MINUTES ◆ FREEZING: NOT SUITABLE ◆ 165 CALS PER SERVING ◆ SERVES 8**

225 g (8 oz) yellow split peas
1 bay leaf
125 g (4 oz) onion, chopped
3 garlic cloves, crushed
60 ml (4 tbsp) light olive oil
salt and freshly ground black pepper
30 ml (2 tbsp) lemon juice
olive oil for drizzling
ground paprika, to garnish

**1** Put the split peas in a large pan with 1.1 litres (2 pints) water. Bring to the boil and skim off any foam from the surface. Add the bay leaf, onion and garlic, cover and simmer for 50-55 minutes or until the peas have softened and absorbed the water to form a coarse purée.
**2** Discard the bay leaf. Beat the purée with the olive oil until smooth. Season very well and add the lemon juice.
**3** Turn into a warm serving dish and drizzle with olive oil. Serve warm or at room temperature, garnished with paprika.

# SMOKED FISH TERRINE

**PREPARATION TIME: 25 MINUTES ◆ COOKING TIME: 15 MINUTES ◆ FREEZING: SUITABLE ◆ 285 CALS PER SERVING ◆ SERVES 8**

450 g (1 lb) smoked haddock
1/2 onion, sliced
1 bay leaf
few peppercorns
125 ml (4 fl oz) double cream
30 ml (2 tbsp) chopped fresh dill
5 ml (1 tsp) paprika
2.5 ml (1/2 tsp) cayenne pepper
30 ml (2 tbsp) lemon juice
11 g (0.4 oz) packet powdered gelatine
175-225 g (6–8 oz) smoked trout, thinly sliced
75-125 g (3–4 oz) each boneless smoked trout fillets

**1** Put the smoked haddock in a shallow pan and add sufficient cold water just to cover. Add the onion, bay leaf and peppercorns. Bring to the boil, then lower the heat and poach gently for 15 minutes or until the fish flakes easily.
**2** Remove the fish from the pan. Strain and reserve 125 ml (4 fl oz) of the poaching liquid. Flake the fish, removing any bones, and leave to cool.
**3** Place the flaked haddock, cream, dill, paprika, cayenne and lemon juice in a food processor and blend until smooth. Season with salt and black pepper.
**4** Put the reserved liquid in a small pan and sprinkle on the gelatine. Leave to soak for 5 minutes, then dissolve over a very low heat. Stir into the fish mixture.
**5** Lightly oil a 900-ml (1 1/2-pint) terrine or loaf pan and line with cling film. Line the base and sides with the smoked trout slices, reserving some for the top. Remove the skin from the trout and mackerel fillets, then halve lengthways
**6** Spoon a third of the fish purée into the terrine and spread evenly. Lay half of the trout and mackerel fillets on top, then cover with half of the remaining purée. Repeat with the remaining fish fillets and purée, smoothing the surface. Cover with the remaining smoked trout slices. Chill for at least 3 hours, until firm.
**7** Turn the terrine out and cut into slices. Serve on a bed of salad leaves.

# SPICED APPLE CAKE WITH BUTTERSCOTCH SAUCE

PREPARATION TIME: 35 MINUTES ◆ COOKING TIME: 1½ HOURS ◆ FREEZING: SUITABLE ◆ 700 CALS PER SERVING ◆ SERVES 8

225 g (8 oz) puff pastry
175 g (6 oz) butter
125 g (4 oz) caster sugar
50 g (2 oz) soft light brown sugar
3 eggs
45 ml (3 tbsp) cider
5 ml (1 tsp) mixed spice
175 g (6 oz) self-raising flour, sifted
4 Granny Smith apples
lemon juice, to brush

**BUTTERSCOTCH SAUCE**
50 g (2 oz) each butter and caster sugar
75 g (3 oz) soft light brown sugar
150 g (5 oz) golden syrup
142 ml carton double cream
few drops vanilla essence
juice of ½ lemon

1  Preheat the oven to 200°C (400°F) Mark 6. Roll out the pastry thinly on a lightly floured surface. Place on a baking sheet and prick all over with a fork. Cook in the oven for 10–12 minutes or until well risen and golden; cool. Lower the temperature to 180°C (350°F) Mark 4.
2  Meanwhile, cream together the butter and sugars until very pale. Beat in the eggs and cider (the mixture will curdle). Fold in the mixed spice and flour. Peel, core and roughly chop 1 apple and fold into the cake mixture.
3  Trim the pastry to fit in the bottom of a shallow 28 x 18 cm (11 x 7 inch) cake tin. Spoon the cake mixture evenly over the pastry and level the surface.

4  Peel, core and halve the remaining apples. Thinly slice each half and press down into the cake mixture. Brush lightly with lemon juice. Bake in the oven for about 1 hour 10 minutes or until firm to the touch.
5  Meanwhile, make the Butterscotch Sauce. Place the butter, sugars and syrup in a pan and heat gently until melted, then stir over a low heat for 5 minutes.
6  Remove from the heat and slowly add the cream. Add the vanilla essence and lemon juice and stir for 1–2 minutes.
7  Dust the cake with icing sugar and serve warm on its own or with Butterscotch Sauce (hot or cold) and vanilla ice cream.

# LEMON SYRUP CAKE

PREPARATION TIME: 20 MINUTES + SOAKING ◆ COOKING TIME: 1 HOUR ◆ FREEZING: SUITABLE ◆ 360 CALS PER SLICE ◆ MAKES 12 SLICES

225 g (8 oz) butter or margarine, softened
finely grated rind of 2 lemons
225 g (8 oz) caster sugar
4 eggs, beaten
225 g (8 oz) self-raising white flour
65 g (2½ oz) candied lemon peel, finely choped (optional)
30 ml (2 tbsp) lemon juice

**SYRUP**
175 g (6 oz) caster sugar
juice of 3 lemons, strained

1  Grease and base-line a deep, 21 cm (8½ inch) round cake tin. Preheat the oven to 180°C (350°F) Mark 4.
2  Cream the butter and lemon rind together in a bowl. Gradually beat in the caster sugar, followed by the eggs. Fold in the flour, candied peel, if using, and lemon juice.
3  Spoon the mixture into the prepared tin and level the surface. Bake in the oven for about 1 hour or until well browned.
4  Meanwhile, prepare the syrup. Place the sugar, lemon juice and 75 ml (5 tbsp) water in a saucepan. Heat gently until the sugar has dissolved, then bring to the boil and bubble for 1 minute; cool.

5  As soon as the cake is cooked, turn out on to an edged dish and immediately spoon over the syrup. Leave for about 30 minutes for the syrup to soak in. Serve warm, with poached fruit if desired. Alternatively, cool completely and store in an airtight tin for up to 3–4 days.

# CHICKEN LIVER AND PISTACHIO PÂTÉ

PREPARATION TIME: **20** MINUTES + CHILLING ◆ COOKING TIME: **15** MINUTES ◆ FREEZING: SUITABLE ◆ **435–350** CALS PER SERVING ◆ SERVES **8–10**

2 rashers rindless streaky bacon, chopped
700 g (1½ lb) chicken livers
about 225 g (8 oz) butter
1-2 garlic cloves, chopped
large pinch of ground allspice
125 g (4 oz) mushrooms, finely chopped
1 onion, finely chopped
200 g (7 oz) low-fat soft cheese
30 ml (2 tbsp) double cream
40 g (1½ oz) shelled pistachio nuts, roughly chopped
45 ml (3 tbsp) chopped mixed fresh parsley, chives and thyme
salt and freshly ground black pepper
parsley and a few shelled pistachio nuts, to garnish

**1** Place the bacon in a heavy-based frying pan and heat gently until the fat starts to run, then increase the heat and cook until lightly browned.
**2** Meanwhile, trim the livers, discard any membranes and the white fibrous bits in the middle and chop roughly.
**3** Add 50 g (2 oz) of the butter to the pan and heat until just melted. Add the livers, garlic and allspice and cook over a high heat until the livers are sealed and browned on the outside but still a little pink on the inside. Remove the bacon and livers with a slotted spoon, set aside.
**4** Add the mushrooms and onion to the pan and cook gently until the onion is softened. Remove from the heat.

**5** Transfer the livers and bacon to a food processor or blender. Add the onion, mushrooms and any butter remaining in the pan. Add the cheese and cream and blend until smooth. Turn into a mixing bowl.
**6** Fold the nuts and herbs into the pâté and season to taste. Spoon into individual dishes and level the tops.
**7** Melt the remaining butter in a small saucepan over a very low heat. Slowly pour into a jug, leaving the milky sediment behind. Slowly pour the clarified butter onto the pâtés to cover them completely (you may need to melt a little more). Immerse the parsley and nuts in the butter to garnish and chill.

# CRAB CAKES WITH MUSTARD SAUCE

PREPARATION TIME: **20** MINUTES + CHILLING ◆ COOKING TIME: **15–20** MINUTES ◆ FREEZING: NOT SUITABLE ◆ **470** CALS PER SERVING ◆ SERVES **6**

300 g (10 oz) white crab meat
4 spring onions, finely chopped
60 ml (4 tbsp) mayonnaise
50 g (2 oz) fresh white breadcrumbs
10 ml (2 tsp) Worcestershire sauce
3–4 drops Tabasco sauce
grated rind of 1 lemon
1 egg yolk
diced tomatoes and black olives
prawns, dill and celery tops, to garnish

**MUSTARD SAUCE**
6 cooked, shell-on prawns
25 g (1 oz) shallots, chopped
25 g (1 oz) button mushrooms, sliced
125 ml (4 fl oz) each white wine and chicken stock
284 ml carton double cream
10 ml (2 tsp) wholegrain mustard

**1** Flake the crab meat and mix with the spring onion, mayonnaise. Season with salt and freshly ground black pepper and stir in 25 g (1 oz) of the breadcrumbs, the Worcestershire and Tabasco sauces, lemon rind and egg yolk. Bind together well.
**2** Divide the mixture into six and shape into round cakes. Coat each cake in the remaining breadcrumbs and chill for at least 2 hours or overnight.
**3** Meanwhile, make the Mustard Sauce. Put the prawns, shallots, mushrooms, wine and chicken stock in a saucepan. Bring to the boil and bubble until the liquid has reduced by two-thirds.
**4** Add the cream and bring slowly to the

boil. Continue to boil until the sauce thickens slightly. Strain the sauce and return to the rinsed saucepan. Stir in the mustard and set aside.
**5** Shallow-fry the crab cakes for 2–3 minutes on each side or until golden and crisp. Reheat the Mustard Sauce. Serve the crab cakes on a bed of diced tomatoes and olives. Garnish with prawns, dill and celery tops and serve with a spinach salad.

# DATE AND GINGER CAKE

PREPARATION TIME: 20 MINUTES ◆ COOKING TIME: ABOUT 1 HOUR ◆ FREEZING: SUITABLE ◆ 210 CALS PER SERVING ◆ MAKES ABOUT 16 SLICES

**Make this sticky cake up to 1 week ahead and store in an airtight cake tin or the freezer.**

2.5 ml (½ tsp) bicarbonate of soda
50 ml (2 fl oz) milk
125 g (4 oz) butter
125 g (4 oz) soft light brown (muscovado) sugar
2 eggs, beaten
150 g (5 oz) golden syrup
150 g (5 oz) black treacle
125 g (4 oz) stoned dates, roughly chopped
50 g (2 oz) stem ginger in syrup, chopped
225 g (8 oz) plain flour, sifted
7.5 ml (1½ tsp) ground ginger
salt

**1** Grease and base-line a 23 cm (9 inch) square cake tin with non-stick baking parchment. Preheat the oven to 150°C (300°F) Mark 2. Stir the bicarbonate of soda into the milk.
**2** Beat together the butter and sugar until pale and light. Slowly add the egg, then stir in the syrup, treacle, milk, dates and stem ginger.
**3** Fold in the flour, ground ginger and a pinch of salt. Pour into the prepared tin and bake in the oven for 1 hour or until a skewer inserted into the centre comes out clean. Leave in the tin for 1 hour, then transfer to a wire rack to cool.
**4** Wrap in greaseproof paper and store until required.

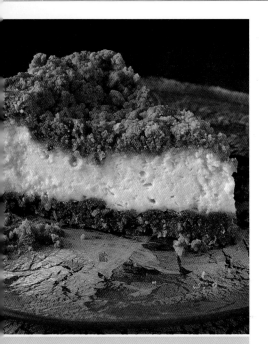

# WARM GINGER RICOTTA CAKE

PREPARATION TIME: 25 MINUTES ◆ COOKING TIME: 1¼ HOURS ◆ FREEZING: SUITABLE (STEP 4) ◆ 715–535 CALS PER SERVING ◆ SERVES 6–8

225 g (8 oz) digestive biscuits
75 g (3 oz) butter, melted
1 piece stem ginger in syrup, plus 15 ml (1 tbsp) syrup
200 g carton full-fat soft cheese
225 g (8 oz) ricotta cheese
60 ml (4 tbsp) double cream
3 eggs, separated
15 ml (1 tbsp) cornflour
125 g (4 oz) icing sugar, sifted

**GINGER AND WHISKY SAUCE**
284 ml carton single cream
10 ml (2 tsp) stem-ginger syrup
10 ml (2 tsp) whisky

**1** Preheat the oven to 200°C (400°F) Mark 6. Crush the biscuits in a food processor or blender to a fine powder. Pour on the melted butter and process for 1 minute.
**2** Line the base of a 20 cm (8 inch) spring-release tin with non-stick baking parchment. Completely cover with just over half of the crumb mixture and set aside.
**3** Finely chop the ginger. Beat or process together the cheeses, cream, egg yolks, cornflour, ginger and syrup; the mixture should be creamy and the ginger roughly chopped through it. Transfer to a large bowl.
**4** Whisk the egg whites until they form

soft peaks. Gradually whisk in the icing sugar, keeping the meringue very stiff and shiny. Fold into the ginger mixture and spoon into the prepared tin. Sprinkle with the remaining biscuit crumbs.
**5** Bake in the oven for 30 minutes. Cover loosely with foil, lower the temperature to 180°C (350°F) Mark 4 and bake for 45 minutes; the cake should feel just set in the centre. Transfer to a wire rack and leave to cool for 15 minutes (it will sink a bit).
**6** Meanwhile, heat all the ingredients for the Ginger and Whisky Sauce together without boiling. Serve just warm with the warm cake.

# MARINATED TROUT

PREPARATION TIME: **15** MINUTES + MARINATING ◆ FREEZING: NOT SUITABLE ◆ **120** CALS PER SERVING ◆ SERVES **4**

2 trout fillets, each about 125 g (4 oz)
salt and freshly ground black pepper
1 pack Thai herbs (see Cook's Tip)
juice of 2 limes and 1 orange
45 ml (3 tbsp) coconut milk powder
30 ml (2 tbsp) honey
1 large bag mixed salad leaves
125 g (4 oz) cooked, peeled prawns
crispy onions, to garnish

**1** Season the trout fillets and sandwich together with the chopped Thai herbs. Place in a shallow, non-metallic dish. Pour over the lime and orange juices, cover and leave to marinate in the fridge overnight.
**2** Thinly slice the trout and divide between 4 serving plates. Blend the coconut milk powder and honey with 200 ml (7 fl oz) water and half of the coriander, lemon grass and chilli from the Thai herbs in the marinade.
**3** Use a little of this dressing to toss the salad leaves and prawns together. Divide between the 4 plates and garnish with crispy onions. Hand the remaining dressing separately.

COOK'S TIP
Look out for packs of Thai herbs in the supermarket. They include all the classic Thai flavourings – fresh coriander, lemon grass and chilli. If you can't find any, this recipe is just as good with coriander and a few drops of Tabasco sauce.

# MINTED PRAWN SALAD

PREPARATION TIME: **10** MINUTES ◆ FREEZING: NOT SUITABLE ◆ **215** CALS PER SERVING ◆ SERVES **6**

225 g (8 oz) cucumber
1 large red chilli, seeded and finely chopped
grated rind and juice of 2 limes
30 ml (2 tbsp) soft brown sugar
salt and freshly ground black pepper
25 ml (1 fl oz) Thai fish sauce (see Cook's Tip)
100 ml (4 fl oz) olive oil
few drops sesame oil
175 g (6 oz) beansprouts
15 g (½ oz) mint or coriander sprigs
450 g (1 lb) cooked king prawns
15 ml (1 tbsp) sesame seeds, toasted
prawn crackers and lime slices, to garnish

**1** Halve the cucumber and remove the seeds, then cut diagonally into thin slices.
**2** Place the chilli in a bowl. Whisk in the lime rind and juice, sugar, seasoning, fish sauce, and oils.
**3** Toss the sliced cucumber, beansprouts, mint or coriander and prawns in the dressing until well coated.
**4** To serve, pile the salad in the centre of 6 individual serving plates, sprinkle with toasted sesame seeds and top with prawn crackers. Garnish with lime slices.

COOK'S TIP
Thai fish sauce, also known as Nam Pla, is available from specialist Asian stores.

# CHOCOLATE LAYER CAKE

PREPARATION TIME: **40** MINUTES ◆ COOKING TIME: ABOUT **1¼** HOURS ◆ FREEZING: NOT SUITABLE ◆ **490** CALS PER SLICE ◆ MAKES ABOUT **12** SLICES

75 g (3 oz) creamed coconut
50 g (2 oz) cocoa powder
350 g (12 oz) self-raising flour
5 ml (1 tsp) baking powder
large pinch of salt
175 g (6 oz) soft light brown sugar
25 g (1 oz) plain chocolate, melted
150 ml (¼ pint) sunflower oil
white and dark chocolate curls and icing sugar, to decorate (optional)

**ICING**
142 ml carton double cream
350 g (12 oz) plain chocolate, in pieces

**1** Grease and line a 1.7 litre (3 pint) loaf tin. Preheat the oven to 180°C (350°F) Mark 4.
**2** Pour 425 ml (17 fl oz) boiling water over the coconut and stir until dissolved. Leave to cool for 30 minutes.
**3** Sift the cocoa powder, flour, baking powder and salt into a bowl; stir in the sugar. Make a well in the centre and add the coconut mixture, melted chocolate and oil. Beat to make a smooth batter.
**4** Pour into the prepared tin and bake in the oven for 40 minutes. Cover with foil and cook for 20–25 minutes or until just firm. Leave in the tin for 10 minutes, then transfer to a wire rack to cool.
**5** To make the icing, place the cream in a pan and bring to the boil. Add the chocolate and stir until melted. Cool, beating occasionally, until thick.
**6** If the cake's surface is uneven, remove a thin slice and turn the cake upside down. Cut in half horizontally and sandwich the layers together with half of the icing. Spread the rest over the cake. Dust with icing sugar and decorate with chocolate curls just before serving, if wished.

## COOK'S TIP

This cake can be stored for 2-3 days in an airtight container.

# STICKY ALMOND CAKE

PREPARATION TIME: **30** MINUTES + RESTING ◆ COOKING TIME: **1** HOUR ◆ FREEZING: SUITABLE (STEP 7) ◆ **675** CALS PER SERVING ◆ SERVES **10**

225 g (8 oz) raisins
125 g (4 oz) currants
175 g (6 oz) citrus peel
60 ml (4 tbsp) almond-flavoured liqueur, eg Amaretto di Soronno
200 g (7 oz) butter
150 ml (¼ pint) milk
125 g (4 oz) caster sugar
450 g (1 lb) strong plain flour
2.5 ml (½ tsp) each salt, grated nutmeg and ground cinnamon
3 cardamom pods
40 g (1½ oz) ground almonds
20 ml (4 tsp) easy-blend yeast (about 2 sachets
grated rind of 1 lemon
1 egg, beaten
250 g (9 oz) white marzipan
icing sugar, to dust

**1** Grease a large bowl and a 30 cm (12 inch) square baking sheet.
**2** Place fruit peel and liqueur in a bowl.
**3** Place 125 g (4 oz) of the butter, the milk and sugar in a pan and heat gently until melted. Cool until just tepid.
**4** Sift the flour, salt and spices into a bowl. Remove the seeds from the cardamom and crush. Add to the bowl with the almonds and yeast and mix together. Make a well in the centre, add the milk mixture, lemon rind and egg and stir until mixed. Tip on to a floured surface and knead for 4 minutes. Knead in the soaked fruit until just combined. Place in the greased bowl, cover and leave to rise in a warm place for 3 hours.
**5** Tip the dough on to a floured surface and knead for 1 minute. Shape into an oval about 30 x 20 cm (12 x 8 inches) and place on the baking sheet.
**6** Roll the marzipan into a sausage almost as long as the dough and place in the centre. Lift one long side over the marzipan, then the other, overlapping in the centre and sealing the ends. Flip over so the sealed ends are underneath. Leave in a warm place for 1 hour. Preheat the oven to 200°C (400°F) Mark 6.
**7** Bake in the oven for 15 minutes, then lower the temperature to 180°C (350°F) Mark 4 and bake for 45–55 minutes.
**8** Melt the remaining butter and brush over the hot loaf. Dust with icing sugar.

# TANDOORI PRAWNS

PREPARATION TIME: **25 MINUTES** ◆ COOKING TIME: **6 MINUTES** ◆ FREEZING: **NOT SUITABLE** ◆ **225** CALS PER SERVING ◆ SERVES **4**

2.5 cm (1 inch) piece fresh root ginger, finely chopped
3 garlic cloves, crushed
20 ml (4 tsp) lemon juice
90 ml (6 tbsp) natural yogurt
salt and freshly ground black pepper
15 ml (1 tbsp) cumin seeds
10 ml (2 tsp) ground paprika
75 g (3 oz) butter
300 g (10 oz) cooked peeled prawns
mini poppadums and naan bread, to serve

**1** Put the ginger, garlic, lemon juice, yogurt, seasoning, cumin seeds and paprika in a bowl and mix well. Cover and set aside for at least 15 minutes.
**2** Melt the butter in a large frying pan, add the yogurt mixture and cook, stirring, for 3–4 minutes or until the butter separates. Stir in the prawns to coat in the butter. Cook for 1–2 minutes or until they are hot.
**3** Serve immediately, with poppadums and naan bread.

# SMOKED SALMON GALETTE

PREPARATION TIME: **20 MINUTES** ◆ COOKING TIME: **5–10 MINUTES** ◆ FREEZING: **NOT SUITABLE** ◆ **285** CALS PER SERVING ◆ SERVES **6**

450 g (1 lb) large potatoes
oil for deep frying
salt and freshly ground black pepper
450 g (1 lb) cucumber (about 2 small)
225 g (8 oz) smoked salmon, cut into strips
15 ml (1 tbsp) chopped fresh dill or 2.5 ml (½ tsp) dried
10 ml (2 tsp) white wine vinegar
90 ml (6 tbsp) crème fraîche
dill sprigs and salmon or trout eggs, to garnish

**1** Slice the potatoes into thin rounds (preferably in a food processor). Cover with cold water.
**2** Drain the potato slices and pat dry on kitchen paper. Heat the oil in a deep-fat fryer to 165–175°C (330–345°F).
**3** Cook the potato slices in batches in the hot oil for 1–2 minutes or until tender but not golden; drain. Cook the potato slices again in slightly hotter oil for 1 minute, until golden and crisp; drain well. Cool, then sprinkle with salt.
**4** Peel the cucumber, slice in half lengthways, then remove the seeds. Using a parer, peel the cucumber into long, wafer-thin strips and mix with the smoked salmon. Mix in the dill and

vinegar and season with black pepper.
**5** Set aside 6 potato slices. Arrange 4 or 5 potato slices in the centre of each serving plate to form a circle. Spoon on a little crème fraîche, then some salmon mixture, more potato and crème fraîche, then the remaining salmon. Top with the reserved potato and garnish with dill sprigs and fish eggs.

# ALMOND, CHOCOLATE AND SWEET POTATO LOAF

**PREPARATION TIME: 20 MINUTES ◆ COOKING TIME: 1–1¼ HOURS ◆ FREEZING: SUITABLE ◆ 435–350 CALS PER SLICE ◆ MAKES 8–10 SLICES**

225 g (8 oz) sweet potato, cut into
chunks
125 g (4 oz) soft margarine
125 g (4 oz) soft light brown
(muscovado) sugar
5 ml (1 tsp) vanilla essence
2 eggs
160 g (5½ oz) self-raising white flour
15 g (½ oz) cocoa powder
5 ml (1 tsp) ground mixed spice
2.5 ml (½ tsp) bicarbonate of soda
30 ml (2 tbsp) milk
125 g (4 oz) milk chocolate, roughly
chopped
75 g (3 oz) flaked almonds, lightly
toasted
icing sugar, to dust

**1** Put the sweet potato in a pan of cold water, bring to the boil and cook for 15 minutes or until softened. Drain well, then mash with a potato masher.
**2** Preheat the oven to 160°C (325°F) Mark 3. Grease a 900 g (2 lb) loaf tin and line the base and long sides with a strip of greaseproof paper.
**3** Put the margarine, sugar, vanilla essence and eggs in a bowl. Sift in the flour, cocoa, mixed spice and bicarbonate of soda. Add the milk and beat well until smooth and creamy.
**4** Stir in the mashed sweet potato, chocolate and 50 g (2 oz) of the almonds. Turn the mixture into the prepared tin and level the surface.

Sprinkle with the remaining almonds.
**5** Bake in the oven for 1–1¼ hours, until well risen and just firm to touch. Leave in the tin for 10 minutes, then transfer to a wire rack to cool. Dust with icing sugar.

## COOK'S TIP

Cook this cake as soon as you have mixed it, as the bicarbonate of soda is activated on blending.

## VARIATIONS

If sweet potatoes are unobtainable, use parsnips instead. Substitute the mixed spice with 2.5 ml (½ tsp) ground coriander and add the finely grated rind of 1 orange.

# PANETTONE

**PREPARATION TIME: 25 MINUTES + RISING ◆ COOKING TIME: 35 MINUTES ◆ FREEZING: SUITABLE ◆ 415–320 CALS PER SERVING ◆ MAKES 10–12 SLICES**

15 ml (1 tbsp) active dried yeast
150 ml (¼ pint) warm milk
450 g (1 lb) strong plain white flour
10 ml (2 tsp) salt
75 g (3 oz) caster sugar
1 egg plus 4 yolks, beaten
finely grated rind of 1 lemon and 1
orange
175 g (6 oz) unsalted butter, softened
75 g (3 oz) chopped mixed candied
orange and citron peel, chopped
125 g (4 oz) raisins

**1** Line a deep 15 cm (6 inch) round cake tin with a double layer of non-stick baking parchment which projects 12.5 cm (5 inches) above the rim.
**2** Dissolve the yeast in 60 ml (4 tbsp) of the milk. Cover and leave in a warm place for 10 minutes, until frothy. Stir in 125 g (4 oz) of the flour and the remaining milk. Cover and leave to rise for 30 minutes.
**3** Sift the remaining flour and salt onto the yeast mixture. Make a well in the centre and add the sugar, beaten egg and citrus rinds. Mix to an elastic dough, adding more flour if necessary, but keeping the dough quite soft. Work in the butter. Cover and leave to rise for

2–4 hours, until doubled in volume.
**4** Preheat the oven to 200°C (400°F) Mark 6. Knock the dough down and knead in the peel and raisins. Place in the prepared tin and cut an X on the top with a very sharp knife. Cover and leave to rise until the dough is 2.5 cm (1 inch) above the top of the tin.
**5** Bake in the oven for 15 minutes, then lower the temperature to 180°C (350°F) Mark 4 and bake for 40 minutes, until well risen. Leave in the tin for 10 minutes, then transfer to a wire rack to cool.
**6** Serve cut into horizontal slices. To store, replace the top, wrap in cling film or foil and keep in the fridge. Bring to room temperature to serve.

# DEEP-FRIED WHITEBAIT WITH HOT SAUCE

**PREPARATION TIME: 20** MINUTES ◆ **COOKING TIME: ABOUT 15** MINUTES ◆ **FREEZING: NOT** SUITABLE ◆ **790** CALS PER SERVING ◆ **SERVES 4**

60 ml (4 tbsp) plain white flour
salt and freshly ground black pepper
700 g (1½ lb) whitebait
oil for deep-frying

**HOT SAUCE**
25 g (1 oz) ground hazelnuts
2-3 red chillies, stems removed
1 small onion, quartered
3 garlic cloves
1 ripe tomato, skinned
15 ml (1 tbsp) mild paprika
10 ml (2 tsp) balsamic or red wine
  vinegar
about 60 ml (4 tbsp) virgin olive oil

**GARNISH**
chopped parsley
paprika
lime or lemon wedges

**1** First make the sauce. Preheat the grill to medium. Spread the hazelnuts in the grill pan and toast until golden brown, shaking the pan occasionally to ensure that they brown evenly.
**2** Put all the sauce ingredients, except the olive oil, in a food processor or blender and blend until smooth. Add a little of the olive oil if the mixture gets stuck around the blades. With the machine running, gradually add the olive oil in a thin stream through the feeder tube, to make a fairly thick sauce. Season with salt and pepper and set aside.
**3** Put the flour in a bowl and season generously with salt and pepper. Add the whitebait and toss to coat in the flour.

**4** Heat the oil in a deep-fat fryer to 190°C (375°F). Test the temperature by dropping a cube of stale bread into the oil – the bread should sizzle immediately on contact with the oil, rise to the surface and become golden brown in about 30 seconds.
**5** Deep-fry the fish in batches in the hot oil for about 3 minutes or until golden brown. Drain on crumpled kitchen paper and keep hot.
**6** Serve the whitebait as soon as they are all cooked, garnished with parsley, a sprinkling of paprika, and lime or lemon wedges. Serve the sauce separately.

# NIÇOISE PLATTER

**PREPARATION TIME: 40** MINUTES ◆ **COOKING TIME: 15** MINUTES ◆ **FREEZING: NOT** SUITABLE ◆ **445** CALS PER SERVING ◆ **SERVES 8**

400 g can cannellini beans, drained
grated rind and juice of 1 lemon
2 garlic cloves, crushed
150 ml (¼ pint) extra-virgin olive oil
30 ml (2 tbsp) chopped fresh parsley
225 g (8 oz) each French beans and
  radishes, trimmed
4 eggs
8 large slices rustic-style bread (or 16
  small slices)
lemon wedges, to garnish

**OLIVE PASTE**
125 g (4 oz) pitted black olives
1 garlic clove, crushed
2 anchovy fillets in oil, drained and
  chopped
30 ml (2 tbsp) chopped fresh parsley
60 ml (4 tbsp) extra-virgin olive oil

**1** First make the Olive Paste. Using a pestle and mortar or a food processor, grind together the olives, garlic, anchovies, parsley and a little freshly ground black pepper until fairly smooth. Gradually blend in the oil. Season to taste and set aside.
**2** Rinse the cannellini beans, drain and place in a bowl. Stir in half of the lemon rind and juice, half of the garlic, 60 ml (4 tbsp) of the oil and the parsley. Season to taste and set aside.
**3** Bring a large pan of water to the boil, add the French beans, bring back to the boil, then simmer for 3 minutes. Drain and immediately refresh under cold running water; dry well. Toss the French

beans with the remaining lemon rind and juice, garlic and a further 60 ml (4 tbsp) of the oil. Season to taste and set aside.
**4** Cut the radishes in half if large. Toss with the remaining oil.
**5** Bring a small pan of water to the boil, add the eggs, bring back to the boil and simmer gently for 7 minutes or longer if a firmer yolk is preferred. Drain and immediately plunge into iced water to cool. Peel and carefully cut in half.
**6** Preheat the grill and toast the bread on both sides. Arrange all the ingredients on one large platter, with the Olive Paste in the centre, and garnish with lemon wedges.

# STICKY GINGERBREAD

PREPARATION TIME: **20** MINUTES ◆ COOKING TIME: **1** HOUR **20** MINUTES ◆ FREEZING: SUITABLE ◆ **350** CALS PER SLICE ◆ MAKES **12** SLICES

150 g (5 oz) stem ginger pieces, plus
45 ml (3 tbsp) syrup from jar
1 large cooking apple, about 225 g (8 oz)
15 ml (1 tbsp) lemon juice
125 g (4 oz) black treacle
125 g (4 oz) golden syrup
175 g (6 oz) molasses or soft dark brown
(muscovado) sugar
175 g (6 oz) unsalted butter
225 g (8 oz) plain white flour
125 g (4 oz) plain wholemeal flour
5 ml (1 tsp) ground mixed spice
7.5 ml (1½ tsp) bicarbonate of soda
2 eggs

**1** Preheat the oven to 160°C (325°F) Mark 3. Grease and line a deep 18 cm (7 inch) square cake tin. Thinly slice the ginger pieces. Peel, core and quarter the apple; immerse in a bowl of water with the lemon juice added to prevent discolouration.
**2** Put the treacle, syrup and sugar in a saucepan. Cut the butter into pieces and add to the pan. Heat gently until the butter has melted; leave to cool slightly.
**3** Sift the flours, spice and bicarbonate of soda into a bowl. Grate three-quarters of the apple into the bowl and toss lightly in the flour. Add the melted mixture, eggs and three-quarters of the ginger pieces. Beat well until combined.

**4** Turn the mixture into the prepared tin, spreading it into the corners. Using a potato peeler, pare the remaining apple into thin slices. Scatter the apple slices and remaining ginger over the surface of the gingerbread and press down lightly into the mixture with the tip of a knife. Bake in the oven for 1 hour 20 minutes or until firm to touch. Leave to cool in the tin.
**5** Turn out the cake and drizzle the ginger syrup over the surface.

### COOK'S TIP

Gingerbread will keep well in an airtight tin for up to 1 week. It's best stored for several days before eating.

# LEMON SEED LOAF

PREPARATION TIME: **20** MINUTES ◆ COOKING TIME: **1** HOUR ◆ FREEZING: SUITABLE (STEP 3) ◆ **200** CALS PER SERVING ◆ MAKES **12** SLICES

3 lemons
50 g (2 oz) butter
250 g (9 oz) caster sugar
250 g (9 oz) self-raising white flour
5 ml (1 tsp) baking powder
1 egg
100 ml (4 fl oz) semi-skimmed milk
30 ml (2 tbsp) plain yogurt
30 ml (2 tbsp) poppy seeds

**1** Grate the rind from 1 lemon. Lightly grease and base-line a 900 g (2 lb) loaf tin. Preheat the oven to 180°C (350°F) Mark 4.
**2** Process the butter in a food processor until soft. Add the lemon rind, 200 g (7 oz) of the sugar, the flour, baking powder, egg, milk, yogurt and poppy seeds and process until smooth.
**3** Turn the mixture into the prepared tin and level the top. Bake in the oven for 55 minutes-1 hour or until cooked through (cover after 40 minutes if necessary to prevent over-browning). Cool in the tin for 10 minutes.
**4** Squeeze the juice from the rindless lemon and 1 more lemon. Thinly slice the

third lemon. Place together in a pan with the remaining sugar and 150 ml (¼ pint) water. Bring to the boil and bubble for 4–5 minutes or until syrupy. Remove from the heat.
**5** Loosen the sides of the cake with a palette knife and turn out onto a wire rack. Pierce the cake in several places with a cocktail stick and spoon over the syrup and lemon slices. Leave until cold.

# CHORIZO SALAD

PREPARATION TIME: **15** MINUTES ◆ COOKING TIME: **15** MINUTES ◆ FREEZING: NOT SUITABLE ◆ **746** CALS PER SERVING ◆ SERVES **4**

225 g (8 oz) chorizo sausage, diced
60 ml (2 fl oz) olive oil
125 g (4 oz) diced French baguette
10 ml (2 tsp) chopped fresh thyme
1 garlic clove, crushed
salad leaves, eg chicory, batavia, rocket
  or spinach
125 g (4 oz) each fennel and cucumber,
  thinly sliced
200 g (7 oz) goat's cheese, diced or
  crumbled

## DRESSING
30 ml (2 tbsp) Dijon mustard
30 ml (2 tbsp) sherry vinegar
1 egg yolk
125 ml (4 fl oz) olive oil
salt and freshly ground black pepper

**1** Place the chorizo in a pan and dry-fry over a high heat until golden, stirring occasionally; set aside.
**2** Heat the oil in the pan, add the baguette and cook until golden. Add the thyme and garlic; set aside.
**3** To make the dressing, whisk together the mustard, vinegar, egg yolk and oil. Season to taste.
**4** Mix the salad leaves with the fennel, cucumber, goat's cheese, chorizo and bread in a salad bowl. Add the dressing, toss well and serve immediately.

# PARMA HAM WITH MANGO AND ORANGE

PREPARATION TIME: **20** MINUTES + MARINATING ◆ COOKING TIME: **5** MINUTES ◆ FREEZING: NOT SUITABLE ◆ **250** CALS PER SERVING ◆ SERVES **4**

1 orange
30 ml (2 tbsp) virgin olive oil
45 ml (3 tbsp) sweet sherry
5 ml (1 tsp) balsamic vinegar
salt and freshly ground black pepper
2 large mangoes
75 g (3 oz) Parma ham
tarragon sprigs, to garnish

**1** Pare the rind from the orange and place in a small bowl with the oil. Cover and set aside for 30 minutes. Divide the orange into segments.
**2** Meanwhile, pour the sherry into a small saucepan, bring to the boil and bubble to reduce by half. Remove from the heat and whisk in the vinegar. Season to taste, then set aside to cool.
**3** Peel the mangoes and halve to remove the stone. Slice the flesh.
**4** Arrange the mango, orange segments and ham on individual plates. Add the orange-flavoured oil to the sherry mixture and drizzle over the mango and Parma ham (see Cook's Tip). Garnish with tarragon.

## COOK'S TIP
Keep orange oil in a cool place for up to one week. Add to salad dressings.

## VARIATION
Omit the mango. Slice the orange (step 1). Add 15 ml (1 tbsp) finely chopped fresh mint to the sherry mixture with the vinegar (step 2). Add the orange oil as before. Sprinkle the ham and orange with pepper just before serving.

# PISTACHIO ICE CREAM

PREPARATION TIME: 15 MINUTES + FREEZING ◆ COOKING TIME: 10–15 MINUTES ◆ FREEZING: SUITABLE ◆ 555 CALS PER SERVING ◆ SERVES 6

15 ml (1 tbsp) cornflour
175 g (6 oz) caster sugar
300 ml (½ pint) milk
4 eggs, beaten
284 ml carton double cream, lightly whipped
125 g (4 oz) pistachio nuts, blanched and chopped (see Cook's Tip)
few drops almond essence
few drops edible green food colouring (optional)

1 Blend the cornflour and caster sugar with a little of the milk in a saucepan to form a smooth paste. Stir in the remaining milk and bring to the boil, stirring constantly.
2 Pour the mixture on to the eggs, stirring constantly. Return to the saucepan.
3 Stir the custard mixture over a medium heat for about 5 minutes or until thickened. Leave to cool.
4 Fold the cream into the custard. Add the pistachio nuts, almond essence and food colouring, if using.
5 Pour the mixture into a freezerproof container, cover and freeze for 1–2 hours or until just firm.

6 Remove from the freezer and beat thoroughly. Return to the freezer for at least 4 hours. Allow to soften at room temperature for 20 minutes before serving.

## COOK'S TIP

To blanch pistachios, plunge the shelled nuts into boiling water for a few minutes, then remove the skins. The blanched nuts are a lovely, bright green.

# MANGO, GINGER AND CITRUS SORBET

PREPARATION TIME: 25 MINUTES ◆ COOKING TIME: 3–4 MINUTES ◆ FREEZING: SUITABLE ◆ 140–95 CALS PER SERVING ◆ SERVES 4–6

2 large mangoes, each about 400 g (14 oz), chopped
25 g (1 oz) preserved stem ginger, finely chopped
50 ml (2 fl oz) syrup from the stem ginger jar
50 g (2 oz) caster sugar
thinly pared rind and juice of 3 limes

1 Place the mango flesh in a food processor or blender and purée until very smooth. Transfer to a bowl and stir in the stem ginger.
2 Place the ginger syrup, sugar, lime rind and juice in a small pan. Add 90 ml (3 fl oz) water and heat gently, stirring until the sugar has dissolved. Bring to the boil, then simmer for 3 minutes. Remove from the heat and leave to cool.
3 Strain the cooled syrup through a fine sieve into the mango mixture and stir well. Transfer to a plastic container and freeze for 2 hours. Remove from the freezer and beat well to break down any ice crystals. Return to the freezer for 1 hour, then beat again. Repeat once

more. Freeze for several hours until firm, or until required.
4 Transfer the sorbet to the refrigerator about 20 minutes before serving to soften slightly. Scoop into individual glass dishes to serve.

## VARIATION

Mango Ice Cream: Heat 284 ml carton double cream with 2 strips of lemon rind until boiling. Remove from the heat and leave to infuse for 30 minutes; strain. Whisk into 3 egg yolks, then heat gently until thickened; do not boil. Cool, then combine with the pureed flesh of 2 large mangoes and 30 ml (2 tbsp) lemon juice. Freeze, stirring every hour, until firm.

# THAI CHICKEN WONTONS

PREPARATION TIME: **20** MINUTES ◆ COOKING TIME: **10–15** MINUTES ◆ FREEZING: NOT SUITABLE ◆ **345** CALS PER SERVING ◆ SERVES **12**

3 large red chillies, finely chopped
3 kaffir lime leaves, finely chopped
6 spring onions, finely chopped
2 x 15 cm (6 inch) stems lemon grass, finely chopped
450 g (1 lb) chicken fillet, roughly chopped
small handful of fresh coriander sprigs
3 garlic cloves, crushed
45 ml (3 tbsp) coconut milk
salt and freshly ground black pepper
225 g (8 oz) filo pastry
1 egg, beaten
oil for deep-frying

**1** Place the chillies, lime leaves, spring onions, lemon grass, chicken, coriander, garlic, coconut milk and seasoning in a food processor and blend for 2–3 minutes.
**2** Cut the pastry into thirty 15 cm (6 inch) squares. Keep the squares covered with cling film as you work. Brush each square with beaten egg. Place 10 ml (2 tsp) of the chicken mixture in the centre of each square. Scrunch the edges roughly together to seal.
**3** Deep-fry the wontons in batches in hot oil (see Cook's Tips) for 4-5 minutes or until they are pale golden brown and cooked through. Drain on kitchen paper. Pile up on a warm serving platter and serve with a dipping sauce. Alternatively, cool and leave for up to 1 hour.
**4** To reheat, place on a baking sheet and reheat at 200°C (400°F) Mark 6 for 5–10 minutes or until piping hot.

## COOK'S TIPS
Look for packets of fresh Thai herbs, containing chillies, lime leaves, lemon grass and coriander. Available from major supermarkets, you'll need three packets for this recipe.
Keep the wontons well apart in the hot oil so that they do not stick together.

# POTATO PANCAKES WITH MUSTARD CHICKEN LIVERS

PREPARATION TIME: **20** MINUTES ◆ COOKING TIME: **25-30** MINUTES ◆ FREEZING: NOT SUITABLE ◆ **335** CALS PER SERVING ◆ SERVES **4**

225 g (8 oz) floury potatoes
1 small egg (size 5), or ½ size 2 egg
30 ml (2 tbsp) milk
20 ml (1½ tbsp) self-raising flour
5 ml (1 tsp) chopped fresh thyme
1.25 ml (¼ tsp) salt
1 egg white
25 g (1 oz) butter
2 shallots, sliced
225 g (8 oz) chicken livers
salt and freshly ground black pepper

## SAUCE
50 g (2 oz) crème fraîche
15 ml (1 tbsp) wholegrain mustard
7.5 ml (1½ tsp) lemon juice
15 ml (1 tbsp) chopped fresh chives

**1** Cut the potatoes into even-size pieces. Cook in lightly salted boiling water for 12–15 minutes, until tender. Drain well and mash until very smooth. Leave to cool slightly, then whisk in the egg, milk, flour, thyme and salt to form a thick smooth batter.
**2** Meanwhile, make the sauce. Mix together the crème fraîche, mustard, lemon juice and chives; set aside.
**3** Whisk the egg white and carefully fold into the pancake batter.
**4** Preheat the oven to its lowest setting. Heat a very thin layer of oil in a frying pan. Pour in 2 large spoonsful of the batter to form small pancakes and cook for 1–2 minutes, until golden. Flip the pancakes over and cook the other side. Drain on kitchen paper and keep warm in the oven. Repeat to make 8 pancakes.
**5** Melt the butter in a small frying pan, add the shallots and fry gently for 5 minutes, until just golden. Increase the heat, add the chicken livers and stir-fry for 3–4 minutes until they are well browned on the outside but still a little pink in the centre. Season with salt and pepper to taste.
**6** Arrange the potato pancakes on warm serving plates. Sit the livers on top, scraping over any pan juices, and add a spoonful of the sauce. Garnish with salad leaves tossed in a little olive oil and lemon juice, chives and lemon wedges.

# SORBET BASKETS WITH RASPBERRY SAUCE

PREPARATION TIME: **45–50** MINUTES ◆ COOKING TIME: **15** MINUTES ◆ FREEZING: SUITABLE ◆ **340** CALS PER SERVING ◆ SERVES **12**

500 ml (15 fl oz) blackcurrant or cassis
  sorbet
12 biscuit baskets
whitecurrants, raspberries and mint,
  sprigs to decorate

**BISCUIT BASKETS**
40 g (1½ oz) butter
40 g (1½ oz) sugar
40 g (1½ oz) flour
40 g (1½ oz) liquid glucose (see Cook's
  Tips)

**RASPBERRY SAUCE**
450 g (1 lb) fresh or frozen raspberries
225 g (8 oz) caster sugar
about 30 ml (2 tbsp) lemon juice

**1** To make the biscuit baskets, blend together the butter, sugar, flour and glucose in a food processor until smooth. Chill in the refrigerator for 30 minutes.
**2** Place 1 tsp of the mixture per basket, wide apart, on silicone parchment-lined baking trays. Cook in batches at 180°C (350°F) Mark 4 for 7 minutes.
**3** Leave to cool for a few seconds, then mould over ramekin moulds to make baskets. Cool.
**4** Chill 2 baking sheets in the freezer. Place about 24 scoops of the sorbet in single layers on the sheets. Return to the freezer for at least 10 minutes.
**5** To make the raspberry sauce, place the raspberries and sugar in a food processor or blender and blend until smooth. Push through a sieve to remove the seeds. Stir in the lemon juice to taste.
**6** Flood 12 serving plates with 30–45 ml (2–3 tbsp) of the sauce. Add 2 scoops of sorbet to each basket and place one on each plate. Decorate with fruit and mint sprigs (see Cook's Tips).

### COOK'S TIP

Liquid glucose is like a stiff syrup. You'll find it at most chemists.
The baskets may be frozen with the sorbet in them. Allow 5 minutes at room temperature before serving.

# APRICOT ICE CREAM

PREPARATION TIME: **30** MINUTES + FREEZING ◆ COOKING TIME: **30–40** MINUTES ◆ FREEZING: SUITABLE ◆ **335** CALS PER SERVING ◆ SERVES **6**

225 g (8 oz) ready-to-eat dried apricots
pared rind of 1 large lemon
45 ml (3 tbsp) orange juice
2 eggs
50 g (2 oz) caster sugar
5 ml (1 tsp) vanilla essence
30 ml (2 tbsp) Cointreau or Grand
  Marnier
284 ml carton double cream, whipped
deep fried orange rind, to decorate
fresh orange juice, to serve

**1** Place the apricots in a bowl, add 450 ml (¾ pint) water, cover and leave to soak overnight.
**2** Place the apricots with their soaking liquid and lemon rind in a saucepan. Bring to the boil; cover and cook over a low heat for 20–30 minutes, stirring occasionally. Uncover and cook until all the liquid has evaporated. Leave to cool a little, then remove the lemon rind. Place the apricots and orange juice in a food processor and process for 20 seconds. Set aside to cool.
**3** Place the eggs and sugar in a large bowl. Using an electric whisk, whisk the mixture over a pan of simmering water for about 10 minutes until a thick mousse forms. Remove from the heat and whisk until cool.
**4** Fold the egg mixture, apricots, vanilla essence and Cointreau or Grand Marnier into the cream. Place in an ice cream maker and freeze until stiff, then transfer to a freezerproof container until required. Alternatively, pour the mixture into a shallow freezerproof container. Freeze for 2½–3 hours, then beat with a fork to break down any ice crystals. Repeat this process twice, then leave to freeze for at least 2 hours, until firm.
**5** Remove the ice cream from the freezer 15 minutes before serving. Serve decorated with the orange rind, with a squeeze of orange juice on top.

# QUICK MOZZARELLA AND SALAMI PIZZAS

PREPARATION TIME: **20** MINUTES ◆ COOKING TIME: **15-20** MINUTES ◆ FREEZING: NOT SUITABLE ◆ **435** CALS PER SERVING ◆ SERVES **4**

**This is an ideal starter for an informal supper – it's quick and easy and tastes absolutely delicious.**

2 ciabatta rolls
60 ml (2 fl oz) olive oil (optional)
30 ml (2 tbsp) sun-dried tomato paste
1 large ripe beefsteak tomato
12 large basil leaves
50 g (2 oz) salami
150 g (5 oz) mozzarella cheese, thinly
  sliced
5 ml (1 tsp) dried oregano
extra-virgin olive oil, for drizzling
basil sprigs, to garnish

**1** Preheat the oven to 220°C (425°F) Mark 7. Cut each roll in half horizontally. Heat the oil in a large frying pan and fry the halved rolls for 2–3 minutes, until crisp and golden on both sides. Drain on kitchen paper. (Alternatively, lightly toast the rolls on both sides.)
**2** Spread the cut sides of the rolls with a little sun-dried tomato paste. Cut the tomato into 4 thick slices and place a slice on each roll half. Top with 3 basil leaves, some salami and mozzarella slices.
**3** Transfer the pizzas to a baking sheet and sprinkle with the oregano. Drizzle with a little olive oil and bake near the top of the oven for 10–15 minutes, until

the cheese is bubbling and golden. Serve immediately, garnished with a little basil.

## VARIATION

Vary the toppings for these pizzas as you wish. Try spreading the fried or toasted halved rolls with olive paste and top the tomato slices with chopped anchovies and capers. Bake as above.

# DIVINE SPARE RIBS

PREPARATION TIME: **15** MINUTES ◆ COOKING TIME: **1½** HOURS ◆ FREEZING: SUITABLE ◆ **280** CALS PER SERVING ◆ SERVES **4**

**In this recipe the ribs are simmered to tenderise the meat before roasting with a tangy Chinese-style glaze – resulting in succulent, tender ribs.**

900 g (2 lb) pork spare ribs
30 ml (2 tbsp) malt vinegar
30 ml (2 tbsp) sesame oil
90 ml (3 fl oz) rice or wine vinegar
60 ml (2 fl oz) dark soy sauce
10 ml (2 tsp) grated fresh root ginger
1 garlic clove, crushed
grated rind of 1 lime
60 ml (4 tbsp) soft brown sugar
2.5 ml (½ tsp) Chinese five-spice powder
90 ml (3 fl oz) water
coriander sprigs and lime wedges, to
  garnish

**1** Wash and dry the spare ribs and place in a saucepan. Cover with plenty of cold water and add the malt vinegar. Bring to the boil, then simmer for 20 minutes, skimming the surface from time to time to remove the scum.
**2** Preheat the oven to 220°C (425°F) Mark 7. Meanwhile, place the remaining ingredients in a small pan, bring to the boil, then simmer for 5 minutes, until reduced and thickened slightly.
**3** Drain the ribs and transfer to a roasting pan that will hold them in a single layer. Pour over the soy mixture and toss the ribs to coat evenly.
**4** Cover loosely with foil and roast in the oven for 30 minutes. Remove the foil

and cook for a further 30 minutes, turning and basting the ribs every 5 minutes. Leave to cool for about 10 minutes before serving.
**5** Garnish with coriander and lime wedges. Provide finger bowls and plenty of napkins to serve.

## VARIATION

Barbecued chicken wings make a tasty alternative to pork ribs. Omit the par-boiling stage. Roast as above, coated with the glaze, for the same time or until glazed and tender.

# SPICED STRAWBERRY SORBET

PREPARATION TIME: **35** MINUTES + STANDING + FREEZING ◆ COOKING TIME: **5** MINUTES ◆ FREEZING: SUITABLE ◆ **115** CALS PER SERVING ◆ SERVES **6**

**Pepper and balsamic vinegar complement strawberries perfectly.**

15 ml (1 tbsp) black peppercorns
125 g (4 oz) caster sugar
700 g (1½ lb) strawberries
30 ml (2 tbsp) balsamic vinegar
sliced strawberries and crushed peppercorns, to decorate

**1** Coarsely grind the peppercorns using a pestle and mortar. Place the sugar and 150 ml (¼ pint) water in a small saucepan and bring to the boil, stirring, until the sugar has dissolved. Stir in the peppercorns, remove from the heat, cover and leave to stand for 1 hour.
**2** Strain the syrup through a fine sieve and discard the peppercorns. Place the syrup and strawberries in a food processor or blender and purée until smooth. Push the mixture through the sieve, discarding the seeds and other solids. Stir in the vinegar.
**3** Turn the mixture into a shallow freezerproof container and freeze for about 2 hours or until mushy.

**4** Beat gently with a fork to break down the ice crystals, return to the freezer for another hour, beat again. Return to the freezer and freeze until firm. Alternatively, churn the mixture in an ice cream machine until thick and almost frozen.
**5** Transfer the sorbet to the fridge for about 30 minutes before serving. Garnish with strawberries and crushed peppercorns to serve.

# CARDAMOM AND PISTACHIO ICE CREAM

PREPARATION TIME: **10** MINUTES + FREEZING ◆ COOKING TIME: **10** MINUTES ◆ FREEZING: SUITABLE ◆ **465** CALS PER SERVING ◆ SERVES **6**

50 g (2 oz) shelled pistachio nuts, toasted and chopped
3 litres (5¼ pints) milk
14 cardamom pods
125 g (4 oz) caster sugar
mango, pineapple and papaya, to serve

**1** Place the milk and cardamom pods in a large heavy-based saucepan. Bring to the boil, then simmer vigorously until reduced to 750 ml (1¼ pints). Strain the milk, discarding the cardamom, then stir in the sugar and nuts.
**2** Cool quickly, then freeze the mixture in an ice cream machine. Alternatively pour into a freezerproof container, cover and freeze for about 2 hours. Beat once to break down the ice crystals, then freeze. Allow to stand at room temperature for 30 minutes before serving.
**3** Serve scoops of the ice cream with sliced exotic fruits.

## COOK'S TIP
A non-stick preserving pan would be ideal for boiling the milk.

# GLAZED CHICKEN WINGS

PREPARATION TIME: **10** MINUTES + MARINATING ◆ COOKING TIME: ABOUT **1** HOUR ◆ FREEZING: NOT SUITABLE ◆ **175** CALS PER SERVING ◆ SERVES **4**

12 small chicken wings
4 garlic cloves, crushed
5-10 ml (1–2 tsp) hot chilli sauce
45 ml (3 tbsp) sweet soy sauce
15 ml (1 tbsp) preserved stem ginger
   syrup or clear honey
15 ml (1 tbsp) lemon juice
5 ml (1 tsp) ground coriander
2.5 ml (½ tsp) ground cinnamon
shredded spring onion and lemon
   wedges, to garnish

**1** Wash and dry the chicken wings and pull out any small feathers that still remain attached. Tuck the tip of each wing under the thickest part of the wing to form a triangular shape. Transfer to a large shallow, non-metallic dish.
**2** Put the remaining ingredients in a bowl, mix well, then pour over the chicken wings. Toss to coat the wings thoroughly. Cover and leave to marinate in a cool place for at least 4 hours, preferably overnight.
**3** Preheat the oven to 220°C (425°F) Mark 7. Transfer the chicken wings and marinade to a roasting pan just large enough to hold them in a single layer. Bake at the top of the oven for 50–60 minutes, basting and turning frequently until the wings are glazed and tender – the flesh should almost fall from the bone. Serve hot, garnished with shredded spring onion and lime and/or lemon wedges. Remember to provide finger bowls.

## VARIATION

Use the sauce as a glaze for pork spare ribs rather than chicken wings. Place 675 g (1½ lb) pork ribs in a pan, cover with cold water and add 30 ml (2 tbsp) malt vinegar. Bring to the boil, then simmer for 20 minutes. Drain and cool. Toss with the marinade and continue as above.

# SPINACH AND RATATOUILLE TERRINE

PREPARATION TIME: **1 ½** HOURS ◆ COOKING TIME: **1¼** HOURS + SETTING ◆ FREEZING: NOT SUITABLE ◆ **135** CALS PER SERVING ◆ SERVES **12**

5 red and 2 yellow peppers
30 ml (2 tbsp) oil
225 g (8 oz) onion, roughly chopped
2 garlic cloves, crushed
30 ml (2 tbsp) tomato paste
125 g (4 oz) ripe tomatoes, chopped
45 ml (3 tbsp) chopped fresh basil leaves
150 ml (¼ pint) white wine
20 ml (4 tsp) powdered gelatine
1 aubergine, thinly sliced lengthways
2 courgettes, thinly sliced lengthways
175 g (6 oz) spinach
basil sprigs, to garnish

**1** Roughly chop 3 red peppers. Heat 30 ml (2 tbsp) oil in a saucepan, add the onions and garlic and cook for 7–10 minutes. Stir in the tomato paste, then add the chopped peppers, tomatoes and basil and cook for 4–5 minutes. Add the wine, bring to the boil and reduce by half.
**2** Add 300 ml (10 fl oz) water, bring to the boil and simmer, uncovered, for 15–20 minutes. Purée the mixture in a liquidiser, sieve and leave to cool. Season
**3** Pour 60 ml (4 tbsp) cold water into a bowl, sprinkle over the gelatine and leave to soak for 2–3 minutes. Place over a pan of gently simmering water for 2–3 minutes, then stir into the tomato sauce.
**4** Brush the remaining peppers and sliced aubergine with 90 ml (6 tbsp) oil. Place on baking sheets and cook at 220°C (425°F) Mark 7 for 20–30 minutes. Cool, peel and de-seed the peppers.
**5** Cook the courgettes in boiling water for 3 minutes. Drain, plunge into iced water and drain again.Put the spinach in a colander and pour over boiling water. Pour over ice-cold water; drain well.
**6** Line a 1.4-litre (2½-pint) terrine with clingfilm, then with the spinach leaves. Cover the base of the terrine with some tomato sauce mixture. Add a layer of yellow pepper, then spoon over tomato sauce to cover.
**7** Continue layering the vegetables with tomato sauce in between, ending with a layer of tomato sauce. Season well between the layers. Cover with spinach leaves, wrap in clingfilm and refrigerate overnight.
**8** To serve, turn the terrine out, remove the clingfilm and cut into slices.

# RASPBERRY AND ORANGE MERINGUES

PREPARATION TIME: 40 MINUTES ◆ COOKING TIME: 1½ HOURS ◆ FREEZING: NOT SUITABLE ◆ 185 CALS PER SERVING ◆ SERVES 6

**MERINGUES**
2 egg whites
125 g (4 oz) caster sugar
grated rind of 1 large orange

**FILLING**
175 g (6 oz) raspberries
15 g (½ oz) icing sugar
125 ml (4 fl oz) Greek-style yogurt
142 ml carton whipping cream, whipped
extra icing sugar, to dust

1  Place the egg whites in a clean grease-free bowl (see Cook's Tip) and whisk with an electric whisk until stiff. Add half of the caster sugar and continue to whisk until stiff and shiny. Fold in the remaining caster sugar and orange rind.
2  Preheat the oven to 100°C (200°F) Mark ¼. Line 3 baking sheets with non-stick baking parchment. Using a cup or glass as a guide, draw six 8.5 cm (3½ inch) circles on each sheet. Turn the parchment over.
3  Put 1 heaped teaspoon of meringue mixture inside each circle, then spread it around the circle with the back of the spoon. Cook in the oven for 1½ hours or until dry, swapping the position of the

trays occasionally to ensure even cooking. Leave to cool on the tray.
4  Set aside about 18 raspberries for decoration. Place the rest in a bowl and sprinkle with the icing sugar. Fold the yogurt and raspberries into the cream.
5  Sandwich 2 meringues together with the cream mixture. Decorate with the reserved raspberries and dust with icing sugar. Repeat with the remaining meringues. Serve within 1 hour.

**COOK'S TIP**
Before whisking egg whites, rub the surface of the mixing bowl with ½ lemon to ensure it is free from grease.

# MERINGUES WITH FRESH FRUITS

PREPARATION TIME: 20 MINUTES + COOLING ◆ COOKING TIME: 1½–2 HOURS ◆ FREEZING: NOT SUITABLE: ◆ 200 CALS PER SERVING ◆ SERVES 6

**MERINGUES**
175 g (6 oz) caster sugar
3 egg whites

**TO SERVE**
fruits in season, eg peaches or
   nectarines, strawberries and
   raspberries
vanilla sugar
whipped cream, crème fraîche or thick
   yogurt

1  Preheat the oven to its lowest setting, maximum 120°C (250°F) Mark ½. Line 2 baking sheets with non-stick baking parchment.
2  Put the caster sugar and egg whites in a large heatproof bowl and place over a pan of gently simmering water. Using an electric whisk, beat on high speed until the mixture is very thick and leaves a 'trail' across the surface when the beaters are lifted. Immediately remove the bowl from the heat and continue whisking for 2 minutes.
3  Using 2 large spoons, shape the meringue mixture into 12 oval rounds, well apart, on the prepared baking sheets. Bake in the oven for 1½–2 hours,

until the meringues are crisp and can be easily peeled away from the baking parchment. Set aside to cool.
4  To serve, prepare the fruits as necessary, slicing the peaches or nectarines. Pile the meringues on a serving plate. Arrange the fruits in a separate dish, sprinkling them with vanilla sugar. Serve with chilled cream, crème fraîche or yogurt. Alternatively, arrange 2 meringues on each plate with the fruits, a spoonful of cream or yogurt and a dusting of vanilla sugar.

# ROOT VEGETABLE BEIGNETS

**PREPARATION TIME: 15 MINUTES ◆ COOKING TIME: 45 MINUTES ◆ FREEZING: NOT SUITABLE ◆ 640-425 CALS PER SERVING ◆ SERVES 4–6**

450 g (1 lb) mixed root vegetables, eg carrots, parsnips, turnips, cut into bite-size pieces
225 g (8 oz) cooked beetroot, cut into wedges
15 ml (1 tbsp) oil
350 g (12 oz) self-raising flour
25 g (1 oz) capers
30 ml (2 tbsp) chopped fresh basil
300 ml (½ pint) lager
sea salt and freshly ground black pepper
1 egg white
oil for deep-frying
basil leaves, to garnish

1 Preheat the oven to 200°C (400°F) Mark 6. Place the vegetables and oil in a roasting pan and cook in the oven for 25–30 minutes or until golden and tender; cool.

2 Place the flour, capers, basil and lager in a food processor or blender and blend until smooth. Season to taste and place in a mixing bowl. Whisk the egg white until soft peaks form, then fold into the batter.

3 Heat the oil in a deep-fat fryer or large saucepan to 190°C (375°F) or until a cube of bread browns as soon as it is put in. Season the vegetables and coat them in the batter. Deep-fry in batches for 1–2 minutes or until golden and crisp.

Drain on kitchen paper. Deep-fry the basil leaves for 30 seconds.

4 To serve, sprinkle the beignets lightly with salt and garnish with the deep-fried basil.

# PUMPKIN AND SAGE GNOCCHI

**PREPARATION TIME: 35 MINUTES ◆ COOKING TIME: 20 MINUTES ◆ FREEZING: NOT SUITABLE ◆ 530-354 CALS PER SERVING ◆ SERVES 4–6**

**This can be served as a supper dish for 4 or a starter for 6.**

350 g (12 oz) pumpkin or butternut squash, cut into 2.5 cm (1 inch) cubes
225 g (8 oz) potato, cut into 2.5 cm (1 inch) cubes
1 egg yolk
125 g (4 oz) plain flour
2.5 ml (½ tsp) salt
freshly ground black pepper
125 g (4 oz) unsalted butter
handful of fresh sage leaves
25 g (1 oz) freshly grated Parmesan cheese
75 g (3 oz) goat's cheese, crumbled
30 ml (2 tbsp) balsamic vinegar (optional)

1 Steam the pumpkin or butternut squash and potato over simmering water for 10–15 minutes or until tender. Push through a vegetable mouli or mash with a potato masher and transfer to a clean pan. Place over a low heat for 1 minute to dry out.

2 Transfer the purée to a bowl. Cool slightly, then beat in the egg yolk, flour, salt, and pepper to taste.

3 Put a large, deep pan of salted water on to boil. As soon as it reaches a rolling boil, drop in about 12 teaspoons of the mixture. The water will calm slightly; once it returns to the boil, simmer the gnocchi fast for 1½ minutes, until they have risen to the surface and are

softening slightly around the edges. Remove with a slotted spoon and drain on kitchen paper. Repeat with the remaining mixture.

4 Melt the butter in a large frying pan, add the sage and fry gently for 1–2 minutes or until the butter starts to turn golden. Immediately add the gnocchi and Parmesan cheese. Stir over a low heat for 30 seconds or until heated through.

5 Spoon the gnocchi on to warm individual plates, sprinkle with the goat's cheese and drizzle with the vinegar, if using. Serve immediately.

# ICED CHRISTMAS ALASKA

**PREPARATION TIME: 30 MINUTES + SOAKING + FREEZING ◆ COOKING TIME: 5-10 MINUTES ◆ FREEZING: SUITABLE ◆ 600 CALS PER SERVING ◆ SERVES 6**

200 g (7 oz) sultanas, chopped
50 g (2 oz) blanched almonds, chopped
25 g (1 oz) ready-to-eat dried apricots, chopped
45 ml (3 tbsp) rum
175 g (6 oz) caster sugar
4 egg yolks and 2 whites
284 ml carton double cream, lightly whipped
150 ml (¼ pint) brandy

**1** Place the sultanas, almonds, apricots and rum in a bowl, cover and soak overnight.
**2** Place 25 g (1 oz) of the sugar and 15 ml (1 tbsp) water in a saucepan and heat gently until the sugar has dissolved, then bring to the boil and bubble for 1 minute. Remove from the heat.
**3** Place the egg yolks in a bowl over a pan of simmering water. Using an electric whisk, whisk until pale, then gradually whisk in the hot sugar syrup, in a thin stream, until thick. Remove from the heat and whisk until cool. Fold in the cream and soaked fruits and nuts. Spoon into a 1 litre (1¾ pint) pudding basin, cover and freeze overnight.

**4** Invert the pudding on to a baking sheet and return to the freezer. Whisk the egg whites with 125 g (4 oz) of the sugar in a bowl over a pan of simmering water until thick and glossy. Cover the pudding completely with the meringue, then return to the freezer for at least 1 hour.
**5** To serve, preheat the oven to 240°C (475°F) Mark 9. Sprinkle the pudding with the remaining sugar and bake in the oven for 5-10 minutes or until golden.
**6** Meanwhile, heat the brandy in a saucepan, set alight and pour over the pudding. Serve immediately, while flaming.

# APPLE DÉLICE WITH CALVADOS AND APPLE SAUCE

**PREPARATION TIME: 25 MINUTES ◆ COOKING TIME: 2–2½ HOURS ◆ FREEZING: NOT SUITABLE ◆ 570 CALS PER SERVING ◆ SERVES 6**

2 egg whites
125 g (4 oz) caster sugar
700 g (1½ lb) dessert apples, eg Granny Smith
50 g (2 oz) butter
284 ml carton double cream, whipped
50 g (2 oz) flaked almonds, toasted
icing sugar, to decorate

**CALVADOS AND APPLE SAUCE**
600 ml (1 pint) apple juice
10 ml (2 tsp) arrowroot
lemon juice and Calvados, to taste

**1** Preheat the oven to 140°C (275°F) Mark 1. Place the egg whites in a large bowl and whisk until stiff. Add 50 g (2 oz) of the sugar and continue whisking until stiff and glossy. Fold in the remaining sugar with a metal spoon.
**2** Line 2 baking sheets with non-stick baking parchment and spread six 8.5 cm (3½ inch) circles of meringue mixture on each baking sheet.
**3** Cook in the oven for 2–2½ hours or until dry. Carefully remove the meringues from the paper and store in an airtight container, interleaved with baking parchment, until required.
**4** Peel, core and slice the apples. Melt a third of the butter in a large frying pan

and fry a third of the apples for 3–4 minutes or until golden. Remove and set aside to cool. Repeat with the remaining butter and apples.
**5** To make the sauce, put the apple juice in a pan, bring to the boil, then bubble until reduced by half. Blend the arrowroot with 15 ml (1 tbsp) water and whisk into the juice. Bring back to the boil, stirring, until thickened. Set aside to cool, then add lemon juice and Calvados to taste.
**6** Sandwich 2 meringues together with the cream and apples, sprinkle with the almonds and dust with icing sugar. Surround with the sauce to serve.

# WARM VEGETABLE SALAD WITH BALSAMIC DRESSING

PREPARATION TIME: **40** MINUTES ◆ COOKING TIME: **20** MINUTES ◆ FREEZING: NOT SUITABLE ◆ **270** CALS PER SERVING ◆ SERVES **6**

450 g (1 lb) thin leeks, cut diagonally
   into 5 cm (2 inch) lengths
salt and freshly ground black pepper
700 g (1½ lb) carrot, thinly sliced
   lengthways
75 ml (5 tbsp) vegetable oil
45 ml (3 tbsp) caster sugar
60 ml (4 tbsp) chopped fresh tarragon
150 ml (¼ pint) white wine
75 ml (5 tbsp) olive oil
45 ml (3 tbsp) balsamic vinegar
2 Little Gem lettuces
1 bunch or 75 g (3 oz) watercress

1  Bring a large pan of salted water to the boil, add the leeks and boil for 30 seconds. Drain and plunge into iced water. Drain again thoroughly and set aside.

2  Bring another pan of salted water to the boil, add the carrot and boil for 30 seconds. Drain and plunge into iced water. Drain again thoroughly and set aside.

3  Heat 30 ml (2 tbsp) of the vegetable oil in a large frying pan. Add the leeks and fry until golden. Remove and set aside.

4  Heat the remaining vegetable oil with the sugar and 45 ml (3 tbsp) of the tarragon. Fry the carrots in 2–3 batches over a high heat, turning regularly, for 3 minutes or until they are brown around the edges. Remove and set aside.

5  Add the wine to the pan, bring to the boil and bubble until reduced by half. Stir in the olive oil, vinegar and remaining tarragon. Season and set aside.

6  Tear the lettuce and mix it with the watercress and warm leeks and carrots. Pour the warm wine dressing over and serve immediately.

# SOURED CREAM AND ONION TARTS

PREPARATION TIME: **20** MINUTES + CHILLING ◆ COOKING TIME: ABOUT **1** HOUR ◆ FREEZING: NOT SUITABLE ◆ **535** CALS PER SERVING ◆ SERVES **6**

700 g (1½ lb) tomatoes, halved
salt and freshly ground black pepper
15 ml (1 tbsp) chopped fresh thyme or
   2.5 ml (½ tsp) dried
30 ml (2 tbsp) olive oil
200 g (7 oz) butter, chilled
175 g (6 oz) plain flour
90-105 ml (6–7 tbsp) soured cream
900 g (2 lb) onion, thinly sliced
125 g (4 oz) Roquefort, feta, or a good
   Red Leicester or Lanark Blue cheese,
   crumbled
fresh thyme sprigs, to garnish

1  Preheat the oven to 160°C (325°F) Mark 3. Place the tomatoes on a baking sheet, season with salt and pepper, sprinkle with the thyme and drizzle with the oil. Cook, uncovered, in the oven for 40 minutes, until slightly shrivelled. Increase the oven temperature to 200°C (400°F) Mark 6.

2  Meanwhile, cut 150 g (5 oz) of the butter into small dice and place in a food processor with the flour. Pulse until the butter is roughly cut up through the flour (you should still be able to see pieces of butter), then add the soured cream and pulse again for 2–3 seconds, until just mixed.

3  On a floured surface, cut the pastry into 6 pieces and thinly roll each into a 12.5 cm (5 inch) round. Place on 2 baking sheets, cover and chill for 30 minutes.

4  Melt the remaining butter in a pan, add the onion and cook gently for about 15 minutes, until very soft. Increase the heat and fry for 3–4 minutes or until well browned and caramelised; cool.

5  Spoon the onion into the centre of the pastry rounds, leaving a 1 cm (½ inch) edge. Sprinkle with the cheese and top with the tomato. Season to taste, then roughly fold up the pastry edge.

6  Cook in the oven for 30 minutes, until golden. Garnish with thyme and serve immediately.

# PEACHES AND FIGS WITH STRAWBERRY CREAM

PREPARATION TIME: 30 MINUTES ◆ COOKING TIME: 25 MINUTES ◆ FREEZING: NOT SUITABLE ◆ 440 CALS PER SERVING ◆ SERVES 12

450 g (1 lb) strawberries
375 g (12 oz) caster sugar
juice of 1 lemon
568 ml carton double cream, lightly
  whipped
600 ml (1 pint) white wine
1 vanilla pod
12 peaches
12 ripe black figs

1  Place the prepared strawberries, 125 g (4 oz) of the sugar and 30 ml (2 tbsp) of the lemon juice in a food processor or blender and blend until smooth, then push through a sieve. Whisk the cream into the purée and add lemon juice to taste. Cover and chill until required.
2  Place the wine, remaining sugar and vanilla pod in a saucepan and bring slowly to the boil, stirring until the sugar has dissolved. Simmer for 5 minutes. Add the peaches and simmer gently until beginning to soften, then add the figs and cook for 5 minutes. Leave in the wine syrup to cool. Skin the peaches.
3  Serve the peaches with the figs, syrup and strawberry cream.

# FRUIT TERRINE WITH STRAWBERRY SAUCE

PREPARATION TIME: 25 MINUTES + SETTING ◆ FREEZING: NOT SUITABLE ◆ 150 CALS PER SERVING ◆ SERVES 6

300 ml (1/2 pint) orange juice
300 ml (1/2 pint) ruby red orange juice
1 1/2 x 11 g (0.4 oz) sachets powdered
  gelatine
15 ml (1 tbsp) Grand Marnier or other
  orange-flavoured liqueur
50 g (2 oz) caster sugar
225 g (8 oz) raspberries
3 oranges

**SAUCE**
225 g (8 oz) strawberries
50 g (2 oz) caster sugar
10 ml (2 tsp) balsamic vinegar (optional)
5–10 ml (1–2 tsp) freshly ground black
  pepper

1  Line a 1.2 litre (2 pint) loaf pan with cling film. Pour 45 ml (3 tbsp) of each orange juice into separate small heatproof bowls. Sprinkle on the gelatine, dividing it equally between them. Leave to soften for a few minutes, then stand the bowls in a pan of hot water until the gelatine has dissolved. Add each gelatine liquid to the appropriate fruit juice.
2  Stir the liqueur and half of the sugar into the orange-coloured jelly, then pour half of this into the prepared mould. Scatter over half of the raspberries. Chill until just set.
3  Meanwhile, cut the peel and pith from the oranges, break into segments, then

cut into 2 or 3 pieces; drain in a sieve.
4  When the first layer of orange jelly has just set, arrange the orange segments on top. Stir the remaining sugar into the ruby red orange jelly, pour gently over the orange jelly and chill until just set.
5  Pour the remaining orange-coloured jelly on top and scatter over the remaining raspberries. Chill until firm.
6  Put all the sauce ingredients in a food processor or blender and purée until smooth. Chill until required.
7  To serve, turn out the terrine on to a board, peel off the cling film and cut into slices with a warm serrated knife. Pour the sauce on to individual plates and place a slice of terrine on top.

# HOT TOMATO SALAD

**PREPARATION TIME: 15 MINUTES ◆ COOKING TIME: 12 MINUTES ◆ FREEZING: NOT SUITABLE ◆ 160 CALS PER SERVING ◆ SERVES 6**

700 g (1½lb) cherry tomatoes (mixed red and yellow, if possible), halved
2 garlic cloves, sliced
30 ml (2 tbsp) capers, drained and rinsed
5 ml (1 tsp) caster sugar
sea salt and freshly ground black pepper
100 ml (4 fl oz) extra-virgin olive oil
1 loaf ready-to-bake olive ciabatta
30 ml (2 tbsp) chopped fresh basil
balsamic or red wine vinegar to taste
basil sprigs, to garnish

**1** Preheat the oven to 200°C (400°F) Mark 6. Place the tomatoes, garlic, capers and sugar in a small roasting pan and stir to mix. Season well and pour in the oil.
**2** Cook in the oven for 10–12 minutes or until the tomatoes are hot and beginning to soften. Pop the bread in the oven to bake alongside.
**3** Remove the tomatoes from the oven, add the chopped basil and a few drops of vinegar to taste and stir to mix. Slice the hot bread and spoon over the warm tomatoes and juices. Garnish with basil sprigs and serve immediately.

# FRENCH ONION TARTS WITH WARM TOMATO SALAD

**PREPARATION TIME: 35 MINUTES + CHILLING ◆ COOKING TIME: 1 HOUR 10 MINUTES ◆ FREEZING: SUITABLE (STEP 7) ◆ 810 CALS PER SERVING ◆ SERVES 6**

225 g (8 oz) plain flour
275 g (10 oz) butter
450 g (1 lb) large onion, halved and sliced
10 ml (2 tsp) chopped fresh thyme
142 ml carton double cream
2 eggs, separated
200 g (7 oz) feta cheese, crumbled
50 g (2 oz) Emmenthal cheese, grated
thyme sprigs, to garnish

**SALAD**
50 g (2 oz) small pitted black olives
45 ml (3 tbsp) olive oil
15 ml (1 tbsp) balsamic or red wine vinegar
salt and freshly ground black pepper
350 g (12 oz) plum tomatoes, sliced

**1** First prepare the salad. Combine the olives, oil, vinegar and seasoning. Arrange the tomatoes in an ovenproof dish, season with pepper and spoon over the olive dressing. Cover and set aside.
**2** Place the flour and 225 g (8 oz) of the butter in a food processor and process until fine crumbs form. Gradually add about 45 ml (3 tbsp) iced water, until it forms a ball. Chill for 30 minutes.
**3** Roll out the pastry on a lightly-floured surface and use to line six 8 cm (3¼ inch) loose-based tart tins. Prick the bases and chill for 30 minutes.
**4** Melt the remaining butter in a heavy-based saucepan. Add the onion, seasoning and thyme. Cover and cook gently, stirring occasionally, for 30 minutes or until soft. Remove the lid, increase the heat and cook until the juices evaporate. Stir in the cream; cool.
**5** Preheat the oven to 200°C (400°F) Mark 6. Bake the pastry cases blind (see page 101).
**6** Combine the egg yolks and cheese with the onion mixture and season well. Whisk the egg whites until stiff, then fold into the mixture.
**7** Spoon into the pastry cases and cook on the top shelf for 20 minutes or until risen. Place the tomatoes in the oven after 10 minutes.
**8** Garnish with thyme and serve with the warm salad.

# GLAZED PEARS

PREPARATION TIME: **10** MINUTES ◆ COOKING TIME: **10** MINUTES ◆ FREEZING: NOT SUITABLE ◆ **300** CALS PER SERVING ◆ SERVES **6**

1 small bought Madeira cake
about 60 ml (4 tbsp) Kirsch
3 small Williams pears
about 25 g (1 oz) butter, melted
15 ml (1 tbsp) caster sugar
good quality almond-flavoured ice
    cream, to serve

**1**  Cut the Madeira cake lengthways into six thin 5 mm (1/4 inch) slices, then stamp out six 6.5 cm (2³/4 inch) rounds. Place on a lightly greased baking sheet and drizzle with the Kirsch.
**2**  Thinly slice the pears and arrange them in an overlapping spiral on the Madeira cake. Brush lightly with melted butter and sprinkle with sugar. Place under a preheated grill for 10 minutes or until pale golden.
**3**  Serve warm with scoops of almond-flavoured ice cream.

### COOK'S TIP

If you are serving ice cream at a dinner party, scoop it in to portions and place on a foil-lined baking sheet in the freezer to firm. When ready to serve, simply lift a pre-shaped scoop on to each individual plate.

# FIGS IN CINNAMON SYRUP

PREPARATION TIME: **15** MINUTES ◆ COOKING TIME: **35** MINUTES + COOLING + CHILLING ◆ FREEZING: NOT SUITABLE ◆ **370** CALS PER SERVING ◆ SERVES **6**

pared rind and juice of 1 orange and
    1 lemon
300 ml (1/2 pint) red wine
50 g (2 oz) caster sugar
1 cinnamon stick
450 g (1 lb) ready-to-eat dried figs
200 g carton mascarpone cheese or
    vanilla ice cream, to serve

**1**  Place the pared rinds, orange and lemon juice, wine, sugar and cinnamon stick in a saucepan and bring very slowly to the boil, stirring occasionally.
**2**  Add the figs and simmer very gently for 20 minutes, until plump and soft. Remove the figs, rinds and cinnamon with a slotted spoon and transfer to a serving bowl.
**3**  Bring the liquid back to the boil and bubble for about 5 minutes, until syrupy. Pour over the figs, leave to cool, then cover and chill until required (see Cook's Tip).
**4**  Serve with mascarpone cheese or ice cream. (If preferred, the figs can be served warm.)

### COOK'S TIP

The figs can be kept in the fridge for up to one week - just stir occasionally. Reheat in the syrup for 3–4 minutes if you wish to serve them warm.

# WARM ASPARAGUS AND HERB MOUSSES

**PREPARATION TIME: 20 MINUTES ◆ COOKING TIME: 1 HOUR ◆ FREEZING: NOT SUITABLE ◆ 590 CALS PER SERVING ◆ SERVES 6**

**It is worth buying shallots for this recipe as they're sweeter in flavour.**

75 g (3 oz) butter
450 g (1 lb) asparagus spears
salt and freshly ground black pepper
3 eggs plus 2 yolks
10 ml (2 tsp) chopped fresh chervil or tarragon
10 ml (2 tsp) chopped fresh chives
568 ml carton double cream
2 shallots or 25 g (1 oz) onion, finely chopped
150 ml (¼ pint) each dry white wine and vegetable stock
chervil sprigs, to garnish

**1** Melt 25 g (1 oz) of the butter and grease six 150 ml (¼ pint) ramekins. Set aside in the fridge. Reserve 12 small asparagus spears for garnish; roughly chop the remainder. Preheat the oven to 200°C (400°F) Mark 6.
**2** Bring a large pan of salted water to the boil, add the chopped asparagus and cook for 4–5 minutes or until tender. Drain, plunge into iced water, then drain again. Cook the reserved asparagus for 1–2 minutes, cover and set aside. Place the chopped asparagus, eggs and yolks in a food processor or blender and blend until smooth. Sieve, then stir in the chopped herbs and 450 ml (¾ pint) of the cream. Season well.

**3** Pour the asparagus mixture into the ramekins and place in a large roasting pan with enough boiling water to come halfway up the sides of the ramekins. Cover the pan loosely with foil and cook in the oven for 30–40 minutes, until set.
**4** Melt the remaining butter in a saucepan, add the shallots or onion and cook, stirring, for 10 minutes, until soft. Add the wine and stock, bring to the boil, then simmer for 10 minutes. Add the remaining cream, season to taste and simmer for 10 minutes.
**5** Reheat the asparagus spears in the hot sauce for 1 minute. Turn out the ramekins on to 6 warm plates, surround with the sauce and garnish with chervil.

# MINI POPPADUMS WITH AUBERGINE PURÉE

**PREPARATION TIME: 5 MINUTES ◆ COOKING TIME: ABOUT 1 HOUR ◆ FREEZING: NOT SUITABLE ◆ 20 CALS PER SERVING ◆ SERVES 8**

**Aubergines are low in calories and fat, but can absorb large amounts during cooking. This dip contains very little added fat and is a slimmer's delight. Serve it with crudités instead of poppadums for even fewer calories.**

2 large aubergines
1-2 garlic cloves, crushed
15 ml (1 tbsp) tahini (see Cook's Tip)
juice of ½ lemon
45 ml (3 tbsp) chopped fresh coriander
salt and freshly ground black pepper
1 packet of mini poppadums (40 in pack)
paprika and coriander sprigs, to garnish

**1** Preheat the oven to 200°C (400°F) Mark 6. Pierce the aubergines several times with a small sharp knife and place on a baking sheet. Cook in the oven for about 1 hour or until very soft; cool.
**2** Peel the aubergines. Wrap the flesh in a clean cloth and squeeze to remove any excess juice. Add the garlic, tahini and lemon juice to the aubergine and mash well with a fork or in a food processor or blender. Stir in the chopped coriander and 150 ml (¼ pint) water to give a dipping consistency. Season to taste. Place a little purée on each poppadum, arrange on a serving plate and garnish with paprika and coriander sprigs.

**COOK'S TIP**
Tahini is a thick creamy paste made from ground sesame seeds. Available in good supermarkets and healthfood shops.

# STICKY ORANGE AND ALMOND CAKE

**PREPARATION TIME: 40 MINUTES + SOAKING ◆ COOKING TIME: 1¼ HOURS ◆ FREEZING: SUITABLE (STEP 2) ◆ 480 CALS PER SERVING ◆ SERVES 8**

175 g (6 oz) each butter and caster sugar
3 eggs
pinch of salt
350 g (12 oz) semolina
300 g (10 oz) ground almonds
7.5 ml (1½ tsp) baking powder
grated rind of 2 oranges, plus the juice
    of 1 orange
icing sugar, to dust

## ORANGES AND DATES IN SYRUP
7 oranges
juice of 3 lemons
75 ml (5 tbsp) caster sugar
1 cinnamon stick
125 g (4 oz) stoned dates, roughly
    chopped

**1** Preheat the oven to 170°C (325°F) Mark 3. Grease and base-line a 23 cm (9 inch) spring-release cake tin. Using an electric whisk, mix together the butter and sugar until pale and fluffy. Beat the eggs with a pinch of salt and whisk in to the mixture a teaspoonful at a time; this should take about 5 minutes. Fold in the semolina, ground almonds, baking powder, orange rind and juice.
**2** Spoon the mixture into the prepared tin and level the surface. Cook in the oven for 1 hour or until a skewer inserted into the centre comes out clean. If the top begins to brown, cover loosely with foil. Cool in the tin for 15 minutes, then turn out on to a wire rack.

**3** To prepare the Oranges and Dates In Syrup, peel and slice 5 oranges. Place the juice of the remaining oranges and the lemon juice in a saucepan with the sugar, cinnamon stick and 450 ml (¾ pint) water. Cook over a low heat until the sugar has dissolved, bring to the boil, then simmer for 4–5 minutes, until syrupy.
**4** Using a skewer, make holes all over the surface of the warm cake. Spoon over half of the warm syrup and leave for about 30 minutes for it to soak in.
**5** Place the sliced oranges and the dates in the remaining syrup and leave to cool.
**6** Dust the cake with icing sugar and serve with the Oranges and Dates in Syrup.

# HEAVENLY MERINGUE PIE

**PREPARATION TIME: 20 MINUTES + CHILLING ◆ COOKING TIME: 1 HOUR ◆ FREEZING: NOT SUITABLE ◆ 725 CALS PER SERVING ◆ SERVES 8**

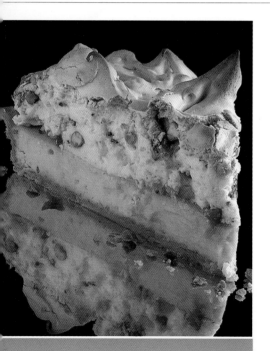

## PASTRY
225 g (8 oz) plain flour
150 g (5 oz) butter
grated rind of 1 lemon
1 egg, beaten

## FILLING
7 eggs
grated rind and juice of 3 large lemons
397 g can condensed milk
142 ml carton double cream
50 g (2 oz) mixed nuts, eg pecans,
    blanched almonds, shelled pistachio
    nuts
225 g (8 oz) icing sugar, sifted

**1** Place the flour, butter and lemon rind in a food processor and process until the mixture resembles crumbs. Add the egg and pulse until the pastry forms a ball. Wrap in cling film and chill for 30 minutes.
**2** Roll out on a floured surface and use to line a 23 x 3.5 cm (9 x 1½ inch) deep, fluted loose-based tart tin. Prick the base and chill for 30 minutes. Preheat the oven to 200°C (400°F) Mark 6 and bake the case blind (see page 101). Cool on a wire rack. Lower the temperature to 180°C (350°F) Mark 4.
**3** Separate 4 of the eggs. Lightly whisk the yolks with the remaining eggs, grated lemon rind and 175 ml (6 fl oz) of the juice. Mix in the condensed milk and cream.

**4** Pour into the pastry case and cook in the oven for 30–35 minutes until just set.
**5** Toast the nuts in the oven for about 5 minutes, cool and chop. Increase the temperature to 200°C (400°F) Mark 6.
**6** Place the egg whites and icing sugar in a large bowl over a pan of barely simmering water and whisk for 10 minutes or until very shiny and thick. Remove from the heat and whisk on a low setting for 5–10 minutes or until the bowl feels cool. Set aside.
**7** Fold the nuts into the meringue and pile on to the lemon mixture. Cook in the oven for 10 minutes or until golden. Serve at room temperature.

# MUSHROOM SAMOSAS

PREPARATION TIME: **40** MINUTES ◆ COOKING TIME: **50** MINUTES ◆ FREEZING: SUITABLE ◆ **350** CALS PER SERVING ◆ SERVES **6**

2.5 cm (1 inch) piece fresh root ginger, finely chopped
3 garlic cloves, crushed
30 ml (2 tbsp) natural yogurt
25 g (1 oz) butter
125 g (4 oz) onion, finely chopped
5 ml (1 tsp) cumin seeds
2.5 ml (½ tsp) turmeric
pinch of cayenne pepper
225 g (8 oz) button mushrooms, chopped
125 g (4 oz) potato, diced
125 g (4 oz) frozen petit pois
30 ml (2 tbsp) chopped fresh coriander
salt and freshly ground black pepper
about 300 g (10 oz) filo pastry
oil for brushing

**1** Combine the ginger, garlic and yogurt and set aside.
**2** Melt the butter in a saucepan, add the onion and cook for 5–7 minutes or until soft. Add the cumin seeds, turmeric and cayenne pepper and cook for 30 seconds. Add the mushrooms and cook over a high heat, stirring, for 2 minutes or until all the liquid has evaporated. Add the yogurt mixture, potato and 150 ml (¼ pint) water. Bring to the boil, then cover and simmer, stirring occasionally, for 25–30 minutes or until the potato is cooked and nearly all the liquid has been absorbed. Add the peas 5 minutes before the end of the cooking time. Set aside to cool, adding the chopped

coriander and seasoning.
**3** Preheat the oven to 200°C (400°F) Mark 6. Cut the filo pastry into 30 x 12 cm (12 x 5 inch) rectangles. Keep covered. Brush a rectangle lightly with oil, fold in half lengthways to form a strip 6 cm (2½ inches) wide and brush again with oil. Place about 10 ml (2 tsp) of the mushroom mixture in the bottom left-hand corner and fold the pastry over to form a triangle. Continue folding until the filling is enclosed in several layers of pastry. Brush with oil. Repeat with the remaining filling and pastry. Cook in the oven for 10 minutes or until a deep golden brown. Leave to cool slightly before serving.

# SWEET ROAST-ONION SALAD

PREPARATION TIME: **5** MINUTES ◆ COOKING TIME: **1½** HOURS ◆ FREEZING: NOT SUITABLE ◆ **340** CALS PER SERVING ◆ SERVES **6**

6 even-size onions, about 700 g (1½ lb) total weight
50 ml (2 fl oz) oil
salad leaves, eg rocket, to serve

**DRESSING**
45 ml (3 tbsp) capers, chopped
grated rind and juice of 1 large lime
7.5 ml (½ tsp) sugar
150 ml (¼ pint) olive oil
30 ml (2 tbsp) chopped flat-leaf parsley
salt and freshly ground black pepper

**1** Preheat the oven to 200°C (400°F) Mark 6. Peel the onions, if wished, and place in an ovenproof dish just large enough to hold them (see Cook's Tip). Pour over the oil and cook in the oven for 1½ hours or until beginning to colour. Cover with foil and cook for 20 minutes or until soft in the centre.
**2** To make the dressing, mix all the ingredients together, with salt and pepper to taste, cover and set aside.
**3** To serve, add any cooking juices to the dressing and adjust the seasoning. Halve each onion, place on a bed of salad leaves and spoon over the dressing.

**COOK'S TIP**

Using a dish just large enough to hold the onions prevents any cooking juices evaporating.

# LEMON CRUNCH

PREPARATION TIME: 20 MINUTES + CHILLING ◆ FREEZING: SUITABLE (STEP 3) ◆ 694 CALS PER SERVING ◆ SERVES 6

175 g (6 oz) ginger or lemon crunch
  biscuits
75 g (3 oz) almonds, toasted
50 g (2 oz) butter, melted
two 397 g cans condensed milk
568 ml carton double cream
grated rind and juice of 4 large lemons,
  about 200 ml (7 fl oz)
caramelised lemon slices, to decorate
  (see Cook's Tip)

1 Lightly brush an 18-20 cm (7-8 inch) spring release tin with oil and base-line with non-stick baking parchment. Alternatively, oil a similar-size deep flan ring and place on an oiled baking sheet.
2 Place the biscuits and almonds in a food processor and process for about 1 minute or until roughly chopped. Add the butter and process to combine. Press the mixture into the base of the tin and chill for at least 30 minutes.
3 Pour the condensed milk into a bowl and stir in the cream. Add the lemon rind and juice a little at a time, stirring constantly; the mixture will thicken dramatically. Pour over the biscuit base and chill overnight.

4 Decorate with caramelised lemon slices, to serve.

## COOK'S TIP

To caramelise lemon slices, place 2 thinly sliced lemons in a shallow saucepan with 300 ml (½ pint) water and 50 g (2 oz) caster sugar. Bring slowly to the boil and bubble until the liquid caramelises around the slices. Cool before using.

# BERRY CRUNCH

PREPARATION TIME: 25 MINUTES + CHILLING ◆ COOKING TIME: 15 MINUTES ◆ FREEZING: NOT SUITABLE ◆ 155 CALS PER SERVING ◆ SERVES 6

50 g (2 oz) jumbo oats (see Cook's Tip)
25 g (1 oz) demerara sugar
25 g (1 oz) butter
225 g (8 oz) strawberries
125 g (4 oz) raspberries
125 g (4 oz) blueberries
15 g (½ oz) caster sugar
300 ml (½ pint) Greek-style yogurt
15 ml (1 tbsp) crème de cassis liqueur
  (optional)

1 Preheat the oven to 190°C (375°F) Mark 5. Place the oats and demerara sugar in a mixing bowl and lightly rub in the butter. Turn the mixture on to a baking sheet, press together with the palm of your hand and bake in the oven for 15 minutes. Set aside to cool, then break into bite-size pieces.
2 Chop the strawberries into bite-size pieces if very large. Place all the prepared berries in a serving bowl, sprinkle with the caster sugar and leave to stand for 15 minutes.
3 Add the yogurt and crème de cassis liqueur, if using, to the berries and mash lightly with a fork to release some of the juices. Cover and chill until required.

4 Just before serving, stir the oat pieces into the berry mixture. Serve immediately.

## COOK'S TIP

If short of time, use a muesli-based cereal instead of the oat mixture.

# SPINACH AND MUSHROOM SHORTBREAD

PREPARATION TIME: **25** MINUTES + CHILLING ◆ COOKING TIME: **12–15** MINUTES ◆ FREEZING: SUITABLE (END STEP 3) ◆ **335** CALS PER SERVING ◆ SERVES **6**

60 g (2½ oz) plain flour
50 g (2 oz) butter
salt and freshly ground black pepper
125 g (4 oz) freshly grated Parmesan cheese
pinch of cayenne pepper
shavings of Parmesan (pared from a block), to garnish

**FILLING**
75 ml (5 tbsp) olive oil
50 g (2 oz) onion or shallot, chopped
3 garlic cloves, crushed
450 g (1 lb) brown-cap or field mushrooms, sliced
450 g (1 lb) small spinach leaves
75 g (3 oz) roughly chopped mixed basil and flat-leaf parsley

**1** Place the flour, butter and a pinch of salt in a food processor and process until the mixture resembles breadcrumbs. Add the Parmesan and cayenne and process in short bursts until the dough comes together. Turn out on to a lightly floured surface and shape into a small flat disc. Wrap in cling film and chill for 30 minutes.
**2** Divide the shortbread into 6 equal balls. Roll out each ball thinly and cut out a round using an 8.5 cm (3½ inch) fluted cutter. Place the rounds on 2 baking sheets; chill for 15 minutes. Preheat the oven to 190°C (375°F) Mark 5.
**3** Cook the shortbread rounds in the oven for 12–15 minutes or until golden brown. Cover and keep warm.

**4** To make the filling, heat 30 ml (2 tbsp) of the oil in a large saucepan, add the onion and garlic and cook for 2–3 minutes until soft. Add the mushrooms and cook over a high heat for 4–5 minutes until soft and all the liquid has gone. Remove from the pan; keep warm.
**5** Heat 15 ml (1 tbsp) of the oil in the pan and add half of the spinach. Cook over a high heat until just wilted and the liquid has evaporated. Remove from the pan. Repeat with the remaining spinach. Add the spinach, mushrooms, herbs and seasoning and stir for 1 minute.
**6** Divide the spinach mixture between the shortbread rounds. Drizzle with the remaining oil and garnish with Parmesan.

# VEGETABLE STACKS

PREPARATION TIME: **15** MINUTES ◆ COOKING TIME: **15** MINUTES ◆ FREEZING: NOT SUITABLE ◆ **340** CALS PER SERVING ◆ SERVES **4**

1 thin aubergine, 350 g (12 oz), thickly sliced
60 ml (4 tbsp) olive oil
60 ml (4 tbsp) pesto sauce
freshly ground black pepper
small bunch of fresh basil
350 g (12 oz) tomato, thickly sliced
150 g (5 oz) mozzarella cheese, thinly sliced
fresh tomato sauce
basil sprigs, to garnish

**1** Brush the aubergine with oil and fry in batches in a large non-stick frying pan until well browned on both sides.
**2** Preheat the oven to 200°C (400°F) Mark 6. Spread the aubergine slices with pesto and season with pepper. Top with a basil leaf, tomato slice and a slice of mozzarella. Repeat to make 4 stacks. Secure each with a cocktail stick.
**3** Warm the tomato sauce gently in a pan, then transfer to an ovenproof dish. Add the aubergine stacks and cook in the oven for 10–15 minutes. Serve immediately, garnished with basil.

# DOUBLE CHOCOLATE TERRINE

**PREPARATION TIME: 1 HOUR ◆ COOKING TIME: 55 MINUTES + CHILLING ◆ FREEZING: SUITABLE ◆ 660 CALS PER SERVING ◆ SERVES 6**

4 eggs, separated, plus 4 yolks
250 g (9 oz) caster sugar
90 g (3½ oz) cocoa powder
65 g (2½ oz) unsalted butter
65 g (2½ oz) plain chocolate
284 ml carton double cream
25 g (1 oz) icing sugar
cocoa powder, to dust

1  Line a 23 x 30 cm (9 x 12 inch) Swiss roll tin with baking parchment. Preheat the oven to 150°C (300°F) Mark 2.
2  Mix 4 egg yolks with 25 g (1 oz) of the caster sugar and 25 g (1 oz) of the cocoa powder. Whisk the egg whites until stiff, then gradually whisk in 75 g (3 oz) of the caster sugar until glossy. Beat a quarter of the meringue into the egg-yolk mixture, then gently fold back into the remaining meringue. Spread in the prepared tin and bake in the oven for 45–55 minutes until just firm in the centre. Cool and cover with a cloth.
3  Place the butter, chocolate and remaining cocoa powder in a bowl and place over a pan of simmering water. Stir until melted, then leave to cool.
4  Whip the cream with the icing sugar until it begins to thicken. Beat the remaining egg yolks with the remaining sugar until thick and light in colour, then beat into the cooled chocolate mixture. Slowly whisk in the cream.
5  Line a 1.3 litre (2 pint) loaf tin with non-stick baking parchment. Cut the cake into 3 rectangles that will fit in the tin. Place a third of the chocolate mousse in the tin and top with a piece of cake. Repeat the layers until all the mousse and cake are used, finishing with cake. Cover with foil and chill overnight.
6  To serve, turn out, cut into thick slices and dust with cocoa powder.

# CHESTNUT AND CHOCOLATE MACAROON

**PREPARATION TIME: 45 MINUTES ◆ COOKING TIME: 1 HOUR 20 MINUTES + CHILLING ◆ FREEZING: SUITABLE (STEP 7) ◆ 750 CALS PER SERVING ◆ SERVES 6**

**MACAROON MERINGUE**
175 g (6 oz) whole hazelnuts, skinned and toasted
300 g (10 oz) icing sugar
2.5 ml (½ tsp) bicarbonate of soda
4 egg whites

**FILLING**
125 g (4 oz) chestnut purée
15 ml (1 tbsp) maple syrup
200 ml (7 fl oz) double cream, lightly whipped
225 g (8 oz) mascarpone cheese
50 g (2 oz) plain chocolate, melted
chocolate curls, hazelnuts, edible gold-coated almonds and icing sugar, to serve

1  Preheat the oven to 130°C (250°F) Mark ½. Draw three 20 cm (8 inch) circles on non-stick baking parchment. Turn the paper over and place on 3 baking sheets. Place the nuts in a food processor and process in bursts for 1–2 seconds, until finely ground. Sift the icing sugar and bicarbonate of soda together.
2  Place the egg whites in a large bowl and whisk with an electric whisk until very stiff. At high speed, whisk in 50 g (2 oz) of the icing sugar. Using a metal spoon, fold in the rest with the hazelnuts.
3  Divide the mixture between the drawn circles and smooth out into even rounds.
4  Cook in the oven for 5 minutes. Lower the temperature to 125°C (225°F) Mark ¼ and cook for 1¼ hours. Cool on a wire rack, then remove the baking parchment.
5  Beat together the chestnut purée and maple syrup until smooth.
6  Fold the cream into the mascarpone cheese. Stir half into the cooled chocolate and half into the chestnut purée mixture. Stir each well to combine.
7  Place a macaroon on a serving platter and cover with chestnut mixture. Place the second macaroon on top and press down firmly. Cover with chocolate cream. Top with the remaining macaroon. Chill for at least 4–6 hours.
8  To serve, decorate with chocolate curls, hazelnuts and almonds; dust with icing sugar.

# SMOKY FISH UNDER A POTATO CRUST

**PREPARATION TIME: 15 MINUTES ◆ COOKING TIME: 50 MINUTES ◆ FREEZING: SUITABLE ◆ 510 CALS PER SERVING ◆ SERVES 6**

450 g (1 lb) smoked haddock fillet, skinned
225 g (8 oz) fresh haddock fillet, skinned
300 ml (½ pint) skimmed milk
75 g (3 oz) butter
125 g (4 oz) red onion, finely chopped
2 garlic cloves, crushed
50 g (2 oz) plain flour
142 ml carton double cream
50 g (2 oz) mayonnaise
5 ml (1 tsp) chopped gherkin
30 ml (2 tbsp) chopped fresh parsley
15 ml (1 tbsp) chopped fresh chives
grated rind and juice of 1 lemon
825 g (1¾ lb) old potato, cut into chunks
salt and freshly ground black pepper
lemon slices, to garnish

**1** Cut the fish into large pieces, place in a frying pan and pour over the milk. Bring slowly to the boil, cover, remove from the heat and leave for 10 minutes.
**2** Meanwhile, melt 25 g (1 oz) of the butter in a large saucepan, add the onion and cook for 5–7 minutes or until softened but not brown. Add the garlic and cook for 1 minute.
**3** Using a slotted spoon, lift the fish out of the milk and set aside; reserve the milk. Add the flour to the onion and cook, stirring, for 1 minute. Remove from the heat and slowly add the reserved milk, stirring until evenly combined. Return to the heat and simmer for about 3 minutes, gradually stirring in the cream. Bring to the boil, then simmer for 1–2 minutes, until lightly thickened. Cool slightly, then add the mayonnaise, gherkin, herbs, lemon rind and juice. Place the fish in a 1.7 litre (3 pint) ovenproof dish and spoon over the sauce. Preheat the oven to 200°C (400°F) Mark 6.
**4** Boil the potato for 10–12 minutes or until almost tender. Drain and cool, then grate coarsely. Melt the remaining butter and stir into the potato with plenty of seasoning. Spoon over the fish.
**5** Cook in the oven for 30–35 minutes or until the topping is golden. Garnish with lemon slices.

# COUSCOUS-CRUSTED SALMON WITH HOT SALSA

**PREPARATION TIME: ABOUT 1 HOUR, + CHILLING ◆ COOKING TIME: 15 MINUTES ◆ FREEZING: SUITABLE (STEP 3) ◆ 590 CALS PER SERVING ◆ SERVES 4**

**The lemony couscous forms a crispy coating and helps keep the salmon moist.**

grated rind and juice of 2–3 large lemons
50 g (2 oz) couscous
salt and freshly ground black pepper
4 salmon fillets, each about 175 g (6 oz)
25 g (1 oz) plain flour
1 egg, beaten
175 g (6 oz) pitted mixed olives
2 anchovy fillets
90 ml (6 tbsp) olive oil
15 ml (1 tbsp) capers or caper berries
30 ml (2 tbsp) chopped fresh flat-leaf parsley
1 garlic clove, sliced
450 g (1 lb) tomato, preferably plum, chopped
grated lemon rind, to garnish

**1** Set aside 15 ml (1 tbsp) of the lemon juice. Place the remainder in a measuring jug and add enough boiling water to make up to 175 ml (6 fl oz). Pour over the couscous and leave for 15 minutes or until the grains have absorbed the liquid.
**2** Stir in the lemon rind and season well. Spread the couscous on a tray and place in a warm place for about 20 minutes to dry out a little.
**3** Season the salmon and dip each fillet into the flour, then the beaten egg and finally the couscous mixture. Cover lightly and chill for 1 hour or overnight.
**4** Place the olives, anchovies, 30 ml (2 tbsp) of the oil and the reserved lemon juice in a food processor or blender and blend for about 5 seconds. Spoon the mixture into a bowl, add the capers, chopped parsley and garlic and set aside.
**5** Drizzle 15 ml (1 tbsp) of the olive oil over the tomato; season well. Heat the remaining oil in a non-stick frying pan, add the salmon and fry for 4 minutes on each side or until golden; keep warm.
**6** Fry the tomatoes, in the oil that's still clinging to them, for 1–2 minutes. Add the olive mixture to the pan and warm through for about 1 minute. Serve with the salmon, garnished with grated lemon rind.

# TRIPLE-CHOCOLATE MERINGUE CAKE

PREPARATION TIME: 45 MINUTES + CHILLING ◆ COOKING TIME: 1½ HOURS ◆ FREEZING: NOT SUITABLE ◆ 760 CALS PER SERVING ◆ SERVES 8

**MERINGUE**
150 g (5 oz) icing sugar
40 g (1½ oz) cocoa powder
5 egg whites
150 g (5 oz) caster sugar

**FILLING**
175 g (6 oz) plain chocolate
75 g (3 oz) butter, softened
30 ml (2 tbsp) liqueur, eg Drambuie
3 egg yolks
75 g (3 oz) caster sugar
284 ml carton double cream

**TO FINISH**
175 g (6 oz) white chocolate
75 g (3 oz) butter
2 egg yolks
284 ml carton double cream,
chocolates and truffles, to decorate

**1** Preheat the oven to 150°C (300°F) Mark 2. To make the meringue, sift together the icing sugar and cocoa powder. Whisk the egg whites until stiff, then slowly whisk in the caster sugar. Fold in the sifted mixture with a large metal spoon. Spread two 23 cm (9 inch) circles of the meringue mixture on to baking sheets lined with non-stick baking parchment. Cook in the oven for 1½ hours until dried out. Leave to cool.
**2** To make the filling, melt the chocolate in a bowl over a pan of barely simmering water. Stir in the butter and liqueur. Whisk the egg yolks with the sugar until pale and thick. Fold the chocolate into the egg yolk mixture, then fold in the lightly whipped cream. Cover and chill for 30 minutes.
**3** Sandwich the meringue rounds together with the filling. Chill.
**4** To complete, melt the chocolate as above, then stir in the butter and egg yolks. Fold into the lightly whipped cream.
**5** Cover the meringue with the white-chocolate cream and chill overnight. Decorate with chocolates or truffles to serve.

# CHOCOLATE AND ORANGE CHEESECAKE

PREPARATION TIME: 35 MINUTES ◆ COOKING TIME: 1 HOUR 10 MINUTES ◆ FREEZING: SUITABLE (STEP 6) ◆ 630–470 CALS PER SERVING ◆ SERVES 6–8

3 eggs, separated
125 g (4 oz) caster sugar
two 200 g cartons full-fat soft cheese
90 ml (6 tbsp) crème fraîche or thick
 Greek yogurt
125 g (4 oz) plain chocolate, melted
grated rind of 2 large oranges

**TO FINISH**
orange segments
chocolate curls
icing sugar

**1** Preheat the oven to 180°C (350°F) Mark 4. Base-line a 23 cm (9 inch) spring-release tin with non-stick baking parchment.
**2** Beat the egg yolks with 50 g (2 oz) of the sugar until pale and thick. Add the cheese and crème fraîche or yogurt and beat until smooth.
**3** Add a third of the cheese mixture to the chocolate, mix until smooth and set aside.
**4** Add the orange rind to the remaining cheese mixture.
**5** Whisk the egg whites until stiff, then gradually whisk in the remaining sugar until the mixture is stiff and shiny.
**6** Fold a third of the egg white into the chocolate mixture, spoon into the prepared tin and smooth the top. Fold the remaining egg white into the orange mixture, spoon on top of the chocolate mixture and level the top.
**7** Bake in the oven for 55–60 minutes or until the centre is just firm to the touch. Turn off the heat and leave the cheesecake in the oven to cool.
**8** Turn out the cheesecake on to a serving plate. Decorate with orange segments and chocolate curls. Dust with icing sugar.

# SALMON WITH BRIOCHE CRUST AND CREAMY LEEKS

PREPARATION TIME: **15** MINUTES ◆ COOKING TIME : **20** MINUTES ◆ FREEZING: NOT SUITABLE ◆ **680** CALS PER SERVING ◆ SERVES **4**

50 g (2 oz) butter
700 g (1½ lb) leeks, finely chopped
75 g (3 oz) frozen broad beans
2 small brioche rolls or about 75 g (3 oz) brioche loaf
30 ml (2 tbsp) chopped fresh parsley
15 ml (1 tbsp) chopped fresh thyme
4 salmon fillets, each about 175 g (6 oz)
30 ml (2 tbsp) white wine
200 g carton crème fraîche
5 ml (1 tsp) wholegrain mustard
1 lime

**1** Preheat the oven to 200°C (400°F) Mark 6. Melt half of the butter in a frying pan, add the leeks and fry for 10 minutes, stirring occasionally. Stir in the beans and cook for 1 minute.
**2** Meanwhile, melt the remaining butter in another saucepan. Place the brioche and herbs in a food processor and process into rough crumbs. Add the melted butter and blend for 1 minute. Press the mixture on to the top of each salmon fillet.
**3** Place the salmon on a baking sheet and cook in the oven for 8 minutes or until cooked through.
**4** Meanwhile, add the wine to the leeks and bring to the boil, then bubble to

reduce to almost nothing. Stir in the crème fraîche and mustard. Squeeze the lime juice over the salmon and serve with the leeks.

# GRILLED SALMON ESCALOPE

PREPARATION TIME: **40** MINUTES ◆ COOKING TIME: **25** MINUTES ◆ FREEZING: NOT SUITABLE ◆ **780** CALS PER SERVING ◆ SERVES **4**

50 g (2 oz) butter
20 ml (4 tsp) sun-dried tomato paste
10 ml (2 tsp) lemon juice
salt and freshly ground black pepper
4 salmon escalopes, about 700 g (1½ lb) total weight

**CUCUMBER AND DILL SALSA**
300 g (10 oz) cucumber
175 g (6 oz) red onion, roughly chopped
30 ml (2 tbsp) capers
30 ml (2 tbsp) chopped fresh dill
30 ml (2 tbsp) dill mustard sauce

**SWEET POTATO STICKS**
700 g (1½ lb) sweet potato
oil for deep-frying
coarse sea salt, to season

**1** Place the butter, tomato paste, lemon juice and seasoning in a small pan and heat gently until melted, stirring to combine.
**2** Season the salmon with black pepper and brush with the butter mixture. Cook under a preheated grill for 2-3 minutes on each side, turning once and brushing with the melted butter.
**3** To make the Cucumber and Dill Salsa, peel and halve the cucumber, scrape out the seeds and finely chop the flesh. Mix all the ingredients together and season to taste.
**4** To make the Sweet Potato Sticks, cut the sweet potato into thick slices, then cut into 3mm (⅛ inch) fine sticks. Deep-

fry in batches for 1–2 minutes or until golden and crisp. Drain on kitchen paper, sprinkle with sea salt and keep warm (see Cook's Tip).
**5** To serve, place the salmon with the pan juices and any remaining butter on 4 warm serving plates. Serve with the Cucumber and Dill Salsa and Sweet Potato Sticks.

**COOK'S TIP**
The sweet potato sticks will keep crisp for up to 30 minutes in a warm oven.

# BRIOCHE SUMMER PUDDINGS

PREPARATION TIME: 20 MINUTES + CHILLING ◆ COOKING TIME: 5-10 MINUTES ◆ FREEZING: NOT SUITABLE ◆ 250 CALS PER SERVING ◆ SERVES 8

300 g (10 oz) brioche or stale white
    bread (see Cook's Tips)
450 g (1 lb) redcurrants
700 g (1½ lb) blackberries
175 g (6 oz) caster sugar
30 ml (2 tbsp) crème de cassis or
    blackcurrant cordial
lemon juice to taste
seasonal berries, to decorate

1  Remove the crusts and cut the brioche into 10–12 slices. Using a 6 cm (2½ inch) plain round cutter, cut 2 circles to form the bases. Halve the remaining slices.
2  Place the circles in the base of two 1.1 litre (2 pint) fluted charlotte moulds (see Cook's Tips) or pudding basins and line the sides with the slices.
3  To make the filling, place the fruit and sugar in a large pan and heat gently, stirring occasionally, for 5–10 minutes, until the fruit releases its juices and the sugar has dissolved. Add the crème de cassis or cordial and a little lemon juice, then use to fill the moulds.
4  Top with any remaining brioche slices, cover with cling film and place on a tray to catch any juices. Weight down the puddings with cans from the storecupboard and chill overnight.
5  To serve, trim any ragged edges of brioche and carefully unmould the puddings on to deep serving plates. Decorate with seasonal berries and serve with clotted cream.

## COOK'S TIPS

If the bread or brioche is very fresh, leave the slices to dry a little before using. Line the charlotte moulds with cling film. This prevents the juices from reacting with the lining of the moulds and also makes it easier to turn out the puddings.

# SPICED PLUM BRÛLÉE

PREPARATION TIME: 40 MINUTES ◆ COOKING TIME: 45 MINUTES ◆ FREEZING: SUITABLE (SEPARATELY STEP 4) ◆ 520 CALS PER SERVING ◆ SERVES 8

6 egg yolks
40 g (1½ oz) caster sugar
5 ml (1 tsp) vanilla essence
568 ml carton double cream
150 ml (¼ pint) syrup from a jar of stem
    ginger
150 ml (¼ pint) red wine
4 cloves
5 cm (2 inch) piece cinnamon stick
pared rind of 1 lemon and 1 orange
700 g (1½ lb) plums, halved and stoned
75 g (3 oz) demerara sugar

1  Place the egg yolks, caster sugar and vanilla essence in a bowl and beat with an electric whisk until thick. Stir in the cream, then cook over a low heat, stirring, for about 10 minutes, until thickened. Watch the froth on the custard – as it begins to thicken, the froth disappears. Do not boil or the custard will curdle.
2  Preheat the oven to 150°C (300°F) Mark 2. Strain the custard into a 1.1 litre (2 pint) shallow dish. Pour hand-hot water into a roasting pan to come halfway up the sides of the dish. Cook in the oven for 45 minutes, until a skin forms and the custard has firmed up slightly. To test, gently shake the dish: if the custard is set, it should have a slight wobble but not be at all runny. Cool, cover and chill for several hours.
3  Place the ginger syrup, wine, cloves, cinnamon and pared rind in a large sauté pan and bring to the boil. Add the plums and bring back to the boil, then simmer for 10 minutes or until just cooked. Drain, reserving the juice in the pan, return the spices and rind and boil for 10 minutes or until reduced to 150 ml (¼ pint); strain over the plums.
4  Arrange the plums (cut side down) on the custard, then spoon over the syrup. Sprinkle with the demerara sugar and place under a preheated grill for 3–4 minutes, until bubbling. Chill for 30 minutes before serving.

# SALMON NIÇOISE

PREPARATION TIME: **20** MINUTES ◆ COOKING TIME: **10–12** MINUTES ◆ FREEZING: NOT SUITABLE ◆ **265** CALS PER SERVING ◆ SERVES **12**

150 g (5 oz) French beans, trimmed
salt and freshly ground black pepper
300 g (10 oz) small new potatoes
4 hen's eggs or 12 quail's eggs
450 g (1 lb) salmon fillets, skinned
200 ml (7 fl oz) white wine
30 ml ( 2 tbsp) white wine vinegar
150 g (5 oz) cucumber, roughly chopped
300 g (10 oz) cherry tomatoes, halved
125 g (4 oz) pitted black olives
150 g (5 oz) mixed salad leaves

**DRESSING**
4 anchovy fillets, roughly chopped
90 ml (6 tbsp) chopped fresh mint
150 ml (¼ pint) olive oil

**1** Cook the French beans in boiling salted water for 3–4 minutes or until just tender. Drain and place in iced water.
**2** Cook the potatoes in boiling salted water for 10–12 minutes or until tender. Drain and leave to cool. Cook the eggs in boiling water: 8–10 minutes for hen's or 3–4 minutes for quail's. Cool in cold water, then peel and quarter or halve.
**3** Place the salmon, wine and vinegar in a shallow saucepan and season to taste. Bring to the boil, cover tightly and remove from the heat. Leave the salmon in the liquid to cool completely, then flake into large pieces; reserve the liquid.
**4** To make the dressing, mix together the anchovy, mint, oil, 60 ml (4 tbsp) of

the salmon liquid, and seasoning to taste.
**5** To serve, drain the beans and transfer to a large salad bowl. Add the cucumber, tomatoes, potatoes, olives, salad leaves and dressing and toss well. Arrange the salmon and eggs on top.

# GOLDEN SALMON

PREPARATION TIME: **20** MINUTES ◆ COOKING TIME: **10** MINUTES ◆ FREEZING: NOT SUITABLE ◆ **635** CALS PER SERVING ◆ SERVES **6**

125 g (4 oz) filo pastry (see Cook's Tip)
6 salmon fillets, preferably tail end,
    about 700 g (1½ lb) total weight
75 g (3 oz) butter, melted
salt and freshly ground black pepper
lemon slices and watercress sprigs, to
    garnish

**SAUCE**
50 g (2 oz) watercress
245 ml jar hollandaise sauce
15 ml (1 tbsp) lemon juice

**1** Preheat the oven to 200°C (400°F) Mark 6. Cut the filo pastry into 30 rectangles roughly the same size as the salmon fillets (see Cook's Tip). Brush the pastry very lightly on one side with melted butter. Arrange on baking sheets and cook in the oven for 3–4 minutes or until the pastry is golden and crisp.
**2** Pan-fry the salmon fillets in the remaining butter for 3–4 minutes. Season well, cover and leave in the pan to keep warm while making the sauce.
**3** Put the watercress in a food processor and process until finely chopped. Put the hollandaise sauce, lemon juice and black pepper to taste in a saucepan and warm through gently. Add the watercress and

heat until the sauce is hot but not boiling.
**4** To assemble, place 2 pastry sheets on each warm plate. Top with a piece of salmon, a spoonful of sauce and 3 pastry sheets.
**5** Garnish with lemon and watercress. Serve with remaining sauce.

**COOK'S TIP**
We used 5 filo pastry sheets per salmon fillet, but 4 will work just as well if you're short of baking sheets and oven space.

# PECAN, MAPLE AND WHISKY PIE

PREPARATION TIME: **40** MINUTES + CHILLING ◆ COOKING TIME: **1** HOUR **20** MINUTES ◆ FREEZING: SUITABLE (STEP **4**) ◆ **890-665** CALS PER SERVING ◆ SERVES **6-8**

**PASTRY**
225 g (8 oz) plain flour
150 g (5 oz) butter

**FILLING**
75g (3oz) butter
75 g (3 oz) soft dark brown or molasses
  sugar
3 eggs, beaten
5 ml (1 tsp) cornflour
50 ml (2 fl oz) maple syrup
225 g (8 fl oz) golden syrup
60 ml (4 tbsp) whisky
5 ml (1 tsp) vanilla essence
200 g (7 oz) pecan nuts, toasted and
  chopped
maple syrup, to finish

**1** To make the pastry, place the flour and butter in a food processor and pulse until the mixture resembles crumbs. Add 45 ml (3 tbsp) iced water, pulse until the mixture comes together in a ball, then wrap in cling film and chill for 30 minutes.
**2** Roll out the pastry on a lightly floured surface and use to line a 23 cm (9 inch) loose-based tart tin. Prick the base well, line with greaseproof paper and baking beans and chill for 30 minutes. Preheat the oven to 200°C (400°F) Mark 6.
**3** Cook the pastry case in the oven for 15 minutes, then remove the paper and beans and cook for 15 minutes or until golden. Brush the base and side of the

pastry with beaten egg and return to the oven for 3–4 minutes. Set aside while preparing the filling. Lower the temperature to 180°C (350°F) Mark 4.
**4** Beat the butter with the sugar until light, then slowly add the remaining beaten egg and cornflour. Stir in the maple syrup, golden syrup, whisky and vanilla essence. (Don't worry if the mixture appears curdled.) Mix in the toasted nuts and pour into the pastry case.
**5** Cook in the oven for 45 minutes or until the filling is just set. Leave to cool slightly, then drizzle with maple syrup. Serve with ice cream or whipped cream.

# APRICOT AND BANANA MASCARPONE TART

PREPARATION TIME: **20** MINUTES + CHILLING ◆ COOKING TIME: **35** MINUTES ◆ FREEZING: SUITABLE (STEP **4**) ◆ **410** CALS PER SERVING ◆ SERVES **8**

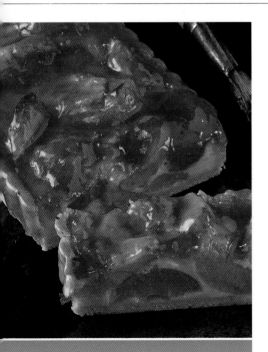

**PASTRY**
175 g (6 oz) plain white flour
50 g (2 oz) caster sugar
75 g (3 oz) butter

**FILLING**
350 g (12 oz) fresh apricots
1 banana
225 g carton mascarpone cheese or 200 g
  (7 oz) full-fat soft cheese blended with
  142 ml carton single cream
2 eggs
1.25 ml (¼ tsp) vanilla essence
25g (1oz) caster sugar
30 ml (2 tbsp) soft dark brown
  (muscovado) sugar
60 ml (4 tbsp) apricot jam

**1** Put the flour and 50 g (2 oz) of the caster sugar in a food processor and pulse until mixed. Add the butter and process until the mixture resembles breadcrumbs. Add 45–60 ml (3–4 tbsp) water and process until the mixture forms a rough dough. Turn on to a floured surface and knead until smooth. Wrap in cling film and chill for 30 minutes.
**2** Roll out and use to line a 33.5 x 11 cm (13½ x 4½ inch) loose-based fluted tranche tin or a 23 cm (9 inch) flan tin. Chill for 30 minutes. Preheat the oven to 200°C (400°F) Mark 6.
**3** Line the pastry case with greaseproof paper and baking beans and cook in the

oven for about 15 minutes or until just set. Remove the beans and paper and return the pastry case to the oven for 15 minutes. Lower the temperature to 170°C (325°F) Mark 3.
**4** Halve and stone the apricots. Slice the banana. Spoon the fruit into the pastry case. Whisk together the cheese, eggs, vanilla essence and remaining caster sugar until smooth. Spoon over the fruit, then sprinkle with the brown sugar. Bake in the oven for about 35 minutes or until just set.
**5** Warm the jam in a saucepan until bubbling, then brush over the tart to glaze. Serve warm, with single cream.

# SALMON FISHCAKES WITH HERB BUTTER SAUCE

**PREPARATION TIME: 16 MINUTES ◆ COOKING TIME: 22 MINUTES + COOLING ◆ FREEZING: SUITABLE (STEP 4) ◆ 737 CALS PER SERVING ◆ SERVES 6**

50 g (2 oz) spring onion, finely chopped
450 g (1 lb) salmon fillet
150 ml (¼ pint) white wine
salt and freshly ground black pepper
65 g (2½ oz) butter
30 ml (2 tbsp) chopped fresh parsley
275 g (10 oz) mashed potato
5-10 ml (1-2 tsp) lemon juice
30 ml (2 tbsp) plain flour
2 eggs, beaten
50 g (2 oz) polenta or 125 g (4 oz) breadcrumbs

**HERB BUTTER SAUCE**
225 g (8 oz) unsalted butter, melted
small bunch of fresh chives, parsley, chervil or dill
30 ml (2 tbsp) lemon juice

1  Place the spring onion, salmon and wine in a shallow saucepan, add enough cold water barely to cover the fish, season and bring to the boil. Remove from the heat, cover and leave the salmon to cool completely in the liquid.
2  Remove the salmon from the liquid with a slotted spoon and set aside. Add 15 g (½ oz) of the butter to the liquid in the pan and bring to the boil. Boil hard for about 10 minutes to reduce to a syrupy consistency.
3  Flake the salmon into a bowl, discarding skin and bones. Mix in 45 ml (3 tbsp) of the reduced liquor, the parsley, mashed potato and lemon juice. Adjust the seasoning. Set aside the rest

of the liquor for the Herb Butter Sauce.
4  Shape the salmon mixture into 12 cakes. Dip into the flour, beaten egg, then polenta or breadcrumbs. Chill for 15 minutes. Preheat the oven to 240°C (475°F) Mark 9.
5  Melt the remaining butter and brush all over the fishcakes. Cook in the oven for 20–25 minutes or until golden brown. Alternatively, shallow-fry in oil.
6  Meanwhile, make the Herb Butter Sauce. Place all the ingredients, with 50 ml (2 fl oz) of the reserved fish liquor in a food processor or blender and blend for 1–2 minutes until creamy and smooth. Season to taste and serve immediately with the fishcakes.

# POACHED SALMON WITH SAFFRON SAUCE

**PREPARATION TIME: 15 MINUTES ◆ COOKING TIME: 35-45 MINUTES ◆ FREEZING: NOT SUITABLE ◆ 675 CALS PER SERVING ◆ SERVES 4**

50 g (2 oz) butter
125 g (4 oz) shallots, finely chopped
450 ml (¾ pint) medium white wine, eg Riesling or Gewurtztraminer
300 ml (½ pint) fish stock
284 ml carton double cream
small pinch of saffron strands
salt and freshly ground black pepper
1 lemon (optional)
175 g (6 oz) young spinach, roughly chopped
75 g (3 oz) watercress, roughly chopped
225 g (8 oz) salmon escalopes or 575 g (1¼ lb) fillets
oil for brushing
chopped fresh chives, to garnish

1  Melt 25 g (1 oz) of the butter in a large frying pan, add the shallots and cook for 5 minutes, stirring. Add the wine, bring to the boil and reduce by two-thirds. Stir in the stock, cream and saffron strands, bring to the boil, then simmer for 15 minutes or until syrupy. Season to taste and add a squeeze of lemon if wished. Set aside. Preheat the oven to 200°C (400°F) Mark 6.
2  Melt the remaining butter in a pan, add the spinach and watercress and toss well. Arrange in 4 piles on a baking sheet and place an escalope on each. Season and brush with oil. Cover with foil and cook in the oven for 5–7 minutes or until just cooked. (If using fillets, increase the

cooking time by 10–13 minutes.) Keep warm.
3  Place a portion of spinach and salmon on each warm plate, spoon the sauce around and garnish with chives.

# BAKED APPLE AND LEMON TARTLETS

PREPARATION TIME: 40 MINUTES + CHILLING ◆ COOKING TIME: 45-50 MINUTES ◆ FREEZING: SUITABLE (STEP 6) ◆ 625 CALS PER SERVING ◆ MAKES 8

**PASTRY**
175 g (6 oz) plain flour
75 g (3 oz) icing sugar
pinch of salt
175 g (6 oz) butter
1 egg, beaten

**FILLING**
700 g (1½ lb) Bramley or Granny Smith apples
grated rind and juice of 2 lemons
125 g (4 oz) butter
225 g (8 oz) caster sugar
5 ml (1 tsp) arrowroot
2 eggs
caster sugar and cinnamon, to dust

1 Place the flour, icing sugar, salt and butter in a food processor and process until the mixture resembles crumbs. Add the egg with 45 ml (3 tbsp) water and pulse until the pastry comes together. Divide into 8 balls and chill for 30 minutes.

2 Roll out the pastry balls on a floured surface and use to line eight 8 x 3 cm (3¼ x 1¼ inch) deep fluted loose-based tartlet tins. Prick and chill for 20 minutes. Preheat the oven to 200°C (400°F) Mark 6 and bake blind (see page 101). Lower the temperature to 180°C (350°F) Mark 4.

3 Peel, core and thinly slice the apples. Toss them in 30 ml (2 tbsp) of the lemon juice. Melt 25 g (1 oz) of the butter in a frying pan, add the apples and fry for 1-2 minutes. Spoon into the pastry cases.

4 Soften the remaining butter and place in the food processor with the caster sugar. Process for 3 minutes or until soft and pale. Add the lemon rind, arrowroot and eggs and process for 2 minutes or until well combined.

5 With the food processor running, add the remaining lemon juice and blend for 1 minute or until combined. Pour over the apples. Dust with caster sugar.

6 Return to the oven and cook for 45–50 minutes or until the pastry is golden and the apples start to caramelise. Remove from the tins and dust with cinnamon. Serve warm or cold.

# GOLDEN PASSION FRUIT TART

PREPARATION TIME: 50 MINUTES + CHILLING ◆ COOKING TIME: 1 HOUR 25 MINUTES ◆ FREEZING: SUITABLE (STEP 4) ◆ 590 CALS PER SERVING ◆ SERVES 8

**FILLING**
8 large ripe passion fruit
150 g (5 oz) caster sugar
4 eggs
200 ml (7 fl oz) double cream

**PASTRY**
225 g (8 oz) plain white flour
50 g (2 oz) icing sugar
grated rind of 1 orange
150 g (5 oz) butter
1 egg, lightly beaten

**TO DECORATE**
1 mango, sliced
2 passion fruit
caster sugar
caramel 'bark' (see Cook's Tip)
edible gold flake

1 To make the pastry, place the flour, icing sugar, orange rind and butter in a food processor and process until the mixture resembles crumbs. Add the egg and pulse until the mixture comes together. Wrap in cling film and chill.

2 Roll out the pastry on a floured surface and use to line a 23 cm (9 inch) fluted loose-based tart tin. Chill for 30 minutes. Preheat the oven to 200°C (400°F) Mark 6 and bake the pastry case blind (see page 101). Lower the temperature to 140°C (275°F) Mark 1.

3 Halve the passion fruit and scoop out the flesh. Add to the rinsed food processor with the caster sugar and process for 1 minute or until the flesh comes away from the seeds. With the machine running, add the eggs and cream, then strain through a fine sieve. Fill the tart case with the mixture and cook in the oven for 1 hour or until the filling has just set in the middle. Set aside to cool, then chill for 2 hours.

4 To decorate, toss the mango in the passion fruit pulp and sugar until heavily coated. Grill until golden. Spoon over the tart. Add caramel 'bark' and gold flake.

### COOK'S TIP

For the caramel 'bark', sprinkle caster sugar over a baking sheet and grill for 4–5 minutes, until liquid. Cool for 10 minutes, then crack into pieces.

# VODKA-POACHED SALMON WITH SALSA VERDE

PREPARATION TIME: **15** MINUTES + CHILLING ◆ COOKING TIME: **25** MINUTES ◆ FREEZING: NOT SUITABLE ◆ **455** CALS PER SERVING ◆ SERVES **6**

grated rind and juice of 2 limes
150 ml (¼ pint) vodka
900 g (2 lb) salmon fillets (preferably tail end), skinned
2 bay leaves
6 black peppercorns

**SALSA VERDE**
50 g (2 oz) rocket or watercress
50 g (2 oz) blanched almonds
1 large garlic clove
5 ml (1 tsp) anchovy paste or 2 mashed anchovy fillets
15 ml (1 tbsp) capers
30 ml (2 tbsp) chopped fresh basil
45 ml (3 tbsp) chopped flat-leaf parsley
juice of 1 small lemon
60 ml (4 tbsp) olive oil
salt and freshly ground black pepper

**1** Mix the lime rind and juice with the vodka. Place the salmon in a shallow non-metallic dish and pour over the vodka mixture. Cover and chill for up to 3 hours.
**2** Preheat the oven to 190°C (375°F) Mark 5. Line an ovenproof dish with a large sheet of greaseproof paper. Place the salmon, vodka mixture, bay leaves and peppercorns in the centre. Fold the edges of the paper together securely to form a parcel, sealing in the fish and liquid.
**3** Cook in the oven for 25 minutes or until the fish is firm and just cooked through.
**4** Meanwhile, place all the Salsa Verde

ingredients (except the oil and seasoning) in a food processor and blend for about 30 seconds or until a rough paste has formed. Lower the speed and slowly add the olive oil (see Cook's Tips). Season to taste.
**5** Lift the salmon from the cooking juices (see Cook's Tips). Serve warm or cold with the Salsa Verde and 1–2 spoonfuls of poaching juice.

## COOK'S TIPS
If you want a runnier sauce increase the amount of oil.
Don't waste the delicious poaching liquid – freeze and use in fish soups or sauces.

---

# SOLE WITH FOAMING HERB AND LEMON SAUCE

PREPARATION TIME: **20** MINUTES ◆ COOKING TIME: **10** MINUTES ◆ FREEZING: NOT SUITABLE ◆ **420** CALS PER SERVING ◆ SERVES **6**

12 sole fillets, each about 50 g (2 oz)
salt and freshly ground black pepper
25 g (1 oz) plain flour
3 eggs, separated
pinch of cayenne pepper
30 ml (2 tbsp) white wine vinegar
juice of 1 lemon
225 g (8 oz) butter
30 ml (2 tbsp) chopped fresh tarragon or a large pinch of dried
30 ml (2 tbsp) chopped chives
chopped fresh chives, lemon wedges and grated rind, to garnish

**1** Season the sole, then dip each fillet in the flour. Shake off any excess, cover and set aside.
**2** Place the egg yolks in a food processor or blender with a pinch of salt and cayenne pepper and blend for 2 minutes.
**3** Place the vinegar and 45 ml (3 tbsp) of the lemon juice in a small saucepan and heat until it just simmers. With the processor at full speed, gradually add the hot liquid to the yolks.
**4** Melt 175 g (6 oz) of the butter in a pan until just bubbling and almost starting to brown (see Cook's Tip). With the processor at full speed, add steadily to the egg yolks. Blend until the butter is incorporated and the sauce is the

consistency of very lightly whipped cream. Fold in the tarragon and chives.
**5** Whisk the egg whites until soft peaks form, then fold into the hot sauce. Adjust the seasoning and keep warm over a pan of barely simmering water.
**6** Melt the remaining butter in a non-stick frying pan, add the sole and cook for 1 minute on each side or until golden.
**7** Garnish with chives, lemon wedges and grated rind, and serve with a mixed salad and the sauce.

## COOK'S TIP
It's important to get the butter really hot in step 4 as it cooks and thickens the yolks lightly.

# PLUM AND ALMOND TART

PREPARATION TIME: 30 MINUTES + CHILLING ◆ COOKING TIME: 40 MINUTES ◆ FREEZING: SUITABLE (STEP 5) ◆ 710–535 CALS PER SERVING ◆ SERVES 6–8

**PASTRY**
150 g (5 oz) butter, chilled and diced
175 g (6 oz) plain flour
105 ml (7 tbsp) soured cream

**TOPPING**
50 g (2 oz) butter
50 g (2 oz) caster sugar
2 eggs, beaten
125 g (4 oz) ground almonds
15 ml (1 tbsp) Kirsch or 3-4 drops almond essence
900 g (2 lb) plums
caster sugar, to dust
50 g (2 oz) blanched almonds
175 g (6 oz) redcurrant jelly

1 Process the butter and flour for 1–2 seconds (you should still be able to see pieces of butter). Add the cream and process for 1–2 seconds, until the dough begins to come together.
2 Turn on to a floured surface and knead very lightly for about 30 seconds, until the pastry just comes together (it should look crumbly). Wrap in cling film and chill for about 30 minutes.
3 Meanwhile, place the butter in a bowl and beat until soft, then add the sugar and beat until fluffy. Beat in the eggs, alternating with the ground almonds. Add the Kirsch or almond essence, cover and set aside. Quarter and stone the plums.
4 Roll the pastry out to a 30 cm

(12 inch) circle, transfer to a baking sheet and prick with a fork. Spread the almond mixture over, leaving a border of about 3 cm (1¼ inches) all the way round. Scatter plums over the almond mixture and fold the pastry up over the fruit.
5 Dust with caster sugar, then chill for 20 minutes. Place another baking sheet in the oven while preheating to 220°C (425°F) Mark 7. Slide the tart on its baking sheet on top of the hot sheet and cook in the oven for 35–40 minutes.
6 Leave to cool for 10 minutes, then slide it on to a wire rack. Arrange the almonds among the fruit. Beat the redcurrant jelly, warm it until smooth, then brush over the fruit; leave to set.

# RHUBARB CRUMBLE TARTS WITH ORANGE SAUCE

PREPARATION TIME: 30 MINUTES + CHILLING ◆ COOKING TIME: 1 HOUR ◆ FREEZING: SUITABLE (END STEP 5) ◆ 370 CALS PER SERVING ◆ SERVES 6

450 g (1 lb) rhubarb, chopped
125 g (4 oz) caster sugar
75 g (3 oz) filo pastry
25 g (1 oz) butter, melted
125 g (4 oz) unsalted butter
150 g (5 oz) plain flour
icing sugar, to dust

**ORANGE SAUCE**
45 ml (3 tbsp) golden syrup
grated rind of 1 orange and juice of 3 oranges
45 ml (3 tbsp) double cream (optional)

1 Mix the rhubarb with 50 g (2 oz) of the sugar, cover and chill overnight.
2 Cut the filo pastry into twelve 15 cm (6 inch) squares. Brush a filo square with melted butter and press down firmly into a deep, 8 x 3 cm (3¼ x 1¼ inch), loose-based tartlet tin. Lay a second piece of buttered filo on top; press down. Repeat with another 5 tins. Chill for 30 minutes. Preheat the oven to 190°C (375°F) Mark 5.
3 Cook the pastry cases in the oven for 5 minutes or until golden and crisp. Cool for 5 minutes, then ease out of the tins on to a baking sheet. Increase the temperature to 200°C (400°F) Mark 6.
4 To make the crumble, rub the unsalted butter into the flour until the mixture

resembles fine crumbs, then stir in the remaining caster sugar.
5 Drain the rhubarb, reserving any juices for the Orange Sauce. Spoon about 15 ml (1 tbsp) of the crumble mixture into each pastry case. Spoon in the rhubarb, then sprinkle with the remaining crumble. Cook in the oven for 30–35 minutes or until golden brown.
6 Meanwhile, make the sauce. Warm the syrup, orange rind, juice and reserved rhubarb juice with 200 ml (7 fl oz) water. Bring to the boil and bubble for 10–15 minutes, until syrupy. Remove from the heat and stir in the cream, if using.
7 Dust the crumble with icing sugar and serve with the sauce.

# SEA BASS BAKED WITH FENNEL

**PREPARATION TIME: 20 MINUTES ◆ COOKING TIME: 30 MINUTES ◆ FREEZING: NOT SUITABLE ◆ 405 CALS PER SERVING ◆ SERVES 4**

1 sea bass, about 1.1 kg (2½ lb), scaled and gutted
4 fresh rosemary sprigs
3 large fennel bulbs
60 ml (4 tbsp) olive oil
juice of 1 lemon
30 ml (2 tbsp) chopped fresh oregano
30 ml (2 tbsp) chopped fresh parsley
salt and freshly ground black pepper
150 ml (¼ pint) dry white wine
20 large green pitted olives

1 Preheat the oven to 220°C (425°F) Mark 7. Wash the fish inside and out, then pat dry with kitchen paper. Place in an oval ovenproof dish and put the rosemary sprigs in the cavity.
2 Cut the fennel bulbs in half lengthways, cut out the core and slice thickly. (See Cook's Tip)
3 Whisk together the oil, lemon juice, chopped herbs and seasoning. Add the fennel slices and toss well. Spoon the fennel over and around the fish, pouring on any remaining marinade. Add the wine and scatter over the olives.
4 Cook in the oven for 30 minutes, stirring the fennel around and basting with the juices halfway through cooking.

Turn off the heat but leave the fish in the oven for 5 minutes to set. Serve immediately.

### COOK'S TIP
If you prefer the fennel to have a softer texture, blanch the slices in boiling salted water for 2 minutes, drain well and continue as above.

### VARIATION
Use a small salmon in place of the sea bass. Replace the olives with chunks of cucumber.

---

# MONKFISH WITH CHILLI OIL

**PREPARATION TIME: 40 MINUTES ◆ COOKING TIME: 1 HOUR ◆ FREEZING: NOT SUITABLE ◆ 600 CALS PER SERVING ◆ SERVES 6**

two monkfish tails, 700 g (1½ lb) each, filleted
30 ml (2 tbsp) chopped fresh parsley
15 ml (1 tbsp) chopped fresh thyme
5 ml (1 tsp) chopped fresh rosemary
salt and freshly ground black pepper
350 g (12 oz) rindless streaky bacon
3 garlic cloves, crushed
dried chilli flakes
90 ml (6 tbsp) olive oil
2 red peppers, cored, seeded and sliced
450 g (1 lb) courgette, sliced
450 g (1 lb) new potatoes, halved or quartered
lemon juice
mayonnaise
250 g (9 oz) French beans
extra-virgin olive oil, to drizzle
lemon wedges, to garnish

1 Preheat the oven to 220°C (425°F) Mark 7. Lay two fish fillets, cut side up, on a board and sprinkle with the parsley, 5 ml (1 tsp) of the thyme, 2.5 ml (½ tsp) of the rosemary and salt and pepper. Place the other two fillets on top and wrap in the bacon. Place in a shallow container just large enough to hold the fish and add the garlic, a large pinch of chilli flakes and 60 ml (4 tbsp) of the oil. Cover and set aside in a cool place.
2 Place the vegetables in a large roasting pan with 1.25 ml (¼ tsp) chilli flakes and the remaining oil. Toss and season well. Cook in the oven for 20–25 minutes, basting and turning occasionally.
3 Brown the monkfish under a

preheated grill for 5 minutes. Place on top of the vegetables, add any juices and return to the oven for 15–20 minutes.
4 Remove the monkfish and vegetables and set aside. Put the pan on top of the stove, stir in the remaining thyme and rosemary, and lemon juice and seasoning to taste. Bring to the boil gently, then bubble until most of the juices have evaporated. Add to the mayonnaise.
5 Cook the French beans in boiling salted water until just tender, drain, then stir into the roasted vegetables and drizzle with a little extra-virgin olive oil.
6 Cut the monkfish into thick slices, garnish with lemon wedges and serve with the vegetables and mayonnaise.

# TARTE TATIN

PREPARATION TIME: **40** MINUTES + CHILLING ◆ COOKING TIME: **45-55** MINUTES ◆ FREEZING: SUITABLE ◆ **750** CALS PER SERVING ◆ SERVES **6**

**PASTRY**
225 g (8 oz) plain flour
150 g (5 oz) butter
1.25 ml (¼ tsp) salt
50 g (2 oz) icing sugar
1 egg
vanilla essence

**CARAMEL**
125 g (4 oz) butter
200 g (7 oz) caster sugar
1.4-1.5 kg (3-3¼ lb) dessert apples
juice of ½ lemon

1  To make the pastry, sift the flour on to a work surface, make a hollow in the centre and add the butter and salt. Work the butter and salt together using the fingers of one hand until smooth and pliable (do not work in the flour). Add the icing sugar to the butter mixture and mix in the same way. Add the egg and vanilla essence and mix with butter mixture until it resembles scrambled egg. Cut the flour into the butter mixture with a palette knife, then knead lightly until smooth. Wrap and chill for 1 hour or until firm.
2  To make the caramel, melt the butter in a 28 cm (11 inch) tarte tatin mould. Add the sugar. Peel, quarter and core the apples. Pack tightly in the mould, preferably standing on one end, and cook over a low heat for 20-25 minutes, until well caramelised. Turn the apples round two-thirds of the way through the cooking time. Add the lemon juice and leave to cool.
3  Preheat the oven to 220°C (425°F) Mark 7. Roll out the pastry on a lightly floured surface so that it is 2.5 cm (1 inch) larger all round than the top of the mould. Place on top of the apples and prick with a sharp knife. Bake in the oven for 25–30 minutes until golden.
4  Leave to cool for 10 minutes, then turn out on to a serving plate. Serve at room temperature.

# PEAR AND PISTACHIO TART

PREPARATION TIME: **25** MINUTES + CHILLING ◆ COOKING TIME: **65** MINUTES ◆ FREEZING: SUITABLE ◆ **670** CALS PER SERVING ◆ SERVES **8**

50 g (2 oz) shelled pistachio nuts
225 g (8 oz) ground almonds
250 g (9 oz) bought puff pastry
3 eggs
175 g (6 oz) butter
175 g (6 oz) caster sugar
30 ml (2 tbsp) plain flour
45 ml (3 tbsp) Poire William (*eau de vie*)
   or Kirsch
411 g can pears in syrup, drained
caster sugar, to sprinkle

1  Place the pistachios and almonds in a food processor and process to a powder.
2  Roll out the pastry thinly on a floured surface and prick with a fork. Place a 20 cm (8 inch) flan ring on a baking sheet and line with the pastry, leaving the excess hanging over the edge. Prick all around the base and into the edge. Chill for 20-30 minutes. Place another baking sheet in the oven while preheating to 200°C (400°F) Mark 6.
3  Place the chilled pastry case on its baking sheet on top of the hot one and cook in the oven for 15 minutes or until just golden brown. Lower the temperature to 180°C (350°F) Mark 4.
4  Press the pastry gently back against the side of the flan ring and trim level; cool. Separate 1 egg. Beat the egg white and brush over the pastry base. Return to the oven for 3-5 minutes.
5  Cream the butter and sugar together until pale and light. Beat the remaining eggs and yolk together and add to the mixture a tablespoon at a time, beating well between additions. Fold in the nuts, flour and Poire William or Kirsch.
6  Fill the pastry case with the nut mixture. Slice the pears and arrange on top. Cook in the oven for 45 minutes or until just firm in the centre. About 5 minutes before the end of the cooking time, brush with the remaining egg white and sprinkle with sugar.

# BAKED MONKFISH BOULANGÈRE

PREPARATION TIME: **40** MINUTES ◆ COOKING TIME: **1** HOUR **10** MINUTES ◆ FREEZING: NOT SUITABLE ◆ **330-220** CALS PER SERVING ◆ SERVES **6-8**

3 lemons
50 g (2 oz) fresh white breadcrumbs
75 ml (5 tbsp) chopped flat-leaf parsley
2 garlic cloves, crushed
30-45 ml (2–3 tbsp) olive oil
salt and freshly ground black pepper
1 kg (2¼ lb) monkfish tails, filleted into 4 pieces (see Cook's Tip)
12 slices Parma ham
75 g (3 oz) butter
900 g (2 lb) new potatoes, quartered
350 g (12 oz) onion, thinly sliced
5 ml (1 tsp) dried thyme
thyme sprigs, to garnish

**1** Preheat the oven to 200°C (400°F) Mark 6. Grate the rind of 2 lemons and place in a food processor with the breadcrumbs, parsley, garlic, 30 ml (2 tbsp) oil and seasoning. Add the remaining oil if the mixture seems dry. Process for 1 minute, until well combined.
**2** Lay the monkfish cut side up on a board. Sprinkle half of the breadcrumb mixture on one fillet; lay the other fillet on top. Repeat with the remaining fish to make 2 parcels.
**3** Wrap each parcel in the Parma ham, making sure the fish is completely covered. Tie at 5 cm (2 inch) intervals and chill while cooking the potatoes.
**4** Quarter the remaining lemon. Use 25 g

(1 oz) of the butter to grease a large roasting pan. Place the potato, onion and lemon in the pan, season to taste and sprinkle with the dried thyme. Dot with the remaining butter and cook in the oven for 50–60 minutes or until golden brown, stirring occasionally.
**5** Place the fish on top of the potato, cover with foil and return to the oven for 20–25 minutes.
**6** Garnish with thyme to serve.

### COOK'S TIP
Two monkfish tails should give you this amount; ask the fishmonger to fillet them for you.

# COCONUT FISH CURRY

PREPARATION TIME: **20** MINUTES ◆ COOKING TIME: **35** MINUTES ◆ FREEZING: SUITABLE (STEP **4**) ◆ **580** CALS PER SERVING ◆ SERVES **4**

2-3 green chillies (optional)
salt and freshly ground black pepper
700 g (1½ lb) cod or haddock steaks
30 ml (2 tbsp) plain flour
75 ml (5 tbsp) oil
225 g (8 oz) onion, finely chopped
2.5 cm (1 inch) piece fresh root ginger, chopped
2 garlic cloves, crushed
2.5 ml (½ tsp) ground turmeric
10 ml (2 tsp) curry paste
400 ml can coconut milk
30 ml (2 tbsp) chopped fresh coriander
30 ml (2 tbsp) chopped fresh mint
45 ml (3 tbsp) lime juice
coriander, to garnish

**1** Split open the chillies, if using; remove the seeds for milder heat, if wished. Season the fish and dust lightly with the flour.
**2** Heat 45 ml (3 tbsp) of the oil in a heavy-based pan, add the fish steaks in batches and fry over a high heat for 1–2 minutes or until well browned. Set aside.
**3** Wipe out the pan and heat the remaining oil. Add the onion and chillies and fry for about 10 minutes or until beginning to soften and turn golden. Add the ginger, garlic, turmeric and curry paste and cook for 1 minute.
**4** Stir in the coconut milk and herbs, then simmer gently for 10–15 minutes or until syrupy. If wished, strain to make a

smooth sauce. Return the fish to the pan to heat through.
**5** Add the lime juice and serve immediately, garnished with coriander sprigs.

# PANETTONE BREAD AND BUTTER PUDDING

PREPARATION TIME: **30** MINUTES + SOAKING + STANDING ◆ COOKING TIME: **1¼** HOURS ◆ FREEZING: SUITABLE (STEP 3) ◆ **705** CALS PER SERVING ◆ SERVES **8**

125 g (4 oz) raisins
100 ml (4 fl oz) brandy
two 500 g cartons fresh custard, about 700 ml (1½ pints)
600 ml (1 pint) milk
panettone, weighing about 700 g (1½ lb) (see Cook's Tip)
75 g (3 oz) butter, softened
200 g (7 oz) plain chocolate, roughly chopped
icing sugar, to dust

**1** Soak the raisins in the brandy overnight. Stir the custard and milk together.
**2** Slice the panettone into circles about 5 mm (¼ inch) thick and spread with the butter. Cut each circle into quarters. Grease a 3.4 litre (6 pint) ovenproof dish and pour in enough custard just to cover the base.
**3** Arrange alternate layers of panettone, raisins, chocolate and custard in the dish, finishing with a layer of custard. Set aside and leave to soak for 1 hour.
**4** Preheat the oven to 180°C (350°F) Mark 4. Place the dish in a roasting pan and pour hot water around the dish to come halfway up the sides. Cook in the oven for 1–1¼ hours or until the custard is set and the top has turned a deep brown. Cover with foil after 40 minutes to prevent the top from burning, if necessary.
**5** Dust the pudding lightly with icing sugar to serve.

## COOK'S TIP

Panettone is a dome-shape yeasted cake with sultanas, orange and citrus peel. You'll find it in major supermarkets and delicatessens.

# CHRISTMAS PUDDING WITH SABAYON SAUCE

PREPARATION TIME: **30** MINUTES + STANDING ◆ COOKING TIME: **4-6** HOURS ◆ FREEZING: SUITABLE ◆ **560** CALS PER SERVING ◆ SERVES **8**

75 g (3 oz) no-soak pitted dried prunes
125 g (4 oz) butter, softened
125 g (4 oz) soft dark brown sugar
2 eggs, beaten
50 g (2 oz) each blanched almonds, walnuts and Brazil nuts, chopped
75 g (3 oz) carrots, coarsely grated
350 g (12 oz) mixed dried fruit
50 g (2 oz) fresh brown breadcrumbs
125 g (4 oz) plain wholemeal flour
50 g (2 oz) plain white flour
15 ml (1 tbsp) ground mixed spice
200 ml (7 fl oz) Guinness
30 ml (2 tbsp) each brandy and treacle
**SABAYON SAUCE**
75 g (3 oz) caster sugar
3 egg yolks
grated rind and juice of 1 lemon
100 ml (4 fl oz) double cream, whipped

**1** Snip the prunes into small pieces. Mix together the butter and sugar, then the eggs. Mix in the remaining ingredients, stirring well. Cover and leave overnight.
**2** Lightly grease a 1.4-1.6 litre (2½–2¾ pint) pudding basin and base-line with baking parchment. Beat the pudding mixture again and spoon into the basin. Pleat a piece of greaseproof paper and foil together and tie over the basin.
**3** Steam the pudding for about 6 hours or stand it in a large saucepan filled with boiling water to come halfway up the side of the basin, cover and boil for about 4 hours. Cool completely, re-cover with greaseproof paper and foil, and refrigerate for up to 2 months.
**4** To make the Sabayon Sauce, place the sugar and 100 ml (4 fl oz) water in a small saucepan. Heat slowly until the sugar has dissolved, then boil for 7–8 minutes, until syrupy with bubbles.
**5** Place the egg yolks in a small bowl and beat with an electric whisk. Pour on the hot syrup in a thin stream and whisk until thick and mousse-like; cool.
**6** Add the lemon rind and juice to the cream, then whip again to soft peaks. Fold into the mousse, cover and chill overnight. Whisk well before serving.
**7** Steam the pudding for about 3 hours or boil for about 2 hours. Turn out on to a warm serving plate and serve with the Sabayon Sauce.

# SPICY FISH WITH TOMATO RELISH

**PREPARATION TIME: 10** MINUTES ◆ **COOKING TIME: 15** MINUTES ◆ **FREEZING: NOT** SUITABLE ◆ **250** CALS PER SERVING ◆ **SERVES 4**

4 skate wings or cod steaks, each about
 175 g (6 oz)
salt and freshly ground black pepper
15 ml (1 tbsp) plain flour
30 ml (2 tbsp) oil
coriander sprigs, to garnish

**TOMATO RELISH**
75 g (3 oz) onion or shallot, finely
 chopped
1 large red chilli, seeded and chopped
2 garlic cloves, crushed
15 ml (1 tbsp) sun-dried tomato paste
200 ml (7 fl oz) white wine
400 g can chopped tomatoes
125 g (4 oz) cherry tomatoes, halved
4 spring onions, roughly chopped
30 ml (2 tbsp) chopped fresh coriander

**1** Season the fish with salt and pepper
and dust with the flour. Heat 15 ml
(1 tbsp) of the oil in a large non-stick
frying pan, add the fish and fry for 3
minutes on each side. Remove from the
pan, cover and keep warm while making
the Tomato Relish.
**2** Heat the remaining oil in the pan, add
the onion or shallot, chilli and garlic and
cook for 2–3 minutes. Add the tomato
paste and wine, bring to boil and bubble
for 5 minutes or until syrupy. Add the
canned tomatoes, bring to the boil and
bubble for 4–5 minutes or until pulpy.
Add the cherry tomatoes, spring onions,
chopped coriander and seasoning and
simmer for 1–2 minutes.

**3** To serve, garnish the fish with
coriander sprigs. Accompany with the
Tomato Relish and fried courgettes.

# AFRICAN SPICED FISH

**PREPARATION TIME: 5** MINUTES + MARINATING ◆ **COOKING TIME: 6** MINUTES ◆ **FREEZING: NOT** SUITABLE ◆ **220** CALS PER SERVING ◆ **SERVES 4**

30 ml (2 tbsp) chopped fresh coriander
15 ml (1 tbsp) chopped fresh parsley
3 garlic cloves, crushed
5 ml (1 tsp) salt
5 ml (1 tsp) ground cumin
10 ml (2 tsp) ground paprika
pinch of cayenne pepper
5 ml (1 tsp) harissa or chilli sauce
50 ml (2 fl oz) olive oil
30 ml (2 tbsp) lemon juice
pinch of saffron
4 haddock, cod or turbot fillets, about
 700 g (1½ lb) total weight
lemon wedges and flat-leaf parsley, to
 garnish

**1** Mix together all ingredients except the
fish. Place the fish in a non-metallic dish
and pour over the marinade. Cover and
leave in a cool place for 1 hour.
**2** Place the fish on a foil-lined baking
sheet and cook under a preheated grill
for 5–6 minutes or until golden and firm
to touch.
**3** Garnish with lemon wedges and
parsley and serve immediately, with
steamed spinach and couscous.

# BRAMBLE AND APPLE CRUMBLE WITH LEMON ICE

**PREPARATION TIME: 45 MINUTES + FREEZING ◆ COOKING TIME: 25 MINUTES ◆ FREEZING: SUITABLE (STEP 4) ◆ 730 CALS PER SERVING ◆ SERVES 6**

**CRUMBLE TOPPING**
50 g (2 oz) plain white flour
25 g (1 oz) plain wholemeal flour
75 g (3 oz) muscovado sugar
50 g (2 oz) ground almonds
50 g (2 oz) unsalted butter

**FILLING**
575 g (1¼ lb) dessert apples
50 g (2 oz) unsalted butter
50 g (2 oz) caster sugar
225 g (8 oz) blackberries

**LEMON YOGURT ICE**
finely grated rind and juice of 3–4 large lemons
2 eggs plus 2 yolks, beaten
200 g (7 oz) caster sugar
75 g (3 oz) unsalted butter, in pieces
500 g (1 lb 2 oz) Greek strained yogurt

**1** First make the Lemon Yogurt Ice. Place the lemon rind in a heatproof bowl and strain on the egg. Add the sugar, butter and 175 ml (6 fl oz) of the lemon juice.
**2** Place over a pan of simmering water and stir for about 20 minutes, until the sugar has dissolved and the mixture thickened. Remove from the pan and leave to cool, stirring occasionally.
**3** When the lemon mixture is cold, fold it into the yogurt until evenly blended. Pour into a freezerproof container and freeze for 3–4 hours, until firm.
**4** To make the crumble topping, sift the flours into a bowl, then tip in any bran from the sieve. Stir in the sugar and ground almonds, then work in the

butter, using your fingertips, to make a very crumbly mixture. Set aside.
**5** Preheat the oven to 190°C (375°F) Mark 5. Butter a 1.7 litre (3 pint) ovenproof dish.
**6** To prepare the filling, quarter the apples, then peel, core and cut into 2.5 cm (1 inch) chunks. Melt the butter in a large frying pan, add the apples and sugar, and cook, stirring, over a high heat for 3–5 minutes, until golden brown and tender.
**7** Spread the apples in the ovenproof dish and sprinkle with the blackberries. Spoon over the crumble and bake in the oven for 25 minutes, until golden brown. Serve warm, with the yogurt ice.

# BANANA TOFFEE CRUMBLES

**PREPARATION TIME: 15 MINUTES ◆ COOKING TIME: 20 MINUTES ◆ FREEZING: NOT SUITABLE ◆ 495 CALS PER SERVING ◆ SERVES 6**

1 small Madeira cake
75 g (3 oz) butter
50 g (2 oz) soft brown sugar
45 ml (3 tbsp) milk
250 g (8 oz) condensed milk
5 ml (1 tsp) lemon juice
4-5 small bananas
icing sugar, to dust
ice cream, to serve

**1** Cut six 5 mm (¼ inch) slices from the cake, then stamp out six 6-7.5 cm (2½-3 inch) rounds, depending on the width of the cake. Crumble the trimmings into fine crumbs.
**2** Melt the butter with the sugar in a saucepan. Bring to the boil and bubble for 1 minute only. Remove from the heat, add the milk and condensed milk and bring to the boil. Stir for 2 minutes or until thick and golden. Add the lemon juice and keep warm. Preheat the oven to 200°C (400°F) Mark 6.
**3** Slice or dice the bananas and stir into the sauce. Place the rounds of cake inside 6 metal pastry cutters on a baking sheet (see Cook's Tip). Spoon in the

banana mixture and sprinkle with the cake crumbs.
**4** Cook in the oven for 15 minutes or until golden. Dust with icing sugar and serve immediately, with ice cream.

**COOK'S TIP**

If you don't have metal pastry cutters, use strips of folded foil stapled together.

# SKATE WINGS WITH OLIVE AND HERB SAUCE

PREPARATION TIME: **10** MINUTES ◆ COOKING TIME: **12** MINUTES ◆ FREEZING: NOT SUITABLE ◆ **600** CALS PER SERVING ◆ SERVES **4**

4 skate wings, each 300–350 g (10–12 oz)
salt and freshly ground black pepper
60 ml (4 tbsp) plain flour
50 g (2 oz) butter
30 ml (2 tbsp) oil
few chives, to garnish

### SAUCE
2 garlic cloves, crushed
8 anchovy fillets, drained and chopped
30 ml (2 tbsp) capers, drained and rinsed
10 ml (2 tsp) black olive paste
15 ml (1 tbsp) sun-dried tomato paste
60 ml (4 tbsp) chopped fresh parsley
15 ml (1 tbsp) chopped fresh chives
60 ml (4 tbsp) extra-virgin olive oil
juice of 1 lemon

**1** First make the sauce. Place all the ingredients in a bowl and mix well.
**2** If the skate wings are very large, cut them into more manageable pieces. Season with salt and pepper and dust with the flour.
**3** Heat the butter and oil in a very large frying pan or two smaller ones. When the butter begins to foam, add the skate wings and fry gently for about 5 minutes on each side or until just cooked. To test, prise a little of the flesh away from the bone with the tip of a knife: if it comes away easily the fish is cooked.
**4** Pour the sauce around the fish and heat through for 1–2 minutes. Serve immediately, garnished with chives.

### COOK'S TIP
Both olive and sun-dried tomato pastes are available from larger supermarkets and good delicatessens. If unavailable, or if you prefer a coarse textured sauce, used chopped pitted olives and sun-dried tomatoes instead.

# KEDGEREE WITH HERB BUTTER

PREPARATION TIME: **10** MINUTES ◆ COOKING TIME: ABOUT **20** MINUTES ◆ FREEZING: NOT SUITABLE ◆ **540** CALS PER SERVING ◆ SERVES **4**

450 g (1 lb) smoked haddock (see Cook's Tip)
150 ml (¼ pint) milk
75 g (3 oz) cooked cockles
225 g (8 oz) basmati rice
5 ml (1 tsp) coriander seeds, crushed
3 hard-boiled eggs, quartered
30 ml (2 tbsp) double cream
45-60 ml (3-4 tbsp) chopped fresh chives
salt and freshly ground black pepper
lemon or lime wedges and extra herbs, to garnish

### HERB BUTTER
50 g (2 oz) butter, melted
5-10 ml (1-2 tsp) lemon juice
30 ml (2 tbsp) chopped fresh tarragon

**1** Place the smoked haddock and milk in a shallow pan. Cover and simmer gently for about 8 minutes, until cooked through. Drain, reserving 30–45 ml (2–3 tbsp) of the juices. Roughly flake the fish, discarding the skin and any bones.
**2** Thoroughly drain the cockles.
**3** Cook the rice in plenty of boiling salted water for 10 minutes or until just tender. Drain, rinse with boiling water and drain well.
**4** Return the rice to the pan and add the flaked haddock, reserved cooking juices, cockles, coriander seeds, eggs, cream and chives. Season lightly with salt and pepper and heat through gently for 2 minutes.

**5** Meanwhile, make the Herb Butter. Pour the butter and lemon juice into a warmed jug, add the tarragon and a little seasoning and stir well.
**6** Spoon the kedgeree onto warm serving plates and garnish with lemon or lime wedges and extra herbs. Serve accompanied by the Herb Butter.

### COOK'S TIP
Choose natural undyed smoked haddock where possible. It's very pale by comparison to the familiar yellow smoked haddock because it doesn't contain colouring and it generally has a superior flavour.

# RICE PUDDING WITH APRICOT SAUCE

PREPARATION TIME: 5 MINUTES ◆ COOKING TIME: 2¹/₂ HOURS ◆ FREEZING: SUITABLE ◆ 220-150 CALS PER SERVING ◆ SERVES 4-6

75 g (3 oz) pudding rice
25 g (1 oz) caster sugar
750 ml (1¹/₄ pints) semi-skimmed milk
2 drops vanilla essence
crushed cardamom seeds and orange
  rind, to decorate

**APRICOT SAUCE**
2 cardamom pods
75 g (3 oz) ready-to-eat dried apricots,
  chopped
150 ml (¹/₄ pint) orange juice
juice of ¹/₂ lemon

**1** Preheat the oven to 170°C (325°F) Mark 3. Place the rice, sugar, milk and vanilla essence in a 1.1 litre (2 pint) shallow ovenproof dish and stir. Cook in the oven for 30 minutes.
**2** Meanwhile, remove and crush the seeds from the cardamom pods. Place the apricots, cardamom, orange juice and 100 ml (4 fl oz) water in a small ovenproof dish, cover with foil and place in the oven with the rice.
**3** Lower the temperature to 150°C (300°F) Mark 2 and cook for 1¹/₂ –2 hours.
**4** Remove the apricots from the oven and purée in a food processor or blender. Add lemon juice to taste and reheat.

**5** Garnish the pudding with crushed cardamom seeds and orange rind and serve with the Apricot Sauce.

# CHOCOLATE, PRUNE AND ORANGE SOUFFLÉS

PREPARATION TIME: 20 MINUTES ◆ COOKING TIME: 20 MINUTES ◆ FREEZING: NOT SUITABLE ◆ 140 CALS PER SOUFFLÉ ◆ MAKES 8

75 ml (5 tbsp) caster sugar
175 g (6 oz) pitted ready-to-eat prunes
30 ml (2 tbsp) vegetable oil
75 ml (3 fl oz) unsweetened orange juice
50 g (2 oz) plain chocolate
grated rind of 1 orange
5 egg whites
1.25 ml (¹/₄ tsp) cream of tartar
pinch of salt
icing sugar, to dust

**1** Lightly grease eight 150 ml (¹/₄ pint) ramekins and sprinkle with 15 ml (1 tbsp) of the caster sugar. Preheat the oven to 180°C (350°F) Mark 4.
**2** Place the prunes, oil and orange juice in a food processor or blender and blend for 2–3 minutes (see Cook's Tip) to form a purée.
**3** Using a sharp knife, chop the chocolate into small pieces and mix with the prune purée, 30 ml (2 tbsp) of the remaining caster sugar and the orange rind.
**4** Place the egg whites, cream of tartar and salt in a clean bowl and whisk until stiff but not dry. Add the remaining sugar and continue to whisk until the

mixture becomes very stiff and shiny.
**5** Using a large metal spoon, beat a quarter of the egg white mixture into the prune mixture, then gently fold in the remainder. Spoon into the prepared ramekins.
**6** Stand the ramekins in a roasting pan and add enough hot water to come halfway up the sides. Cook in the oven for 20 minutes or until just set. Dust with icing sugar and serve immediately.

**COOK'S TIP**

Prune purée can be made up to 3 days ahead and chilled, covered, until required.

# CRISPY-TOPPED FISH RISOTTO

**PREPARATION TIME: 10 MINUTES ◆ COOKING TIME: ABOUT 35 MINUTES ◆ FREEZING: NOT SUITABLE ◆ 620 CALS PER SERVING ◆ SERVES 4**

225 g (8 oz) smoked haddock fillet
600 ml (1 pint) vegetable stock
150 ml (¼ pint) white wine
75 g (3 oz) butter
225 g (8 oz) trimmed leeks, finely chopped
175 g (6 oz) risotto (arborio) rice
45 ml (3 tbsp) chopped fresh chives
175 g (6 oz) Caerphilly or Lancashire cheese, crumbled
45 ml (3 tbsp) freshly grated Parmesan cheese
freshly ground black pepper
30 ml (2 tbsp) fresh breadcrumbs
grated rind of 2 lemons
chives, to garnish

**1** Place the smoked haddock in a saucepan, pour over the stock and wine and bring to the boil. Turn off the heat, cover and leave for 10 minutes. Remove the fish from the pan and skin and roughly flake the flesh. Keep the liquid gently simmering on the hob.
**2** Melt 25 g (1 oz) of the butter in a large saucepan, add the leeks and fry gently for 3 minutes or until beginning to soften. Add the rice and stir well.
**3** Gradually add the simmering liquid, allowing each addition to be absorbed before adding the next – this will take about 25 minutes.
**4** Remove from the heat and add the haddock, chives, crumbled cheese and

15 ml (1 tbsp) of the Parmesan. Season with pepper to taste, then transfer to an ovenproof dish. Melt the remaining butter, add the breadcrumbs, remaining Parmesan and lemon rind and mix well; sprinkle over the risotto. Place under a preheated grill until the topping is crisp and golden. Garnish with chives and serve immediately.

# SPICED MOROCCAN PILAFF

**PREPARATION TIME: 30 MINUTES + MARINATING ◆ COOKING TIME: 1 HOUR ◆ FREEZING: NOT SUITABLE ◆ 695 CALS PER SERVING ◆ SERVES 8**

450 g (1 lb) boned chicken thighs
450 g (1 lb) squid, prawns and scallops
225 g (8 oz) cod or haddock fillet
750 g (1½ lb) mussels in shells, cleaned
125 g (4 oz) celery
2 red peppers, cored and seeded
175 g (6 oz) chorizo sausage
225 g (8 oz) onion, chopped
300 g (10 oz) long-grain white rice
900 ml (1½ pints) chicken stock
400 g can chopped tomatoes

**MARINADE**
3 red chillies, seeded and chopped
75 ml (5 tbsp) chopped fresh coriander
22.5 ml (4½ tsp) each cumin and paprika
9 garlic cloves
150 ml (¼ pint) olive oil
100 ml (4 fl oz) lemon juice

**1** Process the marinade ingredients for 1–2 minutes and season. Place the chicken and half of the marinade in a bowl, cover and chill for at least 2 hours.
**2** Cut the squid into thin rings, shell the prawns, trim and halve the scallops, skin and cut the fish into bite-size pieces. Place in a bowl with the remaining marinade, cover and chill for at least 2 hours. Cover and chill the mussels.
**3** Preheat the oven to 200°C (400°F) Mark 6. Cut the celery, red peppers and chorizo into strips. Heat 30 ml (2 tbsp) oil in a heavy-based flameproof casserole and fry the celery, red pepper and chorizo for 2–3 minutes; set aside.
**4** Drain the chicken and seafood,

reserving the marinade. Return the seafood to the fridge. Fry the chicken in batches for 3–4 minutes; set aside. Fry the onion for 4–5 minutes.
**5** Add the marinade, bring to the boil and bubble for 1–2 minutes. Add the rice and stir for 1 minute. Add the stock and tomatoes. Bring to the boil, stirring, then return the chicken and season. Cover with foil and cook in the oven for 30 minutes, stirring occasionally.
**6** Return the celery, pepper and chorizo to the pan. Place the fish and mussels on top. Cover and return to oven for 10 minutes or until the mussels have opened (discard any that do not). Garnish with coriander and lemon quarters.

# SIZZLING LEMON PANCAKES

PREPARATION TIME: 40 MINUTES ◆ COOKING TIME: 40 MINUTES ◆ FREEZING: SUITABLE (STEP 5) ◆ 420 CALS PER SERVING ◆ SERVES 6

**BATTER**
125 g (4 oz) plain white flour
pinch of salt
1 egg, plus 1 yolk
15 ml (1 tbsp) oil
300 ml (½ pint) milk

**FILLING**
grated rind and juice of 1 lemon
150 ml (¼ pint) milk
1 egg, separated
25 g (1 oz) caster sugar
15 g (½ oz) each plain white flour and
 cornflour
150 g (5 oz) good-quality lemon curd
200 g carton crème fraîche
about 25 g (1 oz) butter, melted
icing sugar, to dust

1 Blend the batter ingredients in a food processor or blender until the consistency of single cream. Cover and set aside in a cool place for at least 30 minutes.
2 Meanwhile, place the lemon rind and milk in a saucepan, bring slowly to the boil, then cover and set aside for 5 minutes. Beat the egg yolk with the sugar until pale. Beat in the flours, then whisk in the milk. Return to the pan and bring to the boil over a low heat, stirring until pale and thick. Cover and cool.
3 Meanwhile, heat and lightly oil an 18 cm (7 inch) pancake pan. Pour in just enough batter to cover the base. Cook until golden underneath, then turn and cook the other side. Make 6 pancakes; set

aside, interleaved with greaseproof paper.
4 Whisk the lemon curd into the custard, then fold in the crème fraîche. Whisk the egg white until it just holds its shape, then fold into the lemon mixture.
5 Divide the filling between the pancakes. Fold the sides into the centre, then fold in the top and bottom to form a parcel. Secure with a wooden cocktail stick. Grease an ovenproof dish with melted butter and add the pancakes.
6 Drizzle with the remaining butter and lemon juice, then dust with icing sugar. Place under a preheated grill for 2 minutes or until the sugar begins to caramelise. Serve immediately, with lemon wedges.

# AUTUMN ALMOND PANCAKES

PREPARATION TIME: 40 MINUTES + STANDING ◆ COOKING TIME: 40-45 MINUTES ◆ FREEZING: SUITABLE (STEP 5) ◆ 275 CALS PER SERVING ◆ SERVES 8

**BATTER**
125 g (4 oz) plain white flour
1 egg, plus 1 yolk
15 ml (1 tbsp) oil
300 ml (½ pint) milk

**FILLING**
300 ml (½ pint) milk
75 g (3 oz) ground almonds
2 eggs, separated
50 g (2 oz) caster sugar
20 ml (4 tsp) plain white flour
25 ml (5 tsp) cornflour
almond essence
30 ml (2 tbsp) double cream
a little melted butter
icing sugar, for dusting
poached plums and blackberries, to
 accompany

1 Blend the batter ingredients in a food processor or blender until the consistency of single cream. Cover and set aside in a cool place for at least 30 minutes.
2 Meanwhile, place the milk and ground almonds in a saucepan, bring slowly to the boil, then cover and set aside for 15 minutes. Beat the egg yolks with 25 g (1 oz) of the sugar until fluffy. Beat in the flours, then blend in the milk. Return to the rinsed pan and bring slowly to the boil, stirring. Add a few drops of almond essence and float the cream on the top to prevent a skin forming. Cover and cool.
3 Whisk the egg whites until stiff, then whisk in the remaining sugar until shiny. Fold into the custard, cover and set aside.

4 Heat and lightly oil an 18 cm (7 inch) pancake pan and make paper-thin pancakes, as above; set aside.
5 Preheat the oven to 220°C (425°F) Mark 7. Lightly butter an 18-20 cm (7-8 inch) round ovenproof dish. Lay a pancake in the bottom, cover with about 30 ml (2 tbsp) of the custard, then lay a second pancake on top. Repeat with the remaining filling, finishing with a pancake. Brush the top with butter.
6 Dust heavily with icing sugar and cook in the oven for 40–45 minutes until hot through. Cover with foil if it becomes too brown. Cut into wedges and serve immediately, with poached plums and blackberries.

# GARLIC RISOTTO WITH FRESH MUSSELS

PREPARATION TIME: **5** MINUTES ◆ COOKING TIME: **30** MINUTES ◆ FREEZING: NOT SUITABLE ◆ **615** CALS PER SERVING ◆ SERVES **4**

50 g (2 oz) butter
175 g (6 oz) onion, finely chopped
4 garlic cloves, crushed
225 g (8 oz) risotto (arborio) rice
450 ml (¾ pint) white wine
450 ml (¾ pint) hot fish or vegetable stock
45 ml (3 tbsp) pesto sauce
50 g (2 oz) freshly grated Parmesan cheese
60 ml (4 tbsp) chopped fresh parsley
1.4 kg (3 lb) mussels in shells or 350 g (12 oz) cooked shelled mussels or prawns (see Cook's Tip)

**1** Melt 25 g (1 oz) of the butter in a large saucepan, add the onion and fry for about 5 minutes or until soft but not coloured. Add half of the garlic and the rice and stir well.
**2** Gradually add 300 ml (½ pint) of the wine and the hot stock a little at a time, allowing each addition to be absorbed before adding the next – this will take about 25 minutes.
**3** Stir in the pesto, Parmesan cheese and 30 ml (2 tbsp) of the parsley. Keep warm.
**4** Place the mussels in a large saucepan with the remaining butter, garlic and wine. Cover with a tight-fitting lid and cook for 3–5 minutes, shaking the pan frequently, until the mussels have opened (discard any that do not open).
**5** Spoon the risotto on to 4 warm serving plates. Pile the mussels on top, allowing the cooking juices to seep into the risotto. Sprinkle with the remaining parsley and serve immediately.

## COOK'S TIP

Fresh mussels are available from most major supermarkets. Look out for ready-prepared marinated mussels or *moules marinières* – quick and easy to use.

# MEDITERRANEAN FISH CASSEROLE

PREPARATION TIME: **10** MINUTES ◆ COOKING TIME: **30** MINUTES ◆ FREEZING: SUITABLE ◆ **330** CALS PER SERVING ◆ SERVES **4**

2 red peppers, cored and seeded
700 g (1½ lb) skinless firm white fish fillets, eg cod, haddock, halibut
30 ml (2 tbsp) olive oil
2 large garlic cloves, finely chopped
2 red onions, sliced
2.5 ml (½ tsp) paprika
100 ml (4 fl oz) dry white wine
two 400 g cans chopped tomatoes
15 ml (1 tbsp) sun-dried tomato paste
salt and freshly ground black pepper
125 g (4 oz) pitted black olives, halved
fresh thyme, to garnish

**1** Cut the peppers into strips and the fish into large bite-size pieces.
**2** Heat the oil in a shallow flameproof casserole, add the garlic and onion, cover and cook gently for about 10 minutes. Add the paprika and red pepper and cook, stirring, for 1 minute. Add the wine, bring to the boil and bubble until reduced by half.
**3** Add the tomatoes, tomato paste and seasoning to taste, bring to the boil, then simmer, uncovered, for 15 minutes. Stir in the fish and simmer for 3–5 minutes, until just cooked. Stir in the olives and garnish with thyme to serve.

# HOT FUDGE PUDDING

PREPARATION TIME: **30** MINUTES + SOAKING ◆ COOKING TIME: **1** HOUR ◆ FREEZING: SUITABLE (STEP 4) ◆ **600** CALS PER SERVING ◆ SERVES **6**

175 g (6 oz) no-soak dried apricots (see Cook's Tip)
two 500 g cartons fresh custard, about 700 ml (1½ pints)
600 ml (1 pint) milk
300 g (10 oz) sweet bread, eg brioche
75 g (3 oz) butter, softened
grated rind of 1 orange
200 g (7 oz) bought fudge, chopped
caster sugar, to dust

**1** Soak the apricots in boiling water for at least 2 hours. Stir together the custard and milk.
**2** Cut the bread into 5 mm (¼ inch) thick slices and spread thinly with the butter. Cut into quarters.
**3** Grease a 2 litre (3½ pint) shallow ovenproof dish and pour in a thin layer of the custard to cover the base.
**4** Drain the apricots and chop roughly. Mix with the orange rind. Arrange alternate layers of bread, apricots, fudge and custard in the basin, finishing with a layer of custard. Leave to soak for about 1 hour.
**5** Preheat the oven to 180°C (350°F) Mark 4. Dust the top of the pudding fairly heavily with caster sugar. Place the dish in a roasting pan and pour in enough hot water to come at least halfway up the sides. Cook in the oven for 1 hour or until the custard has set and the top has turned a rich, deep brown colour. Cover with foil after 40 minutes to prevent the top from burning. Leave to cool for about 10 minutes before serving.

## COOK'S TIP

Although sold as no-soak dried apricots, the fruit will be plumper if soaked.

# MARMALADE PUDDING WITH BURNT WHISKY SAUCE

PREPARATION TIME: **20** MINUTES ◆ COOKING TIME: **45** MINUTES ◆ FREEZING: SUITABLE (STEP 4) ◆ **550** CALS PER SERVING ◆ SERVES **8**

melted butter for greasing
5 large oranges
120 ml (8 tbsp) thin-cut marmalade
250 g (9 oz) butter
250 g (9 oz) caster sugar
3 eggs, beaten
175 g (6 oz) self-raising flour, sifted
45 ml (3 tbsp) whisky

**1** Grease eight 150 ml (¼ pint) metal pudding moulds with melted butter. Base-line with baking parchment and dust with flour. Finely grate the rind and squeeze the juice from 1 orange. Squeeze the juice from another 2. Peel the remaining 2, cut into segments and set aside. Divide 60 ml (4 tbsp) of the marmalade between the moulds.
**2** Cream together 175 g (6 oz) each of the butter and sugar and the orange rind until fluffy. Gradually add the eggs, beating well. Fold in the flour, and 30 ml (2 tbsp) each of the marmalade and orange juice.
**3** Preheat the oven to 190°C (375°F) Mark 5. Divide the mixture between the moulds. Cut 8 pieces of foil and baking parchment, about 18 cm (7 inches) square. Place a piece of foil on a parchment piece and make a pleat. Brush the centre of the parchment with butter. Tie over the basins, parchment side down.
**4** To make the sauce, melt the remaining butter and sugar in a small heavy-based pan. Cook, stirring, for 5 minutes or until golden. Add the whisky and bubble for 1 minute. Add the remaining orange juice, bring to the boil and bubble gently for 15 minutes, until syrupy. Remove from the heat and stir in the remaining marmalade and reserved orange segments. Set aside.
**5** Stand the moulds in a roasting pan and pour boiling water to come halfway up the sides. Cover the pan with foil. Bake in the oven for 40–45 minutes until firm.
**6** Turn out on to warm plates and spoon over the warm sauce to serve.

# MUSHROOM AND TROUT CROÛTES

PREPARATION TIME: **10** MINUTES ◆ COOKING TIME: **10** MINUTES ◆ FREEZING: NOT SUITABLE ◆ **575** CALS PER SERVING ◆ SERVES **4**

8 trout fillets, about 450 g (1 lb) total weight
olive oil
salt and freshly ground black pepper
350 g (12 oz) mushrooms, eg brown cap, shiitake or oyster
small loaf of white crusty bread (unsliced), about 225 g (8 oz)
50 g (2 oz) butter
1 garlic clove, crushed
15 ml (1 tbsp) chopped fresh chives
125 g (4 oz) onion, chopped
200 ml carton crème fraîche
30 ml (2 tbsp) tarragon vinegar or white wine vinegar
50 g (2 oz) watercress

1 Place the trout on a foil-lined baking sheet. Brush with oil, season, then cook under a preheated grill for 3–4 minutes. Leave to cool, then flake the fish. Halve any large mushrooms. Cut the bread into four 1 cm (½ inch) slices and halve diagonally.
2 Melt 25 g (1 oz) of the butter in a non-stick frying pan. Stir in the garlic, chives and black pepper. Add the bread and fry on both sides until crisp and golden. Place on 4 warm serving plates and keep warm.
3 Melt the remaining butter in the pan, add the onion and cook, stirring, for 4–5 minutes. Add the mushrooms and cook for 2–3 minutes, stirring occasionally.

Add the crème fraîche, vinegar and seasoning to taste. Bubble for 2 minutes.
4 Divide the watercress and flaked trout between the croûtes. Spoon over the mushroom mixture and serve immediately.

# PAN-FRIED COD WITH CHANTERELLE MUSHROOMS

PREPARATION TIME: **20** MINUTES ◆ COOKING TIME: ABOUT **20** MINUTES ◆ FREEZING: NOT SUITABLE ◆ **480** CALS PER SERVING ◆ SERVES **4**

4 slices white bread
4 cod steaks, each about 175 g (6 oz)
75 g (3 oz) butter
30 ml (2 tbsp) vegetable oil
salt and freshly ground black pepper
plain flour for dredging
4 spring onions, finely chopped
225 g (8 oz) chanterelle mushrooms or mixed mushrooms
1 garlic clove, crushed
45 ml (3 tbsp) crème fraîche
30 ml (2 tbsp) chopped fresh chives

1 Remove the crusts from the bread and cut the slices into ovals, the same size as the cod steaks. Heat half of the butter and the oil in a frying pan, add the bread and fry on both sides until crisp and golden; keep warm.
2 Season the cod, then coat with flour. Melt the remaining butter in the pan, add the cod and fry for about 5 minutes on each side, until cooked through and lightly golden. Remove from the pan and keep warm.
3 Add the spring onion, mushrooms and garlic to the pan and sauté for 5 minutes, until the juices are just beginning to escape from the mushrooms. Stir in the crème fraîche and heat through gently.

Season to taste and add half of the chives.
4 Place a bread croûte on each warm plate, arrange a cod steak on top and spoon the mushroom mixture on top of the fish. Sprinkle with the remaining chives and serve immediately.

## VARIATION

Any variety of wild mushroom can be used instead of chanterelles.

# BUTTER AND RUM-BAKED APPLES

PREPARATION TIME: **30 MINUTES + MARINATING + CHILLING** ◆ COOKING TIME: **1¼ HOURS** ◆ FREEZING: **SUITABLE (STEP 3)** ◆ **400** CALS PER SERVING ◆ SERVES **6**

50 g (2 oz) dried mango or pineapple, chopped
75 ml (5 tbsp) dark rum or brandy
grated rind of 1 lemon
50 g (2 oz) butter
75 g (3 oz) soft brown sugar
2.5 ml (½ tsp) ground cinnamon
6 small dessert apples
250 g (9 oz) puff pastry
1 egg, beaten
30 ml (2 tbsp) caster sugar
double cream, to serve

1 Put the dried mango or pineapple in a small bowl, add the rum or brandy, cover and marinate for at least 4 hours or overnight.

2 Beat the grated lemon rind, butter, brown sugar and cinnamon together until pale and light. Drain the fruit, reserving the marinade. Beat the marinade into the buttercream and set the fruit aside.

3 Preheat the oven to 200°C (400°F) Mark 6. Slice off the tops of the apples and remove the cores. Fill with the drained fruit and top each with 5 ml (1 tsp) of the rum butter. Place in a roasting pan with 150 ml (¼ pint) water, cover with foil and cook in the oven for 45 minutes or until tender. Set aside in the pan to cool.

4 Roll out the pastry thinly on a lightly floured surface and cut out six 10 cm (4 inch) rounds. Brush with beaten egg and place egg-side down on the cooled apples; press to seal. Brush the pastry with egg, decorate with pastry trimmings and sprinkle with the caster sugar. Chill for 30 minutes.

5 Cook in the oven for 25 minutes or until the pastry is golden. Transfer to a dish. Add the remaining rum butter to the roasting pan and bring to the boil on the hob, stirring (add a little water if the sauce is too thick). Serve the apples with the sauce and double cream.

# GINGER AND ROSEMARY-BAKED BANANAS

PREPARATION TIME: **20 MINUTES** ◆ COOKING TIME: **ABOUT 45 MINUTES** ◆ FREEZING: **NOT SUITABLE** ◆ **240** CALS PER SERVING ◆ SERVES **6**

5 mm (¼ inch) piece fresh root ginger, grated
200 ml (7 fl oz) dark rum
20 ml (4 tsp) sugar
juice of 1 lemon
5 spears of fresh rosemary
50 g (2 oz) butter
4 bananas
3 large oranges, peeled and sliced
ginger or vanilla ice cream, to serve

1 Preheat the oven to 200°C (400°F) Mark 6. Place the ginger, rum, sugar, lemon juice and rosemary in a small saucepan, bring to the boil, then simmer for 10–12 minutes or until syrupy. Add 25 g (1 oz) of the butter and set aside.

2 Slice the bananas lengthways. Melt the remaining butter in a large non-stick frying pan, add the bananas and fry over a high heat for 1–2 minutes, turning occasionally, until golden brown. Place in a shallow ovenproof dish with the oranges, pour over the rum syrup, cover and cook in the oven for 30 minutes.

3 Serve immediately, with ice cream.

## COOK'S TIP

To save time, scoop the ice cream into portions and place on a foil-lined tray in the freezer, ready to serve.

## VARIATION

The fruits can also be divided between 6 pieces of foil and wrapped into parcels to cook.

# GRILLED COD WITH BLACK-OLIVE OIL

**PREPARATION TIME: 20 MINUTES ◆ COOKING TIME: 35–45 MINUTES ◆ FREEZING: NOT SUITABLE ◆ 475 CALS PER SERVING ◆ SERVES 6**

75 g (3 oz) pitted black olives
175 ml (6 fl oz) olive oil
1 garlic clove, crushed
salt and freshly ground black pepper
350 g (12 oz) new potatoes
700 g (1½ lb) leeks, thickly sliced
6 cod fillets, 1 kg (2¼ lb) total weight
chives, to garnish

**1** Place the olives, 100 ml (4 fl oz) of the olive oil, garlic and seasoning in a food processor and process for 1–2 minutes or until the mixture resembles a chunky purée. Cover and set aside.
**2** Cook the potatoes in boiling salted water for 15–20 minutes, until just tender. Drain and cut into wedges.
**3** Heat the remaining oil in a large frying pan. Add the potato and cook for 5–10 minutes or until golden brown on both sides, stirring occasionally. Drain on kitchen paper, season to taste and keep warm. Add the leeks to the pan and cook for 3–4 minutes or until tender; season to taste. Return the potato to the pan.

**4** Place the cod fillets on a baking sheet, season with black pepper and spoon 10 ml (2 tsp) of the olive purée over each fillet. Cook under a preheated grill for about 8 minutes or until the flesh turns white. Spoon a further 5 ml (1 tsp) olive purée on to each fillet and return to the grill for 1 minute to warm through.
**5** To serve, reheat the leek and potato mixture for 1–2 minutes. Arrange on 6 warm plates and place a cod fillet on top. Garnish with chives and serve immediately.

# COD STEAKS WITH FENNEL

**PREPARATION TIME: 10 MINUTES + MARINATING ◆ COOKING TIME: 30 MINUTES ◆ FREEZING: NOT SUITABLE ◆ 175 CALS PER SERVING ◆ SERVES 4**

4 thick cod fillets or steaks, each 150 g (5 oz)
2 fennel bulbs, about 550 g (1½ lb)
15 ml (1 tbsp) vegetable oil
10 ml (2 tsp) sesame seeds

**MARINADE**
15 ml (1 tbsp) hoisin sauce
60 ml (4 tbsp) light soy sauce
60 ml (4 tbsp) dry vermouth
60 ml (4 tbsp) orange juice
2.5 ml (½ tsp) Chinese five-spice powder
2.5 ml (½ tsp) ground cumin
1 garlic clove, crushed

**1** First, make the marinade. Mix all the ingredients together in a small bowl.
**2** Place the cod in a shallow dish, pour over the marinade, cover and leave in a cool place for at least 1 hour.
**3** Thinly slice the fennel, reserving the tops. Remove the fish, reserving the marinade, and cook under a preheated grill or on a lightly oiled hot griddle for 4 minutes. Turn over and cook for 3–4 minutes or until cooked through.
**4** Heat the oil in the sauté pan, add the fennel and cook briskly for 5–7 minutes or until brown and beginning to soften. Add the reserved marinade, bring to the boil and bubble until reduced and syrupy.
**5** To serve, arrange a bed of fennel on 4

warm plates and place the fish on top. Spoon round any pan juices and sprinkle with the sesame seeds. Garnish with the reserved fennel tops.

# FRANGIPANE BAKED PEARS

**PREPARATION TIME: 15 MINUTES + MARINATING ◆ COOKING TIME: 1 HOUR 20 MINUTES ◆ FREEZING: SUITABLE ◆ 575 CALS PER SERVING ◆ SERVES 6**

25 g (1 oz) each raisins, chopped
   almonds and mixed peel
45 ml (3 tbsp) Kirsch or rum
75 g (3 oz) flaked almonds
50 g (2 oz) plain flour
225 g (8 oz) caster sugar
6 pears
15 ml (1 tbsp) apricot jam
125 g (4 oz) butter
2 eggs, beaten
extra-thick cream, to serve

**1** Place the raisins, chopped almonds, mixed peel and Kirsch or rum in a small bowl. Cover and marinate for 6 hours or overnight. Drain, reserving the liquid; set aside.
**2** Place the flaked almonds and flour in a food processor and process until the nuts are very finely ground; set aside.
**3** Place 125 g (4 oz) of the sugar and 900 ml (1½ pints) water in a saucepan and bring to the boil, stirring, until dissolved.
**4** Peel the pears and place, with the peelings, in the syrup. Cover with greaseproof paper and poach for 10–15 minutes or until tender. Drain, discarding the peelings and reserving the liquid in

the pan. Add the jam and bubble for 30 minutes or until syrupy. Set aside.
**5** Cream together the remaining sugar and the butter until fluffy. Gradually add the eggs, beating well. Fold in the flour and almond mixture and reserved Kirsch or rum.
**6** Preheat the oven to 200°C (400°F) Mark 6. Using a teaspoon, scoop out the base of each pear. Combine a spoonful of the creamed mixture with the reserved nuts and fruit and fill the pears. Place in a 900 ml (1½ pint) shallow ovenproof dish and spoon round the remaining creamed mixture. Brush with the glaze.
**7** Cook in the oven for 1 hour or until the frangipane is golden and firm. Brush with glaze and serve with cream.

# GLAZED BERRY PUDDING

**PREPARATION TIME: 20 MINUTES + FREEZING ◆ COOKING TIME: 25 MINUTES ◆ FREEZING: SUITABLE ◆ 430 CALS PER SERVING ◆ SERVES 8**

**Frozen fruits can be used for this pudding.**

vanilla pod or 2.5 ml (½ tsp) vanilla
   essence
4 eggs, separated
50 g (2 oz) caster sugar
25 g (1 oz) plain flour, sifted
142 ml carton double cream
150 ml (¼ pint) milk
225 g (8 oz) icing sugar, sifted
450 g (1 lb) mixed red fruits, frozen
   compôte or conserve
icing sugar, to dust
blueberries and raspberries, to decorate

**1** Lightly butter eight 150 ml (¼ pint) ramekins and place in the freezer to chill. Split the vanilla pod, if using, and scrape the seeds into a bowl with the yolks. Add the caster sugar and beat until pale, then stir in the flour.
**2** Bring the cream and milk to the boil in a small saucepan, then pour over the yolk mixture, stirring. Return the mixture to the pan and cook over a low heat for 2 minutes, stirring until thick and smooth. Turn into a clean bowl, add the vanilla essence, if using, cover and leave to cool.
**3** Place the egg whites and icing sugar in a large bowl over a pan of simmering water and whisk for 10 minutes, until

thick. Remove from the heat and whisk until cool.
**4** Place 30 ml (2 tbsp) of the fruits in the bottom of each ramekin. Fold the meringue into the custard and pile on top of the fruits. Freeze for at least 7 hours or until firm.
**5** Preheat the oven to 220°C (425°F) Mark 7. Place the ramekins on a baking sheet and dust thickly with icing sugar. Cook in the oven for 20 minutes. Decorate with berries and serve immediately.

# CRUSTED COD AND TARTARE SAUCE

PREPARATION TIME: **20** MINUTES ◆ COOKING TIME: **15-20** MINUTES ◆ FREEZING: **NOT** SUITABLE ◆ **210** CALS PER SERVING ◆ SERVES **4**

50 g (2 oz) wholemeal bread, crusts removed
grated rind and juice of 1 lemon
30 ml (2 tbsp) chopped fresh parsley
salt and freshly ground black pepper
4 cod steaks, each about 150 g (5 oz)
40 ml (8 tsp) creamed horseradish
lemon slices and dill sprigs, to garnish

**TARTARE SAUCE**
4 gherkins, chopped
15 ml (1 tbsp) each chopped fresh dill and parsley
150 g (5 oz) reduced-fat crème fraîche

**1** Preheat the oven to 200°C (400°F) Mark 6. Place the bread in a food processor and process to make fine crumbs. Place in a large bowl and stir in the lemon rind, 30 ml (2 tbsp) of the parsley and seasoning.

**2** Place the cod steaks in a roasting pan, spread with the horseradish and season to taste. Divide the breadcrumb mixture between the steaks, pressing on firmly. Cook in the oven for 15–20 minutes or until tender.

**3** Meanwhile, prepare the tartare sauce. Add the gherkins, dill and parsley to the crème fraîche. Flavour with 10–15 ml (2–3 tsp) of the reserved lemon juice and mix well.

**4** Place the cod steaks on warm serving plates and garnish with lemon slices and dill. Serve with a spoonful of the tartare sauce and accompany with seasonal vegetables.

# PLAICE WITH TOMATO AND CAPER DRESSING

PREPARATION TIME: **15** MINUTES ◆ COOKING TIME: **10** MINUTES ◆ FREEZING: **NOT** SUITABLE ◆ **340** CALS PER SERVING ◆ SERVES **4**

8 plaice fillets, about 550 g (1¼ lb) total weight
75 ml (5 tbsp) tapenade (black olive paste)
150 ml (¼ pint) dry white wine
fried garlic slices and basil leaves, to garnish

**DRESSING**
30 ml (2 tbsp) capers
grated rind of ½ lemon
60 ml (4 tbsp) lemon juice
salt and freshly ground black pepper
60 ml (4 tbsp) reserved cooking liquor
60 ml (4 tbsp) olive oil
1 large or 2 small tomatoes, seeded and diced
25 g (1 oz) pitted black olives, sliced

**1** Skin the plaice if necessary, then spread the tapenade over the smoother side and roll up.

**2** Place the fish in a small flameproof casserole and pour around the wine. Bring gently to the boil, then cover and simmer for 8–10 minutes, until just cooked. Using a slotted spoon, remove the fish and place in a warm serving dish. Reserve the cooking liquor.

**3** To make the dressing, whisk together the capers, lemon rind and juice, seasoning, cooking liquor and oil. Add the tomato and olives and spoon over the fish. Garnish with fried garlic slices and basil leaves to serve.

# FENNEL AND ORANGE SALAD

PREPARATION TIME: **15** MINUTES ◆ FREEZING: NOT SUITABLE ◆ **280** CALS PER SERVING ◆ SERVES **4**

**Fennel with orange is a fairly classic combination, though here it is enhanced with olive pesto, which works well with the orange.**

2 large oranges (see Cook's Tips)
1 fennel bulb
1 small red onion, thinly sliced
50 g (2 oz) rocket leaves

**DRESSING**
15 g (½ oz) pitted black olives (see Cook's Tips)
1 sun-dried tomato in oil, drained
1 small garlic clove, crushed
7.5 ml (½ tbsp) chopped fresh parsley
90 ml (6 tbsp) extra-virgin olive oil
10 ml (2 tsp) balsamic vinegar
salt and freshly ground black pepper

**1** First make the dressing. Roughly chop the olives and sun-dried tomato. Place in a food processor or blender with the garlic, parsley and 15 ml (1 tbsp) of the oil and blend to form a fairly smooth paste. Transfer to a bowl and whisk in the remaining oil, vinegar and seasoning to taste.
**2** Remove all the white pith from the oranges, then cut into segments between the membranes and place in a large bowl.
**3** Discard the tough outer layer from the fennel, then slice very thinly.
**4** Add the fennel, onion and rocket to the oranges. Pour over the dressing and toss well. Serve immediately.

## COOK'S TIPS
Blood oranges are the ideal choice when in season, as they have a delicious sweet flavour and pretty ruby-coloured flesh. Although time-consuming, for optimum flavour it is worth buying good quality black olives and stoning them yourself. Alternatively, buy one of the ready-made olive pastes now available from larger supermarkets and specialist food stores.

# SPICED COLESLAW WITH PECANS

PREPARATION TIME: **15** MINUTES + STANDING ◆ FREEZING: NOT SUITABLE ◆ **340** CALS PER SERVING ◆ SERVES **4**

**This is a hot version of the ever-popular coleslaw - the mayonnaise is chilli-flavoured.**

350 g (12 oz) white cabbage
225 g (8 oz) carrots, grated
2-3 celery sticks, thinly sliced
50 g (2 oz) pecans or walnuts (optional)
paprika, for sprinkling
chervil or parsley sprigs, to garnish

**DRESSING**
75 ml (5 tbsp) mayonnaise
30 ml (2 tbsp) olive oil and wine vinegar
5 ml (1 tsp) chilli powder
10 ml (2 tsp) mango chutney (optional)
4 drops of Tabasco sauce
coarse sea salt and freshly ground black pepper

**1** Remove the core from the cabbage and slice finely. Combine the cabbage, carrot and celery in a large bowl.
**2** To make the dressing, put all the ingredients in a screw-top jar and shake vigorously to combine.
**3** Pour the dressing over the salad and toss well. Cover and leave to stand in a cool place for several hours or overnight if possible, to enable the flavours of the dressing to be absorbed.
**4** Just before serving, toss the pecans or walnuts into the salad, if using. Sprinkle with a little paprika and garnish with chervil or parsley.

## VARIATION
To make the dressing suitable for vegans, substitute 125 g (4 oz) tofu for the mayonnaise. Put all the dressing ingredients into a food processor or blender and work until smooth, adding a little more oil to thin if necessary.

# HOT TUNA NIÇOISE

PREPARATION TIME: 20 MINUTES ◆ COOKING TIME: 30 MINUTES ◆ FREEZING: NOT SUITABLE ◆ 540 CALS PER SERVING ◆ SERVES 4

300 g (10 oz) French beans
salt and freshly ground black pepper
450 g (1 lb) new potatoes, halved
250 g (9 oz) cherry tomatoes, halved
50 g (2 oz) pitted black olives, halved
60 ml (4 tbsp) dressing (see Cook's Tip)
30 ml (2 tbsp) olive oil
1 large red onion, sliced
two 200 g cans tuna chunks in oil,
   drained
30 ml (2 tbsp) chopped fresh parsley

1 Cook the beans in boiling salted water for 3–4 minutes. Drain and refresh under cold running water. Cook the potatoes in boiling salted water for about 15 minutes until just tender; drain.
2 Toss the beans, tomatoes and olives in the dressing, season to taste and arrange on a serving platter.
3 Heat the oil in a large non-stick frying pan, add the potato and fry for 3–4 minutes. Add the onion and cook, stirring, for 5–7 minutes or until the potato is golden and the onion beginning to caramelise. Lower the heat and stir in the tuna and parsley.
4 Spoon the mixture on top of the bean and tomato salad and serve immediately.

**COOK'S TIP**

Make whatever dressing you fancy for this salad, or try one of the many ready-made varieties now widely available.

# PINK TROUT WITH ALMOND AND HERB PURÉE

PREPARATION TIME: 20 MINUTES ◆ COOKING TIME: 10-14 MINUTES ◆ FREEZING: NOT SUITABLE ◆ 745 CALS PER SERVING ◆ SERVES 4

**Pink-fleshed trout has the colour of salmon, but a much more delicate taste.**

50 g (2 oz) butter
15 ml (1 tbsp) lemon juice
10 ml (2 tsp) paprika
4 pink-fleshed trout, each about 300 g
   (10 oz), cleaned
75 g (3 oz) blanched whole almonds
1 garlic clove
30 ml (2 tbsp) freshly grated Parmesan
   cheese
50 g (2 oz) fresh parsley sprigs
150 ml (¼ pint) light olive oil
30 ml (2 tbsp) fromage frais
salt and freshly ground black pepper
parsley sprigs, to garnish

1 Place the butter, lemon juice and paprika in a saucepan over a low heat until the butter has melted. Using a sharp knife, make diagonal slashes on both sides of each trout. Place in a foil-lined grill pan and brush with the melted butter.
2 Spread the almonds on a baking sheet and place under a preheated grill for 2–3 minutes, turning frequently, until toasted and golden. Place 50 g (2 oz) of the toasted almonds in a food processor or blender with the garlic, Parmesan, parsley, oil, fromage frais and salt and pepper and blend until smooth. Roughly chop the remaining almonds and set aside.

3 Grill the trout for 5–7 minutes on each side or until opaque and cooked through, basting occasionally with the melted butter.
4 Transfer the trout to warm serving plates. Spoon a good dollop of almond and herb purée on to each plate and scatter over the remaining toasted almonds. Garnish with parsley and serve immediately.

**VARIATION**

Replace the almonds with hazelnuts. Add 15 ml (1 tbsp) hazelnut oil to the olive oil.

# ROASTED ASPARAGUS SALAD

PREPARATION TIME: **10** MINUTES ◆ COOKING TIME: **ABOUT 20** MINUTES ◆ FREEZING: **NOT SUITABLE** ◆ **275–180** CALS PER SERVING ◆ SERVES **4–6**

**Roasting is a great way to cook asparagus. There is no water added so the true flavour of the vegetable is not 'diluted'. The cooking time applies to stalks of medium thickness and should be increased if you are using fatter asparagus stems.**

700 g (1½ lb) asparagus spears
90 ml (6 tbsp) olive oil
45 ml (3 tbsp) lemon juice
coarse sea salt and freshly ground black
    pepper
Parmesan cheese shavings (optional)
rocket leaves and lemon wedges, to
    serve

**1** Preheat the oven to 200°C (400°F) Mark 6. Trim the asparagus spears and use a potato peeler to peel the bottom 5 cm (2 inches) of each stalk. Arrange in a shallow roasting pan.
**2** Spoon 60 ml (4 tbsp) of the oil over the asparagus and shake lightly to mix. Roast in the oven for about 20 minutes, until just tender, turning once during cooking. Leave to cool.
**3** To serve, spoon the remaining oil over the asparagus and sprinkle with the lemon juice. Season with salt and pepper and toss lightly.
**4** Transfer to a serving dish and sprinkle with finely pared shavings of Parmesan, if wished.

**5** Serve with rocket leaves and lemon wedges.

# CLEMENTINE, CHICORY AND PEANUT SALAD

PREPARATION TIME: **20** MINUTES ◆ FREEZING: **NOT SUITABLE** ◆ **395** CALS PER SERVING ◆ SERVES **4**

4 clementines
4 spring onions, sliced
2 heads of chicory, leaves shredded
6 radishes, trimmed and quartered
125 g (4 oz) natural peanuts
30 ml (2 tbsp) snipped fresh chives

**PEANUT DRESSING**
30 ml (2 tbsp) peanut butter
60 ml (4 tbsp) sunflower oil
30 ml (2 tbsp) white wine
15 ml (1 tbsp) white wine vinegar
15 ml (1 tbsp) light soy sauce

**1** Carefully remove any white membrane from the clementines and divide into segments. Place in a salad bowl.
**2** Add the spring onion, chicory leaves and radish and lightly toss together.
**3** To make the dressing, place all the ingredients in a screw-top jar and shake vigorously until well combined.
**4** Pour the dressing over the salad and toss to mix. Scatter over the peanuts and chives. Serve immediately.

## COOK'S TIP

If making the salad in advance, prepare all the vegetables and fruit. Store in plastic bags in the refrigerator until ready to serve, then toss in the dressing.

## VARIATION

Replace the chicory with ½ red cabbage, very finely shredded; replace the chives with 30 ml (2 tbsp) sultanas.

# MADRAS HADDOCK FILLETS WITH RICE AND PEAS

PREPARATION TIME: **10** MINUTES ◆ COOKING TIME: **25** MINUTES ◆ FREEZING: NOT SUITABLE ◆ **550** CALS PER SERVING ◆ SERVES **4**

4 haddock fillets, each about 125 g (4 oz), skinned
1 egg
1/2 onion, grated
5 cm (2 inch) piece fresh root ginger, grated
5 ml (1 tsp) each turmeric and ground coriander
2.5 ml (1/2 tsp) chilli powder
juice of 1/2 lemon

**RICE**
50 g (2 oz) butter
1/2 onion, chopped
10 ml (2 tsp) cumin seeds
200 g (7 oz) long-grain white rice
juice of 1/2 lemon
125 g (4 oz) frozen peas
30 ml (2 tbsp) chopped fresh coriander

**1** First prepare the rice. Melt the butter in a saucepan, add the onion and cumin seeds and cook, stirring, until soft.
**2** Add the rice and stir until it is thoroughly coated in the butter. Add the lemon juice, 450 ml (3/4 pint) water and 5 ml (1 tsp) salt and bring to the boil. Stir in the peas, cover, turn the heat down as low as possible and cook for 12 minutes. Turn off the heat and leave, covered, for a further 10 minutes or so.
**3** Meanwhile, lay the haddock fillets on a plate. Break the egg into a bowl and add the onion, ginger, spices, salt and freshly ground black pepper to taste and lemon juice. Pour over the fish, turning to coat, and leave until the rice is almost ready.

**4** Dredge the haddock fillets with plain flour to coat quite thickly and form a batter with the marinade. Heat a 1 cm (1/2 inch) depth of oil in a frying pan, add the fish and fry for 2–3 minutes on each side. Drain on kitchen paper and keep hot.
**5** Meanwhile, grind black pepper over the rice, sprinkle with the coriander, then fork up lightly. Divide between warm serving plates and top with the fish. Garnish with lemon wedges to serve.

**COOK'S TIP**
If you have time, prepare the marinade first and marinate the fish for up to 1 hour.

# SMOKED HADDOCK FISH CAKES WITH PARSLEY SAUCE

PREPARATION TIME: **20** MINUTES ◆ COOKING TIME: **35–40** MINUTES ◆ FREEZING: SUITABLE ◆ **530** CALS PER SERVING ◆ SERVES **4**

350 g (12 oz) undyed smoked haddock
450 g (1 lb) potatoes, cut into chunks
salt and freshly ground black pepper
6 rashers rindless streaky bacon
25 g (1 oz) butter
4 spring onions, chopped
15 ml (1 tbsp) lemon juice
15 ml (1 tbsp) chopped fresh parsley
1 egg, beaten
50 g (2 oz) fresh white breadcrumbs

**PARSLEY SAUCE**
300 ml (1/2 pint) milk
1 slice onion
1 bay leaf
6 peppercorns
45g (1 3/4 oz) butter
20 ml (1 1/2 tbsp) plain flour
50 g (2 oz) chopped fresh parsley

**1** Place the haddock in a pan and add sufficient water just to cover. Bring to the boil, then lower the heat and poach for 15–20 minutes, until the fish flakes.
**2** Meanwhile, cook the potatoes in boiling salted water until tender. Drain and mash until smooth.
**3** Cook the bacon under a preheated grill until just brown. Chop finely.
**4** Drain and flake the fish. Mix with the mashed potato and bacon.
**5** Melt the butter in a small pan, add the spring onion and cook until beginning to soften. Add to the fish mixture with the lemon juice, parsley and seasoning. Add just enough egg to bind the mixture; it must be firm enough to shape.

**6** With floured hands, shape the mixture into 8 cakes. Brush with egg and coat with breadcrumbs. Chill for 30 minutes.
**7** To make the Parsley Sauce, put the milk in a pan with the onion, bay leaf and peppercorns. Bring to the boil, turn off the heat, cover and leave to infuse for 10 minutes. Melt 20 g (3/4 oz) of the butter in a pan, add the flour and cook, stirring, for 1–2 minutes. Remove from the heat and strain in the hot milk, whisking well. Bring to the boil, stirring. Stir in the parsley, remaining butter and seasoning; keep warm.
**8** Shallow-fry the fish cakes for about 5 minutes each side until golden. Serve with the Parsley Sauce.

# ITALIAN CHEESE AND POTATO SALAD

PREPARATION TIME: **10** MINUTES ◆ COOKING TIME: **10** MINUTES ◆ FREEZING: NOT SUITABLE ◆ **315** CALS PER SERVING ◆ SERVES **4**

350 g (12 oz) new potatoes
175 g (6 oz) creamy Italian cheese, eg taleggio or Gorgonzola, roughly chopped
25 g (1 oz) hazelnuts, toasted
30 ml (2 tbsp) hazelnut or walnut oil
30 ml (2 tbsp) olive oil
salt and freshly ground black pepper

**1** Cook the potatoes in boiling salted water for 10 minutes, until tender. Drain and cut in half.
**2** Place the cheese and warm potatoes in a large mixing bowl.
**3** Mix together the hazelnuts and oils. Season well and toss through the salad. Serve immediately, or place under a preheated grill to melt the cheese.

# BITTER GREEN SALAD WITH CITRUS DRESSING

PREPARATION TIME: **15** MINUTES ◆ FREEZING: NOT SUITABLE ◆ **125** CALS PER SERVING ◆ SERVES **4**

**This delicious salad can be served as a separate course or with rich meats.**

225 g (8 oz) mixed bitter salad leaves, eg rocket, watercress, batavia, sorrel, young spinach (see Cook's Tip)

**CITRUS DRESSING**
grated rind and juice of 1 orange and 1 lime
30 ml (2 tbsp) sunflower oil
15 ml (1 tbsp) walnut oil
15 ml (1 tbsp) dark soy sauce
15 ml (1 tbsp) clear honey
salt and freshly ground black pepper

**1** Wash all the salad leaves and tear into smaller pieces, if necessary. Spin dry in a salad spinner, then transfer to a plastic bag with any water still clinging to the leaves. Leave in the fridge for about 30 minutes to crisp up the salad.
**2** To make the dressing, place 15 ml (1 tbsp) each grated rind in a small bowl with 30 ml (2 tbsp) orange juice and 15 ml (1 tbsp) lime juice. Add the oils, soy sauce and honey and whisk well. Add seasoning to taste. Just before serving the salad, strain the dressing through a fine sieve.
**3** To serve, place the salad leaves in a bowl and pour over the dressing. Toss well and serve immediately.

COOK'S TIP
Rocket is expensive to buy, but grows like a weed in the garden. Try planting some – it will even grow in a window box!

VARIATION
Make the salad with chicory leaves and radicchio for a more colourful version. Add sprigs of herbs, such as basil, chervil, dill and tarragon.

# STIR-FRIED KING PRAWNS ON SESAME NOODLES

PREPARATION TIME: **10** MINUTES ◆ COOKING TIME: **10** MINUTES ◆ FREEZING: NOT SUITABLE ◆ **410** CALS PER SERVING ◆ SERVES **4**

16 raw king prawns
10 ml (2 tsp) sesame seeds
5 ml (1 tsp) salt
150 g (5 oz) mangetout, trimmed
250 g (9 oz) egg noodles
30 ml (2 tbsp) vegetable oil
4 spring onions, chopped
7.5 cm (3 inch) piece fresh root ginger, grated
juice of 1 lime
10 ml (2 tsp) shredded fresh coriander leaves
30 ml (2 tbsp) soy sauce
5 ml (1 tsp) sesame oil
coriander leaves and lime wedges, to garnish

**1** If the prawns are frozen, thaw them in advance; if you buy them fresh, keep them refrigerated until you are ready to cook.
**2** Put the sesame seeds in a small heavy-based pan and shake over a medium heat until they begin to turn golden and develop a toasted aroma. Tip out on to a saucer.
**3** Bring a large pan of water to the boil, add the salt and mangetout and bring back to the boil. Simmer for 30 seconds, then drop in the egg noodles, turn off the heat and leave to stand for 6 minutes.
**4** Meanwhile, heat the oil in a wide frying pan. Add the prawns and cook for

1½–2 minutes. Sprinkle with the spring onion and ginger, turn and cook for a further 1½ minutes. Add the lime juice and sprinkle with the coriander.
**5** Drain the noodles and mangetout, add the soy sauce, sesame oil and toasted sesame seeds and toss well. Transfer to a warm serving dish or individual plates, arrange the prawns on top and garnish with coriander and lime wedges. Serve immediately, with prawn crackers if desired.

# GREEN CURRY OF FISH AND SEAFOOD

PREPARATION TIME: **30** MINUTES ◆ COOKING TIME: ABOUT **10** MINUTES ◆ FREEZING: NOT SUITABLE ◆ **610-410** CALS PER SERVING ◆ SERVES **4–6**

**The best way to clean a squid is under the cold tap. Don't be put off by the preparation – it's not as unpleasant as it sounds! Don't overcook squid or it will be tough.**

350 g (12 oz) squid
350 g (12 oz) raw prawns
450 g (1 lb) firm white fish fillets, eg cod, haddock, halibut, monkfish
15 ml (1 tbsp) vegetable oil
45 ml (3 tbsp) green curry paste
1 lemon grass stalk
few kaffir lime leaves, shredded
450 ml (¾ pint) coconut milk
30 ml (2 tbsp) nam pla (Thai fish sauce)
squeeze of lime juice
chopped coriander, to garnish

**1** Rinse the squid then, holding the body in one hand, firmly pull the tentacles with the other hand. As you do so, the soft contents of the body will come out. Cut the tentacles just in front of the eyes and discard the body contents. Cut the tentacles into small pieces.
**2** Squeeze out the plastic-like quill from the body and discard. Rinse the body under cold running water, making sure that it is clean inside. Rub off the fine dark skin, then cut the body into rings or small rectangular pieces.
**3** Peel the prawns, leaving the small fan-like piece at the end of the tail attached. Using a small sharp knife, make a shallow slit along the outer curve from

the tail to the head end and remove the dark intestinal vein. Rinse under cold running water, drain and pat dry with kitchen paper.
**4** Cut the fish fillets into large pieces.
**5** Heat the oil in a large frying pan, add the curry paste and cook for 2 minutes, stirring. Bruise the lemon grass and add to the pan with the lime leaves. Add the coconut milk and bring to the boil, stirring.
**6** Reduce the heat to a simmer, then add the white fish, prawns and squid. Cook for 1–2 minutes, until opaque.
**7** Add the nam pla and lime juice, garnish with chopped coriander and serve immediately.

# ULTIMATE CAESAR SALAD

PREPARATION TIME: **10** MINUTES ◆ COOKING TIME: **15** MINUTES ◆ FREEZING: **NOT** SUITABLE ◆ **800** CALS PER SERVING ◆ SERVES **4**

3 garlic cloves
3 eggs
15 ml (1 tbsp) lemon juice
5 ml (1 tsp) English mustard powder
5 ml (1 tsp) Worcestershire sauce
50 g (2 oz) freshly grated Parmesan cheese
200 ml (7 fl oz) olive oil
1 small baguette, thinly sliced
350 g (12 oz) small Cos or Romaine lettuce
50 g can anchovy fillets, drained and chopped
Parmesan shavings, to serve

**1** Preheat the oven to 200°C (400°F) Mark 6. Place 1 garlic clove, 1 egg, the lemon juice, mustard powder, Worcestershire sauce and Parmesan cheese in a food processor and blend until smooth. With the machine running, slowly blend in 150 ml (¼ pint) of the oil. Cover and set aside.
**2** Brush the baguette slices with the remaining oil and rub with the remaining garlic cloves. Arrange in a single layer on a baking sheet and cook in the oven for 4–5 minutes or until crisp.
**3** Hard-boil the remaining eggs. Leave to cool, then shell and halve. Tear the lettuce into pieces and place in a salad bowl. Add the anchovy, egg and croûtons, pour over the dressing and toss well. Garnish with Parmesan shavings (pared from a block with a vegetable peeler) to serve.

# HOT AVOCADO SALAD

PREPARATION TIME: **5** MINUTES ◆ COOKING TIME: **20** MINUTES ◆ FREEZING: **NOT** SUITABLE ◆ **370** CALS PER SERVING ◆ SERVES **4**

2 ripe avocados, roughly chopped
few drops Tabasco or chilli sauce
1 small onion, very finely chopped
45 ml (3 tbsp) lime or lemon juice
1 garlic clove, crushed
salt and freshly ground black pepper
4 Little Gem lettuce, halved lengthways
2 beefsteak tomatoes, sliced
175 g (6 oz) Gouda cheese, sliced
salsa and potato wedges, to serve

**1** Preheat the oven to 220°C (425°F) Mark 7. Place the avocados, Tabasco or chilli sauce, onion, lime or lemon juice and garlic in a bowl and mash well. Season to taste.
**2** Cut a little of the core away from each lettuce, then place cut side up in an ovenproof dish. Tuck the tomato and two-thirds of the cheese between the leaves. Season to taste.
**3** Spoon the avocado mixture into the centre and scatter over the remaining cheese. Cook in the oven for 10 minutes or until bubbling. Serve immediately, with salsa and potato wedges.

# SPICY SQUID SALAD

PREPARATION TIME: 20 MINUTES ◆ COOKING TIME: 4 MINUTES ◆ FREEZING: NOT SUITABLE ◆ 120 CALS PER SERVING ◆ SERVES 4

450 g (1 lb) squid, sliced
30 ml (2 tbsp) each finely chopped red chilli and fresh coriander or mint
5 ml (1 tsp) sugar
45 ml (3 tbsp) sherry vinegar
15 ml (1 tbsp) olive oil
8–10 fat spring onions, halved lengthways
lime halves, to serve

1 Clean the squid (see page 44), then cut the body into rings.
2 Mix together the chilli and coriander or mint, sugar, vinegar and oil. Add the squid and toss well to coat.
3 Thread the squid and spring onion on to 4 skewers. Cook under a preheated grill or on the barbecue for 3–4 minutes, turning occasionally.
4 Serve with any remaining dressing and lime halves to squeeze over the fish before eating.

## COOK'S TIP
If you are squeamish, look out for ready-prepared or frozen squid.

## VARIATION
Replace the squid with raw prawns or cubes of firm fish, such as swordfish or monkfish.

# SQUID WITH ROASTED TOMATOES AND HERB SALAD

PREPARATION TIME: 20 MINUTES ◆ COOKING TIME: 50-55 MINUTES ◆ FREEZING: NOT SUITABLE ◆ 340 CALS PER SERVING ◆ SERVES 4

575 g (1¼ lb) squid
90 ml (6 tbsp) extra-virgin olive oil
2 garlic cloves
coarse sea salt and freshly ground black pepper
30 ml (2 tbsp) chopped fresh basil
8 small plum tomatoes, halved lengthways
3 rosemary sprigs
about 75 g (3 oz) mixed salad leaves, eg rocket, lambs lettuce (mâche), frisée, chicory
juice of 1 small lemon
handful of freshly torn flat-leaf parsley

1 Preheat the oven to 200°C (400°F) Mark 6.
2 Clean the squid (see page 44). Cut the body pouches into 7.5 cm (3 inch) squares and score a lattice pattern on each. Leave the tentacles whole.
3 Place the squid in a bowl and spoon over 45 ml (3 tbsp) of the oil. Crush the garlic cloves to a paste with a little coarse sea salt. Add to the squid with the basil, season with pepper and mix well. Cover and chill while preparing the tomatoes.
4 Place the tomatoes cut side up in a shallow baking pan. Tuck the rosemary sprigs among them and season liberally with sea salt. Drizzle over the remaining oil. Roast in the oven for 40–45 minutes,

until tender but still holding their shape.
5 To cook the squid, preheat a dry (not oiled) cast-iron griddle over a high heat for 5 minutes. Lower heat to medium.
6 Add the squid to the hot griddle pan in one layer; you may need to cook it in 2 batches. Allow to sizzle undisturbed for 1 minute, then turn each piece and cook the other side for 1 minute. Add to the tomatoes. Discard the rosemary.
7 Put the salad leaves in a serving bowl and top with the squid and tomatoes. Add the lemon juice to the pan and heat, scraping up the sediment as it sizzles. Trickle over the squid and tomatoes and sprinkle with the parsley. Toss lightly and serve immediately.

# SPICED WINTER SALAD

PREPARATION TIME: **15** MINUTES ◆ COOKING TIME: ABOUT **15** MINUTES ◆ FREEZING: **NOT** SUITABLE ◆ **85** CALS PER SERVING ◆ SERVES **8**

300 g (10 oz) cucumber
300 g (10 oz) carrot
450 g (1 lb) white cabbage
15 ml (1 tbsp) sesame oil
2 garlic cloves, crushed
125 g (4 oz) red pepper, cored, seeded and cut into strips
2.5 ml (1/2 tsp) red chilli paste
150 ml (1/4 pint) white wine vinegar
60 ml (4 tbsp) caster sugar
2.5 ml (1/2 tsp) salt

**1** Halve the cucumber and scoop out the seeds with a teaspoon. Place the carrot and cabbage in a food processor with the shredding disc attached. Process until shredded, then remove and set aside. Shred the cucumber and set aside.
**2** Heat the oil in a large frying pan, add the garlic and cook for 1 minute. Stir-fry the cabbage, carrot and red pepper in batches with the chilli paste. Transfer to a large bowl and toss together.
**3** Add the vinegar, sugar and salt to the pan, bring to the boil and bubble for 5 minutes. Add to the cabbage mixture.
**4** Stir in the cucumber and leave to cool; cover and chill. This salad can be kept in the fridge for up to 4 days.

# GRAPE, AVOCADO AND TOMATO SALAD

PREPARATION TIME: **10** MINUTES ◆ FREEZING: **NOT** SUITABLE ◆ **150** CALS PER SERVING ◆ SERVES **6**

15 ml (1 tbsp) cider or wine vinegar
5 ml (1 tsp) caster sugar
salt and freshly ground black pepper
60 ml (4 tbsp) walnut oil
1 ripe avocado, diced
150 g (5 oz) each seedless grapes and cherry tomatoes
about 200 g (7 oz) mixed salad leaves

**1** Whisk together the vinegar, sugar, seasoning and oil in a large salad bowl.
**2** Add the avocado, grapes, tomatoes and salad leaves and toss well. Serve immediately.

# MINTED SCALLOPS WITH SUMMER VEGETABLES

PREPARATION TIME: **10** MINUTES ◆ COOKING TIME: **20** MINUTES ◆ FREEZING: NOT SUITABLE ◆ **615** CALS PER SERVING ◆ SERVES **4**

45 ml (3 tbsp) chopped fresh mint
100 ml (4 fl oz) vinaigrette
550 g (1¼ lb) shelled scallops or salmon fillet (see Cook's Tip)
salt and freshly ground black pepper
10 ml (2 tsp) olive oil
225 g (8 oz) baby new potatoes
200 g (7 oz) baby carrots
125 g (4 oz) broad beans
125 g (4 oz) asparagus spears
175 g (6 oz) fresh peas
125 g (4 oz) mangetout
15 ml (1 tbsp) vegetable oil

1  Whisk the mint into the vinaigrette and set aside. Pat the scallops dry and slice into 2–3 rounds, or skin and slice the salmon fillet. Season and brush with the olive oil. Set aside.
2  Cook the potatoes in boiling salted water for 10 minutes or until just tender. Drain and transfer to a bowl. While still hot, add half of the vinaigrette and toss well; leave to cool.
3  Cook the remaining vegetables separately in boiling salted water until just tender. Drain, then plunge them into a bowl of iced water to refresh. Leave to cool, then drain well. Add to the potatoes, toss well and season to taste.
4  Heat the vegetable oil in a non-stick

frying pan and quickly fry the scallops or salmon fillet in batches for 1–2 minutes; they should be golden on the outside and just tender on the inside. Serve immediately on a bed of the vegetables with the remaining vinaigrette spooned over.

## COOK'S TIP

If using salmon fillet, replace the mint with 30 ml (2 tbsp) chopped fresh dill.

# PEPPERED PRAWN SALAD WITH LIME AND CHILLI

PREPARATION TIME: **20** MINUTES ◆ COOKING TIME: **2-3** MINUTES ◆ FREEZING: NOT SUITABLE ◆ **160** CALS PER SERVING ◆ SERVES **4**

15 ml (1 tbsp) coriander seeds
5 ml (1 tsp) black peppercorns
juice of 3 limes, about 90 ml (6 tbsp)
10 ml (2 tsp) clear honey
5 ml (1 tsp) salt and freshly ground black pepper
1 red chilli, seeded and finely chopped
350 g (12 oz) cooked peeled king prawns
1 large avocado, sliced
1 bunch of spring onions, sliced
175 g (6 oz) cucumber, thinly sliced
handful of fresh coriander, roughly torn
small naan breads, to serve

1  Crush the coriander seeds and peppercorns. Sieve to remove the husks, then mix with the lime juice, honey and salt. Stir in the chilli, then pour the mixture over the prawns.
2  Add the avocado, spring onion and cucumber to the prawn mixture. Stir in the coriander and season to taste. Serve immediately, on small, warmed naan breads.

# PEASANT BREAD AND CHEESE SALAD

**PREPARATION TIME: 25 MINUTES** ◆ **FREEZING: NOT SUITABLE** ◆ **295 CALS PER SERVING** ◆ **SERVES 6**

175 g (6 oz) ciabatta or pugliese bread
700 g (1½ lb) plum tomatoes
175 g (6 oz) cheese, eg buffalo
  mozzarella, Gorgonzola or Brie
450 g (1 lb) cucumber
30 ml (2 tbsp) red wine vinegar
60 ml (4 tbsp) olive oil
30 ml (2 tbsp) chopped fresh basil
salt and freshly ground black pepper
50 g (2 oz) sun-dried tomatoes in oil,
  drained and thinly sliced
50 g (2 oz) pitted black olives, eg
  Kalamata
125 g (4 oz) young spinach or lambs
  lettuce
fresh basil leaves, to garnish

**1** Cut the bread into 2.5 cm (1 inch) dice, cover with 150 ml (¼ pint) water and leave to soak for 5 minutes. Gently squeeze the bread to remove excess water; set aside.
**2** Cut the plum tomatoes, cheese and cucumber into rough chunks.
**3** Mix together the vinegar, oil and chopped basil; season to taste.
**4** Place the bread, all the tomato, cheese, cucumber, olives and spinach or lettuce in a bowl. Pour over the dressing and toss well. Arrange on a serving dish and garnish with basil leaves.

# MIXED GREEN SALAD WITH ORANGE DRESSING

**PREPARATION TIME: 15 MINUTES** ◆ **FREEZING: NOT SUITABLE** ◆ **130 CALS PER SERVING** ◆ **SERVES 4**

2 oranges
50 ml (2 fl oz) extra-virgin olive oil
30 ml (2 tbsp) cider vinegar
10 ml (2 tsp) poppy seeds
salt and freshly ground black pepper
1 small avocado, sliced
4 spring onions, sliced
about 100 g (3½ oz) mixed salad leaves

**1** Grate the rind and squeeze the juice of 1 orange. Cut the remaining orange into thin slices. Place the grated rind and juice in a bowl, add the oil, vinegar and poppy seeds and whisk well. Season to taste (see Cook's Tips).
**2** Place the avocado, spring onion, salad leaves and sliced orange in a large bowl, add 45 ml (3 tbsp) dressing and toss together lightly. Serve immediately.

## COOK'S TIPS

Any remaining dressing can be stored in a screw-top jar in the fridge.
For calorie counters, 15 ml (1 tbsp) dressing is 43 calories.

# SEAFOOD AND MUSHROOM PAELLA

PREPARATION TIME: **15** MINUTES ◆ COOKING TIME: **1¹/₂** HOURS ◆ FREEZING: NOT SUITABLE ◆ **605** CALS PER SERVING ◆ SERVES **12**

1.1 litres (2 pints) fish stock
300 ml (¹/₂ pint) white wine
1.25 ml (¹/₄ tsp) saffron strands
1 bay leaf
450 g (1 lb) fish fillets, eg cod, salmon or haddock, skinned
125 g (4 oz) wild rice
50 ml (2 fl oz) olive oil
225 g (8 oz) onion, finely chopped
125 g (4 oz) celery, finely chopped
3 garlic cloves, crushed
350 g (12 oz) long-grain rice
salt and freshly ground black pepper
25 g (1 oz) butter
280 g jar wild mushrooms in oil, drained
125 g (4 oz) brown-cap mushrooms
2 bunches of watercress
50 g (2 oz) cooked peeled king prawns

**1** Place the stock, wine, saffron, bay leaf and fish in a large frying pan, cover and slowly bring to the boil. Turn off the heat and leave for 10 minutes. Drain the fish, reserving the stock, and flake into large pieces.
**2** Cook the wild rice in boiling salted water for about 40 minutes or until tender. Drain and set aside. Preheat the oven to 200°C (400°F) Mark 6.
**3** Heat the oil in a large flameproof casserole, add the onion, celery and garlic and cook for 7–10 minutes or until soft. Add the long-grain rice and stir over heat for 1–2 minutes. Add the reserved stock and bring to the boil. Season, then cover and cook in the oven for

30 minutes.
**4** Melt the butter in a large saucepan, add all the mushrooms and cook for 1–2 minutes. Remove from the pan and set aside. Add the watercress to the pan and stir for 1–2 minutes or until wilted.
**5** Gently stir the wild rice, mushrooms, watercress, fish and prawns into the long-grain rice. Adjust the seasoning, cover and return to the oven for 1 minute. Serve immediately.

# SEAFOOD PESTO CHOWDER

PREPARATION TIME: **20** MINUTES ◆ COOKING TIME: **50–55** MINUTES ◆ FREEZING: SUITABLE (STEP 2) ◆ **330** CALS PER SERVING ◆ SERVES **8**

50 g (2 oz) butter
225 g (8 oz) onion, roughly chopped
30 ml (2 tbsp) plain flour
450 ml (³/₄ pint) fish stock
150 ml (¹/₄ pint) white wine
142 ml carton double cream
50 g (2 oz) freshly grated Parmesan cheese
salt and freshly ground black pepper
125 g (4 oz) shelled scallops
300 g (10 oz) each salmon fillet and smoked haddock fillet
350 g (12 oz) tomato, skinned and seeded
50 g (2 oz) chopped fresh basil or parsley
125 g (4 oz) cooked peeled prawns

**1** Melt the butter in a large heavy-based saucepan, add the onion and cook for 10 minutes or until soft and golden. Add the flour and cook, stirring, for 1 minute.
**2** Add the stock, wine and cream and bring to the boil, whisking constantly until smooth, then simmer gently for 10 minutes. Remove from the heat, stir in the Parmesan cheese and season well. Preheat the oven 180°C (350°F) Mark 4.
**3** Rinse the scallops well under cold running water; pat dry. (If they are large, cut in half horizontally.) Cut the fish into 5 cm (2 inch) strips and place in a large ovenproof dish in a single layer. Pour over the sauce, cover loosely with foil and cook in the oven for 25–30 minutes

or until just tender. Add the scallops after 10–15 minutes.
**4** Meanwhile, cut the tomato flesh into strips. Stir the basil or parsley, tomato and prawns into the chowder. Season to taste and serve immediately.

# SPICED POTATOES

PREPARATION TIME: **10** MINUTES ◆ COOKING TIME: ABOUT **40** MINUTES ◆ FREEZING: NOT SUITABLE ◆ **330** CALS PER SERVING ◆ SERVES **4**

**Choose firm potatoes with a good flavour. Look out for Charlotte, La Ratte, Pink Fir Apple, or any other interesting varieties available.**

700 g (1½ lb) small or baby potatoes
coarse sea salt
2 mild green chillies
about 45 ml (3 tbsp) olive oil
3 garlic cloves, finely chopped
30 ml (2 tbsp) coriander seeds, crushed
15 ml (1 tbsp) black peppercorns, crushed
2 spring onions, thinly sliced
50 g (2 oz) butter
large handful of watercress sprigs, to serve (optional)

**1** Preheat the oven to 220°C (425°F) Mark 7. Place the potatoes in a single layer in a roasting pan, sprinkle with salt and roast in the oven for about 40 minutes or until tender. (If the potatoes are very small they may take less time.)
**2** Meanwhile, slice the chillies, removing the seeds if a milder flavour is preferred.
**3** Heat the oil in a small saucepan, add the garlic and cook until just beginning to brown. Add the coriander seeds and peppercorns and cook for 1 minute. Add the chilli, turn off the heat and leave to infuse while the potatoes are cooking.
**4** When the potatoes are cooked, add the spring onion and butter to the spice mixture and heat gently until the butter has just melted.
**5** Pile the potatoes in a warm serving dish. Pour over most of the spiced butter and toss together. Scatter a generous handful of watercress on top, if wished, and pour over the remaining butter. Serve immediately.

### COOK'S TIP

If you're short of time, you could steam or boil the potatoes instead of baking them, but the extra cooking time is worth the heavenly contrast of crisp-baked skin and buttery juices!

# SHREDDED BRUSSELS SPROUTS WITH BACON

PREPARATION TIME: **10** MINUTES ◆ COOKING TIME: **7** MINUTES ◆ FREEZING: NOT SUITABLE ◆ **300** CALS PER SERVING ◆ SERVES **4**

**These buttery shredded sprouts are stir-fried with crispy cubes of bacon. They make an interesting change from traditional boiled or steamed Brussels sprouts and look so attractive. Use lightly smoked bacon, buying it in a piece if possible.**

175 g (6 oz) piece smoked bacon, cut into small cubes
50 g (2 oz) butter
700 g (1½ lb) Brussels sprouts, trimmed and shredded
60 ml (4 tbsp) double cream
10 ml (2 tsp) caraway seeds
salt and freshly ground black pepper
freshly grated nutmeg

**1** Heat a wok or frying pan and add the bacon. Cook over a high heat, stirring constantly, until the fat runs and the bacon is browning and crisp. Stir in the butter.
**2** Toss in the shredded Brussels sprouts and stir-fry over a high heat for 2–3 minutes, until they begin to wilt. Pour in the cream, add the caraway seeds and stir-fry for 1 minute. Season with salt, pepper and nutmeg. Transfer to a warm serving dish. Serve immediately.

### COOK'S TIP

Cubed gammon would be good instead of bacon but you will need to fry it in a little butter rather than dry-fry.

### VARIATION

Replace the Brussels sprouts with Savoy cabbage, or white cabbage.

# THAI-STYLE PRAWN AND PUMPKIN CURRY

**PREPARATION TIME: 20 MINUTES ◆ COOKING TIME: ABOUT 20 MINUTES ◆ FREEZING: NOT SUITABLE ◆ 675 CALS PER SERVING ◆ SERVES 4**

225 g (8 oz) button onions
30 ml (2 tbsp) oil
225 g (8 oz) squash, eg pumpkin, etc, chopped
2.5 cm (1 inch) piece fresh root ginger, sliced
30 ml (2 tbsp) Thai red or mild Indian curry paste
600 ml (1 pint) thin coconut milk
10 ml (2 tsp) sugar
225 g (8 oz) cooked peeled prawns
25 g (1 oz) fresh spinach or basil leaves
juice of 1 lime
225 g (8 oz) broad rice or thread egg noodles
2-3 spring onions, shredded, to garnish

**1** Halve the button onions if large. Heat the oil in a wok or large non-stick frying pan, add the onion, squash and ginger and fry for 5–7 minutes or until golden brown.

**2** Stir in the curry paste, then add the coconut milk and sugar. Bring to the boil then simmer the mixture, uncovered, for 7–10 minutes or until the onion and squash are tender.

**3** Remove from the heat and stir in the prawns and spinach or basil. Add a little fresh lime juice to taste.

**4** Cook the noodles in a large pan of boiling salted water according to packet instructions. Drain well and serve immediately with the curry, garnished with shredded spring onion. Accompany with chilli sauce, if wished.

# LOBSTER WITH BASIL MAYONNAISE

**PREPARATION TIME: 30 MINUTES ◆ COOKING TIME: 8 MINUTES ◆ FREEZING: NOT SUITABLE ◆ 550 CALS PER SERVING ◆ SERVES 4**

4 cooked lobsters, each about 450 g (1 lb)
50 g (2 oz) rocket leaves, to serve

**BASIL MAYONNAISE**
2 egg yolks
5 ml (1 tsp) Dijon mustard
30 ml (2 tbsp) lemon juice
salt and freshly ground black pepper
125 ml (4 fl oz) olive oil
125 ml (4 fl oz) sunflower or groundnut oil
25 g (1 oz) chopped fresh basil

**TOMATO COMPOTE**
30 ml (2 tbsp) olive oil
1 shallot, finely chopped
350 g (12 oz) plum tomatoes, skinned and roughly chopped
15 ml (1 tbsp) sugar
10 ml (2 tsp) balsamic vinegar

**1** First prepare the Basil Mayonnaise. Place the egg yolks in a bowl, add the mustard, 15 ml (1 tbsp) of the lemon juice and a little salt and pepper, and beat well to combine. Continue beating while adding the oils (mixed together), drop by drop. When the mayonnaise begins to thicken, add the oil in a thin steady stream, beating constantly. When the mixture is thick and smooth, add the remaining lemon juice, check the seasoning and stir in the basil. Cover and chill.

**2** To make the Tomato Compote, heat the oil in a pan, add the shallot and cook until softened. Add the tomatoes, sugar and vinegar, stir well, increase the heat and cook for 3 minutes. Transfer the tomatoes to a bowl with a slotted spoon and continue cooking the liquid until reduced and slightly syrupy; add to the tomatoes. Season to taste and leave to cool.

**3** Split the lobsters in half and discard the gravel sac and dark membrane. Snap off the legs and break at the joint. Reserve the smaller claws (and legs if you wish) for garnish. Remove the tail meat and cut into thick slices.

**4** Arrange the lobster and rocket leaves on individual serving plates, placing the claws and legs to one side. Place a spoonful of the mayonnaise and Tomato Compote on each plate. Equip everyone with a lobster pick or fine metal skewer, to extract the meat from the legs.

# CRUNCHY-TOPPED ASPARAGUS AND COURGETTES

PREPARATION TIME: 15 MINUTES ◆ COOKING TIME: 5-6 MINUTES ◆ FREEZING: NOT SUITABLE ◆ 445-300 CALS PER SERVING ◆ SERVES 4-6

**This is a really quick and simple way of serving seasonal vegetables. The crunchy topping provides an excellent contrast to the melting texture of the vegetables below.**

225 g (8 oz) thin asparagus
225 g (8 oz) baby courgettes
salt and freshly ground black pepper
125 g (4 oz) butter
175 g (6 oz) fresh white breadcrumbs
50 g (2 oz) freshly grated Parmesan
   cheese

1 Trim the asparagus and cut into 5 cm (2 inch) lengths. Cut the courgettes into quarters lengthways. Bring a pan of salted water to the boil, add the asparagus and courgette, bring back to the boil and cook for 3 minutes. Drain and refresh immediately in cold water to stop the cooking. Remove with a slotted spoon and drain on kitchen paper.
2 Melt the butter in a frying pan, add the breadcrumbs and fry until lightly golden and crisp. Stir in the Parmesan cheese.
3 Place the asparagus and courgette in a warm shallow flameproof dish. Cover thickly with the crumbs and place under a preheated grill for 2–3 minutes or until the topping is golden and the vegetables are heated through. Serve immediately.

## VARIATION
Replace the asparagus and/or courgettes with any other green vegetable - try broccoli florets, cauliflower, French beans, or even carrots, but be sure to half-cook them before adding the topping.

# POTATO PARSNIP GALETTE

PREPARATION TIME: 25 MINUTES ◆ COOKING TIME: 45 MINUTES ◆ FREEZING: NOT SUITABLE ◆ 380 CALS PER SERVING ◆ SERVES 6

**It is really important to clarify the butter, as it lends a wonderful colour to the potatoes and intensifies the flavour. This galette is a perfect partner to roasts and game dishes.**

900 g (2 lb) firm potato, eg Desirée,
   Romano, Estima or Wilja, thinly sliced
175 g (6 oz) unsalted butter
60 ml (4 tbsp) clear honey
30 ml (2 tbsp) lemon juice
225 g (8 oz) young parsnip, thinly sliced
salt and freshly ground black pepper
freshly grated nutmeg

1 Preheat the oven to 200°C (400°F) Mark 6. Divide the potato into 3 portions – don't worry if they discolour.
2 To clarify the butter, melt it slowly in a small pan, then skim off any white residue or foam; keep warm. Melt the honey and lemon juice together in a small pan; keep warm.
3 Pour 30 ml (2 tbsp) of the butter into a heavy 20 cm (8 inch) non-stick frying pan, suitable for oven use. Arrange one-third of the potato in neat overlapping circles in the pan, seasoning each layer.
4 Cover with half of the parsnip. Brush with the honey mixture and season with nutmeg, salt and pepper.
5 Cover with another third of the potato, brush with butter and season well. Layer the remaining parsnip on top. Brush with the remaining honey mixture and season as before. Finish with the remaining potato and butter; season.
6 Cook on the hob for about 5 minutes or until the underside begins to turn golden brown - test by carefully lifting up the edge with a palette knife.
7 Press down firmly and cover with a lid or buttered kitchen foil. Cook in the oven for 40–45 minutes or until tender and the underside is a deep golden brown.
8 Loosen with a palette knife. Place a warm serving dish over the pan and invert the galette on to the dish. Serve immediately.

# CHICKEN ROASTED IN A LEMON VINAIGRETTE

PREPARATION TIME: **10** MINUTES ◆ COOKING TIME: **40** MINUTES ◆ FREEZING: **NOT** SUITABLE ◆ **360** CALS PER SERVING ◆ SERVES **6**

2 lemons
175 g (6 oz) shallot or onion, thickly
 sliced
30 ml (2 tbsp) balsamic vinegar
30 ml (2 tbsp) sherry vinegar
60 ml (4 tbsp) runny honey
150 ml (¼ pint) olive oil
6 chicken suprêmes or 12 boneless
 thighs, with skin
salt and freshly ground black pepper

**1** Preheat the oven to 200°C (400°F) Mark 6. Grate the rind and squeeze the juice of one lemon; set aside. Thinly slice the remaining lemon. Scatter the lemon slices and shallot or onion over the base of a small roasting pan (see Cook's Tip).
**2** Whisk together the grated lemon rind and juice, vinegars, honey and oil. Place the chicken in the roasting pan, season generously and pour over the lemon vinaigrette.
**3** Cook in the oven, basting regularly, for 35 minutes or until the chicken is golden and cooked through. Transfer the chicken to a warmserving dish and keep warm. Place the roasting pan on the hob, bring the juices to the boil and bubble for 2–3 minutes or until syrupy. Spoon over the chicken to serve.

### COOK'S TIP
Make sure the roasting pan is just large enough to hold the chicken in a single layer.

# CHICKEN CAESAR

PREPARATION TIME: **20** MINUTES ◆ COOKING TIME: **15** MINUTES ◆ FREEZING: **NOT** SUITABLE ◆ **740** CALS PER SERVING ◆ SERVES **4**

6 hen's or 12 quail's eggs
200 g carton crème fraîche (see Cook's
 Tip)
4 sprigs fresh tarragon or pinch of dried
50 g can anchovy fillets
1 garlic clove
dash of Worcestershire sauce
dash of Tabasco sauce
75 g (3 oz) freshly grated Parmesan
 cheese
1 Cos lettuce
½ small ciabatta loaf, cut into 2.5 cm
 (1 inch) cubes
350 g (12 oz) chicken breast fillets,
 skinned
salt and freshly ground black pepper
105 ml (7 tbsp) olive oil

**1** Cook the hen's eggs in a pan of boiling water for 9 minutes (quail's for 3 minutes) until hard-boiled. Plunge them into cold water to cool, then peel.
**2** Meanwhile, put the crème fraîche, tarragon, three-quarters of the anchovy, garlic, Worcestershire sauce, Tabasco sauce and 50 g (2 oz) of the Parmesan in a food processor and process for 5 seconds. Set aside.
**3** Tear the lettuce into bite-size pieces, place in a bowl, cover and chill. Slice the chicken into strips and season.
**4** Heat 45 ml (3 tbsp) of the oil in a wok or large frying pan, add the chicken and stir-fry for 4–5 minutes or until cooked through. Set aside.
**5** Heat the remaining oil in the pan, add the bread and fry until golden. Toss the hot chicken and bread with the lettuce and dressing in a large salad bowl. Cut the eggs into quarters or halves and add to salad with the remaining anchovy and Parmesan. Serve immediately.

### COOK'S TIP
If you use reduced-fat crème fraîche, it reduces the calories to 642 per portion.

### VARIATIONS
Use chopped hot garlic bread instead of the ciabatta croûtons.
This salad is also delicious with grilled bacon instead of chicken.

# COOL-DOWN SALSA

PREPARATION TIME: 30 MINUTES ◆ FREEZING: NOT SUITABLE ◆ 25 CALS PER SERVING ◆ SERVES 6

**A salsa makes a great partner for meat, fish or chicken. This is a delicious fruity variation on the traditional relish made with tomatoes, onions and chillies.**

225 g (8 oz) cucumber
1 red chilli, seeded and chopped
50 g (2 oz) red onion, finely chopped
juice of 2 limes
225 g (8 oz) cantaloupe melon, chopped
225 g (8 oz) Galia or Ogen melon, chopped
30 ml (2 tbsp) chopped fresh flat-leaf parsley
salt and freshly ground black pepper

1  Cut the cucumber in half lengthways, then remove the seeds and roughly chop the flesh.
2  Place in a serving bowl and add the remaining ingredients, with seasoning to taste. Cover and chill until required.

# STEAMED BASIL AND MUSTARD SEED RICE

PREPARATION TIME: 10 MINUTES ◆ COOKING TIME: 25 MINUTES ◆ FREEZING: NOT SUITABLE ◆ 270 CALS PER SERVING ◆ SERVES 4

**Wonderfully fragrant, this rice is a little sticky, but great for mopping up juices. It goes equally well with fish, meat or game. Black mustard seeds impart a nutty flavour to the rice without being too hot. You can, however, use yellow mustard seeds as an alternative - for a hotter flavour.**

225 g (8 oz) basmati rice
30 ml (2 tbsp) sunflower oil
30 ml (2 tbsp) black mustard seeds
5 ml (1 tsp) salt
12 large basil leaves, shredded
basil leaves, to garnish

1  Wash the rice in several changes of cold water or in a sieve under cold running water until the water runs clear; drain well.
2  Heat the oil in a non-stick saucepan, add the mustard seeds and cook for a few minutes, until the seeds start to pop.
3  Stir in the rice, salt and 300 ml (1/2 pint) water. Bring to the boil, stir, then boil rapidly until the water has evaporated and there are steam holes all over the surface.
4  Stir in all but 15 ml (1 tbsp) of the basil and cover very tightly so that no steam can escape. Set on a simmering mat (see Cook's Tip) over a very low heat for 15 minutes for the rice to swell. Fluff up with a fork, adding the reserved basil. Garnish with basil leaves and serve immediately.

### COOK'S TIP

A simmering mat is used here to ensure the heat is very low and evenly distributed. They are available from cookshops and hardware stores. If you do not have one, make sure the heat is kept to a minimum and add a little more water if necessary to prevent the rice sticking.

# CHICKEN WITH OLIVE PASTE

PREPARATION TIME: **20** MINUTES ◆ COOKING TIME: ABOUT **1** HOUR ◆ FREEZING: SUITABLE ◆ **350** CALS PER SERVING ◆ SERVES **4**

4 chicken quarters, about 1.4 kg (3 lb) total weight
30 ml (2 tbsp) olive oil
225 g (8 oz) small onions (not button onions), quartered
2 garlic cloves, crushed
15 ml (1 tbsp) tomato paste
15 ml (1 tbsp) mild paprika
400 g can chopped tomatoes
100 g jar black olive paste (see Cook's Tip)
salt and freshly ground black pepper
1 large green pepper, cored and seeded
400 g can artichoke bottoms or hearts, drained and halved
basil leaves, black olives and chopped parsley, to garnish

1 Cut each chicken quarter in half.
2 Heat the oil in a flameproof casserole and cook the chicken in batches until thoroughly browned on all sides. Remove from the casserole and set aside. Add the onion to the casserole and cook, turning occasionally, until tinged with brown.
3 Add the garlic, tomato paste and paprika and cook for 2 minutes, stirring. Add the tomatoes and olive paste and stir thoroughly. Return the chicken to the casserole and season with salt and pepper. Cover and simmer gently for 45 minutes or until the chicken is tender.
4 Meanwhile, cut the green pepper into very, very thin strips.
5 Add the pepper strips and artichokes to the casserole, cover and cook for 15 minutes or until the pepper strips are tender and the chicken is cooked right through. Adjust the seasoning. Garnish with basil leaves, olives and chopped parsley and serve immediately.

### COOK'S TIP

Some brands of olive paste are very oily. If necessary, drain off a little of the oil from the jar before using.

# PEPPER CHICKEN WITH ORANGE

PREPARATION TIME: **5** MINUTES ◆ COOKING TIME: **25** MINUTES ◆ FREEZING: SUITABLE ◆ **475** CALS PER SERVING ◆ SERVES **6**

salt and freshly ground black pepper
6 chicken breast fillets, with skin
15 ml (1 tbsp) oil
125 g (4 oz) butter, chilled
125 g (4 oz) onion, finely chopped
10 ml (2 tsp) peppercorns in brine
200 ml (7 fl oz) brandy
450 ml (³/₄ pint) chicken stock
pared rind and juice of 1 large orange
flat-leaf parsley, to garnish

1 Preheat the oven to 180°C (350°F) Mark 4. Season the chicken with plenty of ground black pepper.
2 Heat the oil in a non-stick frying pan, add the chicken and cook for about 5 minutes, until golden. Place in an ovenproof dish and cook in the oven for about 20 minutes, until cooked through.
3 Meanwhile, melt 25 g (1 oz) of the butter in the pan, add the onion and peppercorns and cook, stirring, for 10 minutes, until golden and soft. Add the brandy and bubble to reduce by half. Add the stock, orange rind and juice and bubble again for about 7 minutes, until reduced by half.
4 Dice the remaining butter and add to the pan a little at a time, whisking after each addition. Season to taste and keep warm.
5 Pour the sauce over the chicken and garnish with parsley to serve.

# PEAS WITH PESTO

PREPARATION TIME: **5** MINUTES ◆ COOKING TIME: **5** MINUTES ◆ FREEZING: **NOT SUITABLE** ◆ **100** CALS PER SERVING ◆ SERVES **4**

350 g (12 oz) frozen peas
salt and freshly ground black pepper
1 garlic clove, crushed
45 ml (3 tbsp) pesto sauce
fresh basil leaves, to garnish

**1** Place the peas in a pan of boiling salted water, bring back to the boil and boil for 2 minutes.
**2** Drain, reserving 90 ml (6 tbsp) of the cooking liquid. Add the garlic, pesto and peas to the liquid, bring to the boil, season to taste and bubble for 1–2 minutes. Garnish with basil and serve immediately.

### VARIATION

For a main meal, cook 150 g (5 oz) white rice according to packet instructions. Stir into the peas, along with an extra 30 ml (2 tbsp) pesto.

# WILD MUSHROOM RICE

PREPARATION TIME: **20** MINUTES ◆ COOKING TIME: **25** MINUTES ◆ FREEZING: **NOT SUITABLE** ◆ **265** CALS PER SERVING ◆ SERVES **12**

450 g (1 lb) leeks
75 g (3 oz) butter
350 g (12 oz) wild or flat mushrooms, chopped
salt and freshly ground black pepper
450 g (1 lb) long-grain rice
125 g (4 oz) wild rice
fresh chives, to garnish

**1** Halve the leeks lengthways and slice thinly.
**2** Melt the butter in a large heavy-based saucepan, add the leeks and cook, stirring, for 3–4 minutes. Add the mushrooms and cook for 2 minutes, season well and set aside.
**3** Cook the rice according to packet instructions; drain well. Reheat the mushroom and leek mixture and stir into the hot rice. Serve garnished with fresh chives.

# CHICKEN RAREBIT

PREPARATION TIME: **25** MINUTES + COOLING ◆ COOKING TIME: **20** MINUTES ◆ FREEZING: NOT SUITABLE ◆ **570** CALS PER SERVING ◆ SERVES **6**

75-150 ml (5-10 tbsp) milk
350 g (12 oz) mature Cheddar, Gruyère
 or Jarlsberg cheese, grated
15 ml (1 tbsp) plain flour
25 g (1 oz) fresh breadcrumbs
5 ml (1 tsp) English mustard powder
2.5 ml (1/2 tsp) Worcestershire sauce
2 garlic cloves, crushed
salt and freshly ground black pepper
1 egg plus 1 yolk
6 chicken breast fillets, with skin
30 ml (2 tbsp) olive oil
15 ml (1 tbsp) freshly grated Parmesan
 cheese
crispy bacon, to serve

**1** Put the milk and cheese in a saucepan and heat very gently until the cheese has melted. (Use 150 ml [1/4 pint] milk if using Gruyère or Jarlsberg cheese.) Stir in the flour, breadcrumbs and mustard and cook over a low heat, stirring, until the mixture is smooth. Add the Worcestershire sauce, garlic and seasoning to taste. Leave to cool, then beat in all the egg. Cover and chill until required.
**2** Preheat the oven to 200°C (400°F) Mark 6. Make a small horizontal slit in each chicken breast and spoon in about 15 ml (1 tbsp) of the cheese mixture. Reshape the chicken, place in a single layer in a shallow, heatproof serving dish

and drizzle over the oil.
**3** Roast in the oven for 15–20 minutes or until just tender. Remove the chicken skin. Beat any pan juices into the remaining cheese mixture and spread over each chicken breast. Sprinkle with Parmesan cheese and place under a preheated grill for 2–3 minutes or until golden and bubbling. Garnish with crispy bacon and accompany with sauté potatoes and onion.

### COOK'S TIP

The paste can be kept in the fridge, covered, for 4–5 days.

# PARSLEY, WALNUT AND ORANGE CHICKEN

PREPARATION TIME: **15** MINUTES ◆ COOKING TIME: **40** MINUTES ◆ FREEZING: SUITABLE (STEP 2) ◆ **480** CALS PER SERVING ◆ SERVES **6**

**This dish can be cooked ahead and served cold for lunch – but is just as good served hot.**

135 ml (9 tbsp) extra-virgin olive oil
125 g (4 oz) onion, finely chopped
75 g (3 oz) walnuts, finely chopped
grated rind and juice of 1 large orange
90 ml (6 tbsp) chopped fresh parsley
15 ml (1 tbsp) cranberry sauce
1 egg, beaten
salt and freshly ground black pepper
6 chicken breast fillets, with skin
15 ml (1 tbsp) Dijon mustard
fresh herb sprigs, to garnish

**1** Heat 45 ml (3 tbsp) of the oil in a small saucepan, add the onion, cover and cook for 10 minutes or until soft. Leave to cool. Combine the walnuts, orange rind, parsley, cranberry sauce and egg. Season well, then stir in the onion; set aside.
**2** Preheat the oven to 200°C (400°F) Mark 6. Gently ease up the chicken skin and push in the stuffing. Reshape the chicken and place in a large roasting pan. Spread with the mustard and season to taste. Drizzle over 30 ml (2 tbsp) of the oil and roast in the oven for 25–30 minutes, basting occasionally. Set aside to cool. (See Cook's Tip.)
**3** When cold, thickly slice the chicken

and arrange on a serving dish. Whisk together 30 ml (2 tbsp) of the orange juice with the remaining oil and seasoning. Add the strained cooking juices and pour over the chicken. Garnish with herb sprigs to serve.

### COOK'S TIP

If serving hot, keep warm while making the dressing, then serve.

# BAKED BABY BEETROOT

PREPARATION TIME: **15** MINUTES ◆ COOKING TIME: **1½** HOURS ◆ FREEZING: NOT SUITABLE ◆ **90** CALS PER SERVING ◆ SERVES **6**

1.25 kg (2¾ lb) baby beetroot
15 g (½ oz) butter
salt and freshly ground black pepper

**1** Preheat the oven to 200°C (400°F) Mark 6. Trim the beetroot and carefully rinse in cold water, making sure you do not tear the skins.
**2** Rub the butter over one side of a large piece of foil. Place the beetroot on the buttered foil, season and wrap well to form an airtight parcel.
**3** Cook in the oven for 1¼–1½ hours or until soft and the skin comes away easily.
**4** Leave to cool a little, then rub off the skins. Serve hot.

# HONEY-GLAZED SHALLOTS

PREPARATION TIME: **15** MINUTES ◆ COOKING TIME: **25** MINUTES ◆ FREEZING: NOT SUITABLE ◆ **95** CALS PER SERVING ◆ SERVES **4**

450 g (1 lb) shallots
25 g (1 oz) butter
15 ml (1 tbsp) clear honey
juice of ½ lemon
15 ml (1 tbsp) Worcestershire sauce
15 ml (1 tbsp) balsamic vinegar
salt and freshly ground black pepper

**1** Place the peeled shallots in a pan with just enough cold water to cover (see Cook's Tip). Bring to the boil, then simmer for 5 minutes. Drain well.
**2** Add the remaining ingredients to the pan and heat gently until the butter has melted. Stir well to mix.
**3** Add the shallots to the pan and stir to coat with the glaze. Cover and cook over a low heat, stirring occasionally, for about 20 minutes or until the shallots are tender. Remove the lid and cook for 2–3 minutes, until any remaining liquid is thick and syrupy. Serve hot.

## COOK'S TIP

If the shallots are difficult to peel, leave them to soak in a bowl of cold water for 20 minutes.

# GOLDEN CHICKEN LASAGNE

PREPARATION TIME: 40 MINUTES ◆ COOKING TIME: ABOUT 2 HOURS ◆ FREEZING: SUITABLE (STEP 6) ◆ 990 CALS PER SERVING ◆ SERVES 6

1.4 kg (3 lb) oven-ready chicken
300 ml (½ pint) white wine
1 onion
1 celery stick
1 bay leaf
450 g (1 lb) leeks, sliced, trimmings reserved
6 peppercorns
salt and freshly ground black pepper
200 g (7 oz) lasagne
150 g (5 oz) butter
1 garlic clove, crushed
90 g (3½ oz) plain flour
175 g (6 oz) Gruyère cheese, grated
50 g (2 oz) Cheddar cheese, grated
284 ml carton single cream
60 ml (4 tbsp) freshly grated Parmesan cheese
45 ml (3 tbsp) pinenuts

1  Put the chicken in a saucepan, add water to cover the drumsticks, half of the wine, the onion, celery, bay leaf, leek trimmings, peppercorns and 5 ml (1 tsp) salt. Bring to the boil, then cover and simmer for 45–60 minutes; cool.
2  Cut the chicken into bite-size pieces. Bring the cooking juices to the boil, then bubble until reduced to about 1 litre (1¾ pints). Strain and skim.
3  Cook the lasagne in boiling salted water according to packet instructions.
4  Melt 50 g (2 oz) of the butter in a frying pan. Add the leeks and garlic and fry for about 10 minutes. Remove the leeks with a slotted spoon. Preheat the oven to 200°C (400°F) Mark 6.

5  Melt the remaining butter in the pan, stir in the flour and cook, stirring, for 1 minute. Remove from the heat and whisk in the stock and remaining wine. Bring to the boil and cook, stirring, for 4–5 minutes. Remove from the heat and stir in 125 g (4 oz) of the Gruyère cheese, the Cheddar, cream and seasoning.
6  Spoon a little sauce into a 3-litre (5¼-pint) shallow ovenproof dish. Top with a layer of lasagne, then chicken, leeks, Parmesan and sauce. Repeat the layers, finishing with pasta and sauce. Sprinkle with the remaining cheeses and the pinenuts. and cook in the oven for 45–50 minutes.

# SWEET SPICY CHICKEN WITH LIME COUSCOUS

PREPARATION TIME: 30 MINUTES ◆ COOKING TIME: 1 HOUR ◆ FREEZING: NOT SUITABLE ◆ 445 CALS PER SERVING ◆ SERVES 6

45 ml (3 tbsp) olive oil
1.1 kg (2½ lb) chicken joints, with skin
1 onion, about 175 g (6 oz), sliced
1 large red chilli, finely chopped
3.5 cm (1½ inch) piece fresh root ginger, grated
2 garlic cloves, crushed
2.5 ml (½ tsp) ground turmeric
1 cinnamon stick
775 ml (26 fl oz) chicken stock
90 ml (6 tbsp) coconut milk powder
550 g (1¼ lb) tomatoes, skinned
deep-fried onion rings and chilli, to garnish

### LIME AND CORIANDER COUSCOUS
350 g (12 oz) French beans
3 limes
225 g (8 oz) couscous
45 ml (3 tbsp) chopped fresh coriander

1  Heat 15 ml (1 tbsp) oil in a 3.1-litre (5¼-pint) flameproof casserole, add the chicken and fry for about 5 minutes or until browned. Drain on kitchen paper.
2  Add the onion to the pan and fry for about 10 minutes, until soft and golden brown. Add the chilli, ginger, garlic, turmeric and cinnamon stick and fry for 2–3 minutes. Stir in 450 ml (¾ pint) of the stock and the coconut milk powder and bring to a gentle simmer, stirring, then bubble for about 5 minutes.
3  Quarter the tomatoes and add to the pan. Return the chicken to the casserole and simmer, uncovered, for about 25 minutes.
4  Meanwhile, prepare the couscous.

Cook the beans in boiling salted water for about 5 minutes or until tender. Drain and refresh under cold running water. Grate the rind from 2 limes and squeeze the juice from them all.
5  Heat 30ml (2 tbsp) oil in a saucepan, add the couscous and stir for 30 seconds. Stir in the remaining stock and the lime juice, remove from the heat, cover and leave to stand for about 10 minutes, until all the liquid has been absorbed. Stir in the lime rind, coriander and beans and season well.
6  Garnish the chicken with deep-fried onion rings and chilli pieces, and serve with the couscous.

# MASHED POTATOES WITH CHIVE OIL

**PREPARATION TIME: 15** MINUTES ◆ **COOKING TIME: 25** MINUTES ◆ **FREEZING: NOT** SUITABLE ◆ **570-380** CALS PER SERVING ◆ SERVES **4-6**

1.4 kg (3 lb) potato, roughly chopped
salt and freshly ground black pepper
45 ml (3 tbsp) chopped fresh chives
75 ml (5 tbsp) olive oil
100 ml (4 fl oz) warm milk
75 g (3 oz) butter
slices of pastrami or salt beef and French
    mustard, to accompany

**1** Cook the potato in boiling salted water for 15–20 minutes, until tender. Mix together the chives and oil.
**2** Drain the potato and return to the saucepan. Using a vegetable masher, mash over a low heat for 2-3 minutes. Beat in the milk and butter and season well with salt and pepper.
**3** Drizzle with the chive oil and serve immediately. Accompany with slices of pastrami or salt beef and French mustard.

# CARROT AND PARSNIP PURÉE WITH CORIANDER

**PREPARATION TIME: 10** MINUTES ◆ **COOKING TIME: 20** MINUTES ◆ **FREEZING: SUITABLE** ◆ **130** CALS PER SERVING ◆ SERVES **4**

450 g (1 lb) carrot, sliced
450 g (1 lb) parsnip, sliced
salt and freshly ground black pepper
15 ml (1 tbsp) ground coriander
45 ml (3 tbsp) reduced-fat crème fraîche
60 ml (4 tbsp) chopped fresh coriander

**1** Place the carrot and parsnip in a pan of cold salted water. Bring to the boil and cook for 20 minutes, until soft. Drain well.
**2** Place in a food processor with the ground coriander and crème fraîche and process until smooth. Season to taste and stir in the fresh coriander to serve.

# STICKY CHICKEN WITH BLACK BEAN CHILLI

PREPARATION TIME: **25** MINUTES + SOAKING ◆ COOKING TIME: **2** HOURS ◆ FREEZING: SUITABLE ◆ **495** CALS PER SERVING ◆ SERVES **6**

75 g (3 oz) butter
45 ml (3 tbsp) honey
3 garlic cloves, thinly sliced
6 chicken breasts with skin

**BLACK BEAN CHILLI**
225 g (8 oz) dried black beans, soaked overnight, drained and rinsed
225 g (8 oz) onion, finely chopped
1 red pepper, cored and chopped
1 large red chilli, finely chopped
2 garlic cloves, crushed
2.5 ml (1/2 tsp) each mild chilli powder and ground cumin
5 ml (1 tsp) Tabasco sauce
30 ml (2 tbsp) Worcestershire sauce
750 ml (1 1/4 pints) chicken stock
juice of 1 lime
75 g (3 oz) chorizo sausage, chopped

1 First, prepare the Black Bean Chilli. Place the beans in a large pan and cover with cold water. Bring to the boil and boil rapidly for 10 minutes; drain.
2 Meanwhile, heat 15 ml (1 tbsp) oil in a pan, add the onion, red pepper and chilli and fry gently for 7 minutes or until the onion is soft. Add the garlic, chilli powder and cumin and cook, stirring, for 1 minute.
3 Stir in the beans, Tabasco and Worcestershire sauces, stock and lime juice, bring to the boil, then cover and simmer gently for 1 hour 20 minutes or until the beans are tender .
4 Add the chorizo and simmer, uncovered, for 30 minutes or until the

chilli sauce has thickened and the mixture reduced. Season to taste.
5 Meanwhile, prepare the chicken. Preheat the oven to 190°C (375°F) Mark 5. Melt the butter and honey in a pan over a low heat, stirring, set aside.
6 Push the garlic slices under the skin of each chicken breast. Place in a roasting pan, brush with the honey mixture and season to taste.
7 Cook in the oven, basting occasionally, for about 35 minutes or until the skin is beginning to turn dark brown and the chicken is cooked.
8 Garnish with flat-leaf parsley and serve with the beans.

# GRILLED MUSTARD CHICKEN WITH SALSA

PREPARATION TIME: **25** MINUTES ◆ COOKING TIME: **6** MINUTES ◆ FREEZING: NOT SUITABLE ◆ **655** CALS PER SERVING ◆ SERVES **4**

30 ml (2 tbsp) Dijon mustard
60 ml (4 tbsp) olive oil
1 garlic clove, crushed
salt and freshly ground black pepper
450 g (1 lb) chicken breast fillet, cut into large pieces
4 muffins
50 g (2 oz) fresh spinach leaves
15 ml (1 tbsp) lemon juice
45 ml (3 tbsp) mayonnaise

**BEETROOT AND HORSERADISH SALSA**
250 g (9 oz) cooked baby beetroot (see Cook's Tip), roughly chopped
25 g (1 oz) pickled gherkins, roughly chopped
30 ml (2 tbsp) olive oil
30 ml (2 tbsp) horseradish cream

1 Mix together the mustard, 45 ml (3 tbsp) of the oil, garlic and seasoning and use to coat the chicken.
2 Cook under a preheated grill for 2–3 minutes on each side, turning once, until tender and golden. Cover with foil and set aside in a warm place. Toast the muffins.
3 Mix the spinach with the remaining oil, lemon juice and pepper to taste.
4 To prepare the Beetroot and Horseradish Salsa, mix all the ingredients together, adding seasoning to taste.
5 Place an open toasted muffin on each plate and top with the spinach, chicken and a spoonful of mayonnaise. Season with pepper and serve with the salsa.

**COOK'S TIP**
Whole cooked baby beetroot are available from major supermarkets – but don't buy those in vinegar.

# BAKED ANCHOVY POTATOES AND PARSNIPS

PREPARATION TIME: **20** MINUTES ◆ COOKING TIME: **1** HOUR **10** MINUTES ◆ FREEZING: NOT SUITABLE ◆ **385** CALS PER SERVING ◆ SERVES **6**

284 ml carton double cream
300 ml (½ pint) vegetable or chicken stock
15 ml (1 tbsp) Dijon mustard
450 g (1 lb) each potato and parsnip, cut into chunks
salt and freshly ground black pepper
25 g (1 oz) butter, melted
125 g (4 oz) onion, thinly sliced
1 garlic clove, crushed
50 g can anchovies in oil, drained and chopped
flat-leaf parsley, to garnish

1  Preheat the oven to 190°C (375°F) Mark 5.
2  Place the cream, stock and mustard in a large pan and bring to the boil. Add the potato and parsnip and bring back to the boil. Drain immediately. Season to taste and set aside.
3  Grease a 2 litre (3½ pint) ovenproof dish with melted butter. Add the onion and garlic to the remaining butter and cook for 10 minutes. Add the anchovy.
4  Place half of the potato and parsnip mixture in the dish, spoon over the onion mixture and cover with potato.
5  Cook, uncovered, in the oven for 1 hour or until tender and golden brown. Garnish with parsley to serve.

# POTATO BAKE

PREPARATION TIME: **25** MINUTES ◆ COOKING TIME: **2¼** HOURS ◆ FREEZING: NOT SUITABLE ◆ **250** CALS PER SERVING ◆ SERVES **4**

125 g (4 oz) bacon
45 ml (3 tbsp) vegetable oil, plus extra for greasing
300 g (10 oz) onion, sliced
1 garlic clove, crushed
700 g (1½ lb) floury potato, thinly sliced
salt and freshly ground black pepper
300 ml (½ pint) vegetable stock
fresh coriander, to garnish

1  Preheat the oven to 190°C (375°F) Mark 5.  Cut the bacon into strips. Heat the oil in a frying pan, add the onion and bacon and cook over a low heat until the onion begins to brown. Add the garlic and cook for 1 minute.
2  Brush a 1.7 litre (3 pint) ovenproof dish with oil. Add alternate layers of potato and onion, seasoning each layer and finishing with potato.
3  Bring the stock to the boil, then pour over the potato. Cover and cook in the oven for 1 hour. Uncover and baste with stock, then return to the oven for 1–1¼ hours, basting occasionally, until tender and browned. Garnish with coriander to serve.

# BALTI CHICKEN

PREPARATION TIME: 10 MINUTES + SOAKING ◆ COOKING TIME: 35 MINUTES ◆ FREEZING: NOT SUITABLE ◆ 485 CALS PER SERVING ◆ SERVES 4

175 g (6 oz) couscous
30 ml (2 tbsp) olive oil
250 g (9 oz) leeks, thickly sliced
175 g (6 oz) red onion, chopped
5 ml (1 tsp) ground coriander
440 g jar balti curry sauce
700 g (1½ lb) boneless chicken thighs
salt and freshly ground black pepper
30 ml (2 tbsp) lemon juice
baked plum tomatoes, to serve

1  Cover the couscous with 450 ml (¾ pint) cold water. Leave for 30 minutes.
2  Heat the oil in a pan, add the leeks, onion and coriander and cook for 10 minutes.
3  Place the curry sauce in a wide pan. Fill the sauce jar with cold water and add to the pan. Add the chicken, bring to the boil, then simmer, uncovered, for 15–20 minutes. Season to taste and add the lemon juice.
4  Add the couscous to the vegetables and season to taste. Stir over a low heat for 2–3 minutes.
5  Serve the chicken with the couscous and baked tomatoes.

# CREAMY CURRIED CHICKEN

PREPARATION TIME: 15 MINUTES ◆ COOKING TIME: 25 MINUTES ◆ FREEZING: NOT SUITABLE ◆ 410 CALS PER SERVING ◆ SERVES 4

25 g (1 oz) butter
700 g (1½ lb) chicken breast fillets, skinned and cut into bite-size pieces
1 small onion, chopped
4 celery sticks, chopped
30 ml (2 tbsp) mild curry paste
30 ml (2 tbsp) mango chutney
30 ml (2 tbsp) lemon juice
30 ml (2 tbsp) Greek natural yogurt
30 ml (2 tbsp) mayonnaise
45 ml (3 tbsp) milk

1  Melt the butter in a large pan, add the chicken and fry for 15–20 minutes, until cooked; set aside.
2  Add the onion and celery to the pan and fry for 5 minutes, until soft. Stir in the curry paste, chutney and lemon juice and cook, stirring, for 2 minutes.
3  Remove from the heat, add the yogurt, mayonnaise and milk and stir well.
4  Return the chicken to the pan and bring to simmering point. Cook until piping hot, then serve with pilau rice.

# GOLDEN ROAST VEGETABLES

PREPARATION TIME: **10** MINUTES ◆ COOKING TIME: **1** HOUR **35** MINUTES ◆ FREEZING: NOT SUITABLE ◆ **225** CALS PER SERVING ◆ SERVES **8**

**These roasted vegetables are the perfect accompaniment to roast beef. If cooking with a joint, use the fat from the beef for extra flavour.**

700 g (1½ lb) potato, cut into large chunks
450 g (1 lb) each celeriac, swede and parsnip, cut into large chunks
1 lemon, chopped
salt
90-120 ml (6-8 tbsp) vegetable oil or hot fat from beef

**1** Preheat the oven to 220°C (425°F) Mark 7. Place the vegetables and lemon in a large saucepan, cover with cold salted water and bring to the boil. Cook for 5 minutes, drain and return to the pan. Cover and shake well to roughen the edges, then lift the lid to allow the steam to escape and the vegetables to dry.
**2** Heat the oil in a roasting pan, or pour the hot fat from the beef into the pan, add the vegetables and toss in the hot fat.
**3** Cook on the top shelf of the oven, turning occasionally, for 1¼ hours or until crisp and cooked through.
**4** Sprinkle with salt to serve.

# NEW POTATOES WITH PEAS AND BROAD BEANS

PREPARATION TIME: **5** MINUTES ◆ COOKING TIME: **30** MINUTES ◆ FREEZING: NOT SUITABLE ◆ **275** CALS PER SERVING ◆ SERVES **4**

700 g (1½ lb) small new potatoes
salt and freshly ground black pepper
200 g (7 oz) each fresh shelled peas and broad beans
40 g (1½ oz) butter
pinch of sugar
45 ml (3 tbsp) chopped flat-leaf parsley

**1** Cook the potatoes in a large pan of boiling salted water for about 15 minutes or until tender; drain and set aside.
**2** Meanwhile, place the peas and broad beans in a large frying pan with the butter, sugar and 75 ml (3 fl oz) water. Bring to the boil, then cover and simmer for 10 minutes.
**3** Remove the lid from the pan, stir in the potatoes and simmer until all the liquid has evaporated. Season well and stir in the parsley. Serve immediately.

# CHICKEN BAKED WITH SPICES

PREPARATION TIME: **15** MINUTES + MARINATING ◆ COOKING TIME: ABOUT **25** MINUTES ◆ FREEZING: NOT SUITABLE ◆ **260** CALS PER SERVING ◆ SERVES **6**

2 garlic cloves
30 ml (2 tbsp) mild paprika
10 ml (2 tsp) ground coriander
5-10 ml (1-2 tsp) cayenne pepper
finely grated rind and juice of 1 large
    lemon
30 ml (2 tbsp) chopped fresh mint
30 ml (2 tbsp) chopped fresh coriander
200 ml (7 fl oz) thick yogurt
salt and freshly ground black pepper
6 chicken suprêmes, or other portions
ghee, butter or vegetable oil, for
    brushing

## GARNISH
mint and rocket leaves
lemon or lime wedges

**1** Crush the garlic and mash with the paprika, coriander, cayenne pepper and lemon rind and juice. Put the herbs in a bowl and stir in the yogurt. Beat in the garlic mixture and add salt and pepper to taste.
**2** Skin each chicken suprême or portion and make 2 or 3 deep cuts in the thickest part of the flesh.
**3** Drop the chicken portions into the yogurt mixture and turn to coat thoroughly. Make sure that the marinade goes well into the slashes. Leave to marinate in a cool place for at least 30 minutes, or overnight if possible.
**4** Preheat the oven to 200°C (400°F) Mark 6. Arrange the chicken in a single layer in a roasting pan and brush with melted butter, ghee or oil. Cook in the oven, basting occasionally, for about 25 minutes, until the chicken is cooked right through.
**5** Garnish with mint and rocket leaves, and lemon or lime wedges to serve.

### VARIATIONS
To simplify the recipe, replace the spices with 30 ml (2 tbsp) ready-made tandoori paste. If fresh herbs are unavailable, use 5 ml (1 tsp) mint concentrate instead.

# ORIENTAL CHICKEN SKEWERS

PREPARATION TIME: **10** MINUTES + MARINATING ◆ COOKING TIME: **15** MINUTES ◆ FREEZING: NOT SUITABLE ◆ **175** CALS PER SERVING ◆ SERVES **4**

450 g (1 lb) chicken breast fillets or
    boned thighs, skinned
2.5 cm (1 inch) piece fresh root ginger,
    grated
2 large garlic cloves, crushed
30 ml (2 tbsp) dark soy sauce
30 ml (2 tbsp) dry sherry
25 ml (5 tsp) caster sugar
noodles and stir-fried vegetables, to
    accompany

**1** Slice the chicken into thick, finger-length strips (about 12 in total).
**2** Combine the ginger, garlic, soy sauce, sherry and sugar in a non-metallic bowl. Add the chicken and stir well to coat. Cover and chill overnight. Soak 12 wooden satay sticks in water for 30 minutes (this helps to stop them burning).
**3** Thread a strip of chicken on to each stick and place in a foil-lined grill pan with any remaining marinade. Cover the exposed part of the sticks with foil.
**4** Cook under a preheated grill for about 15 minutes, turning occasionally. Serve 3 skewers per person, with noodles and stir-fried vegetables.

# SPRING VEGETABLES IN TARRAGON DRESSING

PREPARATION TIME: **10** MINUTES ◆ COOKING TIME: **15** MINUTES ◆ FREEZING: NOT SUITABLE ◆ **110** CALS PER SERVING ◆ SERVES **6**

300 g (10 oz) small new potatoes
150 g (5 oz) asparagus tips
150 g (5 oz) mangetout

**TARRAGON DRESSING**
15 ml (1 tbsp) wine or cider vinegar
60 ml (4 tbsp) oil
15 ml (1 tbsp) chopped fresh tarragon
salt and freshly ground black pepper

**1** First make the dressing. Whisk together the vinegar, oil, tarragon and seasoning, cover and set aside.
**2** Cook the potatoes in boiling salted water for 10 minutes or until just tender. Drain and plunge into a bowl of iced water to cool.
**3** Bring a large pan of salted water to the boil. Add the asparagus and cook for 2–3 minutes, until just beginning to soften. Drain and cool in iced water.
**4** Repeat with the mangetout.
**5** To serve, drain the vegetables well and toss in the dressing.

# MASHED POTATOES WITH ONIONS AND CHEESE

PREPARATION TIME: **10** MINUTES ◆ COOKING TIME: **20** MINUTES ◆ FREEZING: NOT SUITABLE ◆ **560** CALS PER SERVING ◆ SERVES **4**

**This is a marvellous way of using up odd bits of cheese - use whatever you have in the fridge.**

900 g (2 lb) potato, Desirée if possible, chopped
salt and freshly ground black pepper
45 ml (3 tbsp) olive oil
350 g (12 oz) onion, thinly sliced
75 g (3 oz) butter
90 ml (6 tbsp) single cream or milk
75 g (3 oz) cheese, eg Lancashire, Cheddar, Fontina, Taleggio or Gruyère, coarsely grated or crumbled

**1** Cook the potato in boiling, salted water for about 20 minutes, until tender.
**2** Meanwhile, heat the oil in a frying pan, add the onion and cook, stirring over a medium to high heat, for 10–15 minutes, until golden and some of the onion is crisp.
**3** Drain and mash the potato with the butter and cream or milk. Season to taste and transfer to a warm serving dish.
**4** Stir the cheese into the hot onion, then spoon over the mashed potato. Serve immediately.

# HEARTY CHICKEN STEW

PREPARATION TIME: 15-20 MINUTES ◆ COOKING TIME: ABOUT 1 HOUR ◆ FREEZING: SUITABLE ◆ 580-390 CALS PER SERVING ◆ SERVES 4-6

4 chicken quarters, about 1.4 kg (3 lb) total weight
30 ml (2 tbsp) plain white flour
salt and freshly ground black pepper
30 ml (2 tbsp) olive oil
2 onions, roughly chopped
2 parsnips, 2 large carrots and 2 large potatoes, all cut into chunks
125 g (4 oz) split red lentils
2 bay leaves
2 garlic cloves (optional)
425 g can black-eye or red kidney beans, drained
2 courgettes, sliced
45 ml (3 tbsp) chopped fresh parsley
15 ml (1 tbsp) snipped fresh chives (optional)

**1** Cut each chicken quarter in half, sprinkle with flour and season with salt and pepper.
**2** Heat the oil in a flameproof casserole and cook the chicken in batches until well browned on all sides. Remove from the casserole and set aside.
**3** Add a little extra oil to the casserole if necessary and cook the vegetables until lightly browned.
**4** Return the chicken to the casserole and add the lentils, bay leaves, garlic if using, and 900 ml (1½ pints) water. Cover with a tight-fitting lid and simmer gently, stirring occasionally, for 45 minutes or until the chicken is tender and the lentils soft and mushy.

**5** Rinse the beans, drain and add to the casserole with the courgette. Season to taste with salt and pepper and cook for 15 minutes or until the courgette is just tender and the beans are heated through. If the sauce is too thin, retrieve a few spoonsful of vegetables, mash with a potato masher and return to the stew to thicken it slightly. Sprinkle with the chopped parsley, and chives if using, and serve immediately.

### COOK'S TIP
Before using canned beans, always tip them into a sieve and rinse thoroughly under cold running water to remove the slimy residue.

# CHICKEN WITH LIME AND GINGER MAYONNAISE

PREPARATION TIME: 30 MINUTES ◆ COOKING TIME: 1½ HOURS ◆ FREEZING: NOT SUITABLE ◆ 505 CALS PER SERVING ◆ SERVES 6

7.5 cm (3 inch) piece fresh root ginger
1 chicken, about 1.6 kg (3½ lb)
1 bouquet garni
300 ml (½ pint) dry white wine
3 limes
1 Little Gem lettuce (or Cos lettuce heart), finely shredded
4 spring onions, finely chopped
200 ml (7 fl oz) mayonnaise
142 ml carton double cream
salt and freshly ground black pepper
mixed salad leaves, to serve
2 ripe pears
lime wedges or slices, to garnish

**1** Cut a small piece off the ginger and reserve. Crush the remainder with a rolling pin; there's no need to peel it. Put the chicken in a saucepan into which it fits snugly. Add the crushed ginger, bouquet garni, wine and the pared rind and juice of 1 lime. Pour over enough water just to cover the chicken. Cover and bring to the boil, then simmer for about 1½ hours until tender. Skim off any scum and leave to cool.
**2** Remove the chicken. Strain the liquid into a wide saucepan and boil rapidly until reduced to about 150 ml (¼ pint). Meanwhile, cut the chicken into bite-size pieces.
**3** Add the lettuce and spring onion to the reduced liquid and cook for 1 minute

or until the lettuce is just wilted and the onion softened. Transfer to a food processor or blender and purée until smooth. Leave to cool completely.
**4** Peel and grate the reserved ginger and finely grate the rind from the remaining limes. Add the ginger and lime rind to the cooled purée, then fold in the mayonnaise and cream. Add the juice of 1 lime, or to taste. Season generously. Pour over the chicken and toss to coat.
**5** Quarter the pears and remove the cores. Cut into slices and toss in the remaining lime juice.
**6** Arrange the chicken on a bed of mixed salad leaves. Scatter with the pear slices and garnish with lime to serve.

# CRUSHED ROAST PARSNIP AND APPLE

PREPARATION TIME: 25 MINUTES ◆ COOKING TIME: 50 MINUTES ◆ FREEZING: NOT SUITABLE ◆ 310 CALS PER SERVING ◆ SERVES 6

900 g (2 lb) even-size parsnips, cut into
large chunks
700 g (1½ lb) old potato, cut into large
chunks
2 crisp tart dessert apples, peeled and
chopped
salt and freshly ground black pepper
45 ml (3 tbsp) oil
50 g (2 oz) butter
30 ml (2 tbsp) chopped fresh chives (see
Cook's Tip)

**1** Preheat the oven to 220°C (425°F)
Mark 7. Cook the parsnip, potato and
apple together in a large pan of boiling
salted water for 3 minutes, then drain
well.
**2** Heat the oil in a small roasting pan,
add the vegetable mixture and stir to
coat in the oil. Roast in the oven for
45 minutes or until very tender.
**3** Roughly crush the mixture with the
butter and season to taste. Sprinkle with
the chives to serve.

## COOK'S TIP
If you can't find fresh chives, use the
finely chopped green tops of spring
onions.

# BRAISED RED CABBAGE

PREPARATION TIME: 25 MINUTES ◆ COOKING TIME: ABOUT 3 HOURS ◆ FREEZING: NOT SUITABLE ◆ 210 CALS PER SERVING ◆ SERVES 6

1.4 kg (3 lb) red cabbage, finely
shredded
450 g (1 lb) red onion, thinly sliced
salt and freshly ground black pepper
50 g (2 oz) butter
5 cm (2 inch) piece fresh root ginger,
grated
105 ml (7 tbsp) soft light brown
(muscovado) sugar
105 ml (7 tbsp) red wine vinegar

**1** Preheat the oven to 150°C (300°F)
Mark 2.
**2** Layer the cabbage and onion in a
casserole, seasoning as you go. Melt the
butter in a small pan, add the ginger and
fry for 2–3 minutes. Remove from the
heat and stir in the sugar and vinegar;
pour over the cabbage.
**3** Cover with a tight-fitting lid and cook
in the oven for 3 hours, stirring
occasionally. Adjust the seasoning and
serve.

# PROVENÇALE CHICKEN TART

PREPARATION TIME: **25** MINUTES ◆ COOKING TIME: **30** MINUTES ◆ FREEZING: **NOT** SUITABLE ◆ **625** CALS PER SERVING ◆ SERVES **8**

**PASTRY**
225 g (8 oz) plain white flour
salt and freshly ground black pepper
125 g (4 oz) margarine, in small pieces

**FILLING**
1 large red and green pepper, halved
3 chicken breast fillets, skinned
30 ml (2 tbsp) olive oil
1 garlic clove, finely chopped
2 fresh thyme sprigs
2 eggs
450 ml (³/4 pint) crème fraîche or double
   cream
25 g (1 oz) freshly grated Parmesan
   cheese
handful each of black and green olives
5 sun-dried tomatoes in oil, drained and
   halved

**1** To make the pastry, sift the flour and seasoning into a bowl and rub in the margarine until the mixture resembles fine crumbs. Add about 45 ml (3 tbsp) water to mix to a soft dough. Wrap in cling film and chill for 15 minutes.
**2** Meanwhile, place the peppers, skin-side up, under a preheated grill until charred. Cover with a cloth and leave until cool enough to handle, then peel off the skins. Remove the cores and seeds and cut the flesh into thick strips.
**3** Roll out the pastry on a lightly floured surface and use to line a 25 cm (10 inch) loose-based flan tin. Chill briefly while completing the filling.
**4** Cut the chicken into thin slices. Heat

the oil in a frying pan, add the chicken, garlic and thyme and cook over a high heat, stirring, until the chicken is browned. Lower the heat and cook for 3–5 minutes, until the chicken is cooked. Remove with a slotted spoon and leave to cool. Discard the thyme.
**5** Preheat the oven to 200°C (400°F) Mark 6. Add the eggs, crème fraîche or cream, Parmesan and peppers to the chicken. Mix thoroughly and season to taste. Spoon into the pastry case and sprinkle with the olives and tomatoes.
**6** Put the tart on a baking sheet and bake in the oven for about 30 minutes or until golden brown and just set in the middle. Serve warm or cold.

# GLAZED CHICKEN WITH ROAST LEMONS

PREPARATION TIME: **5** MINUTES ◆ COOKING TIME: **70–75** MINUTES ◆ FREEZING: **NOT** SUITABLE ◆ **380** CALS PER SERVING ◆ SERVES **6**

**The lemons lose their sharpness in cooking and develop a deliciously soft, mellow flavour.**

250 g (9 oz) caster sugar
3 large lemons
6 chicken-breast quarters (breast and
   wing), about 300 g (10 oz) each
salt and freshly ground black pepper
flat-leaf parsley, to garnish

**1** Place the sugar in a large saucepan with 600 ml (1 pint) water and slowly dissolve over a low heat. Bring to the boil and bubble for 2 minutes. Pierce the skin of the lemons with a fork, place in the sugar syrup, then cover and cook for 20 minutes. Remove the lemons, bubble the liquid for about 12 minutes or until reduced by half and a golden caramel colour. Cut the lemons in half. Preheat the oven to 450°F (230°C) Mark 8.
**2** Season the chicken quarters and place skin-side down in a roasting pan just large enough to hold them in a single layer. Add the lemon halves and pour over the sugar syrup.
**3** Cook in the oven for 30–35 minutes

or until cooked through and golden, basting occasionally and turning over halfway through cooking.
**4** Serve each chicken quarter with a lemon half and garnish with parsley.

# ROASTED PEPPER AND EGG STEW

**PREPARATION TIME: 10 MINUTES** ◆ **COOKING TIME: 55 MINUTES** ◆ **FREEZING: NOT SUITABLE** ◆ **540 CALS PER SERVING** ◆ **SERVES 2**

4 tomatoes, preferably large plum,
  halved and seeded
3 red peppers, cored and seeded
225 g (8 oz) red onion, roughly sliced
1 red chilli
6 garlic cloves
5 ml (1 tsp) sugar
salt and freshly ground black pepper
60 ml (4 tsp) olive oil
30 ml (2 tbsp) sun-dried tomato paste
6 small eggs
chopped fresh parsley, to garnish

1  Roughly chop 2 of the tomato halves and the peppers and place in a single layer in a large roasting pan. Add the onion and chilli and the unpeeled garlic cloves. Sprinkle with the sugar and season well. Preheat the oven to 230°C (450°F) Mark 8.
2  Drizzle the tomato mixture with the oil and cook in the oven for 25 minutes, stirring occasionally. Stir in the tomato paste and top with the remaining tomato halves. Return to the oven for 20 minutes or until the peppers are charred.
3  Crack an egg into each tomato half. Season well and spoon the pan juices over. Lower the temperature to 180°C (350°F) Mark 4 and return the pan to the

oven for 7 minutes or until the eggs are just set. Garnish with parsley to serve.

# MIXED ONION CASSEROLE

**PREPARATION TIME: 15 MINUTES** ◆ **COOKING TIME: 1½ HOURS** ◆ **FREEZING: NOT SUITABLE** ◆ **620 CALS PER SERVING** ◆ **SERVES 3**

6 onions
50 g (2 oz) butter
5 garlic cloves, sliced
8 juniper berries, crushed
600 ml (1 pint) vegetable stock
coarse sea salt and freshly ground black
  pepper
6-8 shallots
1 bunch of spring onions, sliced
6 slices French bread, 1 cm (½ inch) thick
125 g (4 oz) mature Cheddar cheese,
  coarsely grated
15 ml (1 tbsp) snipped chives, to garnish

1  Preheat the oven to 180°C (350°F) Mark 4.
2  Cut 4 of the onions crosswise into quarters, leaving the root end intact to ensure the onions do not fall apart during cooking. Slice the remaining onions.
3  Melt the butter in a saucepan, add the sliced onion, garlic and juniper berries. Fry gently until golden. Add 300 ml (½ pint) of the stock and bring to the boil. Season with salt and pepper.
4  Stand the quarter-cut onions upright in a 1.2 litre (2 pint) casserole and add the shallots and spring onion. Spoon the sautéed onion and garlic mixture on top. Cook, uncovered, in the oven for

1½ hours. Check from time to time that the liquid hasn't dried out and top up with more stock as necessary. At the end of the cooking time the liquid should be thick and syrupy.
5  About 15 minutes before the end of the cooking time, butter the slices of French bread and arrange butter-side up on top of the onion mixture. Sprinkle with the cheese and return to the oven to crisp and brown.
6  Sprinkle with the snipped chives and serve immediately.

# HOT RED JUNGLE CURRY

**PREPARATION TIME: 10 MINUTES ◆ COOKING TIME: 15 MINUTES ◆ FREEZING: NOT SUITABLE ◆ 200 CALS PER SERVING ◆ SERVES 4**

350 g (12 oz) chicken breast fillet, skinned
75 g (3 oz) green beans
75 g (3 oz) button or brown-cap mushrooms
15 ml (1 tbsp) oil
30 ml (2 tbsp) red curry paste
125 g (4 oz) aubergine, cut into bite-size pieces
125 g (4 oz) baby sweetcorn, halved lengthways
2-3 kaffir lime leaves (optional)
2.5 cm (1 inch) piece fresh root ginger, thinly sliced
450 ml (³/₄ pint) chicken stock
30 ml (2 tbsp) fish sauce
grated rind of ¹/₂ lime
5 ml (1 tsp) tomato paste
15 ml (1 tbsp) soft brown sugar
pared lime rind, to garnish

**1** Cut the chicken into finger-length strips. Top the beans and halve the mushrooms, if necessary.
**2** Heat the oil in a wok or large sauté pan, add the chicken and cook, stirring, for 5 minutes or until golden brown.
**3** Add the red curry paste and cook for 1 minute. Add the vegetables and lime leaves, if using, and stir well. Add the remaining ingredients, bring to the boil, then simmer gently for 10–12 minutes or until the chicken and vegetables are just tender. Serve immediately, garnished with pared lime rind.

**VARIATION**
Add a drained 227 g can bamboo shoots with the vegetables in step 3.

# BARBECUE CHICKEN HOTPOT

**PREPARATION TIME: 30 MINUTES + MARINATING ◆ COOKING TIME: 1 HOUR 20 MINUTES ◆ FREEZING: NOT SUITABLE ◆ 590 CALS PER SERVING ◆ SERVES 4**

2 spring onions, finely chopped
75 g (3 oz) canned pineapple, chopped
salt and freshly ground black pepper
4 chicken suprêmes or fillets, with skin
100 ml (4 fl oz) bought barbecue sauce or tomato ketchup
50 ml (2 fl oz) maple syrup
30 ml (2 tbsp) distilled malt vinegar
10 ml (2 tsp) lemon juice
2 garlic cloves, crushed
90 ml (6 tbsp) olive oil
450 g (1 lb) small red potatoes, quartered
4 small red onions, about 225 g (8 oz) total weight, quartered
flat-leaf parsley, to garnish

**1** Mix together the spring onion and pineapple and season to taste. Make a shallow pocket in the thickest part of each suprême, spoon in a little of the pineapple mixture and fold over the pocket to enclose. Fasten with a wooden cocktail stick and set aside.
**2** Blend together the barbecue sauce or ketchup, maple syrup, vinegar, lemon juice, garlic and 75 ml (5 tbsp) of the oil. Place the chicken in a shallow, non-metallic dish and pour over half of the marinade. Cover and leave to marinate in the fridge overnight.
**3** Preheat the oven to 230°C (450°F) Mark 8. Toss the potato and onion in the remaining oil, spread over the base of a

large roasting pan and cook for 45 minutes, turning occasionally.
**4** Sit the chicken on the vegetables and pour over the remaining marinade. Return to the oven for 30–35 minutes or until the chicken is tender and everything is golden brown.
**5** Carefully remove the cocktail sticks and lift the chicken and vegetables on to a warm serving dish. Cover and keep warm. Add 60–90 ml (4–6 tbsp) water to the pan juices and bring to the boil on the hob. Spoon the sauce over the chicken and garnish with parsley to serve.

# ROASTED VEGETABLES WITH FRUITY COUSCOUS

PREPARATION TIME: **15** MINUTES ◆ COOKING TIME: **10** MINUTES ◆ FREEZING: NOT SUITABLE ◆ **790** CALS PER SERVING ◆ SERVES **6**

10 ml (2 tsp) chilli purée
60 ml (4 tbsp) mayonnaise
30 ml (2 tbsp) balsamic vinegar
5 ml (1 tsp) sugar
1 garlic clove
300 ml (½ pint) olive oil
300 ml (½ pint) vegetable stock
150 g (5 oz) couscous
75 g (3 oz) no-soak dried apricots
50 g (2 oz) shelled pistachio nuts, toasted
50 g (2 oz) each pinenuts and raisins
60 ml (4 tbsp) chopped flat-leaf parsley
15 ml (1 tbsp) each chopped fresh
    tarragon and chives
300 g (10 oz) each aubergine and
    courgette, sliced
300 g (10 oz) each fennel and onion,
    quartered
450 g (1 lb) peppers, cored and seeded

1  Stir the chilli purée into the mayonnaise, cover and set aside.
2  Whisk together the vinegar, sugar, halved and bruised garlic clove, and salt and freshly ground black pepper. Whisk in 120 ml (8 tbsp) of the oil.
3  Pour the hot stock over the couscous and leave to soak for 5 minutes. Stir in the chopped apricots, nuts, raisins, herbs, seasoning and half of the vinaigrette; set aside.
4  Preheat the oven to 240°C (475°F) Mark 9. Place the aubergine, courgette, fennel, onion and peppers in a roasting pan. Brush with the remaining oil and cook in the oven for 15–20 minutes, until well coloured and softened.

5  Skin the peppers and cut into strips; mix with the vegetables.
6  Stir the remaining vinaigrette, discarding the garlic, into the roasted vegetables. Serve with the couscous and chilli mayonnaise.

## COOK'S TIP

If you do not have any balsamic vinegar, replace with lemon juice.

# CHESTNUT AND ARTICHOKE EN CROUTE

PREPARATION TIME: **30** MINUTES + CHILLING ◆ COOKING TIME: **45-50** MINUTES ◆ FREEZING: SUITABLE (STEP 6) ◆ **560** CALS PER SERVING ◆ SERVES **6**

100 g (3½oz) spinach leaves
50 g (2 oz) butter
75 g (3 oz) shallots, roughly chopped
225 g (8 oz) mixed mushrooms, roughly
    chopped
100 g (3½ oz) vacuum-packed chestnuts,
    roughly chopped
3 garlic cloves, crushed
45 ml (3 tbsp) balsamic vinegar
5 ml (1 tsp) , chopped, fresh thyme
140 ml (5 fl oz) double cream
salt and freshly ground black pepper
200 g can artichoke hearts, chopped
500 g (1lb 2 oz) ready-made puff pastry
1 egg, beaten

1  Plunge the spinach into a pan of boiling water for 1–2 seconds. Drain and refresh with cold water.
2  Melt the butter, add the shallots and cook, stirring, for 2–3 minutes. Add the mushrooms and cook for 3–4 minutes. Stir in the garlic and vinegar and cook for 1 minute. Add the chestnuts, thyme and cream and bubble for 10 minutes. Season and cool; add the artichokes.
3  On a work surface, lay out a large piece of cling film and cover with half of the drained spinach to form a rectangle 20 x 15 cm (8 x 6 inches). Season, then spread with half the chestnut mixture. Roll up carefully; repeat with the rest of the spinach and chestnut; chill.

4  Roll out 125 g (4 oz) of the pastry to a rectangle 30 x 20 cm (12 x 8 inches). Place on a baking sheet and prick well; chill. Preheat the oven to 220°C (425°F) Mark 7. Cook the pastry until golden; cool, then halve to make 2 rectangles.
5  Remove the cling film and place one roll on each piece of pastry.
6  Roll out the remaining pastry to 56 x 23 cm (22 x 9 inches). Halve to give 2 rectangles. Brush with egg then place, egg-side down, over the spinach; trim. Brush with egg, cover with cling film and chill for 30 minutes.
7  Cook at 230°C (450°F) Mark 8 for 20-30 minutes, until golden. Leave to stand for 5 minutes before serving.

# GARLIC AND NUT-BUTTER CHICKEN

PREPARATION TIME: **30 MINUTES** + CHILLING ◆ COOKING TIME: **40 MINUTES** ◆ FREEZING: NOT SUITABLE ◆ **630** CALS PER SERVING ◆ SERVES **12**

225 g (8 oz) roasted salted mixed nuts, roughly chopped
5 large garlic cloves, roughly chopped
450 g (1 lb) unsalted butter, softened
60 ml (4 tbsp) chopped fresh parsley
30 ml (2 tbsp) lemon juice
freshly ground black pepper
225 g (8 oz) puff pastry
1 egg, beaten
15 ml (1 tbsp) each poppy or sesame seeds and caraway seeds
12 small chicken breast fillets
900 ml (1½ pints) chicken stock
fresh chervil sprigs and chives, to garnish

**1** Mix together the nuts, garlic, butter, parsley and lemon juice; season well with pepper. Cover and chill.
**2** Roll out the pastry thinly, on a lightly floured surface, prick well and leave to rest for 30 minutes. Preheat the oven to 200°C (400°F) Mark 6. Brush the pastry with beaten egg, stamp out shapes with a small cutter and sprinkle with the seeds. Cook in the oven for 10 minutes; cool.
**3** Arrange the chicken breasts in a roasting pan and half cover with hot stock. Cover with foil and cook in the oven for 30 minutes or until cooked through.
**4** To serve, melt the prepared butter.

Transfer the chicken to a warm serving platter with a slotted spoon. Spoon over the melted butter and garnish with chervil, chives and pastry shapes.

# LEMON-THYME CHICKEN AND ROAST VEGETABLES

PREPARATION TIME: **25 MINUTES** + MARINATING ◆ COOKING TIME: **ABOUT 1 HOUR** ◆ FREEZING: NOT SUITABLE ◆ **430** CALS PER SERVING ◆ SERVES **6**

1 kg (2¼ lb) chicken breast fillets, with skin
grated rind and juice of 2 lemons
10 ml (2 tsp) chopped fresh thyme
4 garlic cloves, crushed
290 g jar artichoke hearts, in oil
2 large red peppers, cored, seeded and diced
700 g (1½ lb) aubergine, diced
450 g (1 lb) courgette, diced
550 g (1¼ lb) plum tomatoes or 400 g can chopped tomatoes
50 ml (2 fl oz) olive oil
175 g (6 oz) onion, roughly chopped
50 g (2 oz) celery, roughly chopped
60 ml (4 tbsp) white wine vinegar
50 g (2 oz) pitted green olives (optional)
4 anchovy fillets, roughly chopped
thyme sprigs, to garnish

**1** Lightly score the flesh side of the chicken fillets and flatten a little. Mix together the lemon rind and juice, thyme, 2 crushed garlic cloves and seasoning. Place the chicken in a non-metallic dish and pour over the lemon mixture. Cover and marinate in the fridge for at least 1 hour, preferably overnight.
**2** Preheat the oven to 220°C (425°F) Mark 7. Drain the artichoke hearts and reserve the oil.
**3** Place the red pepper, aubergine and courgette in 2 large roasting pans (if you use only one, the vegetables will steam and become soggy) and drizzle over the reserved oil from the artichokes. Roast in

the oven for 25–30 minutes, stirring occasionally. Add the artichoke hearts after 15 minutes.
**4** Roughly chop the fresh tomatoes if using. Heat the olive oil in a large frying pan, add the onion, celery and remaining garlic and cook, stirring, for 5–7 minutes or until soft and golden. Add the tomato, vinegar, olives and anchovy and cook for 10–12 minutes. Add the roasted vegetables and season well.
**5** Meanwhile, cook the chicken under a preheated grill for 5–6 minutes on each side or until just cooked through. Garnish with thyme and serve immediately with the roasted vegetables.

# SWEET POTATO AND CHESTNUT CAKES

PREPARATION TIME: **30 MINUTES + CHILLING** ◆ COOKING TIME: **30 MINUTES** ◆ FREEZING: **SUITABLE (STEP 4)** ◆ **570–380 CALS PER SERVING** ◆ **SERVES 4–6**

450 g (1 lb) sweet potato, cut into large chunks
225 g (8 oz) vacuum-packed chestnuts
75 g (3 oz) butter
6 spring onions, sliced
30 ml (2 tbsp) chopped fresh parsley
2.5 ml ($\frac{1}{2}$ tsp) ground mace
salt and freshly ground black pepper
plain flour, for coating
1 egg (size 1), beaten
125 g (4 oz) fresh white breadcrumbs
sunflower oil, for shallow-frying
flat-leaf parsley sprigs, to garnish
tomatoe sauce, to serve

**1** Place the sweet potato in a steamer and steam for 15-20 minutes, until tender. Remove the basket from the steamer and leave the potato to rest for 2–3 minutes to allow excess moisture to evaporate.
**2** Place the potato and chestnuts in a bowl and mash until smooth.
**3** Melt the butter in a frying pan, add the spring onion and fry for 1 minute, until beginning to soften, then add to the potato with the parsley and mix well. Season with the mace, and salt and pepper to taste. Work the ingredients until the mixture comes together.
**4** Divide the mixture into 8 and roll each portion into a ball, then flatten to make

a thick cake. Transfer to a baking sheet and chill for at least 30 minutes.
**5** Season a little flour and use to coat the cakes. Dip each one into beaten egg, then into the breadcrumbs. Chill for 30 minutes to set.
**6** Heat a 1 cm ($\frac{1}{2}$ inch) depth of oil in a frying pan until a breadcrumb dropped into the pan sizzles in 30 seconds. Fry the cakes in batches on both sides until golden. Drain on kitchen paper. Garnish with parsley and serve immediately with a tomato sauce.

# VEGETABLE BIRYANI

PREPARATION TIME: **25 MINUTES** ◆ COOKING TIME: **40 MINUTES** ◆ FREEZING: **NOT SUITABLE** ◆ **670 CALS PER SERVING** ◆ **SERVES 4**

1 large onion, halved
350 g (12 oz) basmati rice
25 g (1 oz) shelled unsalted pistachios
25 g (1 oz) slivered blanched almonds
25 g (1 oz) raisins
2 large pinches of saffron
1 cinnamon stick
6 each black peppercorns and cloves
4 cardamoms
5 ml (1 tsp) each ground cumin and cayenne pepper
3 garlic cloves, crushed
225 g (8 oz) waxy potatoes, cubed
125 g (4 oz) French beans, halved
2 carrots, sliced
225 g (8 oz) cauliflower florets
75 g (3 oz) shelled peas
150 ml ($\frac{1}{4}$ pint) thick yogurt
garam masala

**1** Cut the onion into very thin semi-circular slices. Wash the rice in a sieve under cold running water; drain.
**2** Heat about 60 ml (4 tbsp) vegetable oil in a heavy-based saucepan, add the onion and cook over a high heat for about 5 minutes until golden. Remove with a slotted spoon, drain on kitchen paper and set aside.
**3** Add the nuts and raisins and cook for 1 minute until lightly browned. Remove with a slotted spoon, drain on kitchen paper and set aside.
**4** Add the spices and garlic to the pan, adding a little extra oil if necessary. Add all the vegetables and cook, stirring, for 2 minutes. Add the yogurt, a spoonful at

a time, stirring well after each addition. Add 60 ml (4 tbsp) water, cover and simmer for 10 minutes or until tender.
**5** Meanwhile, put the rice in another saucepan with 600 ml (1 pint) water and salt to taste. Bring to the boil, then partially cover and simmer for 10 minutes or until just tender and the liquid has been absorbed.
**6** Add the rice to the vegetables, cover and simmer for 5–10 minutes, until tender. Season to taste. Pile on to a warm serving platter and top with the nuts, raisins and fried onion. Sprinkle with garam masala to taste and serve immediately.

# GLAZED CHICKEN WITH CRÈME FRAÎCHE

**PREPARATION TIME: 15** MINUTES + MARINATING ◆ **COOKING TIME: 35** MINUTES ◆ **FREEZING: NOT** SUITABLE ◆ **420** CALS PER SERVING ◆ **SERVES 4**

8 chicken thighs, with skin
grated rind and juice of 2 lemons
15 ml (1 tbsp) each chopped fresh thyme
    and rosemary
3 garlic cloves, crushed
salt and freshly ground black pepper
30 ml (2 tbsp) olive oil
200 ml carton crème fraîche
30 ml (2 tbsp) chopped fresh basil
lemon wedges and flat-leaf parsley, to
    garnish

**1** Place the chicken in a non-metallic bowl with the lemon rind, 60 ml (4 tbsp) lemon juice, thyme, rosemary, garlic, salt and pepper, and olive oil. Leave to marinate in the fridge for 6 hours or overnight, stirring occasionally.
**2** Drain the chicken, reserving the marinade. Place skin side up in a lightly oiled, foil-lined grill pan and cook under a preheated grill for 12 minutes or until brown. Turn and grill for 10 minutes, brushing occasionally with the reserved marinade.
**3** Skim the fat from the cooking juices. Pour the juices into a pan and add the crème fraîche. Bring to boil and bubble for 8–10 minutes. Stir in the basil.

**4** Garnish the chicken with lemon wedges and parsley and serve with the sauce.

# CHICKEN TABBOULEH WITH TOMATO DRESSING

**PREPARATION TIME: 50** MINUTES + MARINATING AND SOAKING ◆ **COOKING TIME: 45** MINUTES ◆ **FREEZING: NOT** SUITABLE ◆ **800** CALS PER SERVING ◆ **SERVES 4**

4 chicken breast quarters, each about
    300 g (10 oz)
1 large red chilli, seeded and chopped
3 garlic cloves, crushed
juice of 4 limes (about 120 ml (8 tbsp))
2.5 ml (½ tsp) ground turmeric
450 g (1 lb) plum tomatoes, chopped
30 ml (2 tbsp) capers
15 ml (1 tbsp) sugar
225 g (8 oz) bulgar wheat
125 g (4 oz) cucumber, chopped
50 g (2 oz) pinenuts, toasted
45 ml (3 tbsp) each chopped fresh
    parsley and chives
50 g (2 oz) raisins
75 ml (5 tbsp) olive oil
225 g (8 oz) onion, thinly sliced
lime slices and flat-leaf parsley, to
    garnish

**1** Make 2 or 3 light cuts in the chicken breasts. Place the chilli, garlic, 45 ml (3 tbsp) lime juice and turmeric in a non-metallic bowl. Add the chicken, toss to coat with the mixture and marinate in the fridge for at least 3 hours.
**2** Meanwhile, mix the tomato with the capers, 30 ml (2 tbsp) lime juice, sugar and salt and freshly ground black pepper.
**3** Place the bulgar wheat in a bowl, cover with 600 ml (1 pint) boiling water and leave to soak for 30 minutes; drain. Stir in the cucumber, pinenuts, herbs, raisins, remaining lime juice and 45 ml (3 tbsp) of the oil. Season to taste. Preheat the oven to 240°C (475°F) Mark 9 .
**4** Drain the chicken, reserving the

marinade, and place skin side up in a roasting pan with the remaining oil and the onion. Cook in the oven for 30–35 minutes or until cooked; set aside. Add the tomato mixture and reserved marinade to the roasting pan and return to the oven for 5 minutes.
**5** Spoon the dressing over the chicken, garnish with lime and parsley and serve with the tabbouleh.

# MIXED VEGETABLE CURRY

PREPARATION TIME: **25** MINUTES ◆ COOKING TIME: **45** MINUTES ◆ FREEZING: SUITABLE ◆ **300** CALS PER SERVING ◆ SERVES **4**

450 g (1 lb) small potatoes or sweet
   potatoes
225 g (8 oz) each spinach, carrot,
   cauliflower and French beans
30 ml (2 tbsp) vegetable oil
1 onion, sliced
6 garlic cloves, finely chopped
50 g (2 oz) creamed coconut, coarsely
   grated
60 ml ( 4 tbsp) mild curry paste
225 g (8 oz) tomato, finely chopped
5 ml (1 tsp) salt
15 ml (1 tbsp) black mustard seeds
fresh coriander, to garnish

**1** Cook the potatoes in boiling salted water for 10 minutes (if using sweet potato, cut into bite-size pieces). Drain and set aside.
**2** Roughly chop the spinach, slice the carrots, divide the cauliflower into bite-size florets and trim the beans.
**3** Heat the oil in a large sauté pan, add the onion and garlic and cook for about 5 minutes, stirring occasionally. Add the coconut and curry paste and cook, stirring, for 1 minute. Add the tomato and cook for 3–4 minutes, until the mixture resembles a thick paste.
**4** Add the carrot, potatoes, cauliflower, salt and 150 ml (¼ pint) water (no more than this or the thick sauce will thin out).

**5** Bring to the boil, then cover and simmer for about 15 minutes. Add the beans, spinach and mustard seeds and cook for 10 minutes or until the vegetables are tender.
**6** Adjust the seasoning and garnish with coriander to serve.

### COOK'S TIP

To use dry spices rather than curry paste, combine 12.5 ml (2½ tsp) ground cumin, 10 ml (2 tsp) ground coriander, 2.5 ml (½ tsp) turmeric and 5 ml (1 tsp) each chilli powder, garam masala and paprika. Fry for 1 minute; add with the coconut.

# MINESTRONE

PREPARATION TIME: **20** MINUTES + SOAKING ◆ COOKING TIME: **2-2½** HOURS ◆ FREEZING: NOT SUITABLE ◆ **540-400** CALS PER SERVING ◆ SERVES **6-8**

**Serve this as a main course, with plenty of crusty bread.**

175 g (6 oz) dried haricot, cannellini or
   flageolet beans, soaked overnight
salt and freshly ground black pepper
2.3 litres (4 pints) vegetable stock
1 dried red chilli
450 g (1 lb) potato, diced
450 g (1 lb) carrot, diced
2 large leeks, thinly sliced
450 g (1 lb) courgettes, diced
225 g (8 oz) French beans, halved
400 g can chopped tomatoes
125 g (4 oz) pastini, or very small pasta
   shapes for soup
50 g (2 oz) freshly grated pecorino or
   Parmesan cheese, to serve

**1** Drain the beans and put them in a large saucepan with enough fresh cold water to cover. Bring to the boil and boil steadily for 10 minutes, then simmer for 1–1½ hours or until tender, adding salt towards the end of the cooking time. Drain well.
**2** Pour the stock into a large saucepan and add the chilli. Bring to the boil, add the beans, potato, carrot and leek, then cover and simmer gently for 25 minutes or until the vegetables are really tender.
**3** Add the courgette, French beans, tomatoes and pasta and season with plenty of salt and pepper. Cover and simmer for 10 minutes or until the pasta is just cooked.

**4** To serve, ladle the soup into warm large soup plates. Hand grated cheese separately.

### VARIATION

Use canned instead of dried beans. You will need two 425 g cans. Drain and rinse thoroughly under cold running water. Add to the soup towards the end of step 3 to heat through.

# CHICKEN, APPLE AND BLUE CHEESE SALAD

**PREPARATION TIME: 30 MINUTES ◆ FREEZING: NOT SUITABLE ◆ 490 CALS PER SERVING ◆ SERVES 4**

**This is a delicious way to use up leftover roast chicken and cheese.**

225 g (8 oz) cooked roast chicken
225 g (8 oz) crisp apples, eg Cox's or Braeburn
400 g (14 oz) mixed salad leaves
30 ml (2 tbsp) sunflower seeds, toasted
175 g (6 oz) blue cheese, eg Roquefort or Stilton, crumbled
small packet potato matchsticks (optional)

**DRESSING**
5 ml (1 tsp) clear honey
15 ml (1 tbsp) Dijon mustard
15 ml (1 tbsp) each white wine vinegar and apple or orange juice
90 ml (6 tbsp) sunflower oil
salt and freshly ground black pepper

**1** To make the dressing, whisk together the honey, mustard, vinegar, fruit juice, oil and seasoning in a large bowl.
**2** Shred the chicken into small pieces and stir them into the dressing. Core the apples and cut into fine strips.
**3** Add the apple, chicken, salad leaves, sunflower seeds, cheese and potato matchsticks, if using, to the dressing and toss well. Serve immediately.

# CHICKEN WITH FENNEL AND TARRAGON SAUCE

**PREPARATION TIME: 5 MINUTES ◆ COOKING TIME: 20 MINUTES ◆ FREEZING: NOT SUITABLE ◆ 465 CALS PER SERVING ◆ SERVES 4**

50 g (2 oz) butter
175 g (6 oz) fennel, cut into fine strips
4 chicken breast fillets, with skin, each about 125 g (4 oz)
125 g (4 oz) onion, roughly chopped
2 garlic cloves, crushed
150 ml (¼ pint) white wine
300 ml (½ pint) chicken stock
142 ml carton double cream
salt and freshly ground black pepper
15 ml (1 tbsp) each chopped fresh tarragon and chives
fresh tarragon, to garnish

**1** Preheat the oven to 200°C (400°F) Mark 6. Melt 25 g (1 oz) of the butter in a frying pan, add the fennel and stir-fry for 2–3 minutes; set aside. Add the chicken skin side down and cook for 3 minutes; turn and cook for 2 minutes. Transfer to a baking sheet and cook in the oven for 10–15 minutes.
**2** Meanwhile, wipe out the pan and melt the remaining butter. Add the onion and garlic and cook for 5 minutes, stirring. Pour in the wine, stock and cream, bring to the boil and bubble for 10 minutes or until syrupy. Season well and stir in the chopped herbs and stir-fried fennel. Garnish the chicken with tarragon and serve with the sauce.

# ROASTED PUMPKIN WITH CUMIN

PREPARATION TIME: **15** MINUTES ◆ COOKING TIME: **45-55** MINUTES ◆ FREEZING: NOT SUITABLE ◆ **210** CALS PER SERVING ◆ SERVES **6**

1.1 kg (2¹/₂ lb) pumpkin
150 g (5 oz) butter
2.5 ml (¹/₂ tsp) cumin seeds
salt and freshly ground black pepper

**1** Preheat the oven to 200°C (400°F) Mark 6. Remove the skin from the pumpkin with a small sharp knife. Cut the pumpkin flesh into thick wedges. Remove and discard the seeds.
**2** Place the pumpkin in a roasting pan large enough for the wedges to fit in a single layer. Melt the butter, then add the cumin seeds and seasoning. Pour over the pumpkin.
**3** Cook in the oven, turning occasionally, for 45–55 minutes or until the pumpkin is very soft and golden brown. Serve with pasta.

# MUSHROOM AND SPINACH PANCAKES

PREPARATION TIME: **1** HOUR + STANDING AND SOAKING ◆ COOKING TIME: **1¹/₂** HOURS ◆ FREEZING: NOT SUITABLE ◆ **375** CALS PER SERVING ◆ SERVES **4**

**PANCAKES**
50 g (2 oz) plain white flour
50 g (2 oz) plain wholemeal flour
1 egg
350 ml (12 fl oz) skimmed milk
pinch of salt

**FILLING**
300 ml (¹/₂ pint) vegetable stock
25 g (1 oz) dried mushrooms
450 g (1 lb) fresh spinach, or 350 g (12 oz) frozen-leaf spinach, thawed
225 g (8 oz) reduced-fat soft cheese
15 ml (1 tbsp) vegetable oil
450 g (1 lb) brown-cap mushrooms, roughly chopped
bunch of spring onions, roughly chopped
flat-leaf parsley, to garnish

**1** Blend the pancake ingredients in a food processor, cover and set aside for 30 minutes.
**2** Pour the stock over the dried mushrooms and soak for 30 minutes.
**3** Lightly oil a small non-stick crêpe pan. When hot, add enough batter to coat the base of the pan thinly. Cook for 1–2 minutes until golden brown, then turn and cook for 30 seconds. Transfer to a plate. Continue with the remaining batter to make 10–12 pancakes.
**4** Cook the spinach in a large saucepan for 2–3 minutes, until just wilted. Cool, squeeze out excess moisture, then chop. Mix with the cheese and season to taste.
**5** Heat the oil in a pan, add the chopped

mushrooms and spring onion and cook for about 10 minutes until lightly browned. Add the dried mushrooms and stock, bring to the boil, then simmer for 15–20 minutes until syrupy. Season to taste. Blend half of the mushroom mixture in a food processor until smooth; return to the pan. Preheat the oven to 200°C (400°F) Mark 6.
**6** Place half of the spinach mixture in a lightly oiled 1.1 litre (2 pint) ovenproof dish. Layer about 6 pancakes with the mushroom mixture and remaining spinach mixture, finishing with mushroom.
**7** Cook in the oven for 30 minutes or until well browned. Garnish with parsley.

# GRILLED CHICKEN IN A CHEESY HERB CRUST

PREPARATION TIME: 15 MINUTES ◆ COOKING TIME: 15 MINUTES ◆ FREEZING: NOT SUITABLE ◆ 445 CALS PER SERVING ◆ SERVES 4

**The crisp cheesy crumbs keep the chicken tender and moist as it cooks.**

125 g (4 oz) olive-oil bread, eg ciabatta
75 g (3 oz) Gruyère cheese, grated
salt and freshly ground black pepper
4 chicken breast fillets, about 450 g (1 lb) total weight, skinned
garlic mayonnaise or hollandaise sauce
20 ml (4 tsp) oil
flat-leaf parsley, to garnish

**1** Roughly chop the bread and process to fine crumbs. Turn into a bowl, stir in the cheese and season well.
**2** Coat each chicken breast with 15 ml (1 tbsp) garlic mayonnaise or hollandaise, then dip in the crumbs until coated. Place on a baking sheet and drizzle each chicken breast with 5 ml (1 tsp) oil.
**3** Cook the chicken under a preheated grill, as far away from the heat as possible, for 5-6 minutes on each side.
**4** Slice the chicken and garnish with parsley. Serve with a tomato salad and garlic mayonnaise or hollandaise.

# CHICKEN WITH SPRING ONIONS AND GRAPES

PREPARATION TIME: 10 MINUTES ◆ COOKING TIME: 40 MINUTES ◆ FREEZING: NOT SUITABLE ◆ 490 CALS PER SERVING ◆ SERVES 4

**It may seem as if there's a lot of vinegar in this dish but don't worry – it reduces to a delicious mellow sauce.**

75 g (3 oz) butter
4 chicken suprêmes, each about 175 g (6 oz), with skin
350 g (12 oz) spring onions, green tops removed
10 ml (2 tsp) sugar
150 ml (¼ pint) each sherry vinegar and sherry
300 ml (½ pint) chicken stock
50 g (2 oz) each seedless black and green grapes
salt and freshly ground black pepper
fresh chives, to garnish

**1** Melt 50 g (2 oz) of the butter in a large frying pan, add the chicken skin side down and cook for 3 minutes or until golden. Turn and cook for another 2 minutes; remove and set aside.
**2** Add the remaining butter, spring onion bulbs and sugar to the pan and cook, stirring occasionally, for 4–5 minutes or until golden. Remove the spring onions and set aside.
**3** Add the vinegar, sherry and stock to the pan and bring to the boil. Return the chicken and spring onions to the pan, cover and simmer gently for 10 minutes. Remove the chicken and spring onions and keep warm. Bubble the sauce for 10 minutes or until reduced and syrupy.

**4** Return the chicken and spring onions to the pan, add the grapes and simmer for 5 minutes to heat through. If the sauce becomes over-reduced and buttery, add 30–45 ml (2–3 tbsp) boiling water or stock. Season well and garnish with chives to serve.

# ROASTED VEGETABLE SALAD

**PREPARATION TIME: 20 MINUTES + STANDING ◆ COOKING TIME: 45–50 MINUTES ◆ FREEZING: NOT SUITABLE ◆ 250 CALS PER SERVING ◆ SERVES 8**

2 aubergines and courgettes
salt and freshly ground black pepper
1 fennel bulb
2 red peppers, cored and seeded
2 small red onions, cut into small wedges
15 ml (1 tbsp) each chopped fresh thyme and sage
60 ml (4 tbsp) olive oil
1 small bulb of garlic
125 g (4 oz) fontina cheese, diced
10 ml (2 tsp) balsamic or sherry vinegar
60 ml (4 tbsp) extra-virgin olive oil
30 ml (2 tbsp) chopped fresh basil
25 g (1 oz) pitted black olives
25 g (1 oz) pinenuts, toasted
basil leaves, to garnish

**1** Preheat the oven to 230°C (450°F) Mark 8. Cut the aubergines and courgettes into 2.5 cm (1 inch) cubes. Layer in a large colander, sprinkling with 10 ml (2 tsp) salt. Set aside for 30 minutes. Rinse thoroughly to remove the salt and dry well with kitchen paper.
**2** Remove the tough outer layer and core from the fennel, then cut into small dice. Cut the peppers into 2.5 cm (1 inch) squares.
**3** Combine all the vegetables in a large bowl. Add the thyme, sage and olive oil, toss well, then transfer to 1 or 2 roasting pans, large enough to hold the vegetables in a single layer.
**4** Discard the top from the garlic bulb,

then place on a small sheet of foil. Drizzle over a little oil, season with salt and pepper and seal the foil to form a parcel. Add to the vegetables and cook for 45–50 minutes, stirring occasionally to ensure they brown evenly. Transfer the vegetables to a large bowl and stir in the cheese.
**5** Unwrap the garlic and scoop out the flesh into a bowl. Add the vinegar and extra-virgin olive oil, season to taste and whisk to combine.
**6** Pour over the vegetables. Add the basil, olives and pinenuts and toss lightly. Serve immediately, garnished with basil leaves.

# ROASTED VEGETABLE TATIN

**PREPARATION TIME: 10 MINUTES ◆ COOKING TIME: 40 MINUTES ◆ FREEZING: NOT SUITABLE ◆ 495 CALS PER SERVING ◆ SERVES 4**

175 g (6 oz) shallots
5 ml (1 tsp) each coriander and fennel seeds
175 g (6 oz) each celeriac, carrot and swede, cut into chunks
45 ml (3 tbsp) olive oil
salt and freshly ground black pepper
3 garlic cloves
125 g (4 oz) leeks, roughly chopped
225 g (8 oz) ready-made puff pastry
50 g (2 oz) butter
10 ml (2 tsp) sugar
15 ml (1 tbsp) lemon juice
75 g (3 oz) ready-to-eat dried apricots, chopped

**1** Preheat the oven to 220°C (425°F) Mark 7. Cut the shallots in half, if large. Finely grind the coriander and fennel seeds in a bowl with the end of a rolling pin.
**2** Place the celeriac, carrot, swede and shallots in a roasting pan with the ground spices, oil and seasoning. Cook in the oven for 20 minutes, then add the garlic cloves and cook for 10–15 minutes. Add the leeks and cook for 10 minutes.
**3** Roll out the pastry on a lightly floured surface and cut into a 25 cm (10 inch) round. Prick well with a fork and chill for 10 minutes.
**4** Meanwhile, melt the butter with the

sugar, lemon juice and 50 ml (2 fl oz) water in a 20 cm (8 inch) heavy-based ovenproof frying pan. When the sugar has dissolved, bubble until the mixture turns a light caramel colour.
**5** Mix the apricots into the vegetables, add to the frying pan and cook for 10 minutes.
**6** Quickly place the chilled pastry on top of the vegetables and cook in the oven for 20 minutes or until golden. Cool for 5 minutes, then turn out pastry side down on to a warm serving plate. Serve immediately.

# TANDOORI CHICKEN WITH MINTED COUSCOUS

PREPARATION TIME: **20** MINUTES + MARINATING ◆ COOKING TIME: ABOUT **20** MINUTES ◆ FREEZING: NOT SUITABLE ◆ **445** CALS PER SERVING ◆ SERVES **6**

6 chicken breast fillets, each 125 g (4 oz)
300 ml (1/2 pint) Greek-style yogurt
2 garlic cloves, crushed
2.5 cm (1 inch) piece fresh root ginger
finely grated rind and juice of 1/2 lemon
10 ml (2 tsp) hot curry paste
5 ml (1 tsp) paprika
2.5 ml (1/2 tsp) salt
225 g (8 oz) quick-cook couscous
4 ripe tomatoes, skinned, seeded and diced
1 small red onion, finely chopped

**DRESSING**
juice of 2 lemons
25 g (1 oz) each caster sugar and mint
125 g (4 oz) cucumber
50 g (2 oz) sultanas
60 ml (4 tbsp) extra-virgin olive oil

**1** Skin the chicken and cut into 2.5 cm (1 inch) cubes. Place the yogurt, garlic, ginger, lemon rind and juice, curry paste, paprika and salt in a large bowl. Add the chicken, toss well to coat and leave in a cool place overnight.
**2** Wash the couscous to moisten and place in a muslin-lined steamer. Place over a pan of simmering water, cover with a tight-fitting lid and cook for 5–6 minutes, until fluffy.
**3** Meanwhile, prepare the dressing. Put the lemon juice and sugar in a saucepan and heat gently until dissolved. Stir in the remaining ingredients, seasoning to taste, and remove from the heat.
**4** Transfer the couscous to a large bowl, add the dressing and stir with a fork until evenly mixed. Add the tomato and onion, season to taste and set aside.
**5** Remove the chicken from the marinade and thread on to 6 skewers. Cook under a preheated grill for 10–15 minutes, turning frequently, until the chicken is charred on the outside and cooked right through. Leave to cool.
**6** Spoon the couscous on to individual plates and top with the skewers. Garnish with lemon wedges and mint to serve.

**COOK'S TIP**
If using bamboo skewers, pre-soak in cold water for 30 minutes to prevent them scorching under the grill.

# COCONUT CHICKEN WITH PINEAPPLE

PREPARATION TIME: **10** MINUTES ◆ COOKING TIME: **25** MINUTES ◆ FREEZING: NOT SUITABLE ◆ **650** CALS PER SERVING ◆ SERVES **6**

125 g (4 oz) fresh pineapple
4 chicken breast fillets, about 450 g (1 lb) total weight, with skin
120 ml (8 tbsp) Jamaican jerk sauce
30 ml (2 tbsp) olive oil
175 g (6 oz) onion or shallots, chopped
2 garlic cloves, crushed
5 cm (2 inch) piece fresh root ginger, chopped
400 ml can coconut milk
caster sugar for dusting
oil for brushing
coriander and toasted coconut, to garnish

**1** Cut the pineapple into long slices (remove the skin, if wished) and set aside. Flatten the chicken a little, then dip into half of the Jamaican jerk sauce.
**2** Heat the oil in a frying pan, add the onion or shallots and fry for 4–5 minutes, until soft. Add the garlic and ginger and cook for 1 minute. Stir in the remaining jerk sauce and the coconut milk, bring to the boil and bubble for 5–6 minutes or until syrupy. Strain and keep warm.
**3** Dust the pineapple with sugar. Place on an oiled baking sheet and cook under a preheated grill or on a griddle pan until golden. Brush the chicken with oil and cook on a foil-lined baking sheet under the grill or on the griddle pan for 4–5 minutes each side.
**4** Garnish with coriander and toasted coconut and serve with the coconut sauce. Accompany with mixed long-grain and wild rice.

# JERUSALEM ARTICHOKE DAUPHINOISE

PREPARATION TIME: **15** MINUTES ◆ COOKING TIME: **1** HOUR **35** MINUTES ◆ FREEZING: NOT SUITABLE ◆ **560–375** CALS PER SERVING ◆ SERVES **4–6**

juice of 1 lemon
700 g (1½ lb) Jerusalem artichokes
50 g (2 oz) butter
225 g (8 oz) onion, thinly sliced
2 garlic cloves, crushed
10 ml (2 tsp) chopped fresh thyme or 5 ml (1 tsp) dried
200 ml (7 fl oz) vegetable stock
150 ml (¼ pint) white wine
142 ml carton double cream
salt and freshly ground black pepper
4-6 potato cakes, toasted (see Cook's Tip)

**1** Add the lemon juice to a bowl of cold water. Roughly chop the artichokes and place in the bowl as you work, to prevent discolouration.
**2** Preheat the oven to 190°C (375°F) Mark 5.
**3** Melt the butter in a frying pan, add the onion, garlic and thyme and cook for 10 minutes or until soft. Add the artichokes, stock and wine and bring to the boil, then simmer for 10 minutes. Stir in the cream and seasoning to taste.
**4** Spoon into an ovenproof dish and cook in the oven for 1–1¼ hours or until tender, golden and bubbling.
**5** Serve hot on the toasted potato cakes and accompany with mixed salad leaves.

**COOK'S TIP**
Potato cakes are available from major supermarkets.

# WINTER SQUASH SALAD

PREPARATION TIME: **15** MINUTES ◆ COOKING TIME: **55** MINUTES ◆ FREEZING: NOT SUITABLE ◆ **275–185** CALS PER SERVING ◆ SERVES **4–6**

75 ml (5 tbsp) olive oil
225 g (8 oz) yellow butternut squash,
2 garlic cloves, crushed
125 g (4 oz) onion, thinly sliced
225 g (8 oz) courgette, thinly sliced
225 g (8 oz) plum tomatoes, thinly sliced
30 ml (2 tbsp) chopped fresh herbs, eg chives, mint or flat-leaf parsley
salt and freshly ground black pepper
50 g (2 oz) mixed black and green olives, chopped
50 g (2 oz) cheese, eg feta, crumbled

**1** Preheat the oven to 200°C (400°F) Mark 6. Heat 30 ml (2 tbsp) of the oil in a saucepan, add the squash and fry for 3–4 minutes or until softened and golden. Remove and set aside. Add the garlic and onion to the pan and cook slowly for 10–15 minutes.
**2** Spoon the squash, courgette and tomato into an ovenproof dish and top with the onion and garlic, herbs, seasoning and remaining oil. Cover with foil and cook in the oven for 15 minutes. Remove the foil and return to the oven for about 40 minutes, until tender.
**3** Serve on individual plates, sprinkled with the olives and cheese. Accompany with warm crusty bread.

# ASIAN SPICED CHICKEN

PREPARATION TIME: 15 MINUTES + MARINATING ◆ COOKING TIME: ABOUT 1 HOUR 20 MINUTES ◆ FREEZING: NOT SUITABLE ◆ 275 CALS PER SERVING ◆ SERVES 6

284 ml carton natural yogurt
60 ml (4 tbsp) olive oil
3 garlic cloves, crushed
7.5 ml (1½ tsp) each ground cumin, curry powder and cayenne pepper
2.5 ml (½ tsp) each dry English mustard, ground ginger and cinnamon
salt and freshly ground black pepper
900 g (2 lb) chicken thighs, with skin
225 g (8 oz) red onion, chopped
225 g (8 oz) cucumber, sliced
two 400 g cans chopped tomatoes
1 lemon, cut into wedges
175 g (6 oz) prepared fresh spinach
sprigs of coriander, to garnish

1  Place the yogurt, 30 ml (2 tbsp) of the olive oil, 1 crushed garlic clove, 2.5 ml (½ tsp) each cumin, curry powder and cayenne pepper, the mustard, ginger, cinnamon and 5 ml (1 tsp) salt in a wide bowl. Stir to blend well. Add the chicken, cover and chill for at least 3 hours or preferably overnight.
2  Heat the remaining oil in a large pan, add the onion, cucumber and remaining garlic and cook for 4–5 minutes or until softened. Stir in the remaining cumin, curry powder and cayenne pepper. Add the tomatoes and simmer for 15-20 minutes. Preheat the oven to 200°C (400°F) Mark 6.
3  Season the sauce and add the lemon wedges. Spoon the tomato mixture into a large, shallow, ovenproof dish – the depth of sauce should be about 1 cm (½ inch).
4  Place the chicken thighs, skin side up, and the marinade on a baking sheet. Place the dish of sauce on the shelf beneath the chicken and cook them together in the oven for 50–55 minutes.
5  About 5 minutes before the end of the cooking time, stir the spinach into the tomato sauce and return to the oven.
6  Garnish the chicken with coriander and serve with the tomato and spinach mixture.

# CHICKEN ENCHILADAS WITH SALSA VERDE

PREPARATION TIME: 30 MINUTES ◆ COOKING TIME: 50 MINUTES ◆ FREEZING: NOT SUITABLE ◆ 720–485 CALS PER SERVING ◆ SERVES 4-6

450 g (1 lb) chicken breast fillet, skinned and cut into strips
5 ml (1 tsp) each dried oregano and cumin seeds
salt and freshly ground black pepper
75 ml (3 fl oz) olive oil
225 g (8 oz) onion, thinly sliced
125 g (4 oz) celery, cut into 'matchsticks'
2 garlic cloves, crushed
50 g (2 oz) sun-dried tomatoes, chopped
225 g (8 oz) brown-cap or shiitake mushrooms, chopped
250 g (9 oz) Cheddar cheese, grated
30 ml (2 tbsp) chopped fresh coriander
30 ml (2 tbsp) lemon juice
6-8 flour tortillas
basil leaves, to garnish

1  Preheat the oven to 180°C (350°F) Mark 4. Place the chicken in a bowl with the oregano, cumin seeds and seasoning. Toss to coat.
2  Heat half of the oil in a large frying pan, add the onion, celery and garlic and cook for 3–4 minutes. Add the tomato and mushrooms and cook for 2–3 minutes. Remove and set aside.
3  Add the remaining oil to the pan and stir-fry the chicken in batches for 2–3 minutes. Mix together the chicken, mushroom mixture, 175 g (6 oz) of the cheese, coriander and lemon juice. Season well.
4  Divide the chicken mixture between the tortillas and roll them up. Place seam-side down in a greased baking dish, then sprinkle with the remaining cheese.
5  Cook in the oven for 25–30 minutes or until golden and bubbling. Garnish with basil leaves to serve.

# MUSHROOM GNOCCHI WITH CHEESE SAUCE

**PREPARATION TIME: 10 MINUTES + SOAKING ◆ COOKING TIME: 30 MINUTES ◆ FREEZING: NOT SUITABLE ◆ 240 CALS PER SERVING ◆ SERVES 4**

15 ml (1 tbsp) porcini pieces or snipped
   dried mushrooms
450 g (1 lb) floury old potatoes, eg
   Desirée or King Edward's
40 g (1½ oz) plain flour
grated Parmesan and Gruyère cheese for
   sprinkling
rocket, to garnish

## CHEESE SAUCE
350 ml (12 fl oz) semi-skimmed milk
15 g (½ oz) plain white flour
25 g (1 oz) freshly grated Parmesan
   cheese
50 g (2 oz) Gruyère cheese, grated
salt and freshly ground black pepper

**1** Soak the porcini in 15 ml (1 tbsp) boiling water for 15 minutes.
**2** To make the sauce, place the milk and flour in a food processor or blender and blend for 1–2 minutes. Transfer to a saucepan, bring slowly to the boil, stirring, then simmer gently for 1 minute. Remove from the heat, stir in the cheeses and season to taste. Cover with damp greaseproof paper and set aside.
**3** Cook the unpeeled potatoes in boiling salted water until very tender. Drain well, cool slightly, then remove the skins and press through a sieve or potato ricer.
**4** While still warm, add 5 ml (1 tsp) salt, the soaked mushrooms with their liquid and the flour. Mix together, then turn

out on to a lightly floured board. If the dough is too soft, add a little more flour (it should be soft but manageable).
**5** Roll into a 2 cm (¾ inch) sausage, then cut into 2.5 cm (1 inch) pieces. Roll each piece with the back of a fork.
**6** Bring a large pan of salted water to the boil; lower the heat to a fast simmer. Drop in 12 gnocchi and cook for 2–3 minutes, until they float to the surface. Remove with a slotted spoon, drain well, then place in an oiled dish and keep warm while cooking the rest.
**7** Gently reheat the sauce, taking care not to let it boil. Pour over the gnocchi, sprinkle with a little cheese and brown under a grill. Garnish with rocket.

# COUSCOUS-FILLED AUBERGINES WITH CORIANDER DRESSING

**PREPARATION TIME: 30 MINUTES ◆ COOKING TIME: 20-30 MINUTES + REHEATING ◆ FREEZING: NOT SUITABLE ◆ 160 CALS PER SERVING ◆ SERVES 4**

two 250 g (9 oz) aubergines
30 ml (2 tbsp) lemon juice
salt and freshly ground black pepper
50 g (2 oz) couscous
6 sun-dried tomatoes in oil, drained and
   chopped
25 g (1 oz) no-soak dried apricots,
   chopped
8 fresh mint sprigs, chopped
15 ml (1 tbsp) pinenuts, chopped
4 spring onions, chopped
coriander sprigs, to garnish

## CORIANDER DRESSING
1 cm (½ inch) piece fresh ginger, grated
1 garlic clove, crushed
grated rind and juice of 1 lime
150 ml (¼ pint) low-fat bio yogurt
30 ml (2 tbsp) chopped fresh coriander

**1** Preheat the oven to 200°C (400°F) Mark 6. Cut the aubergines in half lengthways and score the cut sides deeply, without damaging the skin. Place scored-side up on baking sheet. Rub in the lemon juice and sprinkle with a little salt. Cook in the oven for 20–30 minutes or until soft.
**2** Meanwhile, soak the couscous in 150 ml (¼ pint) boiling water.
**3** Mix together the tomato, apricots, mint, pinenuts and spring onion; season to taste.
**4** Scoop the flesh from aubergines and chop finely (reserve the skins). Fork through the couscous and add the aubergine and the tomato mixture. Stir

gently until evenly mixed, then pile into the skins. Reheat in the oven for 15 minutes if serving hot, or cool then chill if serving cold.
**5** Meanwhile, mix the dressing ingredients together and chill until required.
**6** Garnish the aubergines with coriander and top with the dressing to serve.

# MOROCCAN CHICKEN

**PREPARATION TIME: 25 MINUTES + MARINATING ◆ COOKING TIME: 30 MINUTES ◆ FREEZING: NOT SUITABLE ◆ 360 CALS PER SERVING ◆ SERVES 4**

6 garlic cloves, crushed
5 ml (1 tsp) each salt and ground black peppercorns
5 ml (1 tsp) ground ginger
2.5 ml (1/2 tsp) each ground cumin and paprika
4 chicken breast fillets, skinned
150 ml (1/4 pint) fresh orange juice
pared rind of 1 orange
150 g (5 oz) ready-to-eat apricots
1.25 ml (1/4 tsp) saffron threads
150 ml (1/4 pint) sherry
45 ml (3 tbsp) sherry vinegar
30 ml (2 tbsp) vegetable oil
1 onion, sliced
45 ml (3 tbsp) plain flour
300 ml (1/2 pint) chicken stock
chopped flat-leaf parsley, to garnish

1  Put the garlic, salt, ground black peppercorns, ginger, cumin and paprika in a large bowl and stir well.
2  Slash the surface of the chicken breasts with a sharp knife and add to the bowl. Pour in the orange juice, add the rind and stir well to mix. Cover and chill for at least 4 hours, preferably overnight.
3  Place the apricots, saffron, sherry and sherry vinegar in another bowl. Cover and leave at room temperature for at least 4 hours, preferably overnight.
4  Heat the oil in a large flameproof casserole. Remove the chicken from the marinade with a slotted spoon (reserving the marinade), add to casserole and brown over a high heat; set aside.

Adding a little more oil if necessary, cook the onion for about 5 minutes or until beginning to soften.
5  Add the flour, stir well and cook for 1 minute. Add the marinade, stock and apricots with their soaking liquid, stir well and bring to the boil. Return the chicken to the pan, cover and simmer for about 25 minutes or until the chicken is tender (see Cook's Tip).
6  Garnish with parsley to serve. Accompany with couscous.

## COOK'S TIP

If preferred, cook the chicken in the oven at 180°C (350°F) Mark 4 for 30–35 minutes.

# POUSSINS WITH GOAT'S CHEESE AND PESTO

**PREPARATION TIME: 35 MINUTES ◆ COOKING TIME: 45 MINUTES ◆ FREEZING: NOT SUITABLE ◆ 575 CALS PER SERVING ◆ SERVES 4**

**Many supermarkets sell spatchcock (split and opened) poussins; this stuffing would work equally well in these.**

225 g (8 oz) soft, creamy goat's cheese
30 ml (2 tbsp) pesto sauce
60 ml (4 tbsp) chopped fresh basil
salt and freshly ground black pepper
90 ml (6 tbsp) olive oil
15 ml (1 tbsp) balsamic vinegar
450 g (1 lb) new potato, roughly chopped
3 garlic cloves, crushed
2 poussins, each about 700 g (1 1/2 lb)
225 g (8 oz) broad beans, shelled

1  Preheat the oven to 220°C (425°F) Mark 7. Beat together the goat's cheese, pesto, half of the basil and pepper to taste until smooth. Whisk together 30 ml (2 tbsp) of the oil, the vinegar and seasoning; set aside. Place the potato in a roasting pan with the garlic, remaining oil and 30 ml (2 tbsp) water and roast in the oven for 50 minutes or until tender.
2  Halve the poussins along the breastbone. Gently ease up the skin of the breast and leg and insert the cheese mixture.
3  Place the poussins in a roasting pan and roast above the potato for 40–45 minutes or until cooked, basting occasionally. Remove and set aside to

cool slightly.
4  Meanwhile, cook the beans in boiling salted water for 10 minutes or until tender; drain well. Remove the potato from the oven and mix with the beans and remaining basil. Season to taste. Serve the poussins with the vegetables, roasting juices and the oil and vinegar dressing.

# COURGETTE AND THYME TART

PREPARATION TIME: 45 MINUTES + CHILLING ◆ COOKING TIME: 1 HOUR 10 MINUTES ◆ FREEZING: SUITABLE ◆ 620 CALS PER SERVING ◆ SERVES 6

**PASTRY**
125 g (4 oz) butter chilled and diced
125 g (4 oz) plain flour
pinch of salt
beaten egg, to glaze

**FILLING**
30 ml (2 tbsp) olive oil
1 bunch of spring onions, sliced
350 g (12 oz) courgette, roughly chopped
salt and freshly ground black pepper
15 ml (1 tbsp) small sprigs of thyme
300 g (10 oz) medium-fat soft goat's cheese
2 eggs
200 ml (7 fl oz) double cream
125 g (4 oz) feta cheese, crumbled

**1** To make the pastry, place the butter, flour and salt in a food processor and process for 2–3 seconds. Add 60 ml (4 tbsp) cold water and process for 3–4 seconds or until in a ball. Turn out on to a floured surface and knead until smooth but the butter is still in small pieces. Wrap in cling film and chill for 2 hours.
**2** Heat the oil in a large frying pan, add the spring onion and cook for 1–2 minutes. Add the courgette and cook for 2–3 minutes. Season and add the thyme. Turn into a large bowl to cool.
**3** Add the goat's cheese, eggs, cream and feta cheese to the cooled courgette. Set aside in a cool place.
**4** Roll out the pastry on a floured surface

and use to line a 23 cm (9 inch) loose-based flan tin; chill for 20 minutes. Preheat the oven to 200°C (400°F) Mark 6.
**5** Line the pastry case with greaseproof paper and fill with baking beans. Cook in the oven for 15 minutes, then remove the paper and beans and return to the oven for 10–15 minutes or until a deep brown. Leave to cool for 5 minutes, then brush with egg and return to the oven for 4–5 minutes or until the egg has formed a seal. Pour in the courgette mixture and cook for 30–35 minutes or until just set.
**6** Leave to cool in the tin for 5 minutes, then carefully transfer to a wire rack. Serve warm or cold with salad leaves.

# SPINACH RISOTTO

PREPARATION TIME: 5 MINUTES ◆ COOKING TIME: ABOUT 30 MINUTES ◆ FREEZING: NOT SUITABLE ◆ 345 CALS PER SERVING ◆ SERVES 4

400 g (14 oz) fresh spinach or 125 g (4 oz) frozen leaf spinach
25 g (1 oz) butter
1 onion, finely chopped
1 garlic clove, sliced
225 g (8 oz) arborio (risotto) rice
salt and freshly ground black pepper
750 ml (1¼ pints) vegetable stock
60 ml (4 tbsp) freshly grated Parmesan cheese

**1** Remove any tough stalks from the fresh spinach and chop roughly.
**2** Melt the butter in a heavy-based non-stick saucepan, add the onion and garlic and cook for about 5 minutes or until the onion is beginning to soften.
**3** Add the rice, salt and pepper and cook, stirring, for 2–3 minutes. Add the hot stock a ladleful at a time, stirring gently, allowing the rice to absorb the stock after each addition. This should take about 25 minutes and the rice should then be tender.
**4** Squeeze the excess liquid from the frozen spinach, if using. Stir the fresh or frozen spinach into the rice and heat through for 1–2 minutes or until the

fresh spinach has just wilted.
**5** Remove the pan from the heat and stir in the Parmesan cheese. Adjust the seasoning and serve immediately, with a little extra Parmesan if wished.

# BUTTER-ROASTED TURKEY WITH BAKED APPLES

PREPARATION TIME: **40** MINUTES ◆ COOKING TIME: **3½–4** HOURS ◆ FREEZING: NOT SUITABLE ◆ **865** CALS PER SERVING ◆ SERVES **8–10**

4.5 kg (10 lb) oven-ready turkey
125 g (4 oz) butter, softened
salt and freshly ground black pepper
12 small dessert apples
rosemary and thyme sprigs, to garnish

## CHESTNUT & MUSHROOM STUFFING
225 g (8 oz) Cumberland sausage
40 g (1½ oz) butter
200 g (7 oz) onion, roughly chopped
100 g (3½ oz) celery, roughly chopped
200 g (7 oz) brown-cap mushrooms,
    chopped
100 g (3½ oz) fresh brown breadcrumbs
60 ml (4 tbsp) chopped fresh parsley
20 ml (4 tsp) chopped fresh thyme
1 egg, beaten
30 ml (2 tbsp) orange juice or brandy
225 g (8 oz) vacuum-packed chestnuts

**1** First prepare the stuffing. Remove the skin from the sausage. Melt the butter in a pan, add the onion and cook gently for 10 minutes or until golden and soft. Add the celery and mushrooms and cook briskly for 5 minutes. Leave to cool.
**2** Mix the sausagemeat with the breadcrumbs. Add the herbs, egg, orange juice or brandy, and chestnuts; season well.
**3** Preheat the oven to 190°C (375°F) Mark 5. Loosen skin at the neck end of the turkey, and spoon in the stuffing. Neaten the shape, tuck the neck skin under and secure with skewers or wooden cocktail sticks. Weigh the turkey and calculate the cooking time.
**4** Place the turkey in a roasting pan and spread with the butter. Season with a little salt and plenty of pepper. Cover with foil to make a 'tent'. Cook in the oven for the calculated time, basting regularly.
**5** About 1 hour before the end of the cooking time, remove the foil. About 30 minutes before the end, run a knife around middle of the apples to pierce the skin. Add to the pan and baste.
**6** When the turkey is cooked, place on a carving board, tipping it first to let the juices run back into the pan. Remove the apples, cover and keep warm. Cover the turkey with foil and leave to rest for 30 minutes. Garnish the turkey with herbs and serve with the apples.

# TURKEY AND HAM PIE WITH CHESTNUTS

PREPARATION TIME: **50** MINUTES + COOLING ◆ COOKING TIME: ABOUT **1¼** HOURS ◆ FREEZING: SUITABLE ◆ **945-755** CALS PER SERVING ◆ SERVES **8-10**

450 g (1 lb) each turkey breast and thigh,
    diced
45 ml (3 tbsp) plain flour, seasoned
50 g (2 oz) butter
2 large onions, chopped
750 ml (1¼ pints) chicken stock
freshly grated nutmeg
350 g (12 oz) cooked ham, diced
350 g (12 oz) vacuum-packed chestnuts
15 ml (1 tbsp) chopped fresh thyme
150 g (5 oz) fresh or frozen cranberries
142 ml carton double cream

## PASTRY
1 large potato, diced
450 g (1 lb) plain white flour
125 g (4 oz) butter, cut in small pieces
150 g (5 oz) lard, cut in small pieces
beaten egg, to glaze

**1** Coat the turkey with the seasoned flour. Melt the butter in a large frying pan, and fry the turkey in 2 batches until golden. Remove with a slotted spoon and set aside. Add the onion and cook for about 10 minutes, until soft.
**2** Stir in the stock, plenty of nutmeg and seasoning and cook, stirring, until thickened. Combine the turkey, ham, chestnuts and thyme in a flameproof casserole, pour in the stock, cover and cook very gently for 30 minutes. Stir in the cranberries and cream.
**3** Transfer the mixture to a 2-litre (3½-pint) large shallow pie dish. Place a pie funnel in the centre and add enough of the cooking juices to half fill the dish; cool.
**4** Meanwhile, make the pastry. Cook the potato in boiling salted water until tender. Drain well and mash. Sift the flour into a bowl, rub in the fats, then add the potato. Mix with a round-bladed knife, adding a little cold water to make a smooth firm dough. Wrap in cling film and chill for 30 minutes.
**5** Preheat the oven to 200°C (400°F) Mark 6. Roll out the pastry and use to cover the pie. Make a hole in the centre and decorate with shapes cut from the pastry trimmings if wished; brush with beaten egg. Bake in the oven for 40 minutes until crisp and golden. Serve hot, with seasonal vegetables and any reserved cooking juices in a sauceboat.

# FRENCH ONION BAKE

PREPARATION TIME: **15** MINUTES + CHILLING ◆ COOKING TIME: **30** MINUTES ◆ FREEZING: SUITABLE ◆ **440** CALS PER SERVING ◆ SERVES **4**

225 g (8 oz) bought puff pastry
45 ml (3 tbsp) oil
700 g (1½ lb) onion, thinly sliced
50 g (2 oz) anchovy fillets
125 g (4 oz) pitted black olives

**1** Preheat the oven to 220°C (425°F) Mark 7. Roll out the pastry on a lightly floured surface to a 25 cm (10 inch) square. Prick with a fork and chill for 10 minutes.
**2** Meanwhile, heat the oil in a large non-stick frying pan, add the onion and fry for 10 minutes or until soft and beginning to turn golden brown.
**3** Cook the pastry in the oven for 20 minutes or until golden brown. Lower the temperature to 190°C (375°F) Mark 5.
**4** Spread the onion mixture over the pastry and top with the anchovy and olives. Return to the oven for 10 minutes.

**5** Cut into 4 and serve with a tomato salad.

# THAI GRILLED VEGETABLES

PREPARATION TIME: **20** MINUTES + MARINATING ◆ COOKING TIME: **25** MINUTES ◆ FREEZING: NOT SUITABLE ◆ **350** CALS PER SERVING ◆ SERVES **4**

450 g (1 lb) courgette, thickly sliced
1 bunch of spring onions, thickly sliced
450 g (1 lb) asparagus, trimmed
125 g (4 oz) rice noodles
spring onions and chilli, to garnish

**MARINADE**
2 small red chillies, seeded
15 g (½ oz) fresh root ginger
grated rind and juice of 1 large lime
400 g can coconut milk
2 garlic cloves
15 ml (1 tbsp) nam pla (Thai fish sauce)
5 ml (1 tsp) soft brown sugar
15 ml (1 tbsp) peanut butter
15 cm (6 inch) piece lemon grass, lightly crushed

**1** First make the marinade. Place the chillies, ginger, lime rind and juice, coconut milk, garlic, nam pla, sugar and peanut butter in a food processor or blender and blend until smooth. Add the lemon grass.
**2** Place the courgette, spring onion and asparagus in the marinade, cover and leave in a cool place for at least 1 hour.
**3** Remove the vegetables from the marinade. Discard the lemon grass and reserve the marinade. Grill or barbecue the vegetables in batches, turning occasionally, for 5–10 minutes, until tender.
**4** Cook the noodles in a large pan of boiling salted water for 2–3 minutes,

stirring occasionally. Drain well.
**5** Boil the reserved marinade until reduced to a syrupy consistency. Toss the noodles in the marinade and serve with the vegetables, garnished with spring onions and chilli.

# DUCK TERRINE WITH APPLE, APRICOT AND BRANDY

**PREPARATION TIME:** 1½ HOURS + MARINATING ◆ **COOKING TIME:** 2¼ HOURS ◆ **FREEZING:** SUITABLE ◆ **150** CALS PER SLICE ◆ **SERVES 12**

50 g (2 oz) each pitted prunes and dried apricots, roughly chopped
90 ml (6 tbsp) brandy
350 g (12 oz) turkey breast fillet, cut into 2.5 cm (1 inch) cubes
800 g (1¾ lb) duck breasts, skinned
few thyme sprigs
50 g (2 oz) butter
225 g (8 oz) shallot or onion, chopped
350 g (12 oz) dessert apples, peeled and chopped
225 g (8 oz) minced pork
30 ml (2 tbsp) chopped fresh thyme
1 egg, beaten
50 g (2 oz) shelled pistachio nuts
salt and freshly ground black pepper

1  Place the prunes and apricots in a bowl with 60 ml (4 tbsp) of the brandy, cover and leave overnight.
2  Place the turkey, duck, thyme sprigs and remaining brandy in a roasting pan, cover and chill overnight.
3  Melt the butter in a saucepan, add the shallot or onion and cook for 10 minutes or until soft. Stir in the apple, cover and cook for 5–10 minutes, until soft; cool.
4  Place the turkey, pork and apple mixture in a food processor and process to a rough purée. Combine with the chopped thyme, egg, marinated fruits and nuts; season well. Preheat the oven to 180°C (350°F) Mark 4.
5  Place the duck between sheets of greaseproof paper and flatten with a rolling pin until 1 cm (½ inch) thick.
6  Base-line a 1.1-litre (2-pint) terrine or loaf pan with greaseproof paper or foil. Place a duck breast in the terrine, to cover the base evenly with no gaps. Spread over half of the stuffing. Repeat, finishing with a layer of duck.
7  Cover with foil and place in a roasting pan. Add hot water to come three-quarters of the way up the terrine. Cook in the oven for 2–2¼ hours or until the juices run clear. Transfer to a wire rack, cover with a weighted board and, when cool, chill for 6 hours or overnight.
8  Turn out on to a board and carve into thin slices to serve.

# GUINEA FOWL IN LIME AND GINGER SAUCE

**PREPARATION TIME:** 30 MINUTES + MARINATING ◆ **COOKING TIME:** 1¼ HOURS ◆ **FREEZING:** NOT SUITABLE ◆ **460** CALS PER SERVING ◆ **SERVES 6**

15 cm (6 inch) piece fresh root ginger, grated
grated rind and juice of 1 lime
75 ml (5 tbsp) oil
6 guinea fowl suprêmes, with skin
herb sprigs, to garnish

**LIME AND GINGER SAUCE**
pared rind and juice of 1½ limes
15 cm (6 inch) piece of fresh root ginger, chopped
4-5 sprigs fresh thyme
1.3 litres (2 pints) guinea fowl or chicken stock
150 ml (¼ pint) port
150 ml (¼ pint) Madeira or medium sherry
50 g (2 oz) unsalted butter

1  Mix the grated ginger, lime rind and juice with 60 ml (4 tbsp) of the oil. Place the guinea fowl skin side up in a non-metallic dish. Pour over the marinade, cover and chill for at least 2 hours or overnight.
2  Preheat the oven to 240°C (475°F) Mark 9. To prepare the Lime and Ginger Sauce, cut the pared lime rind into strips. Put into boiling water for 4–5 minutes or until transparent. Drain, place in cold water and set aside.
3  Place the lime juice, ginger, thyme sprigs and half of the stock in a saucepan, bring to the boil and boil until reduced by half. Add the port and Madeira or sherry and reduce by half again. Add the remaining stock and reduce to 450 ml (¾ pint); strain.
4  Place the guinea fowl and marinade in a roasting pan and brush with the remaining oil. Cook in the oven, basting regularly, for 30-35 minutes or until tender and the skin is brown and crisp. Remove, cover with foil and leave to rest for 10 minutes.
5  Heat the sauce to simmering point, then gradually whisk in the butter. Garnish the guinea fowl with the reserved lime rind and herb sprigs, and serve with the sauce.

# RATATOUILLE WITH MOZZARELLA TOASTS

PREPARATION TIME: **20** MINUTES ◆ COOKING TIME: **25** MINUTES ◆ FREEZING: **NOT SUITABLE** ◆ **390** CALS PER SERVING ◆ SERVES **4**

30 ml (2 tbsp) olive oil
225 g (8 oz) aubergine, roughly chopped
225 g (8 oz) courgette, roughly chopped
1 yellow pepper, roughly chopped
1 red pepper, roughly chopped
2 large garlic cloves, crushed
400 g can chopped tomatoes
2.5 ml (½ tsp) caster sugar
30 ml (2 tbsp) chopped fresh basil
salt and freshly ground black pepper
1 small baguette, sliced and toasted
two 125 g packs mozzarella cheese,
    thinly sliced

**1** Heat the oil in a non-stick frying pan, add the aubergine, courgette and peppers and fry for about 10 minutes or until beginning to soften.
**2** Add the garlic, tomatoes, sugar and basil and simmer gently for 10 minutes or until the vegetables are tender and any excess liquid has evaporated. Season to taste.
**3** Divide the mixture between 4 shallow heatproof dishes. Place 4 slices of toasted baguette on each dish and top with the mozzarella. Cook under a preheated grill until the cheese is golden brown. Serve immediately.

# PUMPKIN RISOTTO WITH HAZELNUT BUTTER

PREPARATION TIME: **15** MINUTES ◆ COOKING TIME: **40** MINUTES ◆ FREEZING: **NOT SUITABLE** ◆ **715** CALS PER SERVING ◆ SERVES **4**

900 g (2 lb) pumpkin
50 g (2 oz) butter
175 g (6 oz) onion, finely chopped
2 garlic cloves, crushed
225 g (8 oz) risotto (arborio) rice
600 ml (1 pint) chicken stock
grated rind of ½ orange
50 g (2 oz) freshly grated Parmesan
    cheese

**HAZELNUT BUTTER**
50 g (2 oz) hazelnuts, toasted and finely
    chopped
30 ml (2 tbsp) chopped fresh parsley
125 g (4 oz) butter, softened
salt and freshly ground black pepper

**1** First, prepare the Hazelnut Butter. Stir the hazelnuts and parsley into the butter. Season with pepper. Spoon on to a piece of non-stick baking parchment and roll into a sausage shape; twist the paper at both ends and chill while preparing the risotto.
**2** Cut the pumpkin in half, scoop out the seeds and cut away the skin; there should be about 450 g (1 lb) flesh. Cut into cubes the size of large dice.
**3** Melt the butter in a large saucepan, add the onion and fry until soft but not brown. Add the pumpkin and sauté over a low heat for 5–8 minutes, until just beginning to soften (see Cook's Tip).
**4** Add the garlic and rice and stir until well mixed. Add the hot stock a ladleful at a time, stirring gently, allowing the rice to absorb all the liquid after each addition. This should take about 25 minutes and the rice should then be tender.
**5** Stir in the orange rind and Parmesan and adjust the seasoning. Serve the risotto with a slice of the hazelnut butter melting on top. Accompany with a green salad.

**COOK'S TIP**

If the pumpkin is unripe and very firm, you may need to increase the cooking time to 8–10 minutes.

# GAME AND HERB PIES

PREPARATION TIME: 40 MINUTES + CHILLING ◆ COOKING TIME: 1 HOUR ◆ FREEZING: NOT SUITABLE ◆ 995 CALS PER SERVING ◆ SERVES 8

900 g (2 lb) puff pastry
225 g (8 oz) shallots or button onions
225 g (8 oz) brown-cap mushrooms
700 g (1½ lb) boneless mixed game
15 ml (1 tbsp) crushed green
   peppercorns
25 g (1 oz) plain flour
30 ml (2 tbsp) oil
75 g (3 oz) butter
175 g (6 oz) smoked streaky bacon, in
   one piece if possible, chopped
4 garlic cloves, crushed
600 ml (1 pint) dry white wine
5 ml (1 tsp) dried thyme
450 ml (¾ pint) double cream
700 g (1½ lb) fresh spinach
30 ml (2 tbsp) each chopped fresh basil,
   parsley, mint and tarragon

**1** Preheat the oven to 200°C (400°F) Mark 6. Roll out the pastry to 3 mm (⅛ inch) and use to line eight 7.5 cm (3 inch) brioche moulds. Prick and chill for 10 minutes. Bake blind (see page 101). Lower the heat to 180°C (350°F) Mark 4.
**2** Meanwhile, halve any large shallots or onions and halve or slice any large mushrooms. Cut the game into bite-size pieces, season with the peppercorns and roll in the flour. Heat the oil with 50 g (2 oz) of the butter in a casserole, add the game and bacon in batches and fry for 1–2 minutes, until golden; set aside.
**3** Fry the shallots or onions and garlic for 3–4 minutes, until golden. Add the wine and thyme, bring to the boil, then

bubble for 10 minutes until syrupy.
**4** Add the game and bacon, season and bring to the boil. Add the cream and simmer for 8–10 minutes until the liquid has reduced by half. Cover and simmer for 20 minutes until tender.
**5** Melt the remaining butter in a pan, and fry the mushrooms over a high heat until golden; set aside. Add the spinach and cook for 2–3 minutes, until just wilted and all the excess liquid has evaporated. Drain, squeeze chop and season.
**6** Divide the spinach between the pastry cases. Add the herbs and mushrooms to the game mixture, then spoon into the cases. Cover loosely with foil and cook in the oven for 10–15 minutes, until hot.

# DUCK WITH BEETROOT AND RED ONION RELISH

PREPARATION TIME: 15 MINUTES ◆ COOKING TIME: 30 MINUTES ◆ FREEZING: NOT SUITABLE ◆ 640 CALS PER SERVING ◆ SERVES 4

1 orange, sliced
4 duck breasts, about 175 g (6 oz) each
salt and freshly ground black pepper
flat-leaf parsley, to garnish

**BEETROOT AND RED ONION RELISH**
60 ml (4 tbsp) oil
450 g (1 lb) red onion, thinly sliced
300 ml (½ pint) red wine
grated rind and juice of 2 oranges
2.5 cm (1 inch) piece fresh root ginger,
   grated
7.5 ml (1½ tsp) soft light brown
   (muscovado) sugar
200 ml (7 fl oz) port
about 175 g (6 oz) vacuum-packed
   cooked beetroot, sliced

**1** Preheat the oven to 200°C (400°F) Mark 6.
**2** First prepare the Beetroot and Red Onion Relish. Heat the oil in a frying pan, add the onion and cook, stirring, for 15–20 minutes or until soft and caramelised.
**3** Add the wine and orange juice to the onion, bring to the boil and bubble for about 5 minutes to reduce the liquid to almost nothing. Add the ginger, orange rind, sugar and port, bring to the boil and bubble for 5 minutes or until syrupy. Add the beetroot and season to taste.
**4** Meanwhile, sprinkle the duck with salt and cook with the sliced orange in the oven for 12–15 minutes.

**5** To serve, slice the duck, garnish with the orange slices and parsley and serve with the relish.

# CRISPY RISOTTO

PREPARATION TIME: 15 MINUTES + CHILLING ◆ COOKING TIME: 40 MINUTES ◆ FREEZING: NOT SUITABLE ◆ 765 CALS PER SERVING ◆ SERVES 4

45 ml (3 tbsp) oil
125 g (4 oz) onion, finely chopped
2 garlic cloves, crushed
175 g (6 oz) arborio (risotto) rice
450 ml (³/₄ pint) chicken stock
150 ml (¹/₄ pint) white wine
75 g (3 oz) freshly grated Parmesan cheese
75 g (3 oz) butter
125 g (4 oz) podded peas, fresh or frozen
200 ml carton crème fraîche
30 ml (2 tbsp) chopped fresh sage
salt and freshly ground black pepper
freshly grated Parmesan cheese and sage leaves, to garnish

1  Heat 15 ml (1 tbsp) of the oil in a non-stick saucepan, add the onion and fry gently for about 7 minutes or until soft. Stir in the garlic and fry for 1 minute.
2  Add the rice and stir well. Add the hot stock and wine a ladleful at a time, stirring constantly, allowing the rice to absorb all the liquid after each addition. This should take about 25 minutes and the rice should then be tender. Stir in 50 g (2 oz) of the Parmesan and 25 g (1 oz) of the butter. Cool, cover and chill overnight.
3  Shape the risotto into 8 thin, round, flat patties, about 7.5 cm (3 inches) in diameter. Place on a baking sheet and chill for at least 1 hour.

4  Cook the peas in boiling salted water until tender. Drain, then add the crème fraîche and sage. Season well.
5  Dip each pattie in the remaining Parmesan. Melt the remaining butter and oil in a non-stick frying pan, add the patties and fry for 2 minutes on each side or until golden brown. Bring the crème fraîche sauce to the boil. Garnish the patties with grated Parmesan and sage leaves and serve with the sauce.

# ROASTED VEGETABLE TART

PREPARATION TIME: 20 MINUTES ◆ COOKING TIME: 45 MINUTES – 1 HOUR ◆ FREEZING: NOT SUITABLE ◆ 360–240 CALS PER SERVING ◆ SERVES 4–6

350 g (12 oz) aubergine
450 g (1 lb) courgettes
700 g (1¹/₂ lb) red and yellow peppers
350 g (12 oz) tomatoes, halved
75 ml (5 tbsp) olive oil
salt and freshly ground black pepper
125 g (4 oz) filo pastry

1  Preheat the oven to 200°C (400°F) Mark 6. Slice the aubergine, courgettes and peppers lengthways into strips. Place all the vegetables in single layers in roasting pans, brush with oil and season well. Cook in the oven for about 45 minutes or until the vegetables become charred and soft (see Cook's Tip).
2  Line a deep 18 cm (7 inch) loose-based flan tin with the filo pastry, brushing lightly with oil after each layer. Leave the pastry edges up beyond the edge of the tin and free from oil (they should be dry).
3  Place the tin on a baking sheet and cook in the oven for 5–8 minutes or until

the pastry is crisp and golden. Lower the temperature to 150°C (300°F) Mark 2.
4  Spoon the vegetables into the pastry case, seasoning as you go. Cover loosely with foil and warm through in the oven for 5–10 minutes.
5  Cut into wedges with a very sharp knife and drizzle with any remaining oil or juices from the roasting pans to serve.

## COOK'S TIP

The different vegetables will cook at varying speeds so it's important to keep a close eye on them. Check the vegetables and remove pieces from the oven as they are ready.

# CRISPY DUCK PANCAKES

PREPARATION TIME: **30** MINUTES ◆ COOKING TIME: **2¼** HOURS ◆ FREEZING: NOT SUITABLE ◆ **510** CALS PER SERVING ◆ SERVES **6**

2.3 kg (5 lb) fresh oven-ready duckling
2 bay leaves
5 ml (1 tsp) salt
10 black peppercorns
75 g (3 oz) butter
350 g (12 oz) onion, thinly sliced
2 garlic cloves, thinly sliced
2 red chillies, seeded and sliced
2.5 cm (1 inch) piece fresh root ginger, chopped
2 red peppers
175 g (6 oz) cucumber, seeded
4 spring onions
100 ml (4 fl oz) hoisin sauce
45 ml (3 tbsp) teriyaki sauce
90 ml (6 tbsp) chopped fresh coriander
18 sheets filo pastry, about 225 g (8 oz)
1 egg, beaten

1  Place the duck, bay leaves, salt and peppercorns in a saucepan with cold water to cover. Bring to the boil, then cover and simmer for 2 hours. Drain off the stock. Cool the duck, then cut the meat into strips.
2  Melt 25 g (1 oz) of the butter in a saucepan, add the onion, garlic, chilli and ginger and cook over a low heat for 30 minutes or until soft and golden; cool.
3  Cook the peppers under a preheated grill for 10–15 minutes until the skin is well blackened. Cool, then skin, seed and slice. Cut the cucumber and spring onions into 5 cm (2 inch) matchsticks.
4  Mix the duck meat with the onion mixture, sauces and coriander.

5  Melt the remaining butter. Lay a sheet of filo on a work surface and brush with butter. Cut into a 15 cm (6 inch) square. Repeat with the remaining filo, covering with a damp tea-towel or cling film as you work to prevent it drying out.
6  Lay a few red pepper strips diagonally across the centre of each pastry square, top with a little duck mixture, then with spring onion and cucumber. Brush 2 opposite corners with egg, then roll up into a cigar shape. Repeat with the remaining filling and pastry squares.
7  Heat some oil in a deep-fat fryer or large saucepan to 160°C (325°F). Deep-fry each parcel for 3–4 minutes, until golden. Serve immediately.

# PHEASANT WITH CHESTNUTS

PREPARATION TIME: **10-15** MINUTES ◆ COOKING TIME: **45** MINUTES ◆ FREEZING: NOT SUITABLE ◆ **385** CALS PER SERVING ◆ SERVES **4**

350 g (12 oz) fresh or 225 g (8 oz) canned or vacuum-packed chestnuts (see Cook's Tip)
15 ml (1 tbsp) vegetable oil
25 g (1 oz) butter
4 pheasant breasts, about 450 g (1 lb) total weight, skinned
2 onions, sliced
15 ml (1 tbsp) plain flour
450 ml (¾ pint) beef stock
100 ml (4 fl oz) red wine
salt and freshly ground black pepper
grated rind and juice of ½ orange
5 ml (1 tsp) redcurrant jelly
bouquet garni
celery leaves, to garnish (optional)

1  Skin the chestnuts, if necessary.
2  Heat the oil and butter in a 2.3-litre (4-pint) flameproof casserole, add the pheasant and cook over a high heat for 5 minutes, until golden. Set aside and keep warm.
3  Add the onion to the pan and cook for 5 minutes. Add the fresh chestnuts, if using, and cook until golden. Set aside.
4  Stir the flour into the fat and cook gently for 1 minute. Remove from the heat and gradually stir in the stock and wine. Bring to the boil and cook, stirring, until thickened. Season to taste. Return the pheasant and onion to the pan and add the cooked, canned or vacuum-packed chestnuts.

5  Add the orange rind and juice, redcurrant jelly and bouquet garni, cover and simmer for 30 minutes or until tender.
6  Remove the bouquet garni and adjust the seasoning. Garnish with celery leaves, if wished, to serve.

### COOK'S TIP
Vacuum-packed coked peeled chestnuts are now available from most good supermarkets. They save an enormous amount of time.

### VARIATION
Use chicken breasts instead of pheasant.

# POTATO AND FENNEL GRATIN

PREPARATION TIME: 20 MINUTES ◆ COOKING TIME: ABOUT 1 HOUR ◆ FREEZING: SUITABLE ◆ 340 CALS PER SERVING ◆ SERVES 6

450 g (1 lb) fennel
salt and freshly ground black pepper
284 ml carton double cream
300 ml (½ pint) milk
2 garlic cloves, crushed
700 g (1½ lb) large potato, thinly sliced

**1** Trim the feathery leaves and stalks off the fennel, then halve and thinly slice. Cook in boiling salted water for 2 minutes, drain and set aside.
**2** Place the cream, milk and garlic in a large saucepan and bring to the boil. Add the potato and fennel and simmer over a low heat for 15–20 minutes, stirring occasionally to prevent the potato sticking. Preheat the oven to 200°C (400°F) Mark 6.
**3** Season the potato mixture well, then transfer to a 2 litre (3½ pint) ovenproof dish. Cook in the oven for 40 minutes or until the gratin is golden and tender. Serve immediately.

# MUSHROOM AND PARMESAN RISOTTO

PREPARATION TIME: 5 MINUTES ◆ COOKING TIME: 25 MINUTES ◆ FREEZING: NOT SUITABLE ◆ 465 CALS PER SERVING ◆ SERVES 4

75 g (3 oz) butter
1 onion, finely chopped
225 g (8 oz) brown-cap mushrooms, sliced
175 g (6 oz) arborio (risotto) rice
600 ml (1 pint) vegetable stock
150 ml (¼ pint) dry sherry
290 g jar mushroom antipasto, drained
50 g (2 oz) freshly grated Parmesan cheese
salt and freshly ground black pepper
lemon wedges, to serve

**1** Preheat the oven to 180°C (350°F) Mark 4. Melt the butter in a flameproof casserole, add the onion and mushrooms and cook for 5 minutes or until soft and golden. Stir in the rice, stock and sherry and bring to the boil. Cook, uncovered, in the oven for 20 minutes or until the rice has completely absorbed the liquid.
**2** Stir in the mushroom antipasto and about half of the Parmesan cheese. Adjust the seasoning, sprinkle with the remaining Parmesan and serve with lemon wedges.

# VENISON CASSEROLE WITH SWEDE AND POTATO TOPPING

PREPARATION TIME: **10** MINUTES ◆ COOKING TIME: **1¼** HOURS ◆ FREEZING: SUITABLE (STEP 4) ◆ **375** CALS PER SERVING ◆ SERVES **4**

15 ml (1 tbsp) vegetable oil
450 g (1 lb) diced venison
2 garlic cloves, crushed
30 ml (2 tbsp) plain flour
salt and freshly ground black pepper
150 ml (¼ pint) each beef stock and red wine
45 ml (3 tbsp) tomato paste
5 ml (1 tsp) dried basil
15 ml (1 tbsp) redcurrant jelly
1 red pepper, seeded and chopped
1 onion, chopped
1 head of celery, chopped
25 g (1 oz) sun-dried tomato, chopped
350 g (12 oz) each potato and swede, cubed
30 ml (2 tbsp) warm milk
15 g (½ oz) butter
chopped fresh parsley, to garnish

**1** Preheat the oven to 160°C (325°F Mark 3. Heat the oil in a 1.7-litre (3-pint) flameproof casserole, add the venison and brown over a high heat. Lower the heat, add the garlic and cook for 2 minutes.

**2** Stir in the flour and seasoning. Add the stock, wine, tomato paste and basil and bring to the boil, stirring occasionally. Stir in the redcurrant jelly, then add the red pepper, onion, celery and tomato.

**3** Cover and cook in the oven for 1–1¼ hours or until the meat is tender.

**4** Meanwhile, cook the potato and swede in boiling salted water for 15–20 minutes, until very soft. Drain, then mash with the milk and butter. Season well.

**5** Spoon the mixture over the casserole and return to the oven for 10 minutes to brown. Garnish with parsley to serve.

# PHEASANT WITH SMOKED BACON AND MUSHROOMS

PREPARATION TIME: **35** MINUTES ◆ COOKING TIME: ABOUT **1** HOUR ◆ FREEZING: NOT SUITABLE ◆ **420** CALS PER SERVING ◆ SERVES **4**

15 g (½ oz) dried porcini or mixed dried mushrooms
2 garlic cloves, crushed
2 oven-ready pheasants
25 g (1 oz) butter
10 juniper berries, lightly crushed
1 small onion, finely chopped
125 g (4 oz) smoked bacon, in one piece
10 ml (2 tsp) plain white flour
300 ml (½ pint) red wine
150 ml (¼ pint) chicken stock
175 g (6 oz) chestnut or brown mushrooms
30 ml (2 tbsp) redcurrant jelly

**GARNISH**
125 g (4 oz) puff pastry
15 ml (1 tbsp) chopped fresh rosemary
beaten egg yolk, to glaze
flat-leaf parsley, to garnish

**1** Rinse the dried mushrooms twice and place in a bowl with 300 ml (½ pint) warm water; soak for 20 minutes.

**2** Preheat the oven to 220°C (425°F) Mark 7. Prepare the garnish. Roll out the pastry to about 5 mm (1/4 inch) thickness. Sprinkle with the rosemary, then roll out to about 3 mm (⅛ inch) thickness. Cut out small triangular shapes and transfer to a dampened baking sheet. Brush with egg yolk and bake in the oven for about 8 minutes, until risen; set aside. Lower the oven temperature to 200°C (400°F) Mark 6.

**3** Spread the garlic over the pheasants. Melt the butter in a frying pan and sear the pheasants on all sides. Transfer to a large casserole with the juniper.

**4** Fry the onion and diced bacon for 10 minutes. Stir in the flour, add the wine and stock and bring to the boil. Pour over the pheasants, cover and cook for 25 minutes.

**5** Drain and rinse the dried mushrooms; halve the fresh mushrooms. Add both to the casserole, return to the oven and cook, uncovered, for 20–25 minutes, until tender.

**6** Transfer the pheasants and mushrooms to a serving plate and keep warm. Add the redcurrant jelly to the cooking juices and heat until dissolved. Pour a little over the pheasants, garnish with the pastries and parsley, and serve with the sauce.

# ROASTED VEGETABLE MOUSSAKA

PREPARATION TIME: 35 MINUTES ◆ COOKING TIME: 2 HOURS ◆ FREEZING: SUITABLE ◆ 545 CALS PER SERVING ◆ SERVES 12

700 g (1½ lb) potatoes, preferably sweet potatoes
450 g (1 lb) tomatoes, preferably plum
700 g (1½ lb) aubergine
225 g (8 oz) each courgette and fennel
salt and freshly ground black pepper
450 g (1 lb) each red peppers and red onions
4 garlic cloves
150 ml (¼ pint) olive oil
15 ml (3 tsp) dried thyme
150 ml (¼ pint) white wine
45 ml (3 tbsp) sun-dried tomato paste
10 ml (2 tsp) sugar
450 g (1 lb) passata
350 g (12 oz) goat's cheese, cut into 1 cm (½ inch) slices
50 g (2 oz) freshly grated Parmesan cheese

1 Preheat the oven to 230°C (450°F) Mark 8. Cut the potatoes, tomatoes, aubergine and courgette into 5 mm (¼ inch) slices. Cook the potato in boiling salted water for 4 minutes; drain.
2 Cut the fennel, peppers and onions into large pieces. Place the potato, aubergine, fennel, red pepper, onion, unpeeled garlic and oil in 2 large roasting pans. Season well and sprinkle with 10 ml (2 tsp) of the thyme.
3 Cook in the oven, uncovered, for 45 minutes, stirring occasionally. Add the tomato and courgette for the final 10 minutes. Lower the temperature to 200°C (400°F) Mark 6. Remove the skin from the garlic and lightly mash with a fork. Place in a saucepan with the wine, tomato paste and sugar, bring to the boil and bubble for 2 minutes. Add the passata and bubble for 8 minutes. Season to taste.
4 Layer half of the roasted vegetables in a large ovenproof dish with half of the tomato sauce. Layer the remaining vegetables and sauce. Cover and cook in the oven for 45 minutes.
5 Place the goat's cheese on top, sprinkle with the Parmesan and remaining thyme and return to the oven for 15 minutes. If the cheese does not brown sufficiently, place the dish under a preheated grill for 3 minutes. Serve immediately.

# SAFFRON RISOTTO CAKES

PREPARATION TIME: 5 MINUTES ◆ COOKING TIME: ABOUT 45 MINUTES ◆ FREEZING: SUITABLE ◆ 390 CALS PER SERVING ◆ SERVES 8

pinch of saffron threads
125 g (4 oz) butter
225 g (8 oz) onion, chopped
2 garlic cloves, crushed
300 g (10 oz) arborio (risotto) rice
150 ml (¼ pint) white wine
600 ml (1 pint) chicken or vegetable stock
50 g (2 oz) freshly grated Parmesan cheese
2 eggs, beaten
salt and freshly ground black pepper
75 g (3 oz) fresh white breadcrumbs
30 ml (2 tbsp) oil
chives and parsley sprigs, to garnish

1 Soak the saffron in 150 ml (¼ pint) boiling water.
2 Melt half of the butter in a large heavy-based saucepan, add the onion and garlic and cook, stirring, for 7–10 minutes or until soft. Stir in the rice, wine, saffron and soaking liquid and bring to the boil, stirring gently. Cook, stirring, until all the liquid has evaporated. Add the hot stock a ladleful at a time, stirring gently, allowing the rice to absorb all the liquid after each addition. This should take 20–25 minutes and the rice should then be tender. Add more stock, if necessary.
3 Tip the rice into a bowl and stir in the Parmesan cheese. Cool, then add the eggs and season well. Cover and chill overnight.
4 Shape the risotto into 20 small flat cakes. Roll the cakes in the breadcrumbs. Melt the remaining butter with the oil in a large non-stick frying pan and cook the cakes in batches for about 2 minutes on each side, until crisp and golden. Drain and keep warm, covered with foil, in a low oven. Garnish with chives and parsley to serve.

# MUSTARD VENISON WITH MUSHROOM DRESSING

PREPARATION TIME: 15 MINUTES ◆ COOKING TIME: 25 MINUTES ◆ FREEZING: NOT SUITABLE ◆ 510 CALS PER SERVING ◆ SERVES 4

550 g (1½ lb) strip-loin venison, about
  6 cm (2 ½ inch) diameter
15 ml (1 tbsp) wholegrain mustard
8-10 button onions, thinly sliced
350 g (12 oz) small shiitake or brown-cap
  mushrooms
150 ml (¼ pint) olive oil
30 ml (2 tbsp) chopped fresh parsley and
  thyme
25 ml (5 tsp) balsamic vinegar
salt and freshly ground black pepper
lemon juice

1 Preheat the oven to 230°C (450°F) Mark 8. Rub the venison with the mustard. Scatter the onion and mushrooms around the venison and drizzle over half of the oil. Roast for 30–35 minutes for medium-rare, 40 minutes for well-done.
2 Roll the hot venison in the herbs and place on a warm serving platter with the mushrooms and onion. Cover with foil and keep warm while preparing the dressing.
3 Add the remaining oil and the vinegar to the roasting pan and heat through on the hob, stirring. Season and add lemon juice to taste.
4 To serve, cut the venison into thick

slices. Serve with the sauce and accompany with potato chips, if wished.

## VARIATION

For a spicier version, roll the hot venison in crushed peppercorns instead of herbs.

# RABBIT WITH GRAINY MUSTARD

PREPARATION TIME: 10 MINUTES ◆ COOKING TIME: 1½ HOURS ◆ FREEZING: NOT SUITABLE ◆ 330 CALS PER SERVING ◆ SERVES 4

salt and freshly ground black pepper
4-6 rabbit joints, 700–900 g (1½–2 lb)
  total weight
25 g (1 oz) plain flour
300 g (10 oz) shallots or button onions
225 g (8 oz) carrots
15 ml (1 tbsp) vegetable oil
15 g (½ oz) butter
2 garlic cloves, crushed
45-60 ml (3-4 tbsp) wholegrain mustard
300 ml (½ pint) chicken stock
150 ml (¼ pint) white wine
60 ml (4 tbsp) reduced-fat crème fraîche
chopped fresh herbs, to garnish
shredded cabbage, to serve

1 Preheat the oven to 160°C (325°F) Mark 3. Season the rabbit and toss in half of the flour. If the shallots or onions are large, cut them in half. Slice the carrots diagonally about 1 cm (½ inch) thick.
2 Heat the oil and butter in a 2.3-litre (4-pint) flameproof casserole, add the rabbit and cook over a high heat until browned; remove from the pan and set aside. Lower the heat, add the garlic, onion, carrot and mustard to the casserole and cook for 5 minutes. Add the remaining flour.
3 Add the stock and wine, stir well and bring to the boil. Return the rabbit to the casserole, cover and cook in the oven for

1½ hours or until tender.
4 Stir in the crème fraîche and season to taste. Garnish with herbs and serve with shredded cabbage.

## VARIATION

Replace the rabbit with chicken quarters.

# MUSHROOM AND ROASTED POTATO BAKE

**Preparation time: 45 minutes ◆ Cooking time: 35 minutes ◆ Freezing: Suitable (step 4) ◆ 795 cals per serving ◆ Serves 6**

900 g (2 lb) small potatoes, quartered
90 ml (6 tbsp) olive oil
225 g (8 oz) onion, roughly chopped
450 g (1 lb) mixed mushrooms, eg shiitake and brown cap, chopped
2 garlic cloves, crushed
30 ml (2 tbsp) tomato paste
60 ml (4 tbsp) sun-dried tomato paste
10 ml (2 tsp) chopped fresh thyme
300 ml (½ pint) each white wine and vegetable stock
284 ml carton double cream
400 g (14 oz) large spinach leaves, chopped
175 g (6 oz) Gruyère cheese, grated
125 g (4 oz) freshly grated Parmesan cheese
300 ml (½ pint) Greek-style yogurt
2 eggs, beaten

**1** Preheat the oven to 200°C (400°F) Mark 6. Toss the potato with 60 ml (4 tbsp) of the oil in a large roasting pan. Cook in the oven for 40 minutes or until tender and golden.

**2** Heat the remaining oil in a large heavy-based saucepan, add the onion and cook for 10 minutes or until soft, then add the mushrooms and garlic and cook over a high heat for 5 minutes. Stir in the tomato pastes, thyme and wine, bring to the boil, then simmer for 2 minutes.

**3** Add the stock and cream, bring back to the boil and bubble for 20 minutes or until well reduced and syrupy. Pour into a 2.3 litre (4 pint) ovenproof dish. Stir in the potato, spinach, Gruyère and half of the Parmesan cheese. Season well.

**4** Combine the yogurt and eggs and season to taste. Spoon over the vegetable mixture and sprinkle with the remaining Parmesan.

**5** Cook in the oven for 30–35 minutes or until golden and bubbling. Garnish with sprigs of flat-leaf parsley and thyme to serve, if wished.

# PUMPKIN AND CHEESE BAKE

**Preparation time: 30 minutes ◆ Cooking time: About 1½ hours ◆ Freezing: Not suitable ◆ 600 cals per serving ◆ Serves 6**

350 g (12 oz) leftover cheeses, eg Emmenthal, Cheddar, mozzarella
450 g (1 lb) pumpkin, roughly chopped
60 ml (4 tbsp) olive oil
150 g (5 oz) polenta
7.5 ml (1½) tsp salt
freshly ground black pepper
60 ml (4 tbsp) freshly grated Parmesan cheese
300 g (10 oz) onion, roughly chopped
2 garlic cloves, crushed
5 ml (1 tsp) dried thyme
two 400 g cans chopped tomatoes
30 ml (2 tbsp) sun-dried tomato paste
200 ml (7 fl oz) vegetable stock
5 ml (1 tsp) sugar
marjoram sprigs, to garnish

**1** Preheat the oven to 230°C (450°F) Mark 8. Grate any hard cheese; dice any soft cheese. Place the pumpkin in a roasting pan with 30 ml (2 tbsp) of the oil and cook for 25 minutes or until tender. Lower the temperature to 200°C (400°F) Mark 6.

**2** Meanwhile, line a 25 x 16 cm (10 x 6½ inch) baking pan with greaseproof paper. Bring 900 ml (1½ pints) water to the boil in a large saucepan and add the polenta in a thin stream, stirring constantly over a low heat for about 10 minutes until it stiffens. Season and add 45 ml (3 tbsp) of the Parmesan cheese.

**3** Spread the polenta in the baking pan to about 1 cm (½ inch) thickness. Place cling film on the surface to prevent a skin forming. Cool, then cut into squares.

**4** Heat the remaining oil in a large saucepan, add the onion, garlic and thyme and cook until soft. Add the tomatoes, tomato paste, stock and 200 ml (7 fl oz) water. Bring to the boil and bubble for 10–15 minutes. Add the sugar and season well.

**5** Spoon half of the sauce into a large ovenproof dish, then add half of the polenta, pumpkin and cheese. Repeat the layers, finishing with polenta and cheese. Sprinkle with the remaining Parmesan.

**6** Cook in the oven for 35–45 minutes, until golden. Garnish with marjoram.

# STEAK WITH LAGER AND MUSTARD SAUCE

**PREPARATION TIME: 15 MINUTES ◆ COOKING TIME: 30 MINUTES ◆ FREEZING: NOT SUITABLE ◆ 660 CALS PER SERVING ◆ SERVES 4**

45 ml (3 tbsp) oil
75 g (3 oz) butter
450 g (1 lb) red onion, thinly sliced
45 ml (3 tbsp) demerara sugar
15 ml (1 tbsp) chopped fresh thyme
salt and freshly ground black pepper
300 ml (½ pint) beef stock
600 ml (1 pint) lager
60 ml (4 tbsp) dark French mustard
1 small ciabatta loaf
4 fillet or sirloin steaks, each 175 g (6 oz)
2-3 garlic cloves, crushed
thyme sprigs, to garnish
French beans, to serve

**1** Heat 30 ml (2 tbsp) of the oil and 25 g (1 oz) of the butter in a frying pan until foaming, add the onion and cook for 5 minutes or until beginning to soften. Increase the heat, add 15 ml (1 tbsp) of the sugar and cook until golden brown. Stir in the thyme and season to taste. Transfer to an ovenproof dish and keep warm.
**2** Pour the stock and lager into the pan, bring to the boil and bubble hard for 7–10 minutes until syrupy; season to taste. Add the mustard and remaining sugar, then set aside and keep warm.
**3** Meanwhile, split the ciabatta and cut into 4 pieces to fit the steaks. Toast the crust side under a preheated grill until crisp. Melt the remaining butter, then add the garlic and seasoning to taste. Pour over the untoasted side of the bread and toast until golden brown and crisp; keep warm.
**4** Season the steaks with pepper. Heat the remaining oil in a heavy-based non-stick frying pan or griddle until almost smoking, add the steaks and fry over a high heat for 2–3 minutes on each side for medium-rare. (Timing will vary depending on the thickness of the steaks.)
**5** Place the steaks on the ciabatta, pour over any cooking juices and serve with the onion and sauce. Garnish with thyme and serve with French beans.

# BEEF WITH CHILLI BÉARNAISE SAUCE

**PREPARATION TIME: 15 MINUTES ◆ COOKING TIME: 20 MINUTES ◆ FREEZING: NOT SUITABLE ◆ 740 CALS PER SERVING ◆ SERVES 4**

150 ml (¼ pint) white wine
15 ml (1 tbsp) white wine vinegar
2.5 ml (½ tsp) ground cumin or cumin seeds
125 g (4 oz) onion or shallots, finely chopped
1 red chilli, seeded and finely chopped
225 g (8 oz) unsalted butter
4 egg yolks
5 ml (1 tsp) Dijon mustard
salt and freshly ground black pepper
4 fillet steaks, each about 175 g (6 oz)
broccoli and sauté potatoes, to serve

**1** Put the wine, vinegar, cumin, onion or shallot and half of the chilli in a saucepan. Bring to the boil and bubble until reduced to 30 ml (2 tbsp). Strain and reserve the liquid.
**2** Melt the butter in a saucepan. Put the egg yolks and mustard in a food processor and process for 2 minutes. When the melted butter is very hot (see Cook's Tips), slowly pour it on to the eggs, with the processor running at full speed. Blend for 2–3 minutes or until the sauce has thickened. Add the remaining chilli and the reduced wine. Adjust the seasoning. Transfer to a heatproof bowl and keep warm over a pan of gently simmering water.

**3** Season the steaks with pepper and cook under a preheated grill or pan-fry over a high heat for 4–6 minutes on each side, depending on thickness, for medium rare. Serve with the sauce, broccoli and sauté potatoes.

### COOK'S TIPS

It's vital that the butter is very hot and almost starting to brown when it's poured on to the eggs, as it's this heat that cooks and thickens the sauce. The Béarnaise sauce can be made a few hours ahead and chilled. Serve cold to melt over the hot steaks.

# EGG NOODLES WITH CHICKEN AND VEGETABLES

PREPARATION TIME: **10** MINUTES ◆ COOKING TIME: ABOUT **10** MINUTES ◆ FREEZING: NOT SUITABLE ◆ **730** CALS PER SERVING ◆ SERVES **2**

1 chicken breast fillet, skinned
1 red pepper, cored and seeded
4 spring onions
2 carrots
125 g (4 oz) button mushrooms
250 g packet thin egg noodles
about 30 ml (2 tbsp) vegetable oil
2.5 cm (1 inch) piece fresh root ginger (optional), chopped
1 garlic clove, finely chopped
45 ml (3 tbsp) hoisin sauce
30 ml (2 tbsp) light soy sauce
15 ml (1 tbsp) chilli sauce
shredded spring onion and sesame seeds, to garnish

**1** Cut the chicken into very thin strips. Cut the red pepper into thin strips. Cut the spring onions and carrots into similar-sized strips and halve the mushrooms.
**2** Cook the noodles in a large pan of boiling water according to packet instructions. Drain well, then toss with a little of the oil to prevent them sticking together; set aside.
**3** Heat the remaining oil in a wok or a large frying pan, add the chicken, ginger, if using, and garlic and cook over a very high heat until the chicken is browned on the outside and cooked right through.
**4** Add all the vegetables to the wok or pan and stir-fry over a high heat for a few minutes or until they are just cooked, but still crunchy.
**5** Add the sauces and stir to mix. Add the noodles and cook for a couple of minutes to heat through. Serve immediately, sprinkled with shredded spring onion and a few sesame seeds.

## COOK'S TIP

Vary the vegetable content of this dish according to what you have to hand, but aim to keep a good balance of texture, colour and flavour. If supplies of fresh vegetables are limited, canned sliced bamboo shoots or water chestnuts make a good addition.

# PASTA NIÇOISE

PREPARATION TIME: **10** MINUTES + STANDING ◆ COOKING TIME: **20** MINUTES ◆ FREEZING: NOT SUITABLE ◆ **276** CALS PER SERVING ◆ SERVES **6**

225 g (8 oz) dried pasta shapes, eg shells, bows or twists
salt and freshly ground black pepper
225 g (8 oz) fresh or frozen fine green beans, trimmed
225 g (8 oz) tomatoes, quartered
½ small cucumber, thinly sliced
2 eggs, hard-boiled, shelled and quartered
50 g (2 oz) pitted black olives
15 ml (1 tbsp) capers
60 ml (4 tbsp) olive oil
30 ml (2 tbsp) lemon juice
pinch of sugar
2.5 ml (½ tsp) Dijon mustard
15 ml (1 tbsp) chopped fresh parsley
15 ml (1 tbsp) chopped fresh basil

**1** Bring a large pan of salted water to the boil. Add the pasta and fresh green beans, if using, and cook for 10–12 minutes. If using frozen beans, add to the pan 5 minutes before the end of the cooking time. Drain, rinse thoroughly in cold water and drain again.
**2** Put the pasta and beans in a salad bowl. Arrange the tomato, cucumber, egg, olives and capers on top.
**3** Place the oil, lemon juice, sugar, mustard, salt and pepper in a bowl and whisk well. Add the parsley and basil and mix well together.
**4** Pour the dressing over the salad and toss very lightly. Leave the salad to stand for 30 minutes before serving.

# BEEF CASSEROLE

PREPARATION TIME: 40 MINUTES ◆ COOKING TIME: ABOUT 3 HOURS ◆ FREEZING: SUITABLE (STEP 3) ◆ 560 CALS PER SERVING ◆ SERVES 8

1.4 kg (3 lb) stewing beef
175 g (6 oz) each onion, leek and carrot
450 g (1 lb) celery
225 g (8 oz) mixed wild mushrooms in oil
60 ml (4 tbsp) oil
2 garlic cloves, crushed
1 bottle red wine
600 ml (1 pint) chicken stock
15 ml (1 tbsp) red wine vinegar
2 bay leaves
1 thyme sprig or 1.25 ml ($^1/_4$ tsp) dried
15 ml (1 tbsp) tomato paste
30 ml (2 tbsp) roughly crushed black
    peppercorns
45 ml (3 tbsp) redcurrant jelly
150 ml ($^1/_4$ pint) port
50 g (2 oz) butter
250 g (9 oz) vacuum-packed or canned
    whole peeled chestnuts

1  Cut the beef into 3.5 cm (1$^1/_2$ inch) cubes and chop the onion, leek, carrot and 175 g (6 oz) of the celery. Cut the remaining celery into fine strips, cover and set aside. Drain the mushrooms.
2  Heat 30 ml (2 tbsp) of the oil in a heavy-based saucepan, add the chopped vegetables and garlic and cook for 5 minutes, until soft. Add the wine, stock, vinegar, bay leaves, thyme, tomato paste, peppercorns, redcurrant jelly and port, bring to the boil, then simmer, uncovered, for 30 minutes. Strain the stock and discard the vegetables. Blend 15 ml (1 tbsp) cornflour with 30 ml (2 tbsp) water. Bring the stock to the boil, whisk in the blended cornflour and

cook for 1 minute, until lightly thickened. Season with salt to taste. Preheat the oven to 150°C (300°F) Mark 2.
3  Heat the remaining oil in a flameproof casserole and brown the beef. Add the sauce, bring to the boil, then cover and cook in the oven for 1$^1/_2$–2 hours. Remove the meat and boil the sauce hard for about 10 minutes until reduced, then return the beef to the casserole.
4  Melt the butter in a frying pan, add the reserved celery and stir over a high heat for 3 minutes. Add the mushrooms and chestnuts and cook for 2 minutes. Stir into the beef and heat for 2 minutes. Garnish with flat-leaf parsley and shredded lemon rind to serve.

# RICH BEEF DAUBE

PREPARATION TIME: 35 MINUTES + SOAKING ◆ COOKING TIME: 2$^1/_2$ HOURS ◆ FREEZING: SUITABLE (STEP 4) ◆ 540 CALS PER SERVING ◆ SERVES 6

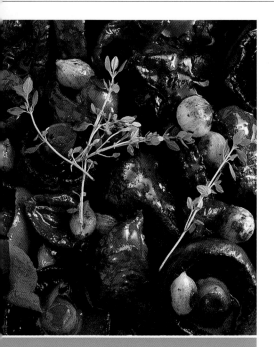

20 g ($^3/_4$ oz) dried wild mushrooms, eg
    porcini, ceps
225 g (8 oz) button onions
900 g (2 lb) stewing steak, cubed
salt and freshly ground black pepper
90 ml (6 tbsp) oil
45 ml (3 tbsp) plain flour
2 large garlic cloves, crushed
2.5 cm (1 inch) piece fresh root ginger,
    chopped
125 g (4 oz) sun-dried tomato, chopped
10 ml (2 tsp) dried mixed herbs
300 ml ($^1/_2$ pint) each red wine and beef
    stock
1–2 large oranges
10 ml (2 tsp) caster sugar
225 g (8 oz) brown-cap mushrooms
125 g (4 oz) pitted black olives
fresh thyme sprigs, to garnish (optional)

1  Rinse the wild mushrooms, then soak in 150 ml ($^1/_4$ pint) water for 1 hour. Peel the onions, leaving the root on, but trim to neaten. Season the stewing steak with salt and pepper. Preheat the oven to 160°C (325°F) Mark 3.
2  Heat 45 ml (3 tbsp) of the oil in a large flameproof casserole and brown the meat in batches over a fairly high heat. Remove from the casserole with a slotted spoon and set aside.
3  Add another 15 ml (1 tbsp) of the oil to the pan, add the onions and fry for 7–10 minutes, until golden. Return the meat to the casserole and stir in the flour, garlic, ginger, tomato and herbs. Cook, stirring, for 1 minute.

4  Add the wild mushrooms with their soaking liquid, the wine, stock, pared rind of 1 orange, about 100 ml (4 fl oz) orange juice and the sugar. Bring to the boil, then cover and cook in the oven for about 2 hours or until very tender.
5  Heat the remaining oil in a frying pan, add the brown-cap mushrooms and cook over a high heat for 2–3 minutes, then add to the casserole. Remove the orange rind and add the olives. Return the casserole to the oven for 15–20 minutes. Adjust the seasoning. Garnish with thyme, if wished, to serve.

# LINGUINI WITH FRIED COURGETTE RIBBONS

PREPARATION TIME: ABOUT 30 MINUTES ◆ COOKING TIME: 20 MINUTES ◆ FREEZING: NOT SUITABLE ◆ 850-565 CALS PER SERVING ◆ SERVES 4-6

400 g (14 oz) dried linguini
45 ml (3 tbsp) freshly grated Parmesan
cheese

**TOMATO SAUCE**
45 ml (3 tbsp) olive oil
1 onion, chopped
1 garlic clove, chopped
400 g can chopped tomatoes
45 ml (3 tbsp) chopped fresh basil
45 ml (3 tbsp) double cream

**COURGETTE RIBBONS**
350 g (12 oz) small courgettes
225 g (8 oz) dry white breadcrumbs
25 g (1 oz) freshly grated Parmesan
cheese
10 ml (2 tsp) dried thyme
2 eggs, beaten

**1** First prepare the Tomato Sauce. Heat the oil in a saucepan, add the onion and garlic and cook, stirring frequently, for 5 minutes, to soften. Add the tomatoes and basil and bring to the boil, then simmer for 10 minutes. Season to taste.
**2** Purée the sauce in a food processor or blender, then sieve the mixture back into the pan. Stir in the cream and set aside.
**3** To make the Courgette Ribbons, use a vegetable peeler to pare the courgettes into long 'ribbons', pressing firmly. Mix the breadcrumbs with the Parmesan, thyme, salt and pepper.
**4** Heat enough oil for deep-frying. Dip the courgette ribbons, one at a time, into the beaten egg, then into the

breadcrumb mixture to coat.
**5** Cook the pasta in a large pan of boiling salted water according to packet instructions.
**6** Meanwhile, deep-fry the Courgette Ribbons, in batches, in the hot oil for 1–2 minutes, until golden and crisp. Drain on kitchen paper and keep warm.
**7** Gently reheat the Tomato Sauce. Drain the pasta well, then return to the pan. Add the sauce and Parmesan and toss lightly. Transfer to a warm serving dish. Pile the Courgette Ribbons on top and serve immediately, accompanied by balsamic vinegar for sprinkling.

# OLIVE TAGLIATELLE WITH PESTO TRAPANESE

PREPARATION TIME: 20 MINUTES + RESTING ◆ COOKING TIME: 2-3 MINUTES ◆ FREEZING: NOT SUITABLE ◆ 565 CALS PER SERVING ◆ SERVES 4

**OLIVE PASTA**
350 g (12 oz) plain white flour
salt
3 eggs (size 2)
45 ml (3 tbsp) black olive paste
basil leaves, to garnish

**PESTO TRAPANESE**
3 ripe tomatoes
4 garlic cloves
salt and freshly ground black pepper
50 g (2 oz) fresh basil leaves
125 g (4 oz) blanched almonds
150 ml (¼ pint) olive oil

**1** To make the pasta, sift the flour and a pinch of salt on to a work surface and make a well in the centre. Beat the eggs and olive paste together, then pour into the well. Gradually mix into the flour, using the fingers of one hand.
**2** Knead the pasta until smooth. The dough should be quite firm; add a little flour if it feels too soft. Wrap in cling film and leave to rest for at least 30 minutes.
**3** Meanwhile, make the pesto. Place all the ingredients in a food processor or blender and blend until smooth. Transfer to a bowl and set aside.
**4** Roll out the pasta as thinly as possible, using a pasta machine if you have one. Dust with flour and roll up like a

sausage. Using a sharp knife cut the pasta into 1 cm (½ inch) strips; unravel and place on a floured tea-towel until required. Alternatively, fit the tagliatelle cutters to your pasta machine and pass the pasta through.
**5** Cook the pasta in a large pan of boiling salted water for 2-3 minutes until tender. Drain well and toss with half of the pesto (see Cook's Tip). Garnish with basil leaves. Serve immediately,

**COOK'S TIP**
It isn't practical to make a smaller quantity of pesto so spoon the rest into a jar, cover with olive oil and seal. Store in the fridge for up to 1 week.

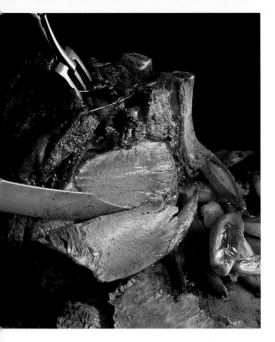

# MUSTARD ROAST RIB OF BEEF

PREPARATION TIME: **5** MINUTES ◆ COOKING TIME: **2½** HOURS + STANDING ◆ FREEZING: NOT SUITABLE ◆ **320–260** CALS PER SERVING ◆ SERVES **8–10**

**Leaving the joint to rest allows the juices that have risen to the surface of the meat during cooking to seep back into the flesh and 'set'.**

2 bone rib of beef, about 2.5–2.7 kg
    (5½–6 lb)
15 ml (1 tbsp) plain flour
15 ml (1 tbsp) mustard powder
salt and freshly ground black pepper
150 ml (¼ pint) Cabernet red wine
600 ml (1 pint) beef stock

**1** Preheat the oven to 230°C (450°F) Mark 8. Place the rib of beef, fat side up, in a roasting pan just large enough to hold the joint.
**2** Mix together the flour and mustard powder and season with salt and pepper. Rub the mixture over the joint. Cook on the centre shelf of the oven for 30 minutes.
**3** Transfer to a shelf at the bottom of the oven, lower the temperature to 220°C (425°F) Mark 7 and roast for 2 hours, basting occasionally.
**4** Place the beef on a carving dish, loosely cover with foil and leave to rest while making the gravy.
**5** Skim any fat off the sediment in the roasting pan. Pour in the wine and bring to the boil on the hob. Boil vigorously until very syrupy. Pour in the stock and boil until syrupy. Add 600 ml (1 pint) water and boil again. Season to taste. There should be about 450 ml (¾ pint) gravy. (See Cook's Tip.)
**6** Remove the rib bone and carve the beef. Serve with the gravy.

### COOK'S TIP

Making the gravy in the roasting pan ensures a rich flavour, using any juices that have escaped from the joint during roasting. If possible, use vegetable cooking water.

---

# AROMATIC BRAISED STEAK

PREPARATION TIME: **15** MINUTES ◆ COOKING TIME: **2½** HOURS ◆ FREEZING: NOT SUITABLE ◆ **520** CALS PER SERVING ◆ SERVES **4**

**This is based on an original French recipe – the anchovies melt during the long slow cooking process, producing a delicious and full-flavoured dish.**

450 g (1 lb) onion, thinly sliced
50 g (2 oz) anchovy, chopped
60 ml (4 tbsp) olive oil
6 large garlic cloves, crushed
30 ml (2 tbsp) chopped capers
60 ml (4 tbsp) chopped fresh parsley
1 kg (2¼ lb) braising steak, cut into large
    bite-size pieces
freshly ground black pepper

**1** Place the onion, anchovy, 30 ml (2 tbsp) of the oil, garlic, capers and parsley in a bowl.
**2** Heat the remaining oil in a 3.4 litre (6 pint) flameproof casserole and brown the braising steak in batches over a high heat. Set aside.
**3** Remove the pan from the heat, add about 45 ml (3 tbsp) water and scrape with a spoon to loosen the brown sediment.
**4** Scatter half of the meat over the bottom of the casserole. Layer the remaining meat alternately with the onion mixture, seasoning with pepper as you go.
**5** Dampen a large piece of greaseproof paper and place on top of the casserole, then cover with a tight-fitting lid. Cook over a low heat for 5–10 minutes. Preheat the oven to 160°C (325°F) Mark 3.
**6** Cook the casserole in the oven for about 2 hours or until the meat is very, very tender.

### COOK'S TIPS

This dish should create its own liquid as it cooks, but check the level after the first hour – you may have to add a little water.
    If the meat is cooked and the sauce a little greasy, add 30–45 ml (2–3 tbsp) boiling water and mix it in.

# PAPPARDELLE WITH ARTICHOKES AND CREAM

PREPARATION TIME: 5-10 MINUTES ◆ COOKING TIME: 10 MINUTES ◆ FREEZING: NOT SUITABLE ◆ 835-555 CALS PER SERVING ◆ SERVES 4-6

400 g (14 oz) dried pappardelle or tagliatelle
25 g (1 oz) butter
2 garlic cloves, chopped
12 artichoke hearts (in oil), drained and sliced
45 ml (3 tbsp) chopped fresh parsley
284 ml carton extra-thick double cream
90 ml (6 tbsp) freshly grated pecorino or Parmesan cheese
salt and freshly ground black pepper

**1** Cook the pasta in a large pan of boiling salted water according to packet instructions.
**2** Meanwhile, prepare the sauce. Melt the butter in a frying pan, add the garlic and cook gently for about 3 minutes to soften; do not allow to brown.
**3** Add the artichoke and 30 ml (2 tbsp) of the parsley and cook, stirring, for 2 minutes. Stir in the cream and bring to a simmer. Stir in the cheese and cook for 1 minute. Season with salt and pepper to taste.
**4** To serve, drain the pasta well, add to the sauce and toss to mix. Serve immediately, sprinkled with the remaining parsley.

### COOK'S TIP

Artichoke hearts preserved in oil are available in jars from many supermarkets and are often sold 'loose' at Italian specialist shops. They are quite superior in flavour to canned artichoke hearts in brine which should not be used for this recipe.

### VARIATIONS

Serve the sauce on finer pasta such as spaghetti or paglia e fieno.
Add 50-75 g (2-3 oz) roughly chopped walnuts to the sauce with the cheese. If available, use 45 ml (3 tbsp) walnut oil in place of the butter.

# PASTA WITH TROUT, PEPPERS AND ALMONDS

PREPARATION TIME: 20 MINUTES ◆ COOKING TIME: ABOUT 30 MINUTES ◆ FREEZING: NOT SUITABLE ◆ 785-525 CALS PER SERVING ◆ SERVES 4-6

3 large red peppers
60 ml (4 tbsp) extra-virgin olive oil
75 g (3 oz) flaked almonds
400 g (14 oz) dried pasta bows, shells or pipes
45 ml (3 tbsp) chopped fresh dill
225 g (8 oz) smoked trout fillets, flaked
40 g (1½ oz) butter
salt and freshly ground black pepper
dill sprigs, to garnish

**1** Place the whole peppers under a preheated grill for about 20 minutes, turning occasionally, until the skin is charred and blistered all over. Cool slightly then, over a bowl to catch the juices, peel away the charred skin and remove the seeds. Cut the flesh into thin strips.
**2** Heat the oil in a large frying pan, add the almonds and cook for about 3 minutes, until lightly browned.
**3** Meanwhile, cook the pasta in a large pan of boiling salted water according to packet instructions.
**4** Add the pepper strips and any reserved juices to the almonds and heat through for 1 minute. Stir in the

chopped dill and flaked trout and heat for 1 minute. Remove from the heat and stir in the butter; this will prevent any further cooking. Season with salt and pepper to taste.
**5** To serve, drain the pasta well. Add to the smoked trout mixture and toss lightly to mix. Serve immediately, garnished with dill.

### COOK'S TIP

To save time the peppers can be cut into quarters before grilling. Grill the pieces skin side up for about 10 minutes until blistered and blackened. However, this method does not retain the sweet juices within the cooked peppers.

# BEEF BRAISED WITH ONIONS AND GUINNESS

PREPARATION TIME: **10** MINUTES ◆ COOKING TIME: **2½** HOURS ◆ FREEZING: SUITABLE ◆ **590** CALS PER SERVING ◆ SERVES **4**

15 g packet dried mushrooms, eg porcini
45 ml (3 tbsp) olive oil
4 braising steaks, about 700 g (1½ lb)
    total weight (see Cook's Tip)
175 g (6 oz) rindless streaky bacon, diced
225 g (8 oz) button onions, halved, or
    shallots
225 g (8 oz) brown-cap or field
    mushrooms, sliced
2 garlic cloves, crushed
30 ml (2 tbsp) plain flour
440 ml  can Guinness
30 ml (2 tbsp) Worcestershire sauce
10 ml (2 tsp) dried thyme
large pinch of sugar

**1** Rinse the porcini and soak in enough warm water to cover.
**2** Heat 15 ml (1 tbsp) of the oil in a 3.4 litre (6 pint) shallow flameproof casserole, add the steaks and fry over a high heat to seal and brown both sides; remove from the pan and set aside. Add the bacon to the casserole and fry until beginning to brown; remove and set aside. Preheat the oven to 160°C (325°F) Mark 3.
**3** Heat the remaining oil in the pan, add the onions or shallots and fry for 2–3 minutes or until beginning to brown. Add the fresh mushrooms and cook, stirring, for 1–2 minutes. Add the garlic and fry for 1 minute.

**4** Add the flour and stir well to coat the mushrooms and onions. Add the soaked mushrooms with their soaking liquid, the Guinness, Worcestershire sauce, thyme and sugar, bring to the boil, then lower the heat to a gentle simmer.
**5** Add the steaks and bacon and push down into the liquid. Cover with a tight-fitting lid and cook in the oven for about 2 hours or until the steaks are tender.

### COOK'S TIP
Choose steaks that have a fine marbling of fat throughout. This is necessary to help tenderise the meat during cooking.

# BEEF IN COCONUT MILK

PREPARATION TIME: **15** MINUTES ◆ COOKING TIME: **1½-1¾** HOURS ◆ FREEZING: SUITABLE ◆ **460** CALS PER SERVING ◆ SERVES **6**

2.5 cm (1 inch) piece fresh root ginger
two 15 cm (6 inch) pieces lemon grass
8 kaffir lime leaves or the grated rind of
    1 lime
225 g (8 oz) shallots or onions
8 garlic cloves
2 large red chillies, seeded and chopped
1 small red pepper, cored, seeded and
    chopped
5 ml (1 tsp) ground cinnamon
5 ml (1 tsp) ground cloves
1.6 litres (2¾ pints) coconut milk
3 bay leaves
900 g (2 lb) stewing beef, cubed
salt
shredded kaffir lime leaves and toasted
    coconut flakes, to garnish

**1** Roughly chop the ginger with the lemon grass, lime leaves, if using, shallots or onions and garlic. Put in a food processor with the chilli, red pepper, cinnamon, cloves, lime rind, if using, and 150 ml (¼ pint) water and blend until smooth.
**2** Place this paste in a large non-stick saucepan with the coconut milk, bay leaves and beef. Season well with salt, then bring to the boil, stirring. Simmer, uncovered, stirring occasionally, for 1½–1¾ hours, until the meat is tender and the milk absorbed to make a thick coating.
**3** Garnish with shredded lime leaves and toasted coconut flakes to serve.

# LINGUINE WITH PARMA HAM AND TOMATOES

PREPARATION TIME: 5 MINUTES ◆ COOKING TIME: 11 MINUTES ◆ FREEZING: NOT SUITABLE ◆ 1020 CALS PER SERVING ◆ SERVES 4

400 g (14 oz) dried linguine or fettucini
salt and freshly ground black pepper
30 ml (2 tbsp) olive oil
125 g (4 oz) Parma ham (about 6 thin
  slices), cut into thin strips
65 g (2½ oz) butter
1 large onion, chopped
2 garlic cloves, crushed
50 g (2 oz) sun-dried tomato, drained
  and cut into strips
142 ml carton double cream
150 g (5 oz) mascarpone cheese
small bunch of marjoram or oregano
  sprigs, leaves pulled from stalks
30-45 ml (2-3 tbsp) pinenuts, toasted
  (optional)

1  Cook the pasta in a large pan of boiling salted water for 10 minutes or until almost tender (al dente).
2  Meanwhile, heat the oil in a frying pan, add the Parma ham and fry quickly for about 1 minute or until frazzled. Remove with a slotted spoon and set aside.
3  Add the butter to the pan and gently fry the onion, garlic and tomato for 2 minutes. Drain the pasta and, while still hot, add to the frying pan. With a fork in each hand, lift the pasta strands a few times, so the buttery mixture coats and separates them.
4  Place the cream and mascarpone in a saucepan and heat gently, stirring, until smooth. Season with salt and pepper, add to the pasta mixture with half of the Parma ham and half of the majoram or oregano leaves.
5  Transfer the mixture to a warm serving bowl and sprinkle with the remaining Parma ham and herbs, and the toasted pinenuts, if using. Serve immediately.

## VARIATIONS

Use strips of pancetta or smoked streaky bacon instead of Parma ham.
Sautéed sliced mushrooms or asparagus tips make tasty additions.

# PENNE WITH OLIVES, ANCHOVY AND CHILLI

PREPARATION TIME: 8-10 MINUTES ◆ COOKING TIME: ABOUT 10 MINUTES ◆ FREEZING: NOT SUITABLE ◆ 660-440 CALS PER SERVING ◆ SERVES 4-6

400 g (14 oz) dried penne
2 garlic cloves, sliced
50 g can anchovies in olive oil
2.5 ml (½ tsp) dried chilli flakes
30 ml (2 tbsp) chopped fresh parsley
225 g (8 oz) pitted mixed black and
  green olives
60 ml (4 tbsp) extra-virgin olive oil
freshly ground black pepper
30-45 ml (2-3 tbsp) freshly grated
  Parmesan cheese
Parmesan cheese shavings, to serve

1  Cook the pasta in a large pan of boiling salted water according to packet instructions.
2  Meanwhile, put the garlic, anchovies with their oil, and chilli flakes in a saucepan and cook over a fairly high heat for 2-3 minutes, stirring with a wooden spoon to break up the anchovies; do not allow the garlic to brown. Stir in the parsley and remove from the heat.
3  Transfer the contents of the pan to a food processor and add the olives and oil. Process for a few seconds to give a coarse paste. Season with pepper to taste (see Cook's Tip).
4  Drain the pasta well, return to the saucepan and add the pounded olive mixture and grated Parmesan cheese. Toss well to coat the pasta. Serve immediately, topped with Parmesan shavings. Accompany with a crisp leafy salad.

## COOK'S TIP

You probably won't need to add salt as the ingredients are naturally salty.

## VARIATION

Add steamed broccoli or cauliflower florets to the pasta and sauce with the grated Parmesan.

# TACO HOTPOT

PREPARATION TIME: 15 MINUTES ◆ COOKING TIME: 35 MINUTES ◆ FREEZING: NOT SUITABLE ◆ 615 CALS PER SERVING ◆ SERVES 4

15 ml (1 tbsp) oil
1 onion, chopped
1 garlic clove, crushed
450 g (1 lb) lean minced beef
425 g can kidney beans, drained and
    rinsed
440 g jar pasta sauce
30 ml (2 tbsp) Worcestershire sauce
15 ml (1 tbsp) chilli sauce
4 tomatoes, chopped
1/2 iceberg lettuce, shredded
125 g (4 oz) Cheddar cheese, grated
125 g (4 oz) tortilla chips, broken up
soured cream, to serve

1  Heat the oil in a frying pan, add the onion and fry for 2–3 minutes until soft. Add the garlic and beef and fry over a high heat for 2–3 minutes to brown.
2  Stir in the kidney beans, pasta sauce and Worcestershire and chilli sauces. Bring to the boil, then cover and simmer for 30 minutes.
3  Stir in the remaining ingredients and serve immediately, topped with spoonsful of soured cream.

# BEEF GULASCH

PREPARATION TIME: 30 MINUTES ◆ COOKING TIME: 2½ HOURS ◆ FREEZING: SUITABLE (STEP 4) ◆ 525 CALS PER SERVING ◆ SERVES 6

30 ml (2 tbsp) plain white flour
salt and freshly ground black pepper
900 g (2 lb) stewing steak, cut into
    chunks
45 ml (3 tbsp) oil
700 g (1½ lb) onion, roughly chopped
225 g (8 oz) pancetta, or thick-cut
    rindless streaky bacon, cubed
2 garlic cloves, crushed
60 ml (4 tbsp) paprika
30 ml (2 tbsp) each chopped fresh thyme,
    parsley and rosemary, or 10 ml (2 tsp)
    mixed dried herbs
400 g  can plum tomatoes
142 ml carton soured cream
chopped fresh parsley, to garnish
pasta noodles, eg tagliatelle, to serve

1  Season the flour with salt and pepper, add the meat and toss well, to coat.
2  Heat 15 ml (1 tbsp) of the oil in a deep flameproof casserole, add the onion and fry for about 5 minutes, until begining to soften and turn golden; remove and set aside. Add the pancetta or bacon to the pan and fry over a high heat until crisp; remove and set aside. Heat the remaining oil in the pan and fry the steak, in small batches, over a high heat, until browned. Preheat the oven to 160°C (325°F) Mark 3.
3  Return the onion and pancetta to the casserole. Stir in the garlic and paprika and cook, stirring, for 1 minute.
4  Add the herbs, tomatoes and 300 ml

(½ pint) water and bring to the boil. Cover and cook in the oven for 1½–2 hours or until tender. Check after 1 hour, adding a little water if dry.
5  Adjust the seasoning, then stir in the cream. Garnish with parsley and serve with pasta noodles.

# SPAGHETTI ALLA CARBONARA

**PREPARATION TIME: ABOUT 15 MINUTES ◆ COOKING TIME: ABOUT 7 MINUTES ◆ FREEZING: NOT SUITABLE ◆ 675-450 CALS PER SERVING ◆ SERVES 4-6**

125-150 g (4-5 oz) smoked pancetta, in slices (see Cook's Tips)
30 ml (2 tbsp) extra-virgin olive oil
25 g (1 oz) butter
1 garlic clove, halved
3 eggs
30 ml (2 tbsp) chopped fresh parsley
30 ml (2 tbsp) dry white wine
40 g (1½ oz) freshly grated Parmesan cheese
40 g (1½ oz) freshly grated pecorino cheese (see Cook's Tips)
salt and freshly ground black pepper
400 g (14 oz) spaghetti

**1** Remove the rind from the pancetta, then cut into tiny strips. Heat the oil and butter in a heavy-based pan, add the pancetta and garlic and cook for 3-4 minutes, until the pancetta begins to crisp. Turn off the heat; discard the garlic.
**2** Meanwhile, in a mixing bowl large enough to hold the cooked spaghetti later, beat the eggs with the parsley, wine and half of each of the grated cheeses. Season with salt and pepper.
**3** Cook the spaghetti in a large pan of boiling salted water according to packet instructions.
**4** When the spaghetti is almost cooked, gently reheat the pancetta in the pan.

Drain the spaghetti well, then immediately add to the egg mixture in the bowl with the pancetta. Toss well to cook the eggs until they are creamy. Add the remaining cheeses, toss lightly and serve immediately.

## COOK'S TIPS

Smoked pancetta is obtainable from Italian delicatessens. If unavailable, use 175-225 g (6-8 oz) smoked bacon. If pecorino cheese is unobtainable, simply double the quantity of Parmesan.

# CRISPY NOODLES WITH VEGETABLES

**PREPARATION TIME: 20 MINUTES ◆ COOKING TIME: ABOUT 10 MINUTES ◆ FREEZING: NOT SUITABLE ◆ 390 CALS PER SERVING ◆ SERVES 4**

125 g (4 oz) thin transparent rice noodles or rice sticks
vegetable oil, for deep-frying
2.5 cm (1 inch) piece fresh root ginger
175 g (6 oz) shiitake or button mushrooms
1 red chilli
15 ml (1 tbsp) peanut or vegetable oil
125 g (4 oz) mangetout
75 g (3 oz) beansprouts
few Chinese leaves, coarsely shredded
30 ml (2 tbsp) each soy sauce and dry sherry
5 ml (1 tsp) sugar

**CORIANDER OMELETTE**
2 eggs
30 ml (2 tbsp) milk
45 ml (3 tbsp) chopped fresh coriander
salt and freshly ground black pepper

**1** First make the omelette. Put the eggs, milk, coriander and seasoning in a jug and whisk together with a fork.
**2** Heat a little oil or butter in an omelette pan or small frying pan, pour in the egg mixture and cook over a high heat. As it sets around the edge, use a palette knife to pull the set mixture towards the middle, letting the uncooked mixture run underneath. Cook until set.
**3** Turn the omelette out onto a sheet of non-stick baking parchment and leave to cool, then roll up and cut into thin slices.
**4** Break the noodles into 7.5 cm (3 inch) lengths. Heat the oil in a deep-fat fryer to 175°C (345°F). Deep-fry the noodles in small batches for about 30 seconds,

until they swell. Remove from the pan with a slotted spoon and drain on crumpled kitchen paper.
**5** Shred the ginger and thickly slice the mushrooms. Slice the chilli, removing the seeds if a milder flavour is preferred.
**6** Heat the oil in a wok. Add the mushrooms and ginger and stir-fry over a high heat for 2 minutes. Add the chilli, mangetout, beansprouts and Chinese leaves and stir-fry for 1 minute. Add the soy sauce, sherry and sugar and cook for 1 minute. Add the noodles and toss to mix, being careful not to crush them.
**7** Turn the vegetables and noodles into a warm serving bowl and top with the omelette shreds. Serve immediately.

# STIR-FRIED BEEF WITH NOODLES AND CHILLI

PREPARATION TIME: 20 MINUTES ◆ COOKING TIME: 15 MINUTES ◆ FREEZING: NOT SUITABLE ◆ 325 CALS PER SERVING ◆ SERVES 4

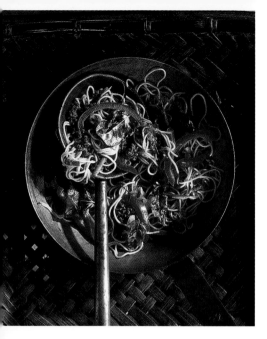

125 g (4 oz) dried egg thread noodles
30 ml (2 tbsp) tamarind paste
15 ml (1 tbsp) Thai fish sauce
10 ml (2 tsp) sugar
90 ml (3 fl oz) beef stock
45 ml (3 tbsp) oil
15 ml (1 tbsp) dark soy sauce
1 small onion, finely chopped
2 garlic cloves, finely chopped
2.5 cm (1 inch) piece fresh root ginger
4 kaffir lime leaves, shredded
225 g (8 oz) lean minced beef
30 ml (2 tbsp) Indian medium curry paste
5 ml (1 tsp) turmeric
2.5 ml (½ tsp) paprika
1.25 ml (¼ tsp) chilli powder
1 red pepper, cored, seeded and sliced
125 g (4 oz) French beans, halved
fresh coriander leaves, to garnish

1  Soak the noodles according to the packet instructions; drain well and pat dry.
2  Place the tamarind paste in a bowl and whisk in the fish sauce, sugar and stock until smooth. Set aside.
3  Heat 15 ml (1 tbsp) oil in a wok or large frying pan, add the noodles and soy sauce and stir-fry for 30 seconds. Remove from the pan and set aside.
4  Heat 30 ml (2 tbsp) oil in the pan, add the onion, garlic, grated ginger and lime leaves and stir-fry for 5 minutes. Add the beef, curry paste and spices and stir-fry for 3 minutes.
5  Add the red pepper and beans and stir-fry for 3 minutes. Blend in the prepared sauce and simmer for 3 minutes. Carefully stir in the noodles and heat through for 2 minutes. Transfer to a warm serving dish. Garnish with coriander leaves and serve immediately.

## VARIATION
Use thin strips of fillet or rump steak instead of mince.

# BEEF SALAD WITH ROASTED VEGETABLE PASTE

PREPARATION TIME: 35 MINUTES + MARINATING ◆ COOKING TIME: 30–35 MINUTES ◆ FREEZING: NOT SUITABLE ◆ 230 CALS PER SERVING ◆ SERVES 4

15 ml (1 tbsp) Szechuan peppercorns
5 ml (1 tsp) each ground black pepper
   and coriander
1.25 ml (¼ tsp) Chinese 5-spice powder
225 g (8 oz) fillet steak
125 g (4 oz) salad leaves
15 ml (1 tbsp) sesame seeds
lime wedges, to garnish

**VEGETABLE PASTE**
225 g (8 oz) shallots
4–8 garlic cloves, chopped
2–3 large chillies, seeded and chopped
2.5 cm (1 inch) piece fresh root ginger
1 lemon grass stalk, finely chopped
5 ml (1 tsp) cumin seeds
15 ml (1 tbsp) tamarind paste
15 ml (1 tbsp) light soy sauce
10 ml (2 tsp) sugar

1  Preheat the oven to 200°C (400°F) Mark 6. Roughly grind the peppercorns and mix with the black pepper, coriander and 5-spice powder. Spread on a board. Press the steak down into the mixture, turning to coat well on both sides. Cover and set aside for 2 hours.
2  Meanwhile, prepare the Vegetable Paste. Halve any large shallots and place in a small roasting pan with the garlic, chilli, chopped ginger, lemon grass and cumin. Pour over 45 ml (3 tbsp) sunflower oil and toss well until evenly combined. Cook in the oven for 30 minutes, until browned and softened. Leave to cool slightly.
3  Transfer the vegetables to a food processor and add the tamarind paste, soy sauce and sugar. Process to form a rough paste, adding a little water if too thick. Add a little salt if necessary.
4  Brush a griddle or heavy-based frying pan with a little oil and heat. As soon as the oil starts to smoke, add the beef and sear by pressing down hard with a fish slice. Fry for 1 minute, turn the steak and repeat with the second side. Remove from the pan and leave to rest for 2 minutes.
5  Divide the salad leaves between 4 serving plates. Thinly slice the beef and arrange on the plates. Spoon on a little of the Vegetable Paste and sprinkle with the sesame seeds. Garnish with lime wedges and serve immediately.

# FRESH PASTA WITH ASPARAGUS AND PARMESAN

PREPARATION TIME: 30 MINUTES + RESTING ◆ COOKING TIME: 6-8 MINUTES ◆ FREEZING: NOT SUITABLE ◆ 585 CALS PER SERVING ◆ SERVES 4

225 g (8 oz) asparagus, trimmed
125 g (4 oz) unsalted butter
2 garlic cloves, sliced
60 ml (4 tbsp) chopped fresh parsley
50 g (2 oz) freshly grated Parmesan cheese
freshly ground black pepper

**PASTA**
225 g (8 oz) type '00' pasta flour
5 ml (1 tsp) salt
2 eggs, plus 1 yolk (all size 3)
15 ml (1 tbsp) extra-virgin olive oil
15 ml (1 tbsp) cold water

1  First make the pasta (see page 112).
2  Divide the pasta dough into 8 pieces and pat flat. Pass each piece twice through each setting of a pasta machine, from the widest through to the narrowest, to form long thin sheets of pasta. Cut each sheet in half crosswise and hang over a clean pole as you go. Leave to rest for 5 minutes.
3  Pass each sheet through the tagliatelle cutter attachment and again hang the noodles over the pole as you go. Curl each group of noodles into 'nests' and place on a floured tea-towel.
4  Bring a large saucepan of water to the boil. At the same time, steam the asparagus over the pan for 3 minutes,

until just tender; drain and cut into 5 cm (2 inch) lengths. Meanwhile, melt the butter in a small pan, add the garlic and cook until it starts to turn brown. Remove from the heat immediately.
5  Add 10 ml (2 tsp) salt to the pasta water. Plunge in the noodles, bring back to the boil and cook for 2-3 minutes until *al dente*. Drain and return to the pan. Add the asparagus, parsley, butter and half of the cheese and toss.
6  Serve immediately, topped with the remaining Parmesan and black pepper.

---

# PASTA WITH CAPER SAUCE AND GRILLED CHEESE

PREPARATION TIME: 30 MINUTES ◆ COOKING TIME: 15 MINUTES ◆ FREEZING: NOT SUITABLE ◆ 755-505 CALS PER SERVING ◆ SERVES 4-6

**Halloumi is a traditional Cypriot cheese with a salty flavour and firm texture. It is wonderful for grilling or frying as it softens - rather than melts - and develops a golden crust.**

2 red peppers
400 g (14 oz) dried penne or rigatoni
225 g (8 oz) halloumi cheese

**CAPER SAUCE**
90 ml (6 tbsp) extra-virgin olive oil
2 onions, chopped
2 garlic cloves, chopped
45 ml (3 tbsp) chopped fresh parsley
50 g (2 oz) capers in wine vinegar, drained (drained weight)

1  Place the peppers under a preheated grill for about 20 minutes, turning occasionally, until the skin is blistered and charred. Cool, then, over a bowl to catch the juices, peel away the skin and remove the seeds and cut the flesh into strips. Add to the bowl and set aside.
2  Meanwhile, make the Caper Sauce. Heat 75 ml (5 tbsp) of the oil in a frying pan, add the onion and cook for 7–8 minutes, stirring frequently, until soft. Stir in the garlic and cook for 2–3 minutes, until the onion is golden. Stir in the parsley, then transfer to a food processor.
3  Rinse the capers and add to the processor. Season with salt and pepper, then process briefly to chop coarsely.

4  Cook the pasta in a large pan of boiling salted water according to packet instructions.
5  Meanwhile, cut the halloumi into 1 cm (½ inch) cubes and place in a baking pan large enough to hold them in a single layer. Add the remaining oil and plenty of pepper. Toss to coat the cheese cubes, then grill, stirring occasionally, for about 8 minutes, until golden.
6  Drain the pasta thoroughly and return to the pan. Add the Caper Sauce and reserved pepper strips and toss to mix. Transfer to a warm serving bowl and sprinkle with the cheese. Serve immediately.

# BAKED STUFFED TOMATOES AND PEPPERS

**PREPARATION TIME: 15 MINUTES ◆ COOKING TIME: 2 HOURS 10 MINUTES ◆ FREEZING: NOT SUITABLE ◆ 560 CALS PER SERVING ◆ SERVES 8**

8 red or yellow peppers
8 large beef tomatoes
salt and freshly ground black pepper
90 ml (6 tbsp) olive oil
225 g (8 oz) onion, finely chopped
2 garlic cloves, crushed
5 ml (1 tsp) ground cinnamon
550 g (1¼ lb) lean minced lamb
225 g (8 oz) long-grain rice
450 ml (¾ pint) stock
50 g (2 oz) pinenuts, toasted
50 g (2 oz) raisins
15 ml (1 tbsp) caster sugar
60 ml (4 tbsp) chopped fresh parsley
25 ml (5 tsp) chopped fresh thyme or
   10 ml (2 tsp) dried
550 g (1¼ lb) potatoes, quartered
thyme sprigs, to garnish

1 Cut the tops off the peppers and tomatoes and reserve. Remove the cores and seeds. Sieve the tomato cores to extract the juice and reserve. Season inside the peppers and tomatoes and leave them upside down on kitchen paper to drain.
2 Heat 15 ml (1 tbsp) of the oil in a saucepan, add the onion, garlic and cinnamon and cook for 10 minutes or until soft and golden. Add the lamb and cook for 10–15 minutes or until lightly browned, stirring occasionally. Add the rice and cook for 1 minute, stirring.
3 Add the reserved tomato juice, stock, pinenuts, raisins, sugar and herbs; season to taste. Bring to the boil, then simmer

gently for 10 minutes or until most of the liquid has evaporated. Adjust the seasoning. Preheat the oven to 200°C (400°F) Mark 6.
4 Pile the stuffing into the peppers and tomatoes and replace the tops. Place the peppers and tomatoes in 2 separate roasting pans. Toss the potatoes in 30 ml (2 tbsp) of the oil and arrange among the peppers to keep them upright. Drizzle the peppers and tomatoes with the remaining oil and season well.
5 Cook the peppers and potatoes in the oven for 1–1¼ hours. Place the tomatoes in the oven after 15 minutes.
6 Garnish with thyme and serve on a large warm platter.

# FRAGRANT LAMB WITH NOODLES

**PREPARATION TIME: 20 MINUTES ◆ COOKING TIME: 2 HOURS 40 MINUTES ◆ FREEZING: NOT SUITABLE ◆ 550–415 CALS PER SERVING ◆ SERVES 6–8**

1.8 kg (4 lb) leg of lamb
2.5 cm (1 inch) piece fresh root ginger,
   sliced
4 garlic cloves, sliced
100 ml (4 fl oz) dry sherry
30 ml (2 tbsp) soft light brown sugar
5 ml (1 tsp) sesame seeds
100 ml (4 fl oz) hoi-sin or teriyaki sauce
1 red chilli, seeded and sliced, or 10 ml
   (2 tsp) harissa sauce, optional
pared rind and juice of 1 orange
pared rind of 1 lemon
125 g (4 oz) egg noodles
1 bunch of spring onions, roughly
   chopped
1 small head of Chinese leaves, thickly
   sliced

1 Preheat the oven to 200°C (400°F) Mark 6. Place the lamb in a deep oiled roasting pan just large enough to hold the joint. Cook in the oven for 15 minutes.
2 Add the ginger, garlic, sherry, sugar, sesame seeds, hoi-sin or teriyaki sauce, the chilli or harissa sauce, if using, pared rinds and orange juice to the roasting pan with 600 ml (1 pint) water. Return to the oven for 15 minutes.
3 Lower the temperature to 160°C (325°F) Mark 3, cover the lamb with a tent of foil and return to the oven for 2 hours or until the lamb is very tender. Baste regularly during cooking.
4 Place the lamb on a warm serving

platter, cover and keep warm in a low oven.
5 Place the roasting pan on the hob and add the noodles to the pan juices. Bring to the boil and bubble gently for about 5 minutes, until tender. Stir in the spring onions and Chinese leaves, bring back to the boil and bubble for 1–2 minutes. Serve immediately, with the carved lamb.

# SPAGHETTI WITH MEATBALLS IN TOMATO SAUCE

PREPARATION TIME: **30** MINUTES ◆ COOKING TIME: **20** MINUTES ◆ FREEZING: SUITABLE (STEP 4) ◆ **965** CALS PER SERVING ◆ SERVES **4**

30 ml (2 tbsp) oil
450 g  jar pasta sauce
450 g (1 lb) spaghetti
oregano sprigs, to garnish
freshly grated Parmesan cheese, to serve

### MEATBALLS
350 g (12 oz) shoulder of pork
175 g (6 oz) piece of gammon
175 g (6 oz) belly pork
2 garlic cloves
5 ml (1 tsp) coarse sea salt
5 ml (1 tsp) sugar
15 ml (1 tbsp) coarsely crushed black
    pepper
5 ml (1 tsp) fennel seeds
1.25 ml (¼ tsp) dried chilli flakes

**1** First make the meatballs. Trim the shoulder of pork, gammon and belly pork of any skin and connective tissue, then cut into rough chunks.
**2** Place the meats in a food processor, add the remaining ingredients and process until smooth. The sausagemeat is ready to use at this stage, but you can cover the bowl and leave in the fridge overnight to mature if preferred.
**3** With moist hands, roll the sausagemeat into small, even-sized balls.
**4** Heat the oil in a frying pan, add the meatballs, in batches if necessary, and fry until evenly browned. Pour over the pasta sauce, bring to the boil, then simmer for 10-15 minutes.

**5** Meanwhile, cook the spaghetti in a large pan of boiling salted water according to packet instructions. Drain well, then toss with the meatballs and sauce. Garnish with oregano and sprinkle with Parmesan cheese, to serve.

### VARIATION
For a quicker version, replace the above meats with 450 g (1 lb) minced pork and 225 g (8 oz) unsmoked streaky bacon, finely chopped.

# SQUASH TORTELLONI WITH SAGE BUTTER

PREPARATION TIME: **40** MINUTES +CHILLING ◆ COOKING TIME: **23** MINUTES ◆ FREEZING: SUITABLE (STEP 6) ◆ **655-640** CALS PER SERVING ◆ SERVES **4-6**

300 g (10 oz) butternut squash, seeded
    and cubed, ie 225 g (8 oz) flesh
1 garlic clove, crushed
10 ml (2 tsp) chopped fresh thyme
30 ml (2 tbsp) olive oil
75 g (3 oz) ricotta cheese
25 g (1 oz) grated Parmesan cheese
pinch of freshly grated nutmeg
squeeze of lemon juice
salt and freshly ground black pepper
125 g (4 oz) unsalted butter, softened
30 ml (2 tbsp) chopped fresh sage leaves

### PASTA
225 g (8 oz) type '00' pasta flour
5 ml (1 tsp) salt
2 eggs, plus 1 yolk, beaten
15 ml (1 tbsp) olive oil

**1** First make the pasta (see page 112).
**2** Preheat the oven to 225°C (425°F) Mark 7. Place the squash, garlic, thyme and oil in a small roasting pan. Toss well and cook in the oven for 20 minutes, until softened. Mash and cool.
**3** Transfer to a bowl and beat in the cheeses, nutmeg, lemon juice and seasoning. Cover and chill for 30 minutes.
**4** Divide the dough into 4 pieces and roll out each one to a thin sheet. Cover all but one of the pasta sheets with cling film. Using a plain 6 cm (2½ inch) pastry cutter, stamp out 6 rounds from the single sheet.
**5** Place 5 ml (1 tsp) of the squash mixture in the middle of each round.

Brush the edge of one half of each round with water, then fold the other half over to enclose the filling. Press the edges together to seal well.
**6** Curve the semi-circular parcel around a finger and pinch the ends together, turning the sealed edge up to form a neat curved tortelloni as you do so. Place on a well floured tea-towel. Repeat to make 48 tortelloni.
**7** Cook in boiling salted water for 2–3 minutes, until *al dente*. Drain well.
**8** At the same time, put the butter and sage in a large frying pan and heat until melted and foaming. Add the tortelloni and toss well. Serve immediately with black pepper.

# SPICED LAMB AND SOURED-CREAM POT

**PREPARATION TIME: 30 MINUTES + SOAKING ◆ COOKING TIME: 2¾ HOURS ◆ FREEZING: NOT SUITABLE ◆ 930 CALS PER SERVING ◆ SERVES 4**

300 g (10 oz) basmati rice
700 g (1½ lb) boneless shoulder or leg of lamb
75 ml (5 tbsp) oil
225 g (8 oz) onion, thinly sliced
5 cm (2 inch) piece fresh root ginger, chopped
2 large garlic cloves, crushed
5 ml (1 tsp) each ground cumin, mace, cinnamon, garam masala and paprika
284 ml carton soured cream
25 g (1 oz) butter
600 ml (1 pint) stock
100 ml (4 fl oz) hot milk
large pinch of saffron strands
25 g (1 oz) chopped fresh coriander or mint
50 g (2 oz) each slivered almonds, toasted, and seedless raisins, to serve

1  Wash the rice in several changes of cold water, cover with cold water and leave to soak for 30 minutes.
2  Cut the lamb into large pieces. Heat 45 ml (3 tbsp) of the oil in an ovenproof casserole and brown the lamb in batches over a high heat; set aside.
3  Lower the heat, add the remaining oil to the casserole and fry the onion for about 10 minutes, until golden. Remove half and set aside. Add the ginger, garlic and spices and cook for 2–3 minutes.
4  Return the lamb to the casserole, add half of the soured cream and bring to the boil. Cover tightly and simmer for 1½ hours or until tender and the sauce well reduced. Stir in the remaining cream.

5  Meanwhile, drain the rice. Melt the butter in a saucepan and stir in the rice. Add the stock and 5 ml (1 tsp) salt, bring to the boil then partially cover and simmer gently for 10–12 minutes or until most of the liquid has been absorbed. Cover the pan and turn off the heat. Leave the rice to steam for 15 minutes. Mix together the hot milk, saffron and coriander or mint. Preheat the oven to 160°C (325°F) Mark 3.
6  Stir the rice into the lamb with the milk mixture. Top with the reserved onion, cover and cook in the oven for 30 minutes. Turn off the heat and leave to rest for 10 minutes. Scatter over the almonds and raisins to serve.

# MARINATED LAMB WITH WATERMELON SALAD

**PREPARATION TIME: 35 MINUTES + MARINATING ◆ COOKING TIME: 30 MINUTES ◆ FREEZING: NOT SUITABLE ◆ 415 CALS PER SERVING ◆ SERVES 6**

700 g (1½ lb) boneless shoulder or leg of lamb
2 garlic cloves
grated rind and juice of 2 oranges
150 ml (¼ pint) medium sherry
30 ml (2 tbsp) balsamic vinegar
15 ml (1 tbsp) clear honey
15 ml (1 tbsp) olive oil
mint sprigs, to garnish

**WATERMELON SALAD**
1.5 kg (3¼ lb) watermelon
2 avocado pears
2 bunches of spring onions, finely chopped
60 ml (4 tbsp) chopped fresh mint
30 ml (2 tbsp) balsamic vinegar
salt and freshly ground black pepper

1  Make a cut along the length of the meat, flatten a little with a rolling pin, then open out into a 'butterfly'. Cut the garlic into thin slivers. Make incisions all over the meat and insert the garlic.
2  Place the orange rind and juice in a bowl with the sherry, vinegar, honey and oil. Immerse the lamb in the marinade, cover and chill for at least 4 hours or overnight, turning occasionally.
3  To prepare the Watermelon Salad, cut the watermelon and avocados into small dice and mix with the spring onion, mint, vinegar and seasoning. Set aside.
4  Remove the lamb from the marinade, reserving the liquid. Cook under a preheated grill for 7–10 minutes on each

side or over a medium heat for 15–20 minutes on each side on the barbecue, basting frequently with the marinade. Alternatively, roast in a preheated oven, 230°C (450°F) Mark 8, for 20 minutes, then at 180°C (350°F) Mark 4 for 20 minutes or until tender, basting frequently. Cover and leave to stand in a warm place. Place the remaining marinade in a pan, bring to the boil and bubble until reduced and syrupy.
5  Carve the lamb into slices and arrange on a warm serving plate. Spoon over the reduced marinade and garnish with mint. Serve immediately, with the salad.

# MEE GORENG

PREPARATION TIME: **30** MINUTES ◆ COOKING TIME: ABOUT **10** MINUTES ◆ FREEZING: NOT SUITABLE ◆ **475-315** CALS PER SERVING ◆ SERVES 4-6

125 g (4 oz) rump steak
2 garlic cloves, crushed
30 ml (2 tbsp) soy sauce
175 g (6 oz) large raw prawns
225 g (8 oz) medium egg noodles
salt
1-2 hot red chillies
2.5 cm (1 inch) piece fresh root ginger
15 ml (1 tbsp) each vegetable oil and
    sesame oil
2-3 spring onions, sliced
450 g (1 lb) prepared squid
30 ml (2 tbsp) hoisin sauce
15 ml (1 tbsp) lemon juice
30 ml (2 tbsp) nam pla (Thai fish sauce)
125 g (4 oz) beansprouts
1 egg, beaten
shredded lettuce and lemon wedges, to
    garnish

1  Cut the steak into wafer-thin slices across the grain. Place in a shallow dish with half of the garlic and half of the soy sauce. Leave to stand.
2  Peel the prawns, leaving the tail end attached. Make a shallow slit along the outer curve from the tail to the head end and remove the dark intestinal vein. Rinse under cold running water, drain and pat dry with kitchen paper.
3  Put the noodles in a large saucepan with a generous pinch of salt and pour over enough boiling water to cover. Bring back to the boil, then turn off the heat. Leave to stand and cook in the residual heat according to packet instructions.
4  Chop the chillies, discarding the seeds

if a milder flavour is preferred. Finely chop the ginger. Heat the oils in a wok or large frying pan, add the remaining garlic, chillies, ginger and spring onion and cook for 2 minutes, stirring.
5  Add the beef and cook for 2 minutes. Add the squid and prawns and cook for 2 minutes. Add the hoisin sauce, lemon juice, nam pla and remaining soy sauce and cook for 2 minutes.
6  Drain the noodles and add to the pan with the beansprouts. Heat through for 2 minutes, then add the beaten egg. Cook briefly until the egg is on the point of setting, then remove from the heat. Serve immediately, garnished with a mound of shredded lettuce and lemon.

# HOT AND SOUR NOODLE AND VEGETABLE SALAD

PREPARATION TIME: **30** MINUTES ◆ COOKING TIME: 3-4 MINUTES ◆ FREEZING: NOT SUITABLE ◆ **345** CALS PER SERVING ◆ SERVES 4

2 carrots
50 g (2 oz) each baby sweetcorn,
    mangetout and broccoli florets
1 small red pepper, seeded
125 g (4 oz) Chinese cabbage or pak choi
50 g (2 oz) canned water chestnuts
45 ml (3 tbsp) peanut or sunflower oil
2 garlic cloves, crushed
5 ml (1 tsp) dried crushed chilli flakes
5 ml (1 tsp) grated fresh root ginger
75 g (3 oz) rice vermicelli noodles
30 ml (2 tbsp) chopped fresh coriander

**DRESSING**
30 ml (2 tbsp) each peanut oil and lime
    juice
5 ml (1 tsp) chilli oil
10 ml (2 tsp) caster sugar
15 ml (1 tbsp) each rice vinegar and nam pla

1  Start by preparing the vegetables. Cut the carrots into matchstick pieces; halve the baby sweetcorn lengthways if large; top and tail the mangetout; cut the broccoli into small florets. Thinly slice the red pepper; roughly shred the Chinese cabbage or pak choi and drain and slice the water chestnuts. Set aside.
2  Place the two oils in a small pan, add the garlic, chilli flakes and ginger and heat until smoking. Strain the oil into a wok or large frying pan. Add the prepared vegetables and stir-fry for 2-3 minutes, until just starting to wilt. Remove the pan from the heat immediately.
3  Soak the noodles according to packet instructions. Meanwhile, whisk all the

dressing ingredients together and season to taste. Strain the cooked noodles and toss with a little of the dressing.
4  Stir the remaining dressing into the vegetables together with the chopped coriander. Arrange the noodles and vegetables on individual warm serving plates. Scatter over 25 g (1 oz) toasted and chopped raw peanuts. Serve immediately or chill for up to 1 hour.

## VARIATION

Include some deep-fried tofu. Cut 125 g (4 oz) plain tofu into cubes and dry well. Deep-fry in hot oil for 2-3 minutes, until crisp and golden. Add to the vegetables and noodles just before serving.

# LAMB STEAKS WITH TARRAGON MUSTARD SALAD

PREPARATION TIME: **10** MINUTES ◆ COOKING TIME: **8** MINUTES ◆ FREEZING: NOT SUITABLE ◆ **480** CALS PER SERVING ◆ SERVES **4**

700 g (1½ lb) onions
120 ml (8 tbsp) olive oil
45 ml (3 tbsp) French mustard
45 ml (3 tbsp) chopped fresh tarragon
1 Cos lettuce, roughly torn
freshly ground black pepper
4 lamb steaks, about 700 g (1½ lb) total weight
tarragon sprigs, to garnish

**1** Halve the onions from root to tip, then thinly slice again from root to tip to make 'petals'.
**2** Heat 30 ml (2 tbsp) of the oil in a large frying pan, add the onion 'petals' and cook gently for 10–15 minutes or until golden brown.
**3** Mix together the mustard, remaining oil and tarragon. Toss half of the dressing through the lettuce with the onion.
**4** Grind black pepper over the lamb steaks, then brush with oil. Cook under a preheated grill or on a barbecue for 3–4 minutes on each side (for medium). Garnish the lamb with tarragon and serve with the salad and any remaining dressing.

# SPICY RACK OF LAMB

PREPARATION TIME: **25** MINUTES + MARINATING ◆ COOKING TIME: **25** MINUTES ◆ FREEZING: NOT SUITABLE ◆ **210** CALS PER SERVING ◆ SERVES **6**

3 racks of lamb, trimmed, about 900 g (2 lb) total weight
3 spring onions, finely chopped
50 g (2 oz) shallots, finely chopped
2.5 cm (1 inch) piece fresh root ginger, chopped
2 red chillies, seeded and chopped
2 garlic cloves, crushed
5 ml (1 tsp) ground allspice
5 ml (1 tsp) ground cinnamon
2.5 ml (½ tsp) cayenne pepper
2.5 ml (½ tsp) ground nutmeg
10 ml (2 tsp) dried thyme
15 ml (1 tbsp) soft dark brown sugar
30 ml (2 tbsp) chilli sauce
75 ml (3 fl oz) fresh orange juice
60 ml (4 tbsp) red wine vinegar
45 ml (3 tbsp) soy sauce
45 ml (3 tbsp) olive oil

**1** Make shallow incisions in the flesh of the racks of lamb, about 2 cm (¾ inch) apart; set aside.
**2** Combine all the remaining ingredients in a bowl. Smear over the lamb, cover and chill overnight.
**3** Preheat the oven to 220°C (425°F) Mark 7. Place the lamb, with the marinade, in a shallow roasting pan and cook for 25 minutes for medium, 30 minutes for well done.
**4** Halve each rack and arrange on warm plates. Spoon over any remaining marinade.

# PRAWN, FRESH PEA AND PASTA SALAD

PREPARATION TIME: **15** MINUTES ◆ COOKING TIME: **10** MINUTES ◆ FREEZING: **NOT SUITABLE** ◆ **510** CALS PER SERVING ◆ SERVES **4**

175 g (6 oz) dried pasta, eg penne, shells or twists
125 g (4 oz) shelled fresh peas, ie about 450 g (1 lb) peas in the pod (see Cook's Tips)
225 g (8 oz) large cooked peeled prawns
30 ml (2 tbsp) chopped fresh mint
15 ml (1 tbsp) chopped fresh chives
50 g (2 oz) hazelnuts, toasted
mint sprigs, to garnish

### DRESSING
60 ml (4 tbsp) hazelnut oil
30 ml (2 tbsp) vegetable oil
45 ml (3 tbsp) freshly squeezed orange juice
15 ml (1 tbsp) lemon juice
2.5 ml (½ tsp) clear honey
salt and freshly ground black pepper

1 Cook the pasta in a large pan of boiling lightly salted water for 8-10 minutes until barely *al dente* (almost cooked but firm to the bite). Drain well and transfer to a large bowl.
2 Meanwhile, prepare the dressing. Place all the ingredients in a screw-top jar and shake well until evenly combined. As soon as the pasta is cooked, pour over two-thirds of the dressing and toss until well coated. Set aside to cool.
3 Blanch the peas in boiling salted water for 1 minute, then drain, refresh under cold running water and pat dry.
4 Assemble the salad just before serving. Add the peas, prawns and herbs to the pasta with the remaining dressing and

toss well. Top with the toasted hazelnuts, garnish with mint and serve immediately.

### COOK'S TIPS
If fresh peas are not in season, use frozen petit pois instead.
Pasta cooking times vary so always check the packet instructions. Undercook the pasta by about 1 minute for this recipe as it will continue to cook as it cools.

### VARIATION
For an enriched version add 60 ml (4 tbsp) mayonnaise or crème fraîche to the pasta along with the dressing.

# SMOKED MUSSEL AND PASTA SALAD

PREPARATION TIME: **15** MINUTES ◆ COOKING TIME: **15-20** MINUTES ◆ FREEZING: **NOT SUITABLE** ◆ **660** CALS PER SERVING ◆ SERVES **4**

**If possible, make the salad in advance to allow the flavours time to mature, but add the avocado just before serving.**

8 spring onions, quartered
2 red peppers, quartered, cored and seeded
90 ml (3 fl oz) olive oil
1 garlic clove, roughly chopped
10 ml (2 tsp) red wine vinegar
salt and freshly ground black pepper
350 g (12 oz) dried pasta shapes,
125 g (4 oz) fresh or frozen peas
two 105 g cans smoked mussels, drained
30 ml (2 tbsp) chopped fresh parsley
1 avocado, cut into chunks
parsley sprigs, to garnish

1 Place the onions and peppers, skin-side up, in a grill pan and drizzle with 15 ml (1 tbsp) of the oil. Cook under a preheated grill until the pepper skins are charred and the onions are nicely browned. (You may need to remove the onions before the peppers.) Place the peppers in a bowl and cover with a plate; the steam created will help to loosen the skins.
2 When the peppers are cool enough to handle, peel away the skins. Place half of the pepper, the garlic, vinegar and remaining oil in a food processor or blender and blend to a purée. Season with salt and pepper to taste.
3 Cook the pasta in a large pan of

boiling salted water according to packet instructions. About 5 minutes before the end of the cooking time, add the peas. Drain well, then immediately refresh under cold running water. Drain thoroughly.
4 Cut the remaining pepper into strips. Transfer the pasta and peas to a large salad bowl, add the pepper dressing and toss well. Add the pepper strips, grilled onions, mussels, parsley and avocado and toss gently to combine. Check the seasoning and garnish with parsley.

# LAMB FILLETS WITH HONEY AND LEMON COUSCOUS

**PREPARATION TIME: 40 MINUTES + MARINATING ◆ COOKING TIME: 1 HOUR 20 MINUTES ◆ FREEZING: NOT SUITABLE ◆ 510 CALS PER SERVING ◆ SERVES 8**

4 best end of neck lamb fillets, about 1 kg (2¼ lb) total weight, fat removed
2 rosemary sprigs
454 g carton thick Greek-style yogurt
3 garlic cloves
300 g (10 oz) soft goat's cheese
90 ml (6 tbsp) chopped mint
250 ml (9 fl oz) olive oil
1 aubergine, about 300 g (10 oz), chopped
300 g (10 oz) onion, chopped
300 g (10 oz) fennel, chopped
60 ml (4 tbsp) each clear honey and white wine vinegar
45 ml (3 tbsp) lemon juice
225 g (8 oz) couscous
1 cucumber, seeded and chopped
300 g (10 oz) plum tomatoes, chopped
90 ml (6 tbsp) chopped fresh parsley

**1** Place the lamb and rosemary in a bowl. Blend the yogurt, garlic and cheese in a processor until smooth. Season and stir in the mint. Mix 60 ml (4 tbsp) with 90 ml (6 tbsp) oil and spread over the lamb. Marinate for at least 6 hours. Chill the remaining yogurt mixture.
**2** Heat 90 ml (6 tbsp) of the oil in a non-stick frying pan. Add the aubergine and onion and cook over a high heat, stirring, for 10 minutes, until soft; cool. Cook the fennel in boiling salted water for 1 minute. Drain, refresh in cold water and drain again; stir into the aubergine.
**3** Place the honey in a small pan, bring to the boil and cook for 2 minutes or until caramelised. Add the vinegar, bring

to the boil and bubble for 1 minute. Remove from the heat and stir in the remaining oil, lemon juice and seasoning.
**4** Place the couscous and 10 ml (2 tsp) salt in a bowl, add 450 ml (¾ pint) water and leave for 15–20 minutes. Break up any lumps, then steam for 10 minutes. Stir into the aubergine mixture with the honey dressing, cucumber, tomato and parsley; adjust the seasoning.
**5** Place the lamb on a foil-lined grill pan and cook under a preheated grill for 6–7 minutes on each side. Pour over any cooking juices and leave to rest for 10 minutes. Carve and arrange on a warm serving plate. Serve with the couscous and reserved yogurt sauce.

# LAMB STEAKS WITH BEANS AND POLENTA CHIPS

**PREPARATION TIME: 15 MINUTES + COOLING ◆ COOKING TIME: 30 MINUTES ◆ FREEZING: NOT SUITABLE ◆ 900 CALS PER SERVING ◆ SERVES 4**

900 ml (1½ pints) chicken stock
175 g (6 oz) quick-cook polenta
75 g (3 oz) freshly grated Parmesan cheese
50 g (2 oz) Emmenthal cheese, grated
50 g (2 oz) butter
salt and freshly ground black pepper
freshly grated nutmeg
50 g (2 oz) plain flour
290 g jar each red and yellow peppers and mixed beans, drained
4 lamb leg steaks, each 175 g (6 oz)
2 garlic cloves, crushed
175 g (6 oz) flat mushrooms, chopped
15 ml (1 tbsp) balsamic vinegar
5 ml (1 tsp) sugar
15 ml (1 tbsp) each sage leaves and chopped fresh parsley

**1** Bring the stock to the boil in a large pan, add the polenta, stirring, then simmer for 5 minutes. Beat the grated cheeses and 25 g (1 oz) of the butter into the polenta. Season well with salt, pepper and nutmeg, transfer to a shallow pan and leave to cool.
**2** Cut the polenta into 5 cm (2 inch) sticks and coat in seasoned flour. Shallow-fry in batches for 2–3 minutes or until golden. Drain on kitchen paper, season with salt and keep warm.
**3** Roughly chop the peppers. Melt the remaining butter in the rinsed pan, add the lamb and fry for 2–3 minutes on each side; remove from the pan and keep warm. Add the garlic and

mushrooms to the pan and cook for 2 minutes. Add the peppers, beans, vinegar, sugar and seasoning to taste and cook for 1 minute. Add the sage and parsley.
**4** Serve the lamb with the bean mixture and polenta chips.

# CHEESE AND PASTA BEEF BAKE

PREPARATION TIME: 25 MINUTES ◆ COOKING TIME: 35 MINUTES ◆ FREEZING: NOT SUITABLE ◆ 825 CALS PER SERVING ◆ SERVES 6

75 g (3 oz) peppered salami, finely chopped
450 g (1 lb) minced beef
3 garlic cloves, crushed
30 ml (2 tbsp) chopped fresh parsley
225 g (8 oz) freshly grated Parmesan cheese
50 g (2 oz) fresh white breadcrumbs
salt and freshly ground black pepper
1 egg, beaten
45 ml (3 tbsp) olive oil
250 g (9 oz) dried pasta
1 kg (2¼ lb) passata (see Cook's Tip)
30 ml (2 tbsp) chopped fresh basil, parsley, thyme or chives, or 10 ml (2 tsp) dried mixed Italian herbs
400 g (14 oz) mozzarella cheese, diced

1 Place the salami, beef, garlic, parsley, 75 g (3 oz) of the Parmesan cheese, breadcrumbs, plenty of seasoning, egg and 150 ml (¼ pint) water in a large bowl. Mix together well with your hands or use a mixer with the flat beater attached. Shape into walnut-size balls and chill for 30 minutes.

2 Preheat the oven to 200°C (400°F) Mark 6. Heat the oil in a non-stick frying pan, add the meatballs in batches and fry for about 5 minutes, until golden brown and cooked through.

3 Cook the pasta in a large pan of boiling salted water according to packet instructions. Drain well, then mix with the passata, herbs, half of the mozzarella, 50 g (2 oz) of the Parmesan and the meatballs. Season generously. Transfer to a greased 3.4 litre (6 pint) ovenproof dish and sprinkle with the remaining mozzarella and Parmesan.

4 Cook in the oven for 30 minutes or until golden brown. Serve immediately.

## COOK'S TIP

Passata - sieved plum tomatoes - is available in most supermarkets.

# SPINACH AND RICOTTA RAVIOLI

PREPARATION TIME: 20 MINUTES + RESTING ◆ COOKING TIME: 3 MINUTES ◆ FREEZING: SUITABLE (STEP 6) ◆ 765-505 CALS PER SERVING ◆ SERVES 4-6

**PASTA**
400 g (14 oz) type '00' pasta flour
pinch of salt
4 eggs, beaten
15 ml (1 tbsp) olive oil

**FILLING**
450 g (1 lb) frozen spinach, thawed and squeezed dry
175 g (6 oz) fresh ricotta or curd cheese
2.5 ml (¼ tsp) freshly grated nutmeg
5 ml (1 tsp) salt
freshly ground black pepper

**TO FINISH**
beaten egg, to seal
75 g (3 oz) butter, melted
25 g (1 oz) Parmesan cheese shavings

1 To make the pasta, sift the flour and salt on to a work surface and make a well in the centre. Pour the beaten egg and oil into the well and gradually mix into the flour, using the fingers of one hand. Knead until smooth, wrap in cling film and leave to rest for at least 30 minutes.

2 To make the filling, place all the ingredients in a food processor or blender and process until smooth. Cover and chill.

3 Cut the dough in half and wrap one piece in cling film. Roll the other piece out thinly on a lightly floured surface to a rectangle. Cover with a clean damp tea-towel; repeat with the remaining pasta.

4 Spoon or pipe small mounds, about 5 ml (1 tsp), of filling in even rows across one piece of the dough, spacing them at 3.5 cm (1½ inch) intervals. Brush the dough between the mounds with egg. Using a rolling pin, carefully lift the other sheet of pasta over the top. Press down firmly between the filling, pushing out any trapped air.

5 Cut into squares, using a ravioli cutter or sharp knife. Transfer to a floured tea-towel and leave to rest for 1 hour.

6 Cook the ravioli in a large pan of boiling salted water for about 3 minutes, until puffy. Drain well and toss with the melted butter. Top with slivers of Parmesan cheese to serve.

# SHOULDER OF LAMB WITH GARLIC AND ROSEMARY

PREPARATION TIME: **35** MINUTES + MARINATING ◆ COOKING TIME: **2** HOURS ◆ FREEZING: NOT SUITABLE ◆ **590–445** CALS PER SERVING ◆ SERVES **6–8**

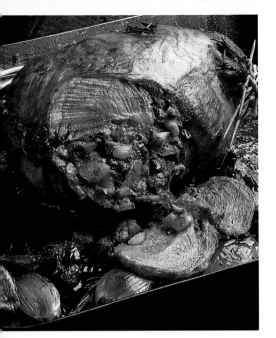

50 g (2 oz) ready-to-eat pitted prunes
25 g (1 oz) each ready-to-eat figs and apricots
300 ml (½ pint) apple juice
25 g (1 oz) butter
125 g (4 oz) each onion and celery
25 g (1 oz) walnuts, roughly chopped
50 g (2 oz) fresh breadcrumbs
2.5 ml (½ tsp) ground allspice
30 ml (2 tbsp) chopped fresh parsley
1 egg yolk
1.4 kg (3 lb) boned shoulder of lamb
30 ml (2 tbsp) oil
2-3 rosemary sprigs
4 garlic bulbs
350 g (12 oz) shallots or button onions
450 ml (¾ pint) lamb stock or water
150 ml (¼ pint) dry white wine

**1** Roughly chop the fruit and soak in the apple juice overnight.
**2** Drain the fruit, reserving the liquid. Preheat the oven to 200°C (400°F) Mark 6. Melt the butter in a frying pan, add the chopped onion and celery and cook for 5–7 minutes, until soft. Leave to cool, then combine in a bowl with the fruit, walnuts, breadcrumbs, allspice, parsley and egg yolk. Season well. Stuff the bone cavity of the lamb with the mixture and secure with wooden cocktail sticks. Season to taste.
**3** Heat the oil in a roasting pan on the hob, add the lamb and cook over a high heat until brown. Place the rosemary under the lamb and add the garlic bulbs and shallots or onions. Cook in the oven for about 1½ hours for pink lamb, 1¾ hours for well done. Baste occasionally and turn the shallots or onions and garlic.
**4** Place the lamb on a carving dish with the shallots and 3 garlic bulbs. Loosely cover with foil and leave to rest in a low oven.
**5** Skim any fat off the sediment in the roasting pan. Crush the remaining garlic bulb to extract the pulp. Add the reserved marinating liquid, stock or water and wine and bring to the boil. Boil vigorously for 5–10 minutes or until syrupy. Adjust the seasoning and strain.
**6** Carve the lamb and serve with the shallots or onions, garlic and gravy.

# SPICED LAMB CHOPS WITH MANGO SALSA

PREPARATION TIME: **15** MINUTES + MARINATING ◆ COOKING TIME: **15** MINUTES ◆ FREEZING: NOT SUITABLE ◆ **350** CALS PER SERVING ◆ SERVES **4**

15 ml (1 tbsp) oil
175 g (6 oz) onion, finely chopped
10 ml (2 tsp) cumin seeds
15 ml (1 tbsp) each mustard and coriander seeds
2.5 ml (½ tsp) cayenne pepper
salt and freshly ground black pepper
300 ml (½ pint) Greek-style yogurt
4 lamb chops, about 175 g (6 oz) each

**MANGO SALSA**
1 large ripe mango, roughly chopped
15 ml (1 tbsp) each chopped fresh parsley and mint
15 ml (1 tbsp) lemon juice
lemon wedges, to serve

**1** Heat the oil in a small frying pan, add the onion and cook, stirring, for 7 minutes or until soft. Add all the seeds and cook for 1 minute. Leave to cool. Place the onion mixture in a shallow non-metallic dish with the cayenne pepper, salt and pepper and half of the yogurt. Add the chops, turning to coat in the mixture, then cover and chill for several hours or overnight.
**2** To prepare the Mango Salsa, mix together the mango, remaining yogurt, herbs, lemon juice and seasoning to taste.
**3** Fold in the end of the chops and secure with a wooden cocktail stick. Cook under a preheated grill for 3–5 minutes on each side. Garnish with lemon wedges and serve with any pan juices and the Mango Salsa.

# SUNSHINE PASTA SALAD

PREPARATION TIME: 15 MINUTES ◆ COOKING TIME: 10 MINUTES ◆ FREEZING: NOT SUITABLE ◆ 460 CALS PER SERVING ◆ SERVES 4

175 g (6 oz) dried pasta, eg orecchiette (ears)
salt and freshly ground black pepper
450 g (1 lb) ripe tomatoes, skinned and seeded
175 g (6 oz) cucumber
175 g (6 oz) celery, sliced
50 g (2 oz) pitted black olives, halved
handful of fresh basil leaves

**DRESSING**
15 ml (1 tbsp) wine or cider vinegar
5 ml (1 tsp) Dijon mustard
120 ml (8 tbsp) olive oil
30 ml (2 tbsp) sun-dried tomato paste
10 ml (2 tsp) paprika
1 garlic clove, chopped

**1** First make the dressing. Put all the ingredients with seasoning to taste in a blender or food processor and blend until smooth. Set aside.
**2** Cook the pasta in a large pan of boiling salted water for 10 minutes. Drain well, then stir in the dressing. Cover and leave to cool.
**3** Cut the tomato into strips. Halve the cucumber lengthways, remove the seeds, then slice the flesh. Place the pasta, tomato, cucumber, celery and olives in a large salad bowl. Season to taste and sprinkle with the basil leaves to serve.

# DILL TAGLIATELLE WITH SMOKED SALMON

PREPARATION TIME: 25 MINUTES + RESTING ◆ COOKING TIME: 12 MINUTES ◆ FREEZING: NOT SUITABLE ◆ 970 CALS PER SERVING ◆ SERVES 4

1 shallot, finely chopped
45 ml (3 tbsp) white wine vinegar
225 g (8 oz) unsalted butter, chilled and cubed
salt and white pepper
squeeze of lemon juice
225 g (8 oz) smoked salmon, cut into strips
40 g (1½ oz) butter, melted
dill sprigs and lemon wedges, to garnish

**PASTA**
300 g (10 oz) type '00' pasta flour or strong white bread flour
pinch of salt
3 eggs
15 ml (1 tbsp) olive oil
50 g (2 oz) fresh dill sprigs

**1** To make the pasta, sift the flour and salt into a mound on a work surface and make a well in the centre. Place the eggs, oil and dill in a food processor or blender and blend until smooth. Pour into the well.
**2** Gradually mix the liquid into the flour, using the fingers of one hand, then bring the dough together. Knead for 5-10 minutes, until smooth and elastic. Wrap in cling film and leave to rest at room temperature for at least 30 minutes.
**3** Using a pasta machine or rolling pin, roll out the pasta dough very thinly in batches. Place on floured tea-towels and leave for 10 minutes to dry slightly. Cut into ribbons, either by machine or hand:

flour the pasta lightly, roll up, then quickly slice with a sharp knife. Leave to dry for 15 minutes on floured tea-towels.
**4** Place the shallot in a small pan with 45 ml (3 tbsp) water and the vinegar. Boil until reduced to 30 ml (2 tbsp). Over a low heat, whisk in the butter, a piece at a time, until creamy and amalgamated; do not allow to boil or the sauce will separate. Season with salt, pepper and lemon juice, stir in the salmon and keep warm.
**5** Cook the pasta in a large pan of boiling salted water for 2 minutes; drain well. Toss the tagliatelle with the melted butter and divide between 4 warm plates. Top with the smoked salmon, garnish with dill and lemon and serve.

# LAMB NOISETTES WITH TARRAGON SAUCE

PREPARATION TIME: 25 MINUTES ◆ COOKING TIME: 25 MINUTES ◆ FREEZING: NOT SUITABLE ◆ 700 CALS PER SERVING ◆ SERVES 4

175 g (6 oz) cucumber
350 g (12 oz) tomatoes
15 ml (1 tbsp) tarragon vinegar
5 ml (1 tsp) caster sugar
salt and freshly ground black pepper
15 ml (1 tbsp) olive oil
8 lamb noisettes, each about 125 g (4 oz)
tarragon sprigs, to garnish

**TARRAGON SAUCE**
15 ml (1tbsp) olive oil
175 g (6 oz) onion, chopped
15 ml (1tbsp) vinegar
150 ml (¼ pint) white wine
142 ml carton double cream
300 ml (½ pint) chicken stock
15 ml (1 tbsp) chopped fresh tarragon

1 Preheat the oven to 200°C (400°F) Mark 6. Halve the cucumber lengthways, remove the seeds and slice the flesh. Plunge the tomatoes into boiling water for 10 seconds, remove the skins and cut in half. Remove the seeds and cut the flesh into strips. Combine with the cucumber, vinegar and sugar. Season to taste and set aside.

2 Heat the oil in a frying pan, add the noisettes and fry for 2 minutes on each side or until browned and the fat is crisp. Place the noisettes in a roasting pan and cook in the oven for 10 minutes for pink, 15 minutes for well done.

3 Meanwhile, prepare the Tarragon Sauce. Heat the oil in the rinsed pan, add the onion and cook for 5–7 minutes, until soft but not coloured. Add the vinegar and wine, bring to the boil and bubble for 2 minutes. Add the cream and stock and bubble for 10 minutes or until syrupy. Season to taste.

4 Remove the string from the lamb. Add the chopped tarragon and roasting juices to the sauce and heat gently. Add the lamb. Garnish with tarragon and serve with the tomato and cucumber salad.

# LAMB AND CHESTNUTS EN CROÛTE

PREPARATION TIME: 30 MINUTES + CHILLING ◆ COOKING TIME: 1 HOUR ◆ FREEZING: SUITABLE (STEP 6) ◆ 560 CALS PER SERVING ◆ SERVES 8

2 racks of lamb, each 350 g (12 oz), trimmed
100 g (3½ oz) fresh spinach
50 g (2 oz) butter
75 g (3 oz) shallots, chopped
225 g (8 oz) mixed mushrooms, chopped
3 garlic cloves, crushed
45 ml (3 tbsp) balsamic vinegar
100 g (3½ oz) vacuum-packed chestnuts, chopped
5 ml (1 tsp) chopped fresh thyme
142 ml carton double cream
salt and freshly ground black pepper
4 thin slices cooked ham
500 g packet puff pastry
1 egg, beaten

1 Cut the meat from the bones in one piece. Plunge the spinach into boiling water, then refresh with cold water; drain.

2 Melt the butter in a saucepan, add the shallots and cook for 2–3 minutes. Add the mushrooms and cook for 3–4 minutes. Add the garlic and vinegar and cook for 1 minute. Add the chestnuts, thyme and cream and boil until reduced to a sticky glaze. Season and cool slightly.

3 Place 2 ham slices on cling film to form a 20 x 15 cm (8 x 6 inch) rectangle. Cover with half the spinach. Season the lamb and place 1 fillet in the middle. Spread with half the mushroom mixture. Wrap tightly; repeat with the other fillet. Chill.

4 Roll out 125 g (4 oz) of the pastry to 30 x 20 cm (12 x 8 inches). Place on a baking sheet, prick well and chill. Preheat the oven to 220°C (425°F) Mark 7. Cook the pastry for 15 minutes. Cool, then cut into 2 rectangles. Increase the heat to 230°C (450°F) Mark 8.

5 Remove cling film from fillets and place on the pastry, trimming to size.

6 Roll out the remaining pastry thinly to 56 x 23 cm (22 x 9 inches). Cut into 2 pieces and brush with egg. Wrap the pastry around the lamb (egg-side down). Trim, leaving 2.5 cm (1 inch) to tuck under the pastry base. Brush with egg and decorate with pastry trimmings; chill.

7 Cook in the oven for 20-30 minutes Cut into thick slices to serve.

# CHILLI-FRIED CHICKEN WITH COCONUT NOODLES

PREPARATION TIME: 15-20 MINUTES ◆ COOKING TIME: 15 MINUTES ◆ FREEZING: NOT SUITABLE ◆ 540 CALS PER SERVING ◆ SERVES 6

30 ml (2 tbsp) plain flour
5 ml (1 tsp) each mild chilli powder and ground ginger
2.5 ml (1/2 tsp) salt
5 ml (1 tsp) caster sugar
6 chicken breast fillets, each about 150 g (5 oz), skinned
250 g (9 oz) thread egg noodles
45 ml (3 tbsp) peanut oil
1 large bunch of spring onions, sliced
7.5 ml (1 1/2 tsp) Thai red curry paste or tandoori paste
150 g (5 oz) roasted peanuts, roughly chopped
90 ml (6 tbsp) coconut milk

**1** Mix the flour, chilli powder, ground ginger, salt and sugar in a bowl. Cut each chicken fillet diagonally into 3 pieces and dip into the spiced flour to coat well.
**2** Cook the noodles in a large pan of boiling salted water according to packet instructions; drain well.
**3** Heat the oil in a frying pan, add the chicken and fry for 5 minutes or until cooked. Remove from the pan and keep warm. Add the spring onion to the pan and fry for 1 minute. Remove from the pan and keep warm.
**4** Add the curry paste to the pan with 75 g (3 oz) of the peanuts and fry for 1 minute. Add the noodles and fry for 1 minute. Stir in the coconut milk and toss the noodles over a high heat for 30 seconds.
**5** Serve the chicken and spring onion on the coconut noodles. Sprinkle with the remaining peanuts.

# CREAMY BROAD BEAN AND BACON PASTA

PREPARATION TIME: 10 MINUTES ◆ COOKING TIME: 20 MINUTES ◆ FREEZING: NOT SUITABLE ◆ 870 CALS PER SERVING ◆ SERVES 4

350 g (12 oz) podded broad beans, ie about 1.1 kg (2 1/2 lb) broad beans in pods
salt and freshly ground black pepper
350 g (12 oz) rindless streaky bacon, finely chopped
350 g (12 oz) dried pasta, eg ravioli
175 g (6 oz) reduced-fat soft cheese
142 ml carton single cream
50 ml (2 fl oz) semi-skimmed milk
chives, to garnish

**1** Cook the broad beans in boiling salted water for about 3 minutes. Drain and plunge into cold water. Remove the outer skins, if wished, to reveal the bright green centres.
**2** Fry the bacon in a non-stick frying pan until crispy. Cook the pasta in a large pan of boiling salted water according to packet instructions.
**3** Meanwhile, soften the cheese over a low heat with the cream and milk. Stir in the beans and bacon and cook for about 1 minute to heat through.
**4** To serve, drain the pasta and arrange on warm plates. Spoon over the hot sauce, season to taste and garnish with chives.

# ROAST RACK OF LAMB WITH BLACK-OLIVE CRUST

**PREPARATION TIME: 40 MINUTES ◆ COOKING TIME: ABOUT 1 HOUR ◆ FREEZING: NOT SUITABLE ◆ 615 CALS PER SERVING ◆ SERVES 4**

50 g (2 oz) ciabatta or focaccia bread, chopped
25 g (1 oz) anchovy fillets in olive oil
60 ml (4 tbsp) milk
30 ml (2 tbsp) olive oil
25 g (1 oz) onion, finely chopped
1 garlic clove, crushed
25 g (1 oz) pitted black olives
1.4 kg (3 lb) mixed butternut squash, potatoes and parsnips
50 g (2 oz) butter
5 ml (1 tsp) sugar
2 racks of lamb, each about 350 g (12 oz), trimmed
30 ml (2 tbsp) Dijon mustard
50 ml (2 fl oz) Madeira or Marsala
450 ml (¾ pint) lamb or beef stock
30 ml (2 tbsp) balsamic or red wine vinegar

**1** Preheat the oven to 220°C (425°F) Mark 7. Bake the bread for 10 minutes or until golden. Drain the anchovies, then soak in the milk for 15 minutes.
**2** Heat 15 ml (1 tbsp) of the oil in a pan, add the onion and cook until soft. Add the garlic and cook for 30 seconds.
**3** Process the bread to make rough crumbs. Drain the anchovies and add to the breadcrumbs with the olives. Process until roughly chopped, mix with the onion and season with pepper.
**4** Cut the vegetables into 2.5 cm (1 inch) cubes. Place in a roasting pan with the butter, 60 ml (4 tbsp) water, sugar and seasoning. Cook in the oven for 40 minutes, mashing roughly as they cook.

**5** Spread each rack of lamb with mustard, then coat with the crumb mixture. Place in a roasting pan and drizzle over the remaining oil. Cook on the top shelf of the oven for 30 minutes; cover with foil after 15–20 minutes.
**6** Remove the lamb, cover with foil and return to a low oven to 'rest' with the vegetables. Skim the fat off any sediment in the pan. Add the Madeira or Marsala, stock and vinegar and bring to the boil on the hob. Bubble fiercely for 10 minutes or until syrupy. Strain and season to taste. Season the vegetables and mash to a rough purée, if wished.
**7** Carve the lamb and serve on the roasted vegetables with the gravy.

# RACK OF LAMB WITH MUSHROOM AND PORT SAUCE

**PREPARATION TIME: 20 MINUTES ◆ COOKING TIME: ABOUT 1 HOUR ◆ FREEZING: NOT SUITABLE ◆ 350 CALS PER SERVING ◆ SERVES 6**

3 trimmed racks of lamb, about 900 g (2 lb) total weight
1 garlic clove, sliced
45 ml (3 tbsp) olive oil

**MUSHROOM AND PORT SAUCE**
50 g (2 oz) butter
2 garlic cloves, crushed
225 g (8 oz) mixed mushrooms , eg shiitake, oyster and chanterelle, sliced
10 ml (2 tsp) plain flour
200 ml (7 fl oz) port
450 ml (¾ pint) red wine
900 ml (1½ pints) chicken stock
10 ml (2 tsp) redcurrant jelly
salt and freshly ground black pepper

**1** First, prepare the Mushroom and Port sauce. Melt the butter in a large frying pan, add the garlic and mushrooms and cook, stirring, for 4 minutes or until they have released their juices and started to colour. Stir in the flour, then add the port, wine, stock and redcurrant jelly. Bring to the boil and bubble furiously for 20 minutes or until the sauce is reduced and syrupy. Season to taste and set aside. Preheat the oven to 200°C (400°F) Mark 6.
**2** Trim the lamb of any excess fat or sinews. Make incisions in the flesh and stud with the garlic. Rub with 30 ml (2 tbsp) of the oil and season.
**3** Heat the remaining oil in a roasting

pan in the oven for 5 minutes. Place the lamb fat side down in the pan and cook for 5 minutes to brown. Turn over, baste and return to the oven for 20–25 minutes for pink lamb, depending on the thickness. Allow an extra 5 minutes for well done.
**4** Carve the lamb and stir any roasting juices into the Mushroom and Port Sauce to serve.

# SPAGHETTI WITH LEMON AND NUT BUTTER

PREPARATION TIME: **10** MINUTES ◆ COOKING TIME: **15** MINUTES ◆ FREEZING: **NOT SUITABLE** ◆ **420** CALS PER SERVING ◆ SERVES **4**

**This dish is delicious served with grilled chicken or fish.**

50 g (2 oz) butter
75 g (3 oz) hazelnuts, toasted and roughly chopped
6 garlic cloves, thinly sliced
grated rind and juice of 2 lemons
450 g (1 lb) fresh spaghetti or 225 g (8 oz) dried
60 ml (4 tbsp) chopped fresh basil
60 ml (4 tbsp) chopped fresh parsley
30 ml (2 tbsp) single cream (optional)
salt and freshly ground black pepper

**1** Melt the butter in a pan until it turns a pale golden brown, add the hazelnuts and garlic and fry for about 30 seconds. Add the lemon rind and set aside.
**2** Cook the spaghetti in a large pan of boiling salted water according to packet instructions. Drain well, then stir into the butter mixture. Stir over a low heat for 2-3 minutes. Stir in the herbs, 60 ml (4 tbsp) lemon juice and the cream, if using. Season with plenty of salt and pepper and serve immediately.

### COOK'S TIP
Prepare the nut butter ahead and reheat while draining the spaghetti.

### VARIATION
Add blanched spring vegetables, such as asparagus tips or broccoli florets, to the drained spaghetti.

---

# FRIED NOODLES WITH TERIYAKI SALMON

PREPARATION TIME: **15** MINUTES + MARINATING ◆ COOKING TIME: **10-15** MINUTES ◆ FREEZING: **NOT SUITABLE** ◆ **495** CALS PER SERVING ◆ SERVES **4**

350 g (12 oz) salmon fillet, thinly sliced
90 ml (6 tbsp) Teriyaki marinade, eg Kikkoman
225 g (8 oz) rice or egg noodles
salt
30 ml (2 tbsp) oil
175 g (6 oz) turnip or tofu, diced
2 garlic cloves, sliced
2.5 ml (½ tsp) hot paprika
juice of 1 lime
15 ml (1 tbsp) tomato paste
25 g (1 oz) roasted peanuts, finely chopped
50 g (2 oz) alfalfa or bean sprouts

**1** Place the salmon in a non-metallic dish and spoon over the Teriyaki marinade. Cover and leave for 30 minutes.
**2** Cook the noodles in a large pan of boiling salted water according to packet instructions. Rinse thoroughly in cold water and leave to drain.
**3** Drain the salmon and place in a single layer on a baking sheet. Cook under a preheated grill for 2-3 minutes, without turning.
**4** Meanwhile, heat the oil in a wok or large non-stick frying pan. Add the noodles, turnip or tofu, garlic and paprika and fry for 1-2 minutes, stirring. Add 45 ml (3 tbsp) of the Teriyaki marinade from the salmon, the lime juice and tomato paste. Cook for 1 minute, stirring gently but continuously.
**5** Stir in the peanuts and alfalfa or bean sprouts and serve immediately with the grilled salmon.

# RED SPICED LAMB

PREPARATION TIME: **5** MINUTES ◆ COOKING TIME: **2** HOURS **25** MINUTES ◆ FREEZING: SUITABLE ◆ **420** CALS PER SERVING ◆ SERVES **6**

2.5 cm (1 inch) piece fresh root ginger, chopped
225 g (8 oz) onion, roughly chopped
8 garlic cloves, crushed
60 ml (4 tbsp) oil
1.1 kg (2½ lb) boned leg of lamb, cut into cubes
10 cardamom pods
2 bay leaves
6 whole cloves
10 peppercorns
2.5 cm (1 inch) stick cinnamon
5 ml (1 tsp) each coriander seeds and cayenne pepper
10 ml (2 tsp) cumin seeds
20 ml (4 tsp) ground paprika
90 ml (6 tbsp) natural yogurt
600-750 ml (1-1¼ pints) lamb stock
5 ml (1 tsp) salt

**1** Preheat the oven to 180°C (350°F) Mark 4. Pour 60 ml (4 tbsp) water into a food processor or blender, add the ginger, onion and garlic and blend until smooth.
**2** Heat the oil in a large flameproof casserole and brown the meat in small batches; set aside (see Cook's Tips). Add a little more oil if necessary and stir in the cardamom pods, bay leaves, cloves, peppercorns and cinnamon. Cook until the cloves begin to swell and the bay leaves to colour, add the onion paste and cook for 4 minutes or until most of the liquid has evaporated, stirring constantly. Add the remaining spices, meat and juices and cook, stirring, for 1 minute.

Add the yogurt a spoonful at a time, cooking and stirring after each addition. Stir in just enough stock to cover the meat. Add the salt and bring to the boil.
**3** Cover and cook in the oven for 1½–2 hours or until the meat is very tender. Spoon off any excess fat before serving (see Cook's Tips).

### COOK'S TIPS

The meat should be well browned, so that the juices have a rich, dark colour. Frying the onion paste gives the sauce body and colour.
Warn your guests to watch out for the whole spices.

# LAMB NOISETTES WITH ITALIAN NOODLES

PREPARATION TIME: **10** MINUTES ◆ COOKING TIME: **15** MINUTES ◆ FREEZING: NOT SUITABLE ◆ **945** CALS PER SERVING ◆ SERVES **4**

**Noisettes are cut from the boned loin. They cook quickly with no waste.**

290 g jar seasoned artichokes
50 g (2 oz) prosciutto ham
12 lamb noisettes
juice of ½ lemon
few fresh basil leaves
salt and freshly ground black pepper
175 g (6 oz) dried pasta noodles
200 ml carton crème fraîche

**1** Preheat the oven to 230°C (450°F) Mark 8. Drain the oil from the artichokes and reserve. Thickly slice the artichokes. Halve the prosciutto ham lengthways and wrap around each noisette. Place on a baking sheet, drizzle with the reserved oil and lemon juice and sprinkle with basil leaves. Season with black pepper. Cook in the oven for 10 minutes for medium-rare, 15 minutes for well done.
**2** Meanwhile, cook the pasta in a large pan of boiling salted water according to packet instructions, until just tender. Drain well, then stir in the artichokes, crème fraîche and any pan juices from the lamb. Stir over a low heat until hot through.

**3** Season generously with black pepper and serve immediately with the lamb noisettes.

# AUBERGINE LINGUINE

PREPARATION TIME: 5 MINUTES ◆ COOKING TIME: 15 MINUTES ◆ FREEZING: NOT SUITABLE ◆ 530 CALS PER SERVING ◆ SERVES 6

**Serve this delicious quick and easy pasta with grilled lamb for a substantial supper dish.**

90 ml (6 tbsp) olive oil
350 g (12 oz) aubergine, finely diced
225 g (8 oz) onion, finely diced
pinch of dried chilli flakes or 1 red chilli, seeded and chopped
150 ml (¼ pint) dry white wine
60 ml (4 tbsp) sun-dried tomato paste
lemon juice to taste
salt and freshly ground black pepper
350 g (12 oz) fresh linguine or spaghetti

1  Heat the oil in a large frying pan, add the aubergine, onion and chilli and fry over a high heat until soft and golden.
2  Stir in the wine and bring to the boil, then bubble to reduce by half. Stir in the tomato paste and lemon juice and season to taste.
3  Meanwhile, cook the pasta in a large pan of boiling salted water according to packet instructions. Drain well, then toss with the aubergine mixture. Serve immediately.

# SEAFOOD LINGUINE 'IN A BAG'

PREPARATION TIME: 30 MINUTES ◆ COOKING TIME: 35 MINUTES ◆ FREEZING: NOT SUITABLE ◆ 630 CALS PER SERVING ◆ SERVES 6

150 ml (¼ pint) olive oil
2 garlic cloves, crushed
400 g (14 oz) can chopped tomatoes
450 g (1 lb) tomatoes, preferably plum, skinned, seeded and chopped
45 ml (3 tbsp) sun-dried tomato paste
500 g (1 lb 2 oz) dried linguine
salt and freshly ground black pepper
5 ml (1 tsp) dried chilli flakes
700 g (1½ lb) cooked mixed seafood, eg peeled prawns, mussels and crab meat
225 g can or jar clams, drained
30 ml (2 tbsp) chopped fresh flat-leaf parsley
flat-leaf parsley sprigs and grated toasted Parmesan cheese to serve (see Cook's Tip)

1  Heat half of the oil in a large heavy-based saucepan, add the garlic and cook for 30 seconds. Add all the tomato and the tomato paste and cook for 5 minutes.
2  Meanwhile, cook the linguine in a large pan of boiling salted water for about 5 minutes, stirring to prevent it sticking. Drain well, place in a bowl and stir through the remaining oil. Add the tomato sauce, chilli flakes, seafood, clams and chopped parsley. Season well.
3  Preheat the oven to 190°C (375°F) Mark 5. Place 6 pieces of greaseproof paper, each about 35.5 cm (14 inches) square, on a work surface and brush lightly with oil. Divide the pasta mixture between the squares, wrap up in a bundle and tie with string. Place on a baking sheet.
4  Cook the seafood parcels in the oven for 20-25 minutes or until heated through. Allow your guests to open their parcel at the table, then sprinkle with parsley sprigs and toasted Parmesan cheese.

### COOK'S TIP

To toast Parmesan, sprinkle the grated cheese on to a baking sheet, then place under a hot grill until golden brown. Scrape up the cheese with a fish slice. Good sprinkled over pasta or salads.

# STUFFED ROAST LAMB WITH FETA AND MINT

PREPARATION TIME: **10** MINUTES ◆ COOKING TIME: **40** MINUTES ◆ FREEZING: NOT SUITABLE ◆ **375** CALS PER SERVING ◆ SERVES **4**

125 g (4 oz) feta cheese
45 ml (3 tbsp) chopped fresh mint
15 ml (1 tbsp) chopped fresh parsley
2 garlic cloves, crushed
salt and freshly ground black pepper
350 g (12 oz) long thin aubergine
45 ml (3 tbsp) olive oil
two racks of lamb, about 450 g (1 lb)
   total weight, trimmed
30 ml (2 tbsp) lemon juice
lemon wedges, to garnish

**1** Mash the feta cheese with the mint, parsley, garlic and seasoning. Cut the aubergine lengthways into 5 mm (1/4 inch) thick slices. Brush lightly with 30 ml (2 tbsp) of the oil and place on a baking sheet. Cook under a preheated grill for 3–4 minutes on each side or until a dark golden-brown colour; set aside. Preheat the oven to 200°C (400°F) Mark 6.
**2** Remove any bones from the lamb to leave only the fillet of meat. Season with pepper. Heat the remaining oil in a heavy-based frying pan, add the lamb and cook for 1–2 minutes until browned all over.
**3** Cut each fillet almost in half

lengthways and fill the cavity with the cheese mixture. Wrap aubergine slices around the fillet to cover completely and secure with wooden cocktail sticks.
**4** Place the remaining aubergine slices in mounds in a small roasting pan and place the lamb on top. Cook in the oven for 20–25 minutes for medium-rare, 30–35 minutes for well done. Sprinkle with the lemon juice and pepper. Cut into thick slices and garnish with lemon wedges to serve. Accompany with a mixture of French and broad beans.

# PAN-FRIED LAMB STEAKS

PREPARATION TIME: **5** MINUTES ◆ COOKING TIME: **10** MINUTES ◆ FREEZING: NOT SUITABLE ◆ **480** CALS PER SERVING ◆ SERVES **4**

15 ml (1 tbsp) lemon juice
30 ml (2 tbsp) orange juice
15 ml (1 tbsp) clear honey
30 ml (2 tbsp) ground coriander
100 g carton garlic butter, softened
4 boneless lamb leg steaks
15 ml (1 tbsp) chopped fresh parsley

**1** Stir the lemon and orange juice, honey and coriander into the garlic butter.
**2** Dry-fry the lamb for 3–4 minutes on each side. Transfer to warm serving plates.
**3** Add the butter to the pan and swirl around until melted, then whisk for 1 minute. Pour over the lamb steaks, sprinkle with the parsley and serve immediately.

# SPICY SAUSAGE AND PASTA SUPPER

PREPARATION TIME: **20** MINUTES ◆ COOKING TIME: **30** MINUTES ◆ FREEZING: NOT SUITABLE ◆ **1080-720** CALS PER SERVING ◆ SERVES **4-6**

200 g (7 oz) spicy sausage, eg chorizo or salami
400 g can pimento, drained and rinsed
15 ml (1 tbsp) olive oil
225 g (8 oz) onion, finely chopped
50 g (2 oz) celery, finely chopped
2 garlic cloves, crushed
400 g passata or can chopped tomatoes
125 g (4 oz) sun-dried tomatoes in oil, drained
600 ml (1 pint) stock
300 ml (½ pint) red wine
15 ml (1 tbsp) sugar
75 g (3 oz) small dried pasta shapes
400 g can borlotti beans, drained and rinsed
284 ml carton soured cream
175 g (6 oz) freshly grated Parmesan cheese

**1** Slice the sausage and chop the pimento.
**2** Heat the oil in a large pan, add the sausage and fry for 5 minutes or until golden and crisp. Drain on kitchen paper.
**3** Add the onion and celery to the pan and fry for 10 minutes or until soft and golden. Add the garlic and fry for 1 minute. Return the sausage with the chopped pimento, passata or chopped tomatoes, sun-dried tomatoes, stock, wine and sugar. Bring to the boil.
**4** Stir in the pasta, bring back to the boil, then cover and simmer for about 10 minutes or until the pasta is cooked through.
**5** Stir in the beans and simmer for

3-4 minutes. Top up with more stock if the pasta is not tender when the liquid has been absorbed.
**6** Ladle into warm bowls and top with soured cream and plenty of Parmesan cheese. Season with salt and freshly ground black pepper and garnish with chopped fresh flat-leaf parsley.

# FETTUCINE WITH SPICY SEAFOOD SAUCE

PREPARATION TIME: **10** MINUTES ◆ COOKING TIME: **40** MINUTES ◆ FREEZING: NOT SUITABLE ◆ **345** CALS PER SERVING ◆ SERVES **4**

175 g (6 oz) dried tagliatelle or 350 g (12 oz) fresh
chopped fresh parsley, to garnish

**SAUCE**
15 ml (1 tbsp) olive oil
1 red onion, sliced
1 red pepper, cored, seeded and chopped
1 red chilli, seeded and chopped
1 fat garlic clove, crushed
2.5 ml (½ tsp) ground coriander
2.5 ml (½ tsp) ground cumin
15 ml (1 tbsp) sun-dried tomato paste
150 ml (¼ pint) red wine
two 400 g cans chopped tomatoes
salt and freshly ground black pepper
350 g (12 oz) cooked prawns

**1** To make the sauce, heat the oil in a large non-stick saucepan. Add the onion, red pepper, chilli and garlic, cover and cook for about 7 minutes or until the onion begins to soften. Add the spices and tomato paste and cook for 1-2 minutes.
**2** Pour in the wine and bring to the boil, then bubble to reduce by half. Add the tomatoes and seasoning and simmer gently, uncovered, for about 30 minutes or until the sauce is reduced and thickened. Add the prawns and heat through for 1-2 minutes. Season to taste.
**3** Cook the pasta in a large pan of boiling salted water according to packet instructions. Drain well.

**4** Stir the sauce through the pasta to serve. Garnish with chopped parsley.

# GINGER AND CORIANDER CHOPS

**PREPARATION TIME: 5 MINUTES ◆ COOKING TIME: 6-10 MINUTES ◆ FREEZING: NOT SUITABLE ◆ 470 CALS PER SERVING ◆ SERVES 4**

5 cm (2 inch) piece fresh root ginger
2 garlic cloves
30 ml (2 tbsp) each clear honey and orange juice
5 ml (1 tsp) Chinese 5-spice powder
125 g (4 oz) butter, softened
salt and freshly ground black pepper
4 lamb chops, each about 175 g (6 oz)
30 ml (2 tbsp) each white wine vinegar and dry sherry
30 ml (2 tbsp) chopped fresh coriander

1 Place the ginger, garlic, honey and orange juice in a food processor or blender and blend until the garlic and ginger are finely chopped. Add the Chinese 5-spice powder and softened butter and blend again until evenly mixed.

2 Season the chops. Heat half of the spiced butter in a frying pan, add the chops and cook for 3–5 minutes on each side, until browned; set aside. Add the remaining spiced butter, vinegar and sherry to the pan, bring to the boil, then add the coriander. Serve immediately, with the chops.

# ITALIAN PORK ESCALOPES

**PREPARATION TIME: 20 MINUTES ◆ COOKING TIME: 6–8 MINUTES ◆ FREEZING: NOT SUITABLE ◆ 370 CALS PER SERVING ◆ SERVES 6**

75 ml (5 tbsp) olive oil
6 garlic cloves, thinly sliced
small bunch of fresh sage leaves
6 pork escalopes, about 350 g (12 oz) total weight
6 slices Parma ham, about 75 g (3 oz) total weight
90 ml (6 tbsp) grated Gruyère cheese
salt and freshly ground black pepper
flour for dusting
200 ml (7 fl oz) crème fraîche
50 g (2 oz) spring onions, chopped
15 ml (1 tbsp) white wine vinegar

1 Heat 45 ml (3 tbsp) of the oil in a frying pan, add the garlic and sage leaves and fry until golden brown. Drain on kitchen paper and leave to cool.

2 Place each escalope between 2 pieces of cling film and beat with a rolling pin until very thin.

3 Place a slice of ham, 15 ml (1 tbsp) of the cheese and some of the garlic and sage leaves on each escalope. Season to taste. Fold the pork in half; season again. Flatten the open edges with a knife to seal. Dust lightly with flour.

4 Heat the remaining oil in a frying pan, add the pork and cook for 3–4 minutes on each side.

5 Meanwhile, mix together the crème fraîche, spring onion and vinegar.

6 Garnish the escalopes with the remaining garlic and sage and serve with the crème fraîche. Accompany with salad leaves.

## VARIATIONS

Use small chicken fillets instead of pork. Parmesan or a blue cheese would be good alternatives to Gruyère.

# ROCKET AND GOAT'S CHEESE WITH PEPPER SALSA

PREPARATION TIME: **20** MINUTES ◆ COOKING TIME: **25** MINUTES ◆ FREEZING: NOT SUITABLE ◆ **390** CALS PER SERVING ◆ SERVES **4**

1 small red pepper
1 small orange pepper
90 ml (6 tbsp) extra-virgin olive oil
1 small red onion, chopped
1 garlic clove, chopped
2 ripe plum tomatoes, skinned, seeded and diced
22 ml (1½ tbsp) balsamic vinegar
pinch of sugar
30 ml (2 tbsp) chopped fresh chervil
salt and freshly ground black pepper
125 g (4 oz) goat's cheese (see Cook's Tip)
125 g (4 oz) rocket leaves
30 ml (2 tbsp) pinenuts, toasted (optional)

1  Preheat the oven to 230°C (450°F) Mark 8. Brush the peppers with a little oil and place in a roasting pan. Roast in the oven for 20 minutes, turning once, until charred. Transfer to a bowl, cover with a tea-towel and set aside to cool.
2  Peel the peppers over the bowl, to catch the juices, then discard the seeds. Dice the flesh and add to the juices.
3  Heat 15 ml (1 tbsp) of the oil in a small pan, add the onion and garlic and fry for about 3 minutes, until softened. Add the tomato and fry gently for 2 minutes. Add to the peppers, toss to mix and set aside to cool.
4  Combine the remaining oil with the vinegar, sugar, chervil and seasoning to taste. Pour over the pepper mixture and toss to mix.
5  Thinly slice the cheese. Divide the rocket between 4 serving plates and arrange the cheese in the centre. Spoon some of the salsa over the cheese and drizzle the rest liberally over the rocket. Sprinkle with the pinenuts, if using, and serve immediately, with olive bread.

### COOK'S TIP

Buy a rindless soft goat's cheese for this recipe, such as Sainte-Maure or a Chabi. For a more pronounced flavour, opt for the *cendré* version of either cheese - they are ripened in wood-ash and have a distinctive grey coating.

# GOLDEN CHEESE AND SPINACH PUDDING

PREPARATION TIME: **20** MINUTES + STANDING ◆ COOKING TIME: **35** MINUTES ◆ FREEZING: NOT SUITABLE ◆ **625** CALS PER SERVING ◆ SERVES **4**

450 g (1 lb) spinach leaves
600 ml (1 pint) milk
3 eggs
60 ml (4 tbsp) freshly grated Parmesan cheese
2.5 ml (½ tsp) chilli seasoning (not powder)
freshly grated nutmeg
salt and freshly ground black pepper
5 large thick slices white crusty bread, about 225 g (8 oz) total weight
225 g (8 oz) Gruyère cheese, grated

1  Cook the spinach, with just the water clinging to the leaves after washing, for 4-5 minutes or until wilted. Drain thoroughly, squeezing out as much excess liquid as possible, then chop.
2  Whisk together the milk, eggs, 45 ml (3 tbsp) of the Parmesan, chilli seasoning and nutmeg. Season with salt and pepper. Halve the bread slices if large.
3  Place half of the spinach in the base of a well buttered 2 litre (3½ pint) ovenproof dish. Cover with half of the bread and sprinkle over two-thirds of the Gruyère. Add the remaining spinach, then top with the remaining bread. Pour over the egg and milk mixture, pressing the bread gently into the milk.
4  Sprinkle with the remaining Gruyère and Parmesan and leave to stand for at least 30 minutes to absorb most of the liquid. Preheat the oven to 220°C (425°F) Mark 7.
5  Place the dish in a roasting pan and pour in enough boiling water to come halfway up the sides of the dish. Cook in the oven for about 30 minutes or until puffed, lightly set and well browned; cover loosely with foil if it browns too quickly. Serve immediately.

# MUSTARD PORK WITH CHERRY TOMATOES

**PREPARATION TIME: 30 MINUTES + STANDING ◆ COOKING TIME: 1¼ HOURS ◆ FREEZING: SUITABLE (STEP 4) ◆ 580 CALS PER SERVING ◆ SERVES 4**

750 g (1½ lb) boned shoulder of pork, cut into chunks
90 ml (6 tbsp) oil
10 ml (2 tsp) chopped fresh rosemary
25 g (1 oz) butter
450 g (1 lb) onions, quartered
3 garlic cloves, crushed
60 ml (4 tbsp) tomato paste
100 ml (4 fl oz) dry sherry
10 ml (2 tsp) plain flour
450 ml (¾ pint) chicken stock
10 ml (2 tsp) dark soy sauce
salt and freshly ground black pepper
450 g (1 lb) small, dark, flat mushrooms
45 ml (3 tbsp) grainy mustard
250 g (9 oz) cherry tomatoes
rosemary and flat-leaf parsley, to garnish

**1** Mix the pork with 30 ml (2 tbsp) of the oil and the rosemary. Cover and set aside in a cool place for 2 hours.
**2** Melt the butter in a flameproof casserole until just beginning to colour. Add the pork in batches and fry over a high heat until golden brown. Remove with a slotted spoon and set aside. Lower the heat, add the onion and cook for 5–7 minutes or until softened and golden. Preheat the oven to 180°C (350°F) Mark 4.
**3** Add the garlic and tomato paste to the pan and fry for 2–3 minutes. Pour in the sherry and bring to the boil, then bubble to reduce by half.
**4** Blend in the flour, stirring until smooth, then pour in the stock and bring to the boil. Return the pork to the pan with the soy sauce and seasoning and simmer for 5 minutes. Cover tightly and cook in the oven for 1–1¼ hours, until tender.
**5** Meanwhile, heat the remaining oil in a large frying pan, add the mushrooms and fry briskly for 3–4 minutes. Season to taste and add to the casserole 10 minutes before the end of the cooking time.
**6** Stir in the mustard, bring back to the boil, add the tomatoes and heat through for 1–2 minutes. Garnish with rosemary and parsley and serve immediately.

# PORK KEBABS WITH MUSTARD MARINADE

**PREPARATION TIME: 20 MINUTES + MARINATING ◆ COOKING TIME: 15 MINUTES ◆ FREEZING: NOT SUITABLE ◆ 175 CALS PER SERVING ◆ SERVES 4**

350 g (12 oz) pork tenderloin, cut into small cubes
2 crisp red dessert apples
fresh sage leaves
rocket or watercress salad, to serve
coarse sea salt, to garnish

**MARINADE**
15 ml (1 tbsp) chopped fresh sage leaves
30 ml (2 tbsp) Dijon mustard
30 ml (2 tbsp) wholegrain mustard
50 ml (2 fl oz) apple juice
30 ml (2 tbsp) cider vinegar
salt and freshly ground black pepper

**1** To prepare the marinade, place all the ingredients in a bowl, with seasoning to taste.
**2** Add the pork, cover and leave in a cool place for at least 1 hour.
**3** Cut the apples into quarters, remove the cores and cut into thick slices. Remove the pork from the marinade with a slotted spoon; reserve the marinade. Thread the pork and apple alternately on to 4 skewers, interspersing them with 1 or 2 sage leaves. Place the skewers under a preheated grill for 10–15 minutes or until the pork is cooked, basting occasionally with the marinade. Serve on a bed of rocket or watercress and garnish with sea salt.

# ROASTED TOMATO AND MOZZARELLA SALAD

PREPARATION TIME: **10** MINUTES + INFUSING ◆ COOKING TIME: 5-6 MINUTES ◆ FREEZING: NOT SUITABLE ◆ 455 CALS PER SERVING ◆ SERVES 4

30 ml (2 tbsp) extra-virgin olive oil
1 garlic clove, crushed
grated rind of 1 lemon
10 ml (2 tsp) chopped fresh thyme
8 ripe plum tomatoes
8 large anchovies in oil, drained
2 Little Gem lettuce
175 g (6 oz) mozzarella cheese
   (preferably buffalo), thinly sliced

**DRESSING**
90 ml (6 tbsp) extra-virgin olive oil
15 ml (1 tbsp) balsamic vinegar
salt and freshly ground black pepper

**1** Place the oil, garlic, lemon rind and thyme in a small bowl and set aside to infuse for several hours if possible.
**2** Halve the tomatoes lengthways and carefully scoop out the seeds. Place the tomatoes cut-side down on a foil-lined grill pan. Brush with a little of the oil mixture and cook under a preheated grill, as close to the heat as possible, for 2 minutes.
**3** Turn the tomatoes over, drizzle over the remaining oil and cook for 2–3 minutes, until softened and lightly charred. Set aside to cool.
**4** Wash and dry the anchovies and cut into thin strips.
**5** Discard the outer leaves of the lettuce,

tear the rest into bite-size pieces and place in a large bowl.
**6** Combine the dressing ingredients in a screw-top jar and shake until well blended. Pour 30 ml (2 tbsp) over the lettuce and toss until coated.
**7** Arrange the lettuce on 4 serving plates and top with the tomatoes, mozzarella and anchovies. Pour over the remaining dressing and serve immediately.

## COOK'S TIP

If you can only find under-ripe tomatoes in the shops, buy them a few days before use and keep in a warm light place to help them ripen naturally.

# RICOTTA QUENELLES WITH FRESH TOMATO SAUCE

PREPARATION TIME: **35** MINUTES + CHILLING ◆ COOKING TIME: 45 MINUTES ◆ FREEZING: NOT SUITABLE: ◆ 505 CALS PER SERVING ◆ SERVES 4

350 g (12 oz) ricotta cheese
45 ml (3 tbsp) freshly grated Parmesan
   cheese
30 ml (2 tbsp) chopped fresh chives
15 ml (1 tbsp) chopped fresh chervil or
   parsley
5 ml (1 tsp) celery salt
1.25 ml (¼ tsp) freshly grated nutmeg
salt and freshly ground black pepper
chives and chervil sprigs, to garnish

**TOMATO SAUCE**
900 g (2 lb) ripe tomatoes
125 ml (4 fl oz) olive oil
finely grated rind of 1 lemon
5 ml (1 tsp) salt
pinch of sugar
30 ml (2 tbsp) chopped fresh basil
15 ml (1 tbsp) balsamic vinegar

**1** First prepare the Tomato Sauce. Immerse the tomatoes in a bowl of boiling water for 30 seconds, remove with a slotted spoon and peel away the skins. Halve, remove the seeds, then dice.
**2** Place the tomato, oil, lemon rind, salt, sugar and a little pepper in a small pan, bring to the boil, then cover and simmer over a low heat for 30 minutes. Remove the lid and simmer for 15 minutes to reduce and thicken. Leave to cool, then stir in the basil and vinegar; chill.
**3** Place the ricotta cheese in a bowl and beat or whisk for several minutes until light and fluffy. Fold in the grated Parmesan, herbs, celery salt, nutmeg and seasoning to taste. Chill for at least 1 hour.

**4** Using 2 dessertspoons, form the chilled ricotta mixture into 12 quenelles or 'egg shapes', by passing the mixture between the spoons.
**5** Spoon the tomato sauce on to 4 serving plates and arrange the ricotta quenelles on top. Garnish with chives and chervil and serve with toasted ciabatta or French bread.

## VARIATION

When fresh tomatoes are not at their best use canned ones instead: you will need two 400 g cans chopped tomatoes. Prepare the sauce as above, omitting the final uncovered simmering stage.

# BRAISED PORK CHOPS WITH PLUMS AND GINGER

**PREPARATION TIME: 15 MINUTES ◆ COOKING TIME: ABOUT 50 MINUTES ◆ FREEZING: SUITABLE ◆ 415 CALS PER SERVING ◆ SERVES 4**

450 g (1 lb) plums
2.5 cm (1 inch) piece fresh root ginger, shredded
salt and freshly ground black pepper
15 g (½ oz) butter
15 ml (1 tbsp) oil
4 pork chops, each about 200 g (7 oz)
60 ml (4 tbsp) white wine
175 ml (6 fl oz) vegetable stock
30 ml (2 tbsp) Greek-style yogurt
30 ml (2 tbsp) chopped fresh tarragon

**1** Preheat the oven to 200°C (400°F) Mark 6. Halve the plums, remove the stones, and cut into slices. Mix with the ginger, then spread evenly in a lightly greased ovenproof dish. Season with salt and pepper and cook in the oven for 15 minutes.
**2** Heat the butter and oil in a frying pan, add the pork chops and fry on both sides until browned. Remove with a slotted spoon and arrange on top of the plums.
**3** Add the wine to the frying pan and cook briskly to reduce by half. Add the stock and cook for 1 minute, scraping up any sediment from the bottom of the pan. Pour over the pork.
**4** Return the dish to the oven and cook

for 20–25 minutes until tender.
**5** Transfer the chops to a warm serving dish or plates. Stir the yogurt and tarragon into the plums, adjust the seasoning, then spoon the plums around the pork. Serve immediately.

# PORK, GARLIC AND BASIL RISOTTO

**PREPARATION TIME: 15 MINUTES ◆ COOKING TIME: 50 MINUTES ◆ FREEZING: NOT SUITABLE ◆ 515 CALS PER SERVING ◆ SERVES 6**

6 thin pork escalopes
about 6 slices Parma ham, 150 g (5 oz) total weight
6 basil leaves
salt and freshly ground black pepper
25 g (1 oz) plain flour
about 65 g (2½ oz) unsalted butter
175 g (6 oz) onion, finely chopped
2 garlic cloves, crushed
225 g (8 oz) risotto (arborio) rice
450 ml (¾ pint) each white wine and stock
45 ml (3 tbsp) pesto sauce
50 g (2 oz) freshly grated Parmesan cheese
60 ml (4 tbsp) chopped fresh parsley

**1** If necessary, pound the escalopes carefully with a rolling pin until they are wafer-thin. Lay a slice of Parma ham on each escalope and top with a basil leaf. Fix in place with a wooden cocktail stick. Season and dip in the flour, dusting off any excess.
**2** Melt a small knob of the butter in a deep ovenproof pan and quickly fry the escalopes in batches for about 1 minute on each side or until lightly golden. Melt a little more butter for each batch. You will need about half of the butter at this stage. Remove from the pan and set aside.
**3** Preheat the oven to 180°C (350°F) Mark 4. Melt about another 25 g (1 oz)

of the butter in the pan, add the onion and fry for about 10 minutes or until soft and golden. Add the garlic and rice and stir well, then add the wine and stock. Bring to the boil and cook, uncovered, in the oven for 20 minutes.
**4** Stir in the pesto, Parmesan and parsley. Push the escalopes into the rice, cover, and return to the oven for 5 minutes or until the rice has completely absorbed the liquid and the escalopes are piping hot. Serve immediately.

### VARIATION

Use British veal or turkey instead of pork.

# TARTE PROVENÇALE

PREPARATION TIME: 40 MINUTES ◆ COOKING TIME: 35–40 MINUTES ◆ FREEZING: SUITABLE ◆ 670–500 CALS PER SERVING ◆ SERVES 6–8

**PASTRY**
225 g (8 oz) plain white flour
pinch of salt
pinch of paprika
125 g (4 oz) butter, diced
50 g (2 oz) Gruyère cheese, grated

**FILLING**
30 ml (2 tbsp) Dijon mustard
300g (10 oz) aubergine, very thinly sliced
1 green pepper, cored, seeded and sliced
3 egg yolks
350 ml (12 fl oz) double cream
1 small garlic clove, crushed
175 g (6 oz) mature Cheddar cheese, grated
2 large tomatoes, seeded and sliced
a few black olives
fresh herbs, eg marjoram and basil

1 To make the pastry, sift the flour, salt and paprika into a bowl, rub in the butter until the mixture resembles fine breadcrumbs, then stir in the Gruyère cheese. Mix in enough water to make a stiff dough, about 45–60 ml (3–4 tbsp).
2 Roll out the pastry on a floured surface and use to line a greased 28 cm (11 inch) flan tin. Spread the mustard over the pastry and chill while preparing the filling.
3 Preheat the oven to 200°C (400°F) Mark 6. Spread the aubergine in a single layer on an oiled baking sheet. Sprinkle with the pepper slices and brush with a little olive oil. Bake in the oven for 20 minutes.

4 Beat together the egg yolks, cream, garlic and Cheddar cheese, and season with salt and freshly ground black pepper.
5 Arrange the tomato slices in a single layer in the pastry case. Top with the aubergine and pepper slices and sprinkle with the olives. Carefully pour the custard mixture over the vegetables so that it comes just to the top of the pastry.
6 Place on a baking sheet and cook in the oven for 30 minutes. Sprinkle with the chopped herbs, then return to the oven for 15–20 minutes, until set. Serve warm or cold.

# SALMON, TOMATO AND EGG TART

PREPARATION TIME: 25 MINUTES + CHILLING ◆ COOKING TIME: 35-40 MINUTES ◆ FREEZING: SUITABLE ◆ 550 CALS PER SERVING ◆ SERVES 4

225 g (8 oz) shortcrust pastry
30 ml (2 tbsp) olive oil
1 shallot or ½ small onion, finely chopped
1 garlic clove, crushed
2 small tomatoes, cut into wedges
25 g (1 oz) sun-dried tomatoes in olive oil, drained and chopped
30 ml (2 tbsp) shredded fresh basil leaves
213 g can salmon, drained and flaked
salt and freshly ground black pepper
2 eggs, beaten
115 ml (4 fl oz) double cream
25 g (1 oz) Parmesan cheese, pared into thin shavings

1 Roll out the pastry on a lightly floured surface to a 30 cm (12 inch) round. Dampen the edge and turn in all the way round to create a wall about 1 cm (½ inch) high. Prick the pastry lightly with a fork, place on a baking sheet and chill for 30 minutes.
2 Heat the oil in a frying pan, add the shallot or onion and garlic and fry over a low heat for 5–8 minutes, until softened and just beginning to brown. Stir in all the tomato and half of the basil. Remove the pan from the heat and lightly stir in the salmon. Season with salt and pepper to taste.
3 Preheat the oven to 190°C (375°F) Mark 5. Spread the tomato mixture over

the pastry base. Whisk together the eggs and cream, season to taste, then carefully pour over the tomato mixture.
4 Bake in the oven for about 30 minutes, until the pastry is crisp and golden and the egg mixture is lightly set. Sprinkle with the remaining basil and the Parmesan shavings and serve immediately.

# BRAISED GAMMON WITH CHERRIES

PREPARATION TIME: **10** MINUTES ◆ COOKING TIME: **2½** HOURS ◆ FREEZING: SUITABLE ◆ **555** CALS PER SERVING ◆ SERVES **6**

1 kg (2¼ lb) unsmoked gammon joint
30 ml (2 tbsp) oil
2 large celery sticks, roughly chopped
150 g (5 oz) carrot, roughly chopped
250 g (9 oz) onion, roughly chopped
200 ml (7 fl oz) dry sherry
900 ml (1½ pints) chicken stock
bouquet garni
60 ml (4 tbsp) golden syrup
50 g (2 oz) blanched almonds, chopped
125 g (4 oz) pitted fresh or frozen cherries
5 ml (1 tsp) cornflour, blended with a little cold water
lemon juice

**1** Place the gammon in a pan, cover with cold water and slowly bring to the boil. Simmer for 30 minutes. Remove and leave to cool.
**2** Meanwhile, heat the oil in a flameproof casserole, add the vegetables, cover and cook for 10 minutes. Add 100 ml (4 fl oz) of the sherry, bring to the boil and bubble to reduce by half. Preheat the oven to 180°C (350°F) Mark 4.
**3** Discard the skin from the gammon and place on the vegetables. Pour in 300 ml (½ pint) of the stock, add the bouquet garni, then boil for 2–3 minutes. Cover and cook in the oven for 1–1¼ hours. Increase the temperature to 200°C (400°F) Mark 6.

**4** Drain the gammon, reserving the liquid. Return to the rinsed casserole, sprinkle with 15 ml (1 tbsp) of the syrup and almonds. Return to the oven and cook for 15 minutes or until golden.
**5** Heat the remaining syrup until a deep caramel colour. Add the remaining sherry, bring to the boil and bubble to reduce by half. Pour on the reserved cooking liquid and remaining stock, bring to the boil and bubble until reduced by a third. Add the cherries for the last 5 minutes.
**6** Add the blended cornflour and bring back to the boil, stirring, until lightly thickened. Add lemon juice to taste. Serve hot with the sliced gammon.

# PEPPERED PORK WITH CIDER AND MUSHROOM SAUCE

PREPARATION TIME: **30** MINUTES ◆ COOKING TIME: **25** MINUTES ◆ FREEZING: NOT SUITABLE ◆ **775** CALS PER SERVING ◆ SERVES **6**

3 pork tenderloins, about 1 kg (2¼ lb) total weight
450 g (1 lb) rindless streaky bacon
9 fresh sage leaves
30 ml (2 tbsp) oil
15 ml (1 tbsp) mixed dried peppercorns, crushed
lemon wedges, to garnish

**CIDER AND MUSHROOM SAUCE**
25 g (1 oz) butter
175 g (6 oz) onion, finely chopped
350 g (12 oz) brown-cap or shiitake mushrooms, thickly sliced
200 ml (7 fl oz) dry cider
150 ml (¼ pint) chicken stock
200 ml carton crème fraîche
5 ml (1 tsp) English mustard
15 ml (1 tbsp) wholegrain mustard
salt and freshly ground black pepper

**1** Preheat the oven to 220°C (425°F) Mark 7. Cut each tenderloin into 3 pieces, place cut side down on cling film, then beat each one into a thick steak with a rolling pin. Stretch the bacon with the back of a knife and loosely wrap around each piece of pork. Place a sage leaf on each one and tie with fine string to secure.
**2** Transfer to a roasting pan just large enough to hold the pork in one layer. Drizzle with oil and sprinkle with the crushed peppercorns. Cook in the oven for 12–15 minutes or until just tender. Keep warm.
**3** Meanwhile, make the sauce. Melt the butter in a saucepan, add the onion and

cook, stirring, for 5–7 minutes or until golden and soft. Add the mushrooms and fry for 4–5 minutes or until golden (adding more butter if necessary). Stir in the cider, bring to the boil and bubble for 2–3 minutes. Stir in the stock, crème fraîche and mustards. Bring back to the boil and bubble for 8–10 minutes, until reduced by half. Adjust the seasoning.
**4** Garnish the pork with lemon wedges and serve with the sauce.

# CRUNCHY CHICKPEA EGGS

PREPARATION TIME: 30 MINUTES + CHILLING ◆ COOKING TIME: 15 MINUTES ◆ FREEZING: NOT SUITABLE ◆ 415 CALS PER SERVING ◆ SERVES 6

two 420 g cans chickpeas, drained and rinsed
2 garlic cloves, crushed
1-2 red chillies, seeded and chopped
2 tomatoes, preferably plum, seeded and chopped
4 spring onions, roughly chopped
125 g (4 oz) pitted black olives, chopped
60 ml (4 tbsp) chopped fresh parsley
salt and freshly ground black pepper
6 hard-boiled eggs
1 egg, beaten
75 g (3 oz) fine fresh white breadcrumbs
oil for deep-frying

## AÏOLI MAYONNAISE
300 ml (½ pint) mayonnaise
4 garlic cloves, crushed
30 ml (2 tbsp) lemon juice

1  First, make the Aïoli Mayonnaise: mix together the mayonnaise, garlic, lemon juice and seasoning. Set aside.
2  Place the chickpeas and garlic in a food processor and process for 1 minute or until roughly chopped. Turn into a bowl and add the chilli, tomato, spring onion, olives and parsley. Season to taste and mix well.
3  Divide the mixture into 6 equal portions. Form each into a flat cake and shape it round the hard-boiled eggs, making it as even as possible (see Cook's Tip). Brush with beaten egg, then roll in the breadcrumbs to coat evenly. Chill, uncovered, for 4 hours or overnight.
4  Heat the oil in a deep-fat fryer or large saucepan to 160°C (325°F) or until a cube of bread begins to sizzle. Gently lower each egg into the oil and deep-fry for 7–8 minutes or until golden brown. Remove and drain thoroughly on kitchen paper. Serve hot with the Aïoli Mayonnaise.

## COOK'S TIP

Make sure the shelled eggs are dry as this will allow the chickpea mixture to stick more easily. The mixture may seem too crumbly, but keep squeezing and pressing it well around the egg and it will stick.

# MOZZARELLA-STUFFED RICE BALLS

PREPARATION TIME: 45 MINUTES ◆ COOKING TIME: 10–15 MINUTES ◆ FREEZING: NOT SUITABLE ◆ 765 CALS PER SERVING ◆ SERVES 4

## RISOTTO
75 g (3 oz) butter
1 red onion, finely chopped
150 ml (¼ pint) dry white wine
300 g (10 oz) arborio (risotto) rice
1 litre (1¾ pints) chicken stock
salt and freshly ground black pepper
25 g (1 oz) freshly grated Parmesan cheese

## TO FINISH
2 eggs, beaten
about 16 small basil leaves
125 g (4 oz) mozzarella cheese, cubed
125 g (4 oz) dried white breadcrumbs
oil for deep-frying

1  To make the risotto, melt the butter in a large saucepan, add the onion and fry gently for 5 minutes or until soft but not coloured. Pour in the wine and boil rapidly until almost totally reduced.
2  Add the rice and stir to coat with the butter and wine. Add a ladleful of stock and simmer, stirring, until absorbed. Continue adding the stock ladle by ladle until the rice is tender and creamy but still has some bite to it; this should take about 20 minutes. Make sure each addition of stock is absorbed before adding the next. (You may not need to use all of the stock.) Season generously and stir in the Parmesan. Leave to cool.
3  Beat the eggs into the cold risotto.

With moistened hands, take 15 ml (1 tbsp) risotto and spread in the palm of one hand. Lay a basil leaf and cube of mozzarella in the middle. Take another 15 ml (1 tbsp) risotto and place over the mozzarella and basil to enclose completely. Shape to form a smooth round ball. Repeat until all the risotto is used up, making about 16 rice balls. Roll them in the breadcrumbs until evenly covered.
4  Heat the oil in a deep-fryer to 180°C (350°F) or until a crumb dropped into the hot oil sizzles immediately. Fry the rice balls, a few at a time, for 3–5 minutes, until golden and crisp. Drain on kitchen paper, sprinkle with salt and keep hot. Serve immediately.

# PORK FILLETS WITH FIGS AND TALEGGIO CREAM

**PREPARATION TIME: 20 MINUTES ◆ COOKING TIME: ABOUT 40 MINUTES ◆ FREEZING: NOT SUITABLE ◆ 715 CALS PER SERVING ◆ SERVES 6**

**If you worry about making sauces, this one is foolproof. All the suggested cheeses have a buttery flavour and can be found in supermarkets and delicatessens.**

12 ready-to-eat figs
100 ml (4 fl oz) white wine
2 large sprigs fresh rosemary
2 pork fillets
salt and freshly ground black pepper
225 g (8 oz) Taleggio, Fontina, Delice de Bourgogne or Vignotte cheese
about 75 g (3 oz) Parma ham, sliced
30 ml (2 tbsp) olive oil
25 g (1 oz) butter
284 ml carton double cream

**1** Soak the figs overnight in the wine with 1 rosemary sprig.
**2** Preheat the oven to 200°C (400°F) Mark 6. Drain the figs, reserving the wine, and remove the hard stalks. Split both pork fillets open lengthways like a book, cover with cling film and beat with a rolling pin until double in size. Season.
**3** Cut 25 g (1 oz) of the cheese into 12 dice, and push a piece into each fig.
**4** Place the Parma ham down the centre of each fillet, arrange the figs on top and fold over the ham. Reshape the fillets and tie at intervals with fine string.
**5** Place the pork on the remaining rosemary sprig in a roasting pan and drizzle over the oil. Pour in the reserved wine. Cook in the oven for 30–35 minutes, until just tender.
**6** Meanwhile, chop the remaining cheese and place in a saucepan with the butter. Pour in the cream and heat gently until melted and blended. Season lightly.
**7** Spoon or brush a little cheese sauce over the pork for the last 15 minutes of cooking time. Cover the remainder and keep warm just off the heat.
**8** Transfer the fillets to a board and cover with foil. Put the pan on the hob, bring the juices to the boil and bubble for 3-4 minutes until only 45-60 ml (3–4 tbsp) liquid remains. Stir into the remaining cheese sauce and serve with the thickly sliced pork.

# STICKY GLAZED HAM WITH SPICED ORANGES

**PREPARATION TIME: 15 MINUTES + SOAKING ◆ COOKING TIME: 1½ HOURS ◆ FREEZING: NOT SUITABLE ◆ 170 CALS PER SERVING ◆ SERVES 6**

1.1 kg (2½ lb) gammon joint
125 g (4 oz) each carrot, onion and celery, roughly chopped
15 ml (1 tbsp) Dijon mustard
15 ml (1 tbsp) soft light brown (muscovado) sugar
45 ml (3 tbsp) marmalade
300 ml (½ pint) cider

## SPICED ORANGES

1.1 kg (2½ lb) oranges
750 ml (1¼ pt) wine vinegar
1.1 kg (2½ lb) sugar
½ cinammon stick
30 cloves

**1** Soak the gammon overnight in cold water.
**2** Drain the gammon and place in a large saucepan with the vegetables and just enough water to cover. Bring slowly to the boil, then cover and simmer very gently for 1 hour. Leave to cool in the water for about 1 hour, then drain and remove the rind.
**3** Preheat the oven to 200°C (400°F) Mark 6. Place the gammon in a small roasting pan. Combine the mustard with the sugar and marmalade and spread over the gammon fat. Pour in the cider and cook in the oven for 20–30 minutes, until the fat is crisp and golden, basting occasionally.
**4** Leave to cool slightly, then carve into thin slices and serve with Spiced Oranges (see below)
**5** To make Spiced Oranges, place the thinly sliced oranges in a pan with water to cover. Bring to the boil, simmer for 5 minutes; drain and set aside.
**6** Add the vinegar, sugar, cinnamon stick and cloves to the pan and bring to the boil. Return the oranges and simmer for 30 minutes.
**7** Place the orange slices in sterilised jars, boil the remaining syrup until reduced and then pour into the jars. Cover and leave to infuse for 2 weeks.

# HOT GOAT'S CHEESE PÂTÉ

**PREPARATION TIME: 15 MINUTES ◆ COOKING TIME: 25 MINUTES ◆ FREEZING: NOT SUITABLE ◆ 375 CALS PER SERVING ◆ SERVES 6**

50 g (2 oz) butter
300 ml (½ pint) milk
50 g (2 oz) plain white flour
225 g (8 oz) creamy goat's cheese
4 eggs, separated
30 ml (2 tbsp) chopped fresh thyme or large pinch of dried
salt and freshly ground black pepper

**1** Preheat the oven to 180°C (350°F) Mark 4. Butter six 200 ml (7 fl oz) ovenproof teacups. Melt the butter in the milk, then bring to the boil. Put the flour in a food processor or blender and pour on the boiling milk with the machine running. Continue to blend for 1 minute or until thick and smooth.
**2** Blend in the cheese, egg yolks, thyme and seasoning to taste. Transfer to a bowl.
**3** Whisk the egg whites until stiff. Using a metal spoon, fold the egg white into the cheese mixture. Spoon into the cups. Stand the cups in a roasting pan with enough warm water to come halfway up their sides. Cook in the oven for 25 minutes or until well-risen and golden. Serve immediately.

## COOK'S TIPS

Serve the pâté with one of the following delicious suggestions:
Halve and season 9 tomatoes. Place on a baking sheet and sprinkle with thyme sprigs. Cook with the pâté. To serve, sprinkle the pâté with grated Parmesan cheese and drizzle the tomatoes with balsamic vinegar.
Garnish the pâté with black olives and thyme sprigs. Serve with toasted olive bread.
Serve the pâté with rocket in vinaigrette.

# THAI CHICKEN OMELETTE

**PREPARATION TIME: 30 MINUTES ◆ COOKING TIME: 20 MINUTES ◆ FREEZING: NOT SUITABLE ◆ 350 CALS PER SERVING ◆ SERVES 4**

30 ml (2 tbsp) peanut satay sauce (see Cook's Tip)
15 ml (1 tbsp) soy sauce
5 ml (1 tsp) soft brown sugar
30 ml (2 tbsp) tomato ketchup
225 g (8 oz) chicken breast fillets,
6 eggs
60 ml (4 tbsp) chopped fresh coriander
freshly ground black pepper
60 ml (4 tbsp) sunflower oil
2 garlic cloves, crushed
2.5 cm (1 inch) piece fresh root ginger, chopped
125 g (4 oz) red pepper, cored, seeded and cut into strips
125 g (4 oz) baby corn, halved lengthways
50 g (2 oz) beansprouts
4 spring onions, chopped

**1** Put the satay sauce, soy sauce, sugar and ketchup in a bowl and mix well. Cut the chicken into thin 2.5 cm (1 inch) long strips, toss in the marinade, cover and chill.
**2** Lightly beat the eggs with half of the coriander and pepper to taste; set aside.
**3** Heat 30 ml (2 tbsp) of the oil in a large non-stick frying pan. Cook the chicken in batches with the garlic and ginger for 1–2 minutes or until golden. Add all the vegetables and cook, stirring, for 3 minutes or until just tender. Turn into a bowl and stir in the remaining coriander.
**4** Wipe out the pan, add the remaining oil and half of the beaten egg. Cook for 2-3 minutes or until the outside edge of the omelette is golden brown and the middle nearly set. Add half of the chicken mixture and fold the omelette over. Remove from the pan and keep warm. Repeat with the remaining egg and chicken mixture, adding more oil if necessary. Serve half an omelette per person.

## COOK'S TIP

Satay sauce is delicious with chicken and is available from most supermarkets.

# PORK WITH TOMATO AND BASIL MARMALADE

**PREPARATION TIME: 25 MINUTES ◆ COOKING TIME: ABOUT 1½ HOURS ◆ FREEZING: NOT SUITABLE ◆ 540 CALS PER SERVING ◆ SERVES 6**

4–5 cardamom pods
900 g (2 lb) ripe tomatoes, preferably plum
120 ml (8 tbsp) olive oil
2 each red and yellow peppers
225 g (8 oz) onion, chopped
2 garlic cloves, crushed
5 cm (2 inch) piece fresh root ginger, chopped
grated rind and juice of 1 lime
20 ml (4 tsp) balsamic vinegar
45 ml (3 tbsp) caster sugar
5 ml (1 tsp) chilli sauce, eg Tabasco
salt and freshly ground black pepper
6 pork chops or boneless steaks, each about 175 g (6 oz)
45 ml (3 tbsp) chopped fresh basil
basil sprigs, to garnish

1  Preheat the oven to 230°C (450°F) Mark 8. Remove the cardamom seeds from their pods and lightly crush.
2  Blanch the tomatoes in boiling water for 10 seconds, then immediately plunge into cold water. Remove the skins, cut into quarters and remove the seeds. Place in a roasting pan with 30 ml (2 tbsp) of the oil and cook in the oven for 1 hour, until beginning to colour at the edges. Lightly crush.
3  Meanwhile, place the peppers in a separate roasting pan with 15 ml (1 tbsp) of the oil and cook in the oven for 45 minutes or until the skins blister. Place in a bowl, cover with cling film and leave to stand for 15–20 minutes. Peel away the skin, remove the seeds and dice.
4  Heat 45 ml (3 tbsp) of the oil in a large frying pan, add the onion, garlic, ginger and cardamom seeds and cook for 7–10 minutes, until soft. Add the peppers, tomato, lime rind and juice, vinegar, sugar and chilli sauce. Bring to the boil and bubble, uncovered, for 10–15 minutes until pulpy. Season and keep warm.
5  Season the pork chops. Heat the remaining oil in a heavy-based frying pan or griddle pan and cook the chops for 4–5 minutes on each side.
6  To serve, simmer the marmalade for 1 minute, then add the chopped basil. Garnish the pork with basil and serve with the sauce.

# DEVILLED GAMMON SALAD

**PREPARATION TIME: 20 MINUTES ◆ COOKING TIME: 10 MINUTES ◆ FREEZING: NOT SUITABLE ◆ 670 CALS PER SERVING ◆ SERVES 4**

4 gammon steaks, about 450 g (1 lb) total weight
30 ml (2 tbsp) olive oil
15 ml (1 tbsp) each mango chutney and English mustard
450 g (1 lb) ripe peaches or nectarines, thickly sliced
about 225 g (8 oz) mixed salad leaves
30 ml (2 tbsp) mixed herb sprigs, eg chives, chervil, parsley
50 g (2 oz) pecan nuts or walnuts, lightly toasted
125 g (4 oz) cherry tomatoes, halved

**VINAIGRETTE**
15 ml (1 tbsp) wine or cider vinegar
5 ml (1 tsp) Dijon mustard
salt and freshly ground black pepper
60 ml (4 tbsp) olive oil
60 ml (4 tbsp) walnut oil

1  Brush the gammon steaks with half of the oil and cook under a preheated grill for 7–8 minutes, turning once or twice, until brown on both sides.
2  Mix together the mango chutney, mustard and remaining oil. Cut the warm gammon into bite-size pieces and toss in the chutney mixture.
3  To make the vinaigrette, mix together the vinegar, mustard and seasoning. Whisk in the oils and set aside.
4  Place the peaches or nectarines under the grill until lightly browned. Place the salad leaves, herbs, tomato and nuts in a salad bowl, add the vinaigrette and toss well to coat. Top with the gammon and peaches and serve immediately.

# MATTAR PANEER

PREPARATION TIME: 20-30 MINUTES + PRESSING ◆ COOKING TIME: 20 MINUTES ◆ FREEZING: SUITABLE ◆ 375 CALS PER SERVING ◆ SERVES 4

**Paneer is a kind of curd cheese that's really easy to make.**

2.3 litres (4 pints) full-fat milk
about 75 ml (5 tbsp) strained lemon juice
45 ml (3 tbsp) ghee or vegetable oil
1 onion, chopped
5 cm (2 inch) piece fresh root ginger, chopped
5 ml (1 tsp) each ground turmeric and coriander
5 ml (1 tsp) cumin seeds
2.5-5 ml (1/2-1 tsp) cayenne pepper
450 g (1 lb) ripe tomatoes, chopped
350 g (12 oz) shelled fresh or frozen peas
5 ml (1 tsp) sugar
30 ml (2 tbsp) chopped fresh coriander
garam masala, to taste

1 Bring the milk to the boil in a deep saucepan. As soon as it boils, remove from the heat and add the lemon juice. Stir thoroughly, then return to the heat for about 1 minute; the curds and whey should separate very quickly. Immediately remove from the heat. If they don't separate, add 15 ml (1 tbsp) lemon juice and repeat.
2 Line a large sieve or colander with a double thickness of muslin or cheesecloth and place over a large bowl. Pour in the curds and whey and leave to drain.
3 When the muslin is cool enough to handle, gather it up around the curds and squeeze to remove the excess whey. Cover and chill 120 ml (4 fl oz) whey.

4 Wrap the cheesecloth tightly around the curds and place on a chopping board. Put a second board on top and weight it down. Leave for 4 hours or until the cheese feels firm. Cut into cubes.
5 Heat the ghee or oil in a frying pan, add the paneer and cook until golden; remove with a slotted spoon. Add the onion and ginger to the pan and cook until golden. Add the spices and cook for 2 minutes, stirring. Add the tomato and reserved whey, bring to the boil, then simmer for 2–3 minutes. Add the peas, cheese, sugar and seasoning.
6 Cover and until the peas are tender. Stir in the coriander. Sprinkle with garam masala and serve.

# STILTON, WALNUT AND BACON FLAN

PREPARATION TIME: 20 MINUTES + CHILLING ◆ COOKING TIME: 50 MINUTES ◆ FREEZING: SUITABLE ◆ 610–405 CALS PER SERVING ◆ SERVES 4-6

175 g (6 oz) plain white flour
pinch of salt
75 g (3 oz) butter, chilled and diced
40 g (1½ oz) walnuts, finely chopped

**FILLING**
125 g (4 oz) rindless back bacon, diced
10 ml (2 tsp) olive oil
2 celery sticks, chopped
75 g (3 oz) Stilton cheese, crumbled
1 egg plus 1 yolk
142 ml carton single cream
salt and freshly ground black pepper

1 To make the pastry, mix together the flour and the salt in a bowl. Add the fat and rub into the flour with your fingers until the mixture resembles breadcrumbs. Stir in the walnuts, then add 45 ml (3 tbsp) chilled water, stirring with a round-bladed knife until the mixture begins to stick. Collect it into a ball, wrap in cling film and chill for 30 minutes.
2 Roll out the pastry on a floured surface and use to line a 20 cm (8 inch) flan tin. Prick the base with a fork and chill for 20 minutes. Preheat the oven to 200°C (400°F) Mark 6 and bake the flan case blind (see Cook's Tip).
3 Meanwhile, prepare the filling. Dry-fry the bacon for 5 minutes to release the

fat. Add the oil to the pan with the celery and fry for 2 minutes. Scatter the bacon, celery and Stilton over the flan.
4 Beat the egg and yolk into the cream and season with salt and pepper. Pour into the pastry case and bake in the oven for 30 minutes, until just set and golden. Serve warm or cold.

### COOK'S TIP

To bake blind, line the pastry case with greaseproof paper and fill with baking beans. Cook in the oven for 15–20 minutes, remove the paper and beans and return to the oven for 5–10 minutes. If wished, brush with egg and return to the oven for 2 minutes to seal.

# SMOKED HAM AND POTATO FRITTATA

**PREPARATION TIME: 5 MINUTES** ◆ **COOKING TIME: 30 MINUTES** ◆ **FREEZING: NOT SUITABLE** ◆ **390 CALS PER SERVING** ◆ **SERVES 4**

400 g packet long-life sliced potato
125 g (4 oz) young spinach or watercress
4 eggs
150 ml (¼ pint) milk
150 g (5 oz) mature Cheddar cheese, grated
150 g (5 oz) wafer-thin smoked ham
freshly ground black pepper

**1** Place the potato in a large non-stick frying pan and fry gently for about 20 minutes or until the potato is beginning to turn golden brown. Add the spinach or watercress and cook for about 2 minutes or until it starts to wilt.
**2** Whisk together the eggs, milk and cheese. Place the ham on top of the spinach and potato, then pour over the egg mixture. Season with pepper and cook over a low heat for about 5 minutes or until the egg mixture has just set.
**3** Place under a preheated grill for 3–4 minutes or until the cheese is bubbling and golden brown. Cut into wedges and serve immediately.

# SAUSAGES

**PREPARATION TIME: 45 MINUTES** ◆ **COOKING TIME: 10–15 MINUTES** ◆ **FREEZING: SUITABLE** ◆ **340 CALS PER SERVING** ◆ **SERVES 6**

**Real sausages – made with pure pork and highly seasoned with black pepper – are easy to make. The secret lies in mincing or hand-chopping the meat coarsely, and using a proportion of gammon to give the right salty taste. This mixture can be filled into sausage skins, made into meatballs or patties, or used as sausagemeat.**

450 g (1 lb) shoulder of pork
225 g (8 oz) piece unsmoked gammon
225 g (8 oz) belly of pork
2 large garlic cloves, crushed (optional)
15 ml (1 tbsp) coarse sea salt
15 ml (1 tbsp) granulated sugar
30 ml (2 tbsp) coarsely crushed black pepper

**1** Trim the shoulder of pork, gammon and belly pork of any skin or connective tissue, then cut into rough chunks. Pass through the coarse blade of a mincer or chop with a large sharp knife or cleaver.
**2** Place the meat in a large bowl. Add the garlic, if using, sea salt, sugar and pepper and mix thoroughly.
**3** Shape the mixture into patties or roll into balls and dust with flour before cooking. Alternatively, use to fill sausage casings as follows. Spoon the sausagemeat into a large piping bag fitted with a large plain plastic nozzle. Rinse the casings in cold water and roll the open end over the nozzle. Hold the first 5 cm (2 inches) of the casing closed and squeeze the filling into the casing to form the first sausage, easing the casing from the nozzle as it fills. Stop when the sausage is big enough and twist gently before filling the next one. Tie the loose end of the casing on the first sausage. Continue until all the filling is used up. If you like, tie the sausages with fine string at two points between the links, then cut into individual sausages.
**4** To cook, heat a little oil in a frying pan and gently fry the sausages for 10–15 minutes, turning once or twice, until cooked. Alternatively, cook under a preheated grill for 5 minutes on each side. Serve as desired.

# SPINACH AND FETA CHEESE PIZZA

PREPARATION TIME: **30** MINUTES ◆ COOKING TIME: **15–20** MINUTES + REHEATING ◆ FREEZING: SUITABLE ◆ **295** CALS PER SERVING ◆ SERVES **6**

**PIZZA DOUGH**
125 g (4 oz) strong plain white flour
125 g (4 oz) wholemeal flour
50 g (2 oz) semolina
15 g (½ oz) butter or margarine
15 ml (1 tbsp) chopped fresh rosemary
0.5 g sachet easy-blend dried yeast

**TOPPING**
450 g (1 lb) fresh spinach leaves, shredded
30 ml (2 tbsp) sun-dried tomato paste
2 courgettes, sliced diagonally
3 tomatoes, sliced
125 g (4 oz) feta or goats' cheese
2 garlic cloves, crushed
12 black olives
15 ml (1 tbsp) olive oil

**1** To make the pizza dough, place the flours, semolina and a pinch of salt in a bowl and mix well. Rub in the butter or margarine, add the rosemary and yeast, then stir in about 200 ml (7 fl oz) warm water (enough to form a soft dough). Knead lightly until smooth, then return to the bowl. Cover with a clean tea-towel and leave to rise in a warm place for about 45 minutes.

**2** Meanwhile, prepare the topping. Cook the spinach in a covered pan with just the water that clings to the leaves after washing. Cook for 3 minutes or until wilted. Refresh under cold running water, dry well and squeeze out any excess moisture.

**3** Preheat the oven to 220°C (425°F) Mark 7. Roll out the pizza dough into one large 30 cm (12 inch) circle or two 20 cm (8 inch) circles and place on greased baking sheet(s). Spread with the tomato paste, then scatter over the spinach. Cover with courgette slices, then top with tomato slices.

**4** Crumble the cheese over the vegetables and sprinkle with the garlic. Season with freshly ground black pepper, scatter with olives and drizzle over the oil.

**5** Bake the pizza in the oven for 15–20 minutes or until well risen. Using a fish slice, lift on to a wire rack and leave to cool for a few minutes. Serve with a crisp green salad.

# PISSALADIÈRE PARCEL

PREPARATION TIME: **1** HOUR **40** MINUTES + RISING ◆ COOKING TIME: **1¾** HOURS ◆ FREEZING: NOT SUITABLE ◆ **470–353** CALS PER SERVING ◆ SERVES **6-8**

60 ml (4 tbsp) olive oil
900 g (2 lb) onion, thinly sliced
3 garlic cloves, thinly sliced
1 rosemary sprig or 5 ml (1 tsp) dried
200 g (7 oz) goat's cheese, crumbled
8 anchovy fillets, chopped

**DOUGH**
375 g (12 oz) strong plain white flour
2.5 ml (½ tsp) easy-blend dried yeast
30 ml (2 tbsp) olive oil
5 ml (1 tsp) salt
1 egg, beaten
small rosemary sprigs and sea salt, to sprinkle

**1** Heat the oil in a saucepan, add the onion, garlic and rosemary, cover with greaseproof paper, then a tight-fitting lid and simmer 45 minutes, stirring occasionally and adding water if the onion looks dry. Drain, reserving the liquid.

**2** To prepare the dough, stir together the flour and yeast in a large bowl. Make a well in the centre, add the onion liquid made up to 300 ml (½ pint) with warm water, oil and salt, stirring until a soft dough is formed. Knead for 10 minutes (4–5 minutes in a mixer). Shape into a ball, place in an oiled bowl and leave for 45 minutes, until doubled in size.

**3** Mix the cheese and anchovy into the onion mixture.

**4** Roll out the dough on a floured surface to a 30 cm (12 inch) round. Lift on to a lightly floured baking sheet and spread with the onion mixture, leaving a 6 cm (2½ inch) border. Brush the border with water and pull up to the centre to cover the filling; seal well. Place a non-stick baking sheet on top of the parcel and invert it. Press down lightly.

**5** Make deep, diagonal slashes across the top of the parcel, 1 cm (½ inch) apart. Leave to stand for 30 minutes or until spongy. Preheat the oven to 220°C (425°F) Mark 7.

**6** Brush with egg and sprinkle with rosemary and salt. Cook for 45–50 minutes. Cool slightly before serving.

# SWEET AND SPICY PINEAPPLE PORK

**PREPARATION TIME: 5 MINUTES** ◆ **COOKING TIME: 35 MINUTES** ◆ **FREEZING: NOT SUITABLE** ◆ **240 CALS PER SERVING** ◆ **SERVES 6**

425 g can pineapple pieces in natural juice
700 g (1½ lb) pork tenderloin or 4 pork steaks
15 ml (1 tbsp) oil (see Cook's Tips)
2 garlic cloves, crushed
15 ml (1 tbsp) mild curry paste
30 ml (2 tbsp) each lemon juice and mango chutney
chopped fresh parsley, to garnish

**1** Preheat the oven to 200°C (400°F) Mark 6. Drain the pineapple pieces, reserving the juice, and chop roughly.
**2** Heat a non-stick frying pan and dry-fry the pork over a high heat for 4 minutes or until golden brown. Set aside in a small ovenproof dish (see Cook's Tips).
**3** Lower the heat, add the oil, garlic and curry paste and fry for 30 seconds (see Cook's Tips). Stir in the pineapple and juice, lemon juice and chutney, bring to the boil, then pour over the pork.
**4** Cook in the oven for about 25 minutes, basting occasionally. Cut into thick slices and serve with the sauce (see Cook's Tips). Garnish with chopped parsley and accompany with lentils.

### COOK'S TIPS
Omit the oil if using pork steaks.
The ovenproof dish needs to be just large enough to hold the pork in a single layer and deep enough to take the juice.
If you'd like a slightly thicker sauce, bubble the pan juices in a saucepan to reduce by half.

# WINTER HOTPOT

**PREPARATION TIME: 20 MINUTES + MARINATING** ◆ **COOKING TIME: 2½ HOURS** ◆ **FREEZING: SUITABLE (STEP 4)** ◆ **685 CALS PER SERVING** ◆ **SERVES 8**

1.4 kg (3 lb) boned shoulder of pork
6 garlic cloves, crushed
105 ml (7 tbsp) oil
30 ml (2 tbsp) red wine vinegar
60 ml (4 tbsp) soft brown sugar
10 ml (2 tsp) minced chilli
15 ml (3 tsp) dried oregano
10 ml (2 tsp) dried thyme
450 g (1 lb) onion, sliced
30 ml (2 tbsp) tomato paste
two 400 g cans haricot or flageolet beans
two 400 g cans chopped tomatoes
300 ml (½ pint) red wine
4 bay leaves
25 g (1 oz) butter
125 g (4 oz) white breadcrumbs from French bread or ciabatta
125 g (4 oz) Gruyère cheese, grated

**1** Cut the pork into 2.5 cm (1 inch) cubes. Place in a large bowl with the garlic, 30 ml (2 tbsp) of the oil, vinegar, sugar, chilli, 10 ml (2 tsp) of the oregano, thyme and salt and freshly ground black pepper to taste. Mix well, cover and chill for at least 8 hours. Drain the pork, reserving the marinade.
**2** Preheat the oven to 180°C (350°F) Mark 4. Heat 45 ml (3 tbsp) of the oil in a large flameproof casserole and fry the pork in batches until well browned; set aside. Heat the remaining oil in the pan, add the onion and cook for 10 minutes over a high heat, stirring occasionally, until soft and caramelised. Add the tomato paste and cook for 1 minute.

**3** Drain the beans, reserving the juice. Return the meat to the casserole, add the bean juice, tomatoes, wine, bay leaves and reserved marinade. Bring to the boil, stirring, then cover and cook in the oven for 2 hours or until the pork is very tender.
**4** Increase the temperature to 200°C (400°F) Mark 6. Stir the beans into the pork and transfer to a lower shelf. Melt the butter in a roasting pan, add the breadcrumbs, remaining oregano and salt and pepper. Place on the top shelf of the oven for 10 minutes, until browned.
**5** To serve, sprinkle the hotpot with the breadcrumbs and cheese and garnish with thyme sprigs.

# ENGLISH BREAKFAST SALAD

PREPARATION TIME: 10 MINUTES ◆ COOKING TIME: 10 MINUTES ◆ FREEZING: NOT SUITABLE ◆ 600 CALS PER SERVING ◆ SERVES 4

**Serve this unusual salad for a weekend brunch.**

5 ml (1 tsp) Dijon mustard
120 ml (8 tbsp) vinaigrette
75 g (3 oz) frisée lettuce
45 ml (3 tbsp) oil
225 g (8 oz) rindless streaky bacon, cut into strips
225 g (8 oz) red onion, chopped
225 g (8 oz) mixed mushrooms, eg button and oyster, chopped
2 large beefsteak tomatoes, halved
salt and freshly ground black pepper
pinch of sugar
4 eggs
15 ml (1 tbsp) chopped fresh chives, to garnish

**1** Whisk the mustard into the vinaigrette and set aside. Tear the lettuce into pieces and place in a bowl.
**2** Heat 15 ml (1 tbsp) of the oil in a large, non-stick frying pan. Add the bacon strips and cook until crisp. Drain on kitchen paper, then add to the lettuce. Heat the remaining oil, add the onion and cook, stirring, for about 7 minutes or until golden. Increase the heat, add the mushrooms and cook, stirring, for 2–3 minutes. Drain on kitchen paper, then add to the bacon and lettuce.
**3** Season the tomatoes with salt, pepper and sugar. Add a little extra oil to the pan if necessary and cook the tomatoes

cut side down for 2–3 minutes, until soft and beginning to colour; turn and cook for 1 minute. Remove from the pan and keep warm. Fry the eggs.
**4** To serve, add the vinaigrette to the lettuce, bacon and mushroom mixture and toss well. Divide between 4 plates. Place a tomato half in the centre of each plate and top with a fried egg. Season generously with black pepper, sprinkle with chives and serve immediately.

# GRILLED GOAT'S CHEESE SALAD

PREPARATION TIME: 25 MINUTES ◆ COOKING TIME: 5-10 MINUTES ◆ FREEZING: NOT SUITABLE ◆ 435 CALS PER SERVING ◆ SERVES 8

142 ml carton double cream
225 g (8 oz) crisp dessert apples
175 g (6 oz) no-soak dried apricots
four 150 g round goat's cheese (see Cook's Tip)
400 g (14 oz) mixed salad leaves, eg frisée, oakleaf and radicchio
175 g (6 oz) walnuts or pecan nuts, toasted and chopped

**DRESSING**
5 ml (1 tsp) clear honey
5 ml (1 tsp) Dijon mustard
15 ml (1 tbsp) white wine vinegar
salt and freshly ground black pepper
30 ml (2 tbsp) sunflower oil
60 ml (4 tbsp) walnut oil
15 ml (1 tbsp) small sprigs fresh thyme or 2.5 ml (½ tsp) dried

**1** First make the dressing. Whisk together the honey, mustard, vinegar, seasoning, oils and thyme. Set aside.
**2** Bring the cream to the boil and bubble to reduce by three-quarters, stirring constantly.
**3** Peel and core the apples. Cut the apples and apricots into fine strips. Stir the apples into the dressing to prevent discolouring. Cut the goat's cheese in half horizontally, place on a lightly oiled baking sheet and put a teaspoonful of the reduced cream on each round.
**4** Brown the cheese rounds under a preheated grill for 3 minutes or until golden brown. Meanwhile, toss the salad leaves with the dressing, apricots and

nuts. Pile on to individual plates.
**5** Top each salad with a grilled round of goat's cheese and serve immediately.

### COOK'S TIP

Not all goat's cheeses are suitable for this recipe. Use either small firm cheeses such as Rigotte or Crottin de Chevignol, or slices cut from a log of Bûcheron.

# POACHED EGGS WITH SMOKED HADDOCK AND MUFFINS

PREPARATION TIME: **10** MINUTES ◆ COOKING TIME: **10** MINUTES ◆ FREEZING: NOT SUITABLE ◆ **430** CALS PER SERVING ◆ SERVES **6**

50 g (2 oz) butter
225 g (8 oz) fresh spinach
salt and freshly ground black pepper
225 g (8 oz) smoked haddock fillets,
  thinly sliced
15 ml (1 tbsp) vinegar
6 eggs
3 English muffins
60 ml (4 tbsp) bought Béarnaise sauce

**1** Melt 25 g (1 oz) of the butter in a saucepan, add the spinach and cook over a high heat until just wilted; season and set aside.
**2** Melt the remaining butter in the pan with 15 ml (1 tbsp) water, add the haddock and cook for 1 minute on each side. Set aside.
**3** Bring a large shallow non-stick pan of water to a gentle simmer and add the vinegar. Carefully break the eggs into the water and cook for 2–3 minutes or until the whites are just set. Remove and drain on kitchen paper.
**4** To assemble, split the muffins and lightly toast under a preheated grill until golden. Divide the spinach between each

muffin half and top with smoked haddock. Place an egg on each muffin and coat with 10 ml (2 tsp) Béarnaise sauce.
**5** Cook under the grill for 2–3 minutes or until the Béarnaise is golden and bubbling. Serve immediately.

# CHEESE AND APPLE PARCELS

PREPARATION TIME: **35** MINUTES + CHILLING ◆ COOKING TIME: ABOUT **15** MINUTES ◆ FREEZING: SUITABLE (STEP **5**) ◆ **260** CALS PER PARCEL ◆ MAKES **10**

**PASTRY**
225 g (8 oz) plain white flour
pinch of salt
175 g (6 oz) firm unsalted butter, diced
5 ml (1 tsp) lemon juice
beaten egg, to glaze

**FILLING**
125 g (4 oz) Cheshire cheese, crumbled
1 large dessert apple
45 ml (3 tbsp) chopped fresh parsley
salt and freshly ground black pepper
herb and leaf salad, to serve

**1** To make the pastry, sift the flour and salt into a bowl. Add the butter, lemon juice and 100 ml (3½ fl oz) very cold water. Using a round-bladed knife, mix to a soft dough, adding a little extra water if the mixture is too dry.
**2** Knead lightly, then roll out on a lightly floured surface to an oblong, about 30 x 10 cm (12 x 4 inches). Fold the bottom third of the strip up and the top third down, keeping the edges straight, then give the pastry a quarter turn. Repeat the rolling, folding and turning 4 more times. Wrap in greaseproof paper and chill for at least 30 minutes.
**3** To make the filling, place the cheese in a bowl. Peel, core and quarter the apple,

then cut into small dice. Add to the bowl with the parsley and seasoning.
**4** Preheat the oven to 220°C (425°F) Mark 7. Roll out half of the pastry and cut out five 12 cm (5 inch) rounds.
**5** Brush the edge of the circles with beaten egg, then spoon a little filling on to one side of each round. Fold the other half over the filling and press the edges together to seal. Lightly flute the edge and score the top. Repeat with the remaining pastry and filling.
**6** Transfer to a lightly greased baking sheet and brush with egg. Bake in the oven for about 15 minutes, until risen and golden. Serve warm with a lightly dressed herb and leaf salad.

# ASPARAGUS, BEAN AND PARMESAN FRITTATA

PREPARATION TIME: 35 MINUTES ◆ COOKING TIME: 15–20 MINUTES ◆ FREEZING: NOT SUITABLE ◆ 720–360 CALS PER SERVING ◆ SERVES 2–4

175 g (6 oz) small new potatoes
225 g (8 oz) asparagus
225 g (8 oz) frozen broad beans, thawed
6 eggs
salt and freshly ground black pepper
50 g (2 oz) freshly grated Parmesan
cheese
45 ml (3 tbsp) chopped mixed fresh
herbs, eg parsley, oregano and thyme
50 g (2 oz) butter

**1** Cook the potatoes in boiling salted water for 15–20 minutes, until tender. Leave to cool, then slice thickly.
**2** Meanwhile, trim the asparagus, removing any woody parts of the stems. Steam for 12 minutes until tender, then plunge into cold water to set the colour and cool completely.
**3** Slip the broad beans out of their waxy skins. Drain the asparagus, pat dry, then cut into short lengths. Mix with the beans.
**4** Put the eggs in a bowl with a good pinch of salt, plenty of pepper and half of the Parmesan cheese. Beat thoroughly until evenly blended, then stir in the asparagus, beans and herbs.

**5** Melt 40 g (1½ oz) of the butter in a 25 cm (10 inch) non-stick heavy-based frying pan. When foaming, pour in the egg mixture. Turn down the heat to as low as possible. Cook for about 15 minutes, until the frittata is set and the top is still a little runny.
**6** Scatter the potato over the frittata and sprinkle with the remaining Parmesan cheese. Dot with the remaining butter.
**7** Place under a preheated grill to brown the cheese lightly and just set the top; don't allow it to brown too much or it will dry out. Slide the frittata on to a warm dish and cut into wedges to serve.

# FLORENTINE TARTLETS

PREPARATION TIME: 20 MINUTES + CHILLING ◆ COOKING TIME: 50 MINUTES ◆ FREEZING: NOT SUITABLE ◆ 645 CALS PER SERVING ◆ SERVES 6

225 g (8 oz) plain flour
30 ml (2 tbsp) freshly grated Parmesan
cheese
pinch of ground paprika
125 g (4 oz) butter
350 g (12 oz) fresh spinach
salt and freshly ground black pepper
freshly grated nutmeg
6 rashers rindless streaky bacon
6 eggs
180 ml (12 tbsp) double cream
fresh spinach leaves, to garnish

**1** Place the flour, Parmesan cheese, paprika and butter in a food processor and process until the mixture resembles fine breadcrumbs. Add 45 ml (3 tbsp) cold water and blend until the pastry comes together in a ball. Wrap and chill for 30 minutes.
**2** Meanwhile, place the spinach in a saucepan with just the water clinging to the leaves after washing. Cover and cook over a low heat for 3–4 minutes or until wilted. Drain, squeezing out any excess liquid, and roughly chop. Season with salt, pepper and nutmeg.
**3** Grill the bacon, leave to cool, then cut in half. Line six 8.5 cm (3½ inch) loose-based flan tins with the pastry and chill

for 30 minutes. Preheat the oven to 190°C (375°F) Mark 5.
**4** Line the pastry cases with foil and cook for 20 minutes. Remove the foil and cook for 5–8 minutes, until golden and cooked through. Lower the temperature to 180°C (350°F) Mark 4.
**5** Divide the spinach between the pastry cases and place 2 pieces of bacon in each. Make a hollow in the centre and break an egg into it. Drizzle 30 ml (2 tbsp) of the cream over each egg, season to taste and cook in the oven for 20 minutes or until the egg is just set. Serve immediately.

# HOT CHEESE AND GARLIC LOAF

PREPARATION TIME: 15 MINUTES ◆ COOKING TIME: ABOUT 15 MINUTES ◆ FREEZING: NOT SUITABLE ◆ 830 CALS PER SERVING ◆ SERVES 4

4 ready-to-bake garlic loaves
2 Little Gem lettuce
1 avocado, thickly sliced
100 ml (4 fl oz) olive oil
30 ml (2 tbsp) white wine vinegar
pinch of caster sugar
30 ml (2 tbsp) crème fraîche, mayonnaise
   or soured cream
30 ml (2 tbsp) parsley sprigs
5 ml (1 tsp) Dijon mustard
125 g (4 oz) Shropshire Blue, Stilton or
   other blue cheese, crumbled
salt and freshly ground black pepper

**1** Cook the garlic loaves as directed.
**2** Meanwhile, roughly tear the lettuce and place in a bowl with the avocado. Blend together the oil, vinegar, sugar, crème fraîche, mayonnaise or soured cream, parsley sprigs and Dijon mustard. Stir in the cheese and season to taste. Add to the lettuce and avocado and toss well.
**3** Split open the hot loaves and fill with the salad mixture. Halve the loaves and serve immediately.

### VARIATIONS

This recipe is also delicious served as a salad – roughly chop the hot bread and toss it through the salad leaves.
The blue-cheese dressing makes a perfect topping for baked potatoes. It will also add flavour to and cheer up vegetables such as broccoli.

# MARINATED CHEESE AND CHILLI SALAD

PREPARATION TIME: 15 MINUTES ◆ COOKING TIME: 20 MINUTES + WARMING ◆ FREEZING: NOT SUITABLE ◆ 425 CALS PER SERVING ◆ SERVES 4

250 g (9 oz) ricotta cheese
225 g (8 oz) creamy fresh goat's cheese
75 g (3 oz) freshly grated Pecorino,
   Romano or Parmesan cheese
2 egg whites
salt and freshly ground black pepper
150 ml (¼ pint) olive oil
pinch of caster sugar
5 ml (1 tsp) Dijon mustard
10 ml (2 tsp) Balsamic or red wine
   vinegar
1 green chilli, seeded and sliced
15 ml (1 tbsp) capers
about 12 pitted black and green olives
focaccia bread, to serve

**1** Preheat the oven to 200°C (400°F) Mark 6. Blend the ricotta, goat's and Pecorino or Parmesan cheeses with the egg whites. Season carefully as Pecorino is salty.
**2** Base-line a shallow ovenproof dish about 18 x 23 cm (7 x 9 inches) with non-stick baking parchment. Spoon in the cheese mixture and drizzle over 25 ml (1 fl oz) of the oil. Cook in the oven for about 20 minutes or until just firm. Cool.
**3** Meanwhile, stir together the remaining oil, sugar, mustard and vinegar. Stir in the chilli, capers and olives.
**4** Turn out the cooked cheese and cut

into 2.5 cm (1 inch) squares. Place in a shallow non-metallic dish, spoon over the dressing, cover and marinate overnight.
**5** To serve, warm the cheese in a moderate oven, 180°C (350°F) Mark 4, for 5 minutes. Serve with warm focaccia bread.

### VARIATION

If you do not like goat's cheese, use 450 g (1 lb) ricotta instead.

# BLUE CHEESE AND SWEET ONION TART

PREPARATION TIME: ABOUT 20 MINUTES + CHILLING ◆ COOKING TIME: ABOUT 1¼ HOURS + COOLING ◆ FREEZING: NOT SUITABLE ◆ 670 CALS PER SERVING ◆ SERVES 4

**PASTRY**
150 g (5 oz) plain flour
125 g (4 oz) butter
125 g (4 oz) freshly grated Parmesan cheese
pinch of cayenne pepper
1 egg yolk, white reserved

**FILLING**
25 g (1 oz) butter
175 g (6 oz) onion, finely chopped
10 ml (2 tsp) caster sugar
225 g (8 oz) fresh spinach
a grating of nutmeg
450 ml (¾ pint) double cream
3 eggs
175 g (6 oz) soft blue cheese, eg Dolcelatte, Roquefort, Bleu d'Auvergne or Lanark Blue, crumbled

**1** In a processor, blend the flour with the butter until fine crumbs form. Add the Parmesan, cayenne and egg yolk, and blend until the mixture forms a crumbly dough. Turn on to a floured surface, knead lightly, wrap and chill while making the filling.
**2** Melt the butter in a small frying pan, add the onion and cook gently with the sugar for at least 20 minutes, or until very soft.
**3** Cook the spinach in a saucepan for 2–3 minutes until just wilted. Drain and squeeze dry. Chop roughly and season well with salt, pepper and nutmeg. Whisk together the cream and eggs;
**4** Line a 23 cm (9 inch) flan tin with the pastry and chill for 30 minutes. Preheat

the oven to 200°C (400°F) Mark 6. Cover the pastry with foil. Make a hole in the centre of the foil and place baking beans around the edge. Cook in the oven for 20–25 minutes or until the pastry looks dry. Remove the foil and beans and return to the oven for 5 minutes. Brush with the reserved egg white, return to the oven for 3–5 minutes. Lower the temperature to 170°C (325°F) Mark 3.
**5** Spoon the onion mixture into the flan. Scatter over the cheese and spinach and pour on the egg mixture. Cook in the oven for about 50 minutes or until lightly set. Cool in the tin for 15 minutes before serving.

# CHEESE AND HAM PIE

PREPARATION TIME: 30 MINUTES ◆ COOKING TIME: 1¼ HOURS ◆ FREEZING: SUITABLE (STEP 5) ( 565 CALS PER SERVING ◆ SERVES 6

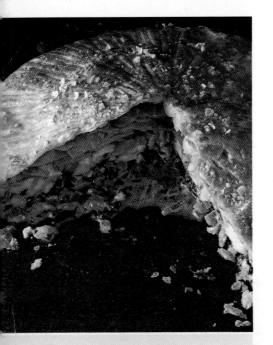

450 g (1 lb) puff pastry
25 g (1 oz) butter
2.5 ml (½ tsp) dried rosemary
300 g (10 oz) onion, finely chopped
60 ml (4 tbsp) crème fraîche
450 g (1 lb) frozen leaf spinach
salt and freshly ground black pepper
grated nutmeg
175 g (6 oz) Roquefort, Bleu d'Auvergne or Stilton cheese, crumbled
175 g (6 oz) sliced cooked ham
beaten egg, to glaze

**1** Preheat the oven to 200°C (400°F) Mark 6. Roll out half of the pastry to a 30 cm (12 inch) square. Place on a baking sheet, prick well and bake in the oven for about 12 minutes or until golden and crisp. Using a 25 cm (10 inch) dinner plate as a template, cut a round of cooked pastry. Set aside on the baking sheet.
**2** Melt the butter with the rosemary in a frying pan, add the onion and fry gently for 10–12 minutes, until very soft. Stir in the crème fraîche, remove from the heat and leave to cool.
**3** Meanwhile, squeeze the excess liquid from the spinach and stir over a low heat until it is completely dry. Chop and

season with salt, pepper and nutmeg.
**4** Roll out the remaining pastry to a 30 cm (12 inch) circle.
**5** Spread the cooled spinach over the cooked pastry round. Top with the onion, then the cheese, then a layer of ham. Lay the uncooked pastry round over the top. Trim the excess pastry, leaving just enough to tuck neatly under the base.
**6** Brush with egg and cook in the oven for 40–45 minutes or until well risen and deep golden; cover with foil if it browns too quickly. Serve immediately.